*Policy Issues
in Urban Education*

MARJORIE B. SMILEY
HARRY L. MILLER
Editors

Policy Issues
in
Urban Education

New York: THE FREE PRESS
London: COLLIER-MACMILLAN LIMITED

First Printing

PREFACE

This collection of readings results from a project under Grant Number 62201 of the United States Office of Juvenile Delinquency and Youth Development. The Project, entitled TRUE, or *Teachers and Resources for Urban Education,* has been conducted at the Hunter College Curriculum Center since 1962.

The book of readings, of which this volume constitutes the second section, has been used experimentally in a number of classes at Hunter College and other institutions providing special courses for teachers of disadvantaged youth. The first section of the original work, published as a separate volume, *Education in the Metropolis,* contains selections that contribute to an understanding of the various social and economic problems out of which arise the specific public and professional policy issues discussed here.

M.B.S.
H.L.M.

ACKNOWLEDGMENTS

Mrs. Helen Randolph, Miss Joan Roberts, and Mrs. Steven Zuckerman assisted in the research and the selection of materials.

A number of people were involved in the production of this collection. We wish to express our appreciation to Miss Elaine Paul for her careful typing; Miss Carol Ratner for art work and layout; Miss Carol Gibbons and Mr. Richard Meyer for performing a variety of tasks among which were layout and reproduction; Mrs. Susan Stein for general supervision of production; and Dr. Stuart A. Selby and Mr. Mark Feldstein for their coordination of all these efforts to produce the experimental edition.

For his assistance in editing and preparing the manuscript for the present edition, we express our appreciation to Mr. Norman Bailey.

Special thanks are due to faculty members of the Hunter College Education Department for testing the readings in their classes and for providing constructive suggestions for revision.

CONTENTS

Preface   v

Acknowledgments   vii

Introduction: An Approach to Issues...   1

Part I
CHALLENGE TO THE TEACHER

Not Like Other Children   25
    BERNARD ASBELL

Who Would Teach Here . . .   48
    MARJORIE B. SMILEY

The Strategy of Style   55
    FRANK REISSMAN

Bridges to Slum-Ghetto Children   66

The First Semester in a Slum School   78

ix

Auxiliary School Personnel   100
    GARDA W. BOWMAN and GORDON J. KLOPF

Part II
WHAT CURRICULUM FOR THE DISADVANTAGED? PATTERNS AND ISSUES

National Policy for Alienated Youth   134
    ROBERT J. HAVIGHURST AND LINDLEY J. STILES

Teach Them the Arts of Freedom   148
    LAWRENCE C. HOWARD

Reaching the Culturally Deprived   156
    TERRY BORTON

Life Is Fun in a Smiling, Fair-Skinned World   167
    OTTO KLINEBERG

Color Me Brown—I'm Integrated   177
    THEODORE B. DOLMATCH

Balance and Imbalance: New History Texts and the
    Negro   182
    IRVING SLOAN

The Negro in History: New Textbooks Are Targets of
    Backlash   201
    GERALD GRANT

Textbooks for Inner City Children   205

A Sustained Program of Language Learning   228
    WALTER LOBAN

Academic Instruction and Preschool Children   239
    CARL BEREITER

Conflict and Reform   250
    DOUGLAS PEDERSEN

A Concept-Centered Curriculum for the Disadvantaged   266
    VIRGINIA FRANK

Part III
REDRESSING THE IMBALANCE
OF THE URBAN SCHOOL

Slums and Schools   287
    CHRISTOPHER JENCKS

The Negro as an American   309
    JOSEPH P. LYFORD

Legal Decisions Affecting School Desegregation   324
    LEE O. GARBER

The New Rochelle Decision   333

School Integration: A Case Study   345

Review of Evidence Relating to Effects of Desegregation
  on the Intellectual Performance of Negroes   400
    IRWIN KATZ

Equality Through Education: A Report on Greenburgh
  School District No. 8   443
    NAOMI and ARNOLD BUCHHEIMER

Equal Schools or Equal Students?   450
    JAMES S. COLEMAN

Should There Be "Compensation" for Negroes?   460
    WHITNEY M. YOUNG, JR., and KYLE HASELDEN

Index   473

Introduction: An Approach to Issues

The companion volume of readings, *Education in the Metropolis,* described the many dimensions of the problems that the inner-city school faces: poverty, and the migrations South to North and from the country to the city; technological change and its increasing demands on schooling; differences in culture and value systems between the poor and the middle-class mainstream; cognitive and linguistic disadvantages of the lower-class child in a school run by and for the middle class. As the school searches for alternative answers to these problems, a number of issues arise among educational professionals, parents, and in some cases the public generally. Such diffusion of concern is typical of school problems, not only because the public supports the schools and thus has the right to a voice in educational policy, but because the school as an institution intersects all other major institutions at their most important point, the thrust into the future.

The readings in *Policy Issues in Urban Education* are grouped for their relevance to fairly large areas that demand policy-formation by either the public or by school professionals, or both: what should be taught in the inner-city school, which determines what the slum child shall become as a worker and citizen; what changes must be made in teaching; and the need to redress the racial imbalance in the urban schools. No one of the specific issues within these areas is simple, and most are, in fact, extraordinarily complex, despite the tendency of some pressure groups and editorial writers to look for the simple answer. One can approach them from a purely technical position and ask whether we have the knowledge or skill to move in certain directions, or raise moral and ethical questions, or ask about the social consequences of suggested policies, or apply already determined political and social positions.

Any discussion of the issues raised in this volume is likely to involve consideration of all these levels of analysis at once and is consequently unlikely to get much beyond a ventilation of views. It may be helpful here, then, to indicate in some detail the various approaches which are relevant to these problems.

THE DOMAIN OF VALUE

The most fundamental questions one can raise are those which ask, what is right, what is best, what is fair, and to whom? One issue argued in these readings which can hardly be discussed at all at any other level is that of "special" compensation for the Negro. After several hundred years of enslavement and discrimination, the argument runs, the society owes the Negro much more than equality, it owes him a period at least of better-than-equal treatment to make up for the harm done to him. This would entail, presumably, a higher per-pupil expenditure in those slum schools which are predominantly Negro, higher not merely than they are at present, which could only bring them to equality, but higher than that of middle-class white schools.

There is, of course, a purely political problem involved; it is doubtful that the most powerful elements in the society would agree to the doctrine of overcompensation for the Negro, and the courts might well rule it an unequal use of public funds. But there are many precedents for preferential treatment for special groups in our society, and one can always apply pressure on the power structure, and sometimes win, so it is not very useful, on this level of discussion, to concentrate on these practical matters. To arrive at a judgment of one's own on the matter one must directly confront the strength of the moral demand for overcompensation, and explore the question of how much responsibility the present generation of Americans must accept for the historical wrongs committed by our forebears.

Similarly, the issues surrounding *de facto* school segregation in the Northern cities, although it involves other levels of argument, pose a fundamental ethical question. The positions most people take on this issue orient themselves, in one way or another, to that most extreme view which argues that school segregation, whatever its causes, must be eliminated whatever the cost of that elimination might be. A basic assumption of the position is, as the Supreme Court argued in its 1954 decision, that segregation is inherently unequal because it induces in the segregated child feelings of inferiority which inhibit learning. Segregation, then, whether it is the result of the neighborhood preferences of Northern city whites or the laws of Southern states, wrongs the child and is morally indefensible.

At the other extreme are those who take the position that, however deplorable the pattern of city segregation, it is the result of historical accident and must be corrected without interfering with the fundamental right of parents to send their children to a neighborhood school. Thus, the question resolves to the issue of which is more important, the advantages to the Negro child of attending an integrated school, or the maintenance of the neighborhood-school concept. Whose rights should be paramount—the Negro parents' to an environment that will not be psychologically harmful to their children, or the white parents' to a school environment that they may have sought at considerable cost through real-estate investment? Like many American conflicts, the basic issue reflects value conflict between property and human rights, as well as the necessity to decide which of two groups in a given circumstance will be hurt the most.

The curriculum issues, too, reflect some moral conflicts. All European school systems recognize difference in class status by sending children of different classes through different courses of training, often with some provision for moving the bright and talented working-class child into an essentially middle-class curriculum that leads to higher education. Our own system, against the equalitarian grain of the society, has developed very much the same sorting mechanism, particularly in the large cities, where specialized high schools have proven to be financially feasible.

The problem of sorting, in a real sense, however, arises not at the high-school level where the decisions about the future have usually already been made, but in the elementary grades where, theoretically, each child's potential is at yet undetermined. From the point of view of such educational militants as Kenneth Clark, the school must treat the Negro child exactly as it treats the white, that is, on the assumption that he will later aspire to higher education and a white-collar or professional career. By making the opposite assumption, the school prejudges the future of the child and leads him to conform to this expectation in a kind of "self-fulfilling prophecy."

The conservative opponents of this view base their position on the realities of social class, arguing that there are few signs of a social millennium in which class differences will disappear. They point out that, in fact, the majority of lower-class children will end up as working-class adults, and to treat them in school as if they were all going on to college is unfair to them; it not only subjects many to a sense of failure and increases their alienation, but fails to provide for their real needs, such as a knowledge of the world of work into which they will go and a firm grounding in the skills now required for any position in a technical society. Where one stands on this issue clearly depends on what "reality" one sees in the social order and how flexible or unchanging one conceives that order to be.

The level at which people explore what is best and fairest

for the child is similar to the one at which some raise the question of what is best for the society, and whether we must make good on our historical conviction that the school implements the democratic order by providing an institution in which children of all classes and ethnic backgrounds come to know one another on equal terms. Because curriculum differences almost inevitably result in separate grouping of pupils, the earlier we begin special training the less chance we have to make the school an instrument for democracy. Inevitably, then, the question resolves itself to a most basic one of what we conceive the nature of the school to be.

THE DOMAIN OF TECHNOLOGY

A very different level of analysis relevant to most of the policy issues discussed in this volume approaches them through the technical problems one must consider in choosing among alternative policies. It may be all very well to decide what is just and right, fair and best, but do we know enough to be sure we are on firm practical grounds in making such a decision, and can we carry it out?

Many concerned educators feel, for example, that there is little question of the superior morality of a better racial balance in Northern city schools. Beyond the broader social morality, if segregation per se results in lower levels of learning, how can one in all conscience as a professional permit the operation of segregated schools? But the obvious large-scale technical problems involved in obtaining a better racial mixture in such large segregated areas as Harlem or Watts are not the only ones schools must confront. One persistent proposal for correcting imbalance is to transport children from one school to another; can we control the situation in the receiving school sufficiently to make the experience of attending an integrated school useful for the child? In many cities, children on specified grade levels are divided into classes on the basis of ability, either IQ scores or reading levels. In practice, bussed-in Negro, Puerto Rican, or Indian children end up in classrooms that are just as segregated as those they have left behind them. New York City has recently decreed an end to the practice of homogeneous grouping by IQ, but even if each school were to assign children more or less at random within the grade, there is considerable cause to doubt that teachers will relinquish grouping within the classroom.

Very formidable technical questions remain to be solved in relation to the issues that surround teaching and teacher preparation. Although the examples of successful teachers presented in several of the selections in this volume suggest a number of characteristics the effective slum school teacher should have, there is not much agreement about how teachers of this kind can be either identified or trained. There is some measure of agreement that academic teacher training ought to inform the future teacher realistically about the background problems of the child of the inner city she will later confront, but even this relatively mild prescription gains by no means universal assent. Some educators disagree, arguing that such preparation might lead teachers to see problems where there are none, and develop stereotypes that would block good teaching.

Even if we were agreed on how to go about the job of training teachers for these children, the demands on the training institutions are staggering. One of the requirements, for example, for teaching alienated and socially handicapped youngsters is, it seems reasonable to suppose, the ability to stimulate and interest them in the materials and tasks that lead to school success. This is a quality that almost every educational theory of the past two centuries has demanded of teaching, with little evidence of success in instilling it in generations of teachers. Or, to take an even more difficult example, an ability to empathize, to feel *with,* those who are different from oneself is clearly an advantage in the inner-city classroom, but whether we can help students acquire that ability is at least doubtful— some would say clearly impossible.

Similar technical questions arise in the areas of materials and curriculum structure. Klineberg's piece on the beautiful, white, smiling world of the early readers suggests that special stories and texts with which the lower-class child can identify more readily might help improve achievement. Some readers already have been produced, samples of which are included, and seem experimentally to be somewhat effective; many of them, however, seem to be as dull as the originals. Some educators argue that standardized texts are of little value with these children, anyway, and that the technique which Sylvia Ashton-Warner describes in her book *Teacher,* the construction of a special verbal world to fit the real world of the specific child, is necessary. But this *does* require teachers with imagination and flexibility, and there is some question whether we can get them in sufficient numbers to staff all the urban schools.

THE DOMAIN OF POLITICS

A third level of analysis requires consideration of what are essentially political questions, involving power and institutional resistance to change. Most of the issues explored here have some fairly obvious political implications, notably the argument over racial imbalance, over which community pressure groups struggle in the streets and in the courts.

A more subtle and complex source of political difficulty resides in the school as an institution. When enough people put enough pressure on a social institution, it is likely to change; but institutions demonstrate varying degrees of resistance, and they accommodate to pressure more or less creatively. All the problems discussed in this volume require change of a considerable magnitude on the part of urban school systems if we are to solve them even minimally, but, as we grope toward viable solutions, the past record of the urban school bureaucracies offers little reassurance about their future creative response.

The public often gets the impression that education must be very hospitable to innovation as it reads about what appears to be almost constant experimentation in the schools: the growth of programmed instruction, ungraded primaries, new alphabets and new ways of teaching reading, language laboratories, and the like. Yet one educational historian wrote in some exasperation that it takes easily fifty years for a new educational idea to be adopted. What accounts for the difference between these impressions is probably that the widely publicized experiments seldom penetrate deeply into the more than one million classrooms that comprise the national public school institution. It is likely, for example, that the impression one gets of the overwhelming "progressive" tinge to education in the past several decades is far from being a true picture, and that the methods called progressive were restricted, in any real sense, to a relatively small minority of schools throughout the country.

The reasons why the school as an institution is essentially resistant to change are instructive:

First, as are all institutions on which public concern focuses and which are open to public pressures, the school is, in most important matters, conservative. In the suburbs, administrators and teachers are subject to open and direct pressures from the community; in the large city the system must adapt to whatever complex political forces operate in the specific city governments. And, the almost unvarying first principle of local government is, "Don't rock the boat."

Second, to an extent paralleled in few other institutions, the teacher is in command of her own classroom and can make or break innovation. To the extent that teachers remain within the system, change must compete against values and techniques which they carry over from a previous generation; to the extent that the career attracts young women who see teaching as a stopgap job, the school has always a large number of inexperienced, hence insecure, practitioners, who prefer the tried and true.

Third, particularly in the large city, the frightening size of the institution makes necessary the development of a classic bureaucratic solution, the centralization of policy and initiative, and the routinization of tasks. This inevitably produces a climate in which forms and procedures are perceived as fundamentally more important than the solution of problems, and a civil-servant attitude that makes prerogative and status more important than the task itself.

As each of these domains of discussion demands different kinds of rational exploration, so do the problems they represent seem more or less resolvable. Most educators and citizens of good will accept the moral necessity of dealing in some way with the problems that urban poverty and the heritage of centuries of slavery create, although they differ about remedies and their cost. The technical problems are more resistant, but they are at least amenable to scientific investigation and the rigor of experimentation. The political problems remain the most obdurate, and do much, as well, to contaminate the other two areas; for it is all too easy to take morally righteous positions while refusing in private to do what is necessary to bring about change, and eagerness to make political capital of some not very successful experiment can lead us to adopt procedures that lack very substantial evidence of effectiveness.

Before most of the articles included in this volume we have placed crucial questions for group discussion or for individual consideration; in some instances the questions lie wholly within one or another of the domains described in this introduction, in others, they point to connections between them. The reader will find it useful, in discussing or thinking about the implication of these pieces, to consider separately the value, technological, or political problems involved in these complex policy issues before determining their interrelationships or the direction in which one must seek solutions.

PART I

Challenge to the Teacher

Many of the most bitter attacks on the slum school focus on those who teach in it, who are accused of being uninterested in the children, of stereotyping them as academic failures, of being ineffective in doing the job they are supposed to do. One might expect that the almost general agreement on the crucial role of the teacher in the achievement of the disadvantaged child would result in a great deal of experimentation in teaching procedures and teacher selection. But, although a large literature on education for the disadvantaged is rapidly accumulating, a remarkably small proportion of the work reported deals directly with the teaching process.

Indeed, so confused is the present state of the discussion of the role of teaching in urban education that it is difficult in this introduction to identify and analyze very precisely the major issues confronting policy-making. The best one can do is to discuss the general areas in which both educators and laymen appear to have conflicting expectations, hopes, and conceptions of the teacher: the instructional roles most appropriate for the slum school; the most effective personal relationships for teachers to build with pupils; and the process of selection and training of teachers.

There is a prior question that in some measure influences the discussion of all of these issues; that is, how much can we realistically expect the school to accomplish in reversing motivational and cognitive handicaps that a number of children of lower socioeconomic status bring with them to school? For, although the school includes curriculum, learning materials, administration, and supportive services as well as teachers, the teacher's role is at least central, if not crucial.

Both of the extreme answers to this question are naive, and tend to be concerned with fixing blame rather than in finding solutions. Many teachers and administrators in slum schools argue that nothing can be done; after trying what they consider to be their best, without positive results, they conclude that the school cannot succeed in the struggle to repair the handicaps of background. It is the child and his family who must change. Only if the child comes to school docile, in the original meaning of the term as well as the behavioral one, can teachers be expected to cope successfully with him. Nor is this the view only of the dogmatically unsophisticated or prejudiced; as thoughtful and eminent an educator as Broudy has put the problem in this form.

At the other extreme a number of parents, following the lead of the more militant wings of ethnic minority pressure groups, claim that it is all the fault of the teachers, whose failure to treat their children as they would any middle-class white child results inevitably in lower levels of achievement. Though the argument in this form is made as often by the very well-educated as by the poor parent, one seldom hears it from professional schoolmen.

Few educators with any prolonged and first-hand experience with the process of education are likely to agree that either of these recriminatory positions are very useful, or can be supported by the available evidence. Most professional educators who have addressed themselves to the problem would probably agree with Coleman's analysis reprinted in the next section, which assumes on good evidence that lower-class children do indeed come as a group to the urban school with a considerable handicap; but the failure of the schools to compensate for the original gap in the preparation of children from different social backgrounds is unlikely to be due simply to the attitudes of the teachers. In the national survey of educational equality on which Coleman reports there must surely have been schools with teaching staffs of very different quality, but these differences are not reflected in measured achievement gains of minority-group pupils.

There is so little hard evidence of any kind that a particular type of teacher or teaching style is related to achievement levels among these children in the long run, that one is compelled to view any argument for one style rather than another with some reservation.

INSTRUCTIONAL STYLE

The most persistent model of teaching in this country, as in Western culture generally, is the *taskmaster*. The role is based on several important assumptions about the nature of knowledge and of the child. One is that the society, through the school personnel, must decide on a common body of knowledge to be learned to the point of recall and skills to be mastered. A second is that this body of material can be broken down into manageable, small tasks of increasing complexity as the child grows in understanding, and it is the teacher's role to explain the tasks and supervise the child's performance of them, reinforcing correct responses and eliminating incorrect ones until mastery is achieved.

Although many of the classroom taskmasters we remember are those whose enthusiasm for their subjects infected us to the point of initial interest in doing strange and often puzzling tasks, motivation is of only peripheral concern to this view of the teacher's role. Every teacher is now taught to "motivate the lesson," but one has only to observe the average run of classrooms to understand how perfunctory and general are such attempts to interest the child.

The second major teaching model, which one might call the *motivator,* concentrates almost totally on developing the child's interest, or on beginning with what already interests him. The fundamental assumptions of this view, which in its modern form derives from Dewey's early influential books on education, are that the school's job is to help the child grow, that each child's growth is a function of his unique individuality as a whole person, and that learning, at whatever stage, must have immediate relevance and value to the learner rather than holding merely a remote promise of usefulness. The teacher's role is to help children devise experiences that are of immediate interest to them and to help work through the problematic features of those experiences. By setting meaningful goals, by dealing over and over again with the barriers to their achievement, and by learning to test alternative choices in moving toward the goal, the children are, in a sense, partly their own teachers.

The present status of these two roles is somewhat ambiguous. As several generations of teacher-training institutions discovered, in the first flush of the progressive education movement, it is difficult to find students who accept the motivational role naturally, and next to impossible to train for it those who do not find it congenial. As a result, and more than a little ironically, most teachers with the skills of this second role are probably teaching in expensive private experimental schools or in upper middle-class suburbs, where children are already sufficiently motivated to learn, if not, indeed, overmotivated. Though most teacher-training institutions today still stress the concepts of the "whole child," individual differences, and developmental lessons, the role one finds most often played in the public-school classroom is that of the taskmaster, despite the training.

There are a number of sufficient reasons for the general failure of training to transfer to the reality. Teachers have had sixteen years of schooling themselves, most of it under taskmaster teachers; thirty or so credits of education courses are unlikely in most instances to overcome such an extensive period of model-setting, particularly since most of the teachers of professional education courses themselves play the taskmaster. The first several years of teaching comprise a period of extraordinary stress and insecurity, in which the generalizations of the college classroom do not seem to work at all; most young teachers, consequently, turn for advice to the old-timers and are thus often reinstructed in the instructional style to which they are most accustomed.

Most importantly, perhaps, the taskmaster model fits perfectly into the large-scale bureaucracies that urban school systems have developed. Major learning objectives can easily be fragmented into daily tasks appropriate for the grade by the central authority and entombed in curriculum memoranda. Each teacher's daily lesson plan can be submitted to the principal's office, which thus has a check on the correspondence between policy and practice. With classrooms as large as thirty pupils, or larger, in which the possibility for dealing with the individual child seldom arises in any event, the bureaucratic system ensures at least some standardization.

In the absence of evidence, one can only speculate about which of these styles is more effective for the average child in the slum school, and speculation about what is primarily a question of technology is not very helpful. Nor are those who take sides on the matter distinguishable by their status as professionals or laymen. Those who regard motivation as crucially important are, to be sure, primarily to be found among professional educators, who see the slum child's alienation from the middle-class life, values, and goals that dominate the school as an important reason for his failure in it. From this point of view the role of the taskmaster, with its concentration on the externally imposed task rather than on the child makes little sense applied to the children in the inner-city school, who do not find those tasks very meaningful, who are bored and restless or openly defiant, or who retreat into a shell of conviction about their own inevitable failure to cope with them.

Most of the teachers favorably described in the Smiley and Asbell articles in this section provide examples of a style in which motivation and interest are centrally important. But they are far from representative of the real model of progressive teaching, in which the children themselves are involved in planning their own experiences, and discussing their implications. There is some measure of agreement among observers of the slum school that intensive efforts to motivate and involve pupils do not work very well. It is possible that their failure is due to a lack of skill and insight among teachers; some attempts to produce materials that touch on the children's own lives and problems have proven successful in arousing interest and motivation for sustained learning.

The proponents of the taskmaster role in one version or another comprise a diverse group including representatives from professional education as well as most of the nonprofessionals who have some relation to the problem. Those parent groups which are vocal about the schools' failure to deal with their children appear to believe that the teachers are just not making them work hard enough, a complaint that is reasonably consonant with lower-class child-rearing values that emphasize behavioral control. But more sophisticated critics, such as Kenneth Clark, make the same charge, attributing the problem to teachers' stereotypes, which lead them to expect less of the Negro slum child, and therefore to demand less. And for the claim that expectation does influence performance there is some evidence, and not only in the laboratory; Rosenthal's experiment in a California school, soon to be published as *Pygmalion in the Classroom,* provides evidence of a real link between expectation and achievement.

Educators and clinicians suggest different reasons for a primary emphasis on the task. In an article included in our companion volume, *Education in the Metropolis,* Ausubel, an educational psychologist of some note, argues that despite the apparent importance of motivation and interest for the learning process, the most enduring basis we can build for an improved level of school achievement for the socially disadvantaged child is the feeling of reward that learning itself provides. He suggests, therefore, a heavy reliance on programmed instruction, which permits the child to work at his own pace and in which the reinforcement is immediate and constant. Frank Reissman, in his article included in this section, seems similarly to favor a concentration on the cognitive processes of the child over attempts to deal with his psychological difficulties in the classroom. The taskmaster role, he appears to be saying, fails only because we insist that the task be approached in a specific way.

THE TEACHER-PUPIL RELATIONSHIP

A second question has to do with the most desirable relation for a teacher to establish with the children of the slum school. The discussion has focused on two different aspects of the relationship: that which involves the teacher as an authority figure in the classroom, and that which is personal and human; as to the first, at least, one can see some fairly general agreement.

The authority relationship demands from the teacher, at a minimum, a disposition toward order and organization, and the ego strength necessary to impose them, when necessary, in the classroom. Most of the important analytic investigations of teaching in general in the past decade have isolated some factor such as this as a correlate of successful teaching, but it seems particularly necessary in the slum school classroom. Lower-class child-rearing styles emphasize external behavioral controls rather than internalized ones; the children tend to be physically, rather than verbally, expressive.

It is most important here to distinguish order from regimentation, the meaningless imposition by external authority of regulatory systems largely for the ease and convenience of the authority, such as the rule of silence in the halls of most urban schools, or the white line dividing the hallways which children passing from one class to another must not cross. One teacher in a city school, much admired by her administrative superiors, has trained her class of brighter-than-average children to proceed to the science room for special lessons by marching silently in single file first to a point in the hall ten feet from their room, then wait until she appears to give the signal to go on the remaining twenty-five feet.

The orderliness of the classroom referred to here as desirable is at the opposite pole from such controls, which are not productive of the kind of behavior that schools in a democracy should strive to achieve. The order that grows out of the learning task, that conforms to its demands, is not necessarily the enemy of exuberance and activity. It is allied to the kind of basic need for order which Pribram, the physiologist, has recently proposed is one of the most dominant needs of the human organism, the impulse to make sense out of things, to make satisfactory relationships out of the inchoate.

No matter how basic the need may be, however, external order must first be imposed, and many young people first going into teaching are not sure enough of themselves to do it very effectively, and a considerable proportion of them, it is reasonable to guess, are not themselves well-enough organized personalities ever to bring real order into classroom learning. These would, it seems clear, do far less harm in a middle-class school where they are likely, at worst, to amuse the children, than in an inner-city classroom where they will probably subside into despair.

The second aspect of the teacher-pupil relationship is the personal one she builds with the children, which is a far more complicated matter. It is in some ways easier to describe what that relationship does *not* necessarily include than it is to state precisely what it *should*. It certainly does not have to be, and probably ought not to be, a relation based on the sentimental, idealized yearning to help the downtrodden that one finds sometimes in young women. Such an idealization of role often gets in the way of clearly perceiving and realistically reacting to the individual child. A genuine kindness in the teacher is probably a useful quality in the relationship, but apparently not a necessary one; experienced observers cite numerous cases of tough martinets who get along very well with children in the slum classroom, who respond to them without fear.

There is very little evidence, in fact, that the sentimental image of the schoolteacher which the educational establishment likes to project is a particularly useful one. Some years ago the National Educational Association produced a film about a poor girl, the daughter of a migrant worker family, who determinedly enrolled in school in every town near which her family stopped to work the crops; eventually, with the help of a multitude of sympathetic and warm teachers, she graduated and planned to go on to college. One scene, which invariably evokes floods of tears from any sophomore class of college girls who are planning to teach, describes a kindly, middle-aged lady who notices that the heroine is having difficulty reading small print. She sends the girl to a doctor, and after class one day presents her with a pair of glasses, explaining that once when she was young and poor someone had done the same for her.

Aside from the sticky unreality of the film (Edward Murrow's angry film documentary about migrant workers made at about the same time points out that we do not know of one case of a migrant child going to college), the image of the teachers in the film indicates the extent to which the profession still clings to the rural context of schooling, where such kindly ladies, in legend, at any rate, once abounded. It is not of much help in the urban school, where the children often know a great deal more about the realities of life than their teachers, and require a different relationship.

The description often advanced of the most necessary ingredient of that relationship is that the teacher must *respect* the child. This term is vague, however; those who use it seldom go on to a more explicit denotation of the word, and people probably mean a variety of different things by it. It can become useful for the purposes of selection and training only if we can give it more precision.

Hilgard, the Stanford psychologist, has suggested that any human relationship is healthy if each person contributes to the growth of the other, and does not exploit the other purely for the satisfaction of his own needs. In the teacher-pupil relationship, obviously, growth has several meanings. The teacher contributes to the child's growth in knowledge, skill, and understanding, but this clinical definition also requires that she aid, or at least not inhibit, growth of the self.

Here is the heart of the difficulty. For the experiences that contribute to the self of the lower-class child are different enough from those of the middle-class world that teachers tend

to want to change him into something else that will better conform to her image of what a child should be. Perhaps such
change may be necessary as part of healthy growth, but the
clinical dictum applies: real growth usually requires acceptance
of the person as he is now. If this is what is meant by respecting
the child, then what it demands of the teacher in the slum
school is that she learn to widen her definition of what constitutes an acceptable self.

Among the many problems in doing so is the fact that the
school is such an alien and fearful environment for many lower-
class youngsters that their behavior tends to cover up and defend the self, rather than reveal it. The teacher, consequently,
needs to have a sufficiently firm concept of her own self to
enable her to make the distinction between the self and the
behavior of children, instead of being seduced into responding
to the behavior alone. One of the warming qualities of Bel
Kaufmann's book, *Up the Down Staircase*, was her ability to
make such a discrimination, from the point at which she took
her friend's advice to respond to the greeting, "Hey, teach,"
with a "Hey, pupe."

This requirement for a good teacher-pupil relationship in
the inner-city school raises the question of whether it does not
demand more than we can get, to which the answer probably is
that it does. Under the current conditions, at least, in which
the urban teaching career line leaves faculty vacancies primarily
in the inner-city schools to be filled by the youngest and least
experienced teachers, we are least likely to find among them
the kind of person described. Young college graduates are too
close to their own struggle to define selfhood to have the confidence necessary to accept very different images of self in others.
Even if there were more teachers available who are capable of
sustaining the kind of human relationship we have described,
they might have considerable difficulty operating within the
human climate of the average urban school as recent sociological observations describe it, and to which some behavioral scientists apply the term *ressentiment*.

Such a climate consists of a pervasive sense of irritability
and ill-humor, a petty preoccupation with rules and forms
rather than with persons and what is happening to them, and

disapproval of any free expression of human impulsiveness and liveliness. *Ressentiment* as a dominant quality of any institution has been explained as a function of the rise to power of the middle class and the development of its favorite institutional form, bureaucracy. Thus, the school is staffed by persons striving for middle-class status (whether to achieve it through social mobility or to maintain it) who, in the course of training and occupational indoctrination, had severely to repress their own impulses and creative self-expression to conform to the demands of the class culture. One has only to discuss high-school or college life with the ordinary student to realize how clearly they do perceive the great pressures toward "acceptable" behavior. When such people actually achieve the status they have striven for, however, the rewards turn out to be considerably less than they had envisioned, in social deference, authority, economic comfort. Their chronic disappointment and small bitterness give rise to the typical climate of the institutions in which they predominate, and account for the repression of any form of exuberance or creative difference in others which they forfeited for themselves.

Everything we know about the way in which group attitudes are transmitted to entering members suggests that beginning teachers, entering a school pervaded by such an atmosphere, either adapt to it by taking over the dominant norms, or sooner or later leave. Those who stay on often develop their own kind of bitterness, as witness this description of big-city teachers by one who has taught a number of years in the system. It is excerpted from a paper on inner-city school human relations submitted in a graduate class.

> I have a vision of the system as it exists today:
>
> At the top—tough, authoritarian, political, Irish Catholics who send their kids to parochial school and despise the teachers and the children who don't have the guts or the money to get out.
>
> In the middle, teachers and supervisors-up-to-principals, who come from lower class white minority backgrounds, many of which (like the Italians and the Jews) are strongly tinged with cultural masochism.
>
> And at the bottom, the children.

The system is certainly one of the most secure and protected of all the secure and protected civil-service jobs; it is, to judge by its personnel, quite adequately paid and rewarded and vacationed and pensioned.

But it is medieval serfdom; and the serfs are willing and active participants. They complain, and dissipate their energies in complaining. They hate, and dissipate their hatred in suffering, in provoking guilt, in destroying the children around them, and then they stand over the corpses, weeping, weeping at the terrible system, this deus ex machina, this THING that did it, that did it to THEM, that did not let them succeed. They drive with a passionate and single-minded overpowering drive toward failure, and in this, at least, and overwhelmingly, they succeed.

And don't tell me they don't fail with the middle-class kids too: only the failure is one of mind and imagination and openness and courage, not the paper skills of math tables and reading achievement.

Alinsky says a democracy lacking in popular participation dies of paralysis. But participation requires courage and strength. The school system, lacking courage and strength and participation, dies of paralysis every day.

Maybe what the teachers of the immigrants of fifty years ago had was not better kids (don't tell me the babies out of Italy with the evil-eye and the garlic around the neck weren't less culturally deprived than the PR's today) but more courage, more self-respect, and a fair share of faith in their jobs and themselves and their children.[1]

The picture is no doubt overdrawn, but it is a better description than any sociologist's of what *ressentiment* looks like.

TEACHER SELECTION AND TRAINING

Assuming that we could somehow change the climate of the school, and there are occasional heartening examples of urban schools infused with enthusiasm and dedication, the problems

---

1. Thanks are due to Miss Gloria Channon for permission to use this excerpt.

of defining, selecting, and training the effective teacher for them have hardly begun to be solved. Some progress, however, can be reported. Syracuse University, for example, with a Ford Foundation grant, developed an ingenious testing device for college graduates without education training who volunteered to become teachers in slum schools. Each candidate was instructed to prepare a fifteen-minute classroom presentation introducing herself as to a new class and beginning a lesson. She delivered it to a group of three staff members who role-played the pupils and who, during the brief period, presented the teacher with three problems to handle. In one instance, two of them began a fight; in another, one interrupted her to inquire, "Hey, teach, why ain't you married?"; finally, one used an obscene expression.

The response of these candidates to later experience in real classrooms is instructive, as they were rated on the basis of this test on both sensitivity to the pupils and ability to handle the problems firmly. Those who were very sensitive, but unable to deal with the provocations, adapted very poorly to the slum classroom. Those with a great deal of positive firmness tended to survive the real experience well, but their pupils did not learn very much. It required a person with both qualities to make the effective teacher.

Regrettably, the results of such imaginative experimentation have not widely been made use of in the many special programs of teacher training aimed at improving slum school teaching. The U.S. Office of Education, for example, has provided for the past several years very substantial funds for summer institutes for teachers of disadvantaged youth. During the first year there were about seventy such institutes held at universities throughout the country and, with an admirable restraint, the funding agency imposed few guidelines on the curricula, permitting each institution to develop its own program. This devout regard for local control resulted in a large number of training institutes which did little more than what an ordinary teacher training course would do, with some emphasis on special lectures and reading.

If we read correctly the lesson of the Syracuse experiments, what is required is to select those who are already capable of firmness and orderliness in the classroom, and train them to be more sensitive and accepting. Although such training is difficult and time-consuming, we know at least how to do it better than we know how to help weak and disorganized persons become stronger. And, difficult as it is, the evidence is very strong that we cannot do much about changing the behavior of teachers in the classroom by asking them to listen to lectures and read books. Any serious attack on the problems of supplying adequate teaching for the slum school requires totally new methods of teacher training as well as the development of sophisticated selection devices. Money is not quite enough, if we do not know as yet how to spend it wisely.

"The guilt often turns to hate, and the hate may be turned upon the child."

NOT LIKE OTHER CHILDREN*

Bernard Asbell

Asbell, a professional writer, comes, on the basis of his observations, to many of the same conclusions as numbers of educators and behavioral scientists do about teaching in the slum school; the most significant element he sees in the situation appears to be the teacher's conviction that the children will not succeed. Yet, at one point, he suggests that teaching in an inner-city classroom is "a crushing task," so perhaps it is an oversimplification of his point of view to point out only his great emphasis on the teacher's attitude as crucial. Although it is a fine, warm piece of writing, it does suffer from this ambivalence which marks so many descriptions of the slum school—it's a terribly difficult task, and it is the teachers' fault that it is not being adequately done.

The article provides a rich catalogue of teacher insensitivities in these schools. If one considers all of these he describes, do they seem to have some elements in common? If so, how could one describe it?

* From *The New Improved American* by Bernard Asbell. Copyright © 1963, 1964, 1965 by Bernard Asbell. McGraw-Hill Book Company. Used by permission of author, McGraw-Hill Book Company, and Curtis Brown, Ltd.

WHEN I began work on this article about schools in the vast slums of our cities, I made the error of setting out to inspect the condition of schoolhouses instead of the lives of the children who spend their days in them. Almost everybody makes the same error. The week I began, a committee of six congressmen, concerned by a growing educational failure in the nation's capital, as well as by rising racial tensions, proceeded to investigate the problem. How did they do it? They went to look at dilapidated schoolhouses, which were not hard to find.

In Pierce School, built in 1894 for 280 pupils, they found 400 enrolled in eight rooms, no hot-lunch room, no auditorium, no health room, no library. Ceiling plaster drops on desks; windows are shaded by sheets of wrapping paper. The congressmen expressed shock.

I had no trouble finding schoolhouse squalor either. In New York, at Public School 103, I didn't get as far as the principal's office before suffering an assault of sickening fumes—pervasive odors of decayed plaster and stale urine, too impregnated in the ancient walls ever to be washed away.

Such observations, of course, are shocking and deserve exposure. But they are also peculiarly comforting. They help strengthen a favorite American myth. The myth is that we can ride a bulldozer to higher national literacy merely by knocking down old, deteriorated classrooms and building glassy, gleaming new ones. But the reality is that schools in the central sections of our major cities are factories of failure, and the school buildings that house them have little to do with the matter. In the struggle to educate the children of the impoverished, whole school systems are surrendering on a mass scale and blaming their failure on the victims—the children and their parents.

In brand-new, gaily painted buildings as well as antiquated shabby ones, the eyes of the children are dull, detached and uninterested, the faces of the teachers harassed and helpless. From open doors the most frequently heard sound is a teacher's *"Shhhhhhhh!"* Sometimes a desperate variation—

"James, sit *down* and shut *up!*" In the streamlined teachers' lunchrooms of these new buildings, shoptalk about pupils includes a high incidence of the word "dumb." Ask a teacher why the kids are so "dumb" and you hear, after a troubled shrug, "I try every way I know to teach them, but they don't *want* to learn. After all, *look at their IQs.*"

That is the teacher's ultimate condemnation. One of the rules she memorized at teachers college is that an intelligence quotient describes the classroom potential of a child. If his IQ is low, the child is unteachable, "dumb."

Recently the idea has crystallized in the minds of a few people—a school superintendent here, a Ford Foundation official there, a professor of psychiatry here, a school social worker there—that the slum child is a child of another world. Our laws do not bind him, our standard middle-class ambitions do not inspire him, our IQs do not measure him and, most of all, his teacher is not reaching him. Rules she learned in teachers college clearly don't work in the slum school, but she clings to them, for no one has taught her different rules. Teachers in first to third grades feel the child slipping away. By the fourth grades he has fallen behind. By the eighth grade he may be as many as three years back, his mind closed, his behavior rebellious. By high-school age he is more than likely a dropout, headed for chronic unemployment, disdaining the "outside" middle-class world that already disdains him, secretly contemptuous of himself, a waste of a human being. A failure.

The few people trying to understand this child have given him a name—not a satisfactory name, but a name; they call him "culturally deprived." What defines him is not an absence of money or nice clothes or good furniture or cars or food, although all these objects are relatively lacking. These children suffer from a poverty of experience. Perhaps their lives are rich with experiences their teachers know nothing about. But they are growing up unequipped to live in an urban, primarily middle-class world of papers and pens, books and conversations, machines and desks and time clocks.

Their numbers are staggering. While in 1950 one child out of every ten in America's 14 largest cities was "culturally deprived," by 1960 the figure had become an alarming one out of three. This is an estimate made for the Ford Foundation by a group of big-city school boards organized as the Great Cities School Improvement Studies. By 1970 one of every two big-city children is expected to be "culturally deprived."

Some of these deprived children are the sons and daughters of coal miners and "branch water" farmers of the Southern Appalachian backwoods driven to the cities when their land would no longer support an ever-growing population. Some are children of Puerto Ricans, Mexicans, refugees from American Indian reservations.

But mostly they are the children of Negroes. Chicago's elementary-school enrollment is 46 per cent Negro. Philadelphia's and Baltimore's are about the same. New York City's is 27 per cent (Negroes and Puerto Ricans in Manhattan total 76 per cent). The percentage of Negro children in Washington public schools is a lopsided 85. These proportions are constantly, inexorably growing.

Ten years from now when many of these children, like their parents, will be on relief, unemployable in a society demanding increased human skills, and when *their* children in even vaster numbers are failing to learn from their bewildered teachers, a congressman will rise, as many do every year, to protest that the cost of the dole is killing us. How, he will ask, can we dare mortgage our grandchildren by the cost of today's handouts? Yet so few men of responsibility are asking what investment may be made in today's classrooms—to change the architecture not only of walls but of lives—so that millions of our young may be saved from defeat, economic uselessness and spiritual hopelessness.

What investment can be made? This is what I tried to find out as I talked to teacher after teacher, child after child, in school after school, city after city. The problems may not be as hopeless as they seem. But the problems are not what most of us think they are, either.

I met Tracy in a classroom in Milwaukee. Two years ago he came to Milwaukee from Mississippi, one unnoticed soul in the great migratory wave from declining southern farmlands to northern industrial cities. Tracy (that is not his real name) is 12 years old. When his mother took him to enroll in the strange northern schoolhouse, he looked and acted "dumb"—sullen, staring without focus when spoken to, responding to questions not in sentences but in monosyllabic grunts. He was given a standard intelligence test for "nonverbal" children and scored a 66. That number confirmed, as almost any certified teacher will vow, that Tracy, like so many of his slum schoolmates, was a lost cause. The proof was in the pudding; at the age of ten he was unable to muddle through a first-grade reader.

Was he really so unteachable? Was it possible that his IQ, his manner and even the color of his skin were a curtain hiding from his teachers an active, eager intelligence starved for experience to nourish it? By chance Tracy was chosen at random from thousands for an experimental class of 20 children, one of seven such classes in Milwaukee subsidized by the Ford Foundation. His classmates' IQs were like Tracy's, 73, 64, 81, 71, 77. Illiterates and near illiterates all. Some were old enough for junior high school, but all were classified as "first to fourth grade, ungraded."

In a year and a half his teacher, Mrs. Marguerite Stangel, a stocky, stern-looking woman, ignoring Tracy's "unteachability," succeeded in teaching him. "A child does what's expected of him," she told me. "His teachers had convinced him he couldn't do anything. They convinced his mother. She told me, 'Teacher, I hope you can learn him. Nobody I ever saw could learn him.' Whenever I got him to learn something, I'd make him write it on the board and I'd say, 'There—you did it.' He'd look astonished, as if to say, 'I didn't know it was that easy. I *did* it!'"

Mrs. Stangel led me to a bulletin board covered with papers of careful writing. Not just lists of words, or even sentences, but poems—original poems—for Lincoln's Birthday. I liked Tracy's best. Decorated by a neatly scissored silhouette of Lincoln, his poem read:

> Abraham Lincoln grew up to be a very nice man.
> He believed in freedom for every man.

> He went to a theater one fine night.
> And a half crazy actor shot him at sight.

It was less than Shakespearian. But as the work of a child who a few months earlier couldn't read "Look, Dick, look," it brought on a tremor of dreadful wonder at how many intelligences are buried beneath a teacher's conclusion that a child is "dumb."

I called Tracy over. The class had already been let out, but a few boys were still there, doing chores. Mrs. Stangel told me they had not been ordered to stay; they just liked to. Tracy was lining up desks in precise military formation. His body was alive with boyish fidgeting but his face was dull. He would not focus his eyes on me.

"What are you going to do when you're all finished with school?" I asked.

"Go down the gym. Play basketball."

"I don't mean today," I said. "I mean when you're all finished going to school. What do you want to be when you grow up?"

He looked out the window, eyes unsteady and gently blinking. He said nothing. As I waited he droned a note as if on the edge of a pronouncement, but no thought would come.

I had asked this question of dozens upon dozens of boys in slum schools—young white mountaineers and young Negroes. The mountain children would often try for a few seconds to understand the odd question. Then their concentration would melt away. No words. The question was too strange. Young Negroes—six or seven years old—would usually produce an answer, and it was almost always the same:

"Baseball player."

"What team?"

"San Francisco Giants."

"What position?"

"Center field."

Everyone knows who plays there. Willie Mays.

"What if there's no job for you on a baseball team?"

"Be basketball player."

"What if all the teams have all the players they need? What if you get a job to do work? What kind of job would you get?"

Then the Negro child's mind, like the mountain boy's, strains for a moment and seems to go blank.

These, of course, were six-year-olds. But Tracy was 12 years old—almost old enough to drop out of school. He was old enough to know there can be only one Willie Mays. What other worthwhile ambitions remained? Like most 12-year-olds I asked, Tracy grappled with the question wordlessly.

"What does your father do?" I asked.

"My father? When?"

"What does he do when he works?"

"Sometimes they call him. He—I guess he wash cars."

"All right. Now, what kind of work do you want to do when you grow up?"

Now that he knew what I was getting at, he squinted thoughtfully, as though to take inventory of all the far-ranging occupations he could imagine. But none seemed to come to mind.

Mrs. Stangel came to my aid. "Did you ever see anybody working whose work you would like to do?"

After a strained silence Tracy finally said, "Like to be the boss in a store."

"What kind of store?" I asked.

The question confounded him again.

"A department store?" Mrs. Stangel prodded him.

Silence. His forehead began to sweat. I don't think he knew about department stores. Then he said, apparently reaching out as far as his worldly knowledge would take him: "Groc'ry store."

"Why," I asked, "would you like to be a boss in a grocery store?"

His answer was ready and reasonable.

" 'Cause anything that was there you could get."

If he was stretching his imagination strenuously to understand the meaning of my questions, I had to stretch mine just as strenuously to get the meaning of his answers. It is difficult to comprehend the world of a child who has hardly ever seen

a man of his color performing any task honored by society
except playing baseball or doing something musical. Adults in
his world do not ask a child what he wants to be when he
grows up. They do not generally talk about work. The working
day is when they are held in lowest esteem, by themselves as
well as by others. Grown men of dark color, if not great stars
like Willie Mays, are part-time car washers like Tracy's father.
But hardly anything in between, as far as Tracy has ever seen.
Ambition for a career is either unreasonable or untenable;
such an unfruitful thought does not ordinarily come to mind.

In a classroom in a slum school in Chicago, a conscientious
white teacher proudly showed me some drawings made by her
sixth graders. Only one pictured a person. It was a remarkably
skilled rendition of a boy, wearing a straw Huckleberry Finn
hat, sucking a weed, fishing at a riverbank. The boy in the picture was white.

I looked around. Not a white child in the class. The teacher,
sensing my unspoken question, handed me an elementary
reader, a Dick and Jane story. "Do you see any children here,"
she asked quietly, "who aren't white? The boy has never seen
a picture of a Negro child. At least not a real picture in a book.
He already knows a colored child isn't good enough to be in a
picture."

Does he ever see *any* Negro in a school reader?

"Yes," the teacher said. "When Dick and Jane go to visit
their grandmother in the country—which these children don't
understand because Grandmother lives with *them*—and they
ride on a train to get there—these children have never ridden
on a train—they are served by a Negro porter. The book isn't
about children like them. It's a silly fairy tale about things they
can't imagine. Why learn to read it? In fact, why learn to read?"

Because the books seem stupid, the children's negative response to them appears stupid. Other elements in the background of the slum child help complete a classical portrait, as
described in standard teacher education, of stupidity.

"How can I teach them," I was asked by teacher after
teacher, "when they have no attention span? They just *won't*
concentrate."

Psychologists are beginning to discern that the slum child's inattention may be a high skill, the result of intensive training. When a child lives with 11 people in three rooms separated by thin walls from other households of 11 people in three other rooms, smelling their cooking, sharing their toilets, knowing when the man is drunk next door and the baby awake downstairs—a child must *learn* to be inattentive to survive. His ears become skilled at not hearing, his eyes at not seeing.

Dr. Martin Deutsch, of the Institute for Developmental Studies, tells of a boy who seemed a social misfit. A school psychologist, moved to investigate, learned that the boy liked to lock himself in a closet. This had ominous Freudian implications, such as a need to withdraw to the dark comfort of the womb. To confuse the implications, however, the boy showed a predilection for a certain closet in which he could turn on an electric light. On investigating this deviation, the psychologist discovered that the boy—indeed a misfit among his peers— merely liked to read. He would go to all lengths to do so in quiet, including locking himself in a closet. This eccentricity had led his family and school to suspect that he was seriously out of his head.

Most teachers hardly suspect other forms of the slum child's poverty of—or differences in—experience. Dr. Deutsch's staff has found that kindergarten children often have not learned to tell one color from another, except red and blue. No one has told them to wear the pink dress today or wondered aloud in their presence about the advisability of getting lavender draperies to go with the gray rug. They may be unaware of shapes—blocks, circles, squares, the idea of short and long. The teacher assumes a knowledge of these things. She often cannot conceive of a child's not knowing colors and shapes—except a very "dumb" child. One teacher, trying to teach reading through a story about a snowman, was baffled to learn that some children assumed a snowman is a man who shovels snow from city streets; they had seen one of those, but knew of no other kind. She later found that one of her children was sure a fire engine's purpose was to bring fire. No one had ever told him otherwise.

In fact, no one ever tells slum children much about anything. Conversation is not a highly developed art in their families. Suddenly the child, accustomed to learning through his
senses, is obliged to sit still all day before a talkative teacher—
she can talk for hours without stopping. Moreover, she seems to
think the most important thing in the world is to make out
printed words on a page. About half the children surveyed by
Dr. Deutsch came from homes that did not possess a single
book. Instead of bringing the middle-class teacher and the
impoverished pupil closer together, words may only help to
alienate them, underlining the distance between their worlds.

The teacher of early grades may remain largely unaware
that her pupils aren't following her. The fifth- and sixth-grade
teachers find out with a jolt.

"Those are the grades," says Dr. Deutsch, "when learning
depends more and more on abstractions. What is a nation?
What happened in the past? Suddenly it's discovered that these
children are unprepared for skilled use of such basic abstract
ideas as bigger and smaller, higher and lower, round and
square. They are untrained in ideas that grow from numbers.
A child may know that Yankee Stadium holds a large number
of people, but he doesn't know if that large number is closer to
one hundred or one hundred thousand.

"He is comparatively unprepared to deal skillfully with the
idea of time, the past, the future, planning, scheduling. The
middle-class American notion of the value of time or the careful allotment of it appears to be comparatively absent in the
culture of the slums, just as it is almost entirely absent in the
life of certain Indian tribes. This is extremely difficult for most
time-oriented Americans to grasp. Often a teacher interprets a
child's disregard for time as a form of rebellion or stupidity,
instead of a problem of cultural difference."

By the time the child is old enough to drop out of school,
he is well insulated from other standard American values.

"It's hard for outsiders to understand," says Mrs. Zenobia
Baxter, a school counselor in Chicago working with dropouts,
"that for many of these children work is only a word. They
have never seen anyone work. If there's a man at home, there's

a good chance he's unemployed. But in fifty per cent of these homes there is no man at the head of the house at all."

Mrs. Baxter organizes visits to offices and factories to demonstrate what people do when they work—how a knowledge of words and numbers helps them live better. She organizes trips to the Loop, Chicago's downtown district, for teen-agers and parents who have never been there, even though it is only 30 blocks from the heart of the slums. They never had occasion to go because they can't get jobs in Loop offices and do not feel welcome in the stores.

After these visits Mrs. Baxter leads the teen-agers in discussing what wages are, what one must do to get them, how one's life is improved when one has money of his own. These elementary ideas are often startlingly new to young people of the slums. Mrs. Baxter has found that while many understand the idea of "a job"—something hard to get—few have any real notion that jobs separate into many specialized occupations. They do not know that a house is built from the separate efforts of carpenters, bricklayers, painters, truck drivers, architects, mortgage bankers. No one they know has such specialized occupations. A low-status, unskilled worker speaks simply of "going to work."

But don't adults of the slums lead their children into wanting something better? Why don't they see school as the obvious avenue of progress? Says Edward Ponder, the energetic, zealous director of the Milwaukee experimental project:

"We can't begin to understand why these people don't accept school as a real part of their lives until we begin to understand how they have been rebuffed by every element of the organized community for more than a hundred years. They have become convinced—'You may live here, but you don't really belong here.' Even the supposedly helpful, friendly agencies contribute to this negative education. Recently we sent the father of one of our pupils to a social agency to get advice on budgeting. He had no conception of how to allot the little money he brought home. The social agency sent him back with a note saying, 'This family doesn't earn enough to budget. We cannot give them any advice.' That father, against all the lessons of his experience, had been willing to give those strange people in organized society another try, and again they found him useless, as they always had.

"Repeated experiences like that are what helped long ago to make the people of the slums the lost population. The school children grow up absorbing the environment and experience of their parents. They create a world apart from agencies, officials, laws, policemen, schools and teachers, and far away from middle-class ideas of success. How do you begin to introduce the idea of 'goal' into the life of a child who grows up in that other world?"

The task of introducing the idea of "goal" to such a child must fall, for lack of anyone else to assume it, upon his teacher. It is a crushing task, particularly for one untrained for it, who probably did not choose it and who frequently does not comprehend the problem. With the exception of three courses of small enrollment in the entire United States, teachers colleges that are turning out certified educators by the thousands offer no special instruction in helping the child of the slums. It is no wonder that teachers by the thousands, no matter how conscientious, fail at the task. And it is a terrible burden for a weary, bewildered teacher to go home from the classroom after each harassing day, carrying the weight of failure. The guilt often turns to hate, and the hate may be turned upon the child.

"My bunch is pretty rough," a husky male teacher in his middle 30s told me in the lunchroom of a Chicago slum school. "But drop in. If you don't mind, I don't mind." Everywhere, I found principals and teachers surprisingly willing to throw open their classrooms. The few effective ones want to show the good that can be done. The many helpless ones want to free themselves of the burden of failure; they want to display how terrible the children are.

When I called on the teacher who had invited me, I found him standing in front of his class, hands locked behind him, chest out, shoulders back, springing up and down rhythmically on the balls of his feet, overseeing the sullen, dark-skinned faces that filled the room. It was the authoritative stance of a cop on a beat.

"Most of the time I'm a policeman, not a teacher," he said. "This is what new teachers get to cut their teeth on. Of course, I really don't mind. I was in the Army for years and I just got out of teachers college a year ago. Maybe this is a good place for me 'cause I'm a big bruiser. But they'll take some tender young girl right out of college and throw her into a bunch like this to get her started. She has to wait it out until she's got enough seniority to transfer to a decent place. Naturally, the experienced teachers want the better spots. *Someone's* got to do this, so the new ones get it."

All this was said in what I can only call a softened loud tone. The comments were directed at me, but the class heard every word. A dozen times I had heard teachers talk in that special tone. It was more than an expression of contempt; it seemed a form of revenge upon the pupils.

"How do you get them interested when they don't *want* to get interested?" the teacher went on. "Like in art. I put something on the board, some kind of design, and tell them to copy it, except to change it a little so it will be original. They just look at me. They don't understand. They don't try to understand, so what can I do?"

His class of sixth graders seemed old enough for high school. The boys were big-boned, muscular, some at the age of shaving. The girls were plump and bosomy. They sat in a hodgepodge of slovenly postures, facing almost every way except straight forward, where the teacher's desk was. Yet there was a liveliness in the room. An unspoken language of defiance seemed to flit through the air, by a subtle flicking of eyes, the dropping of a book, two heads disappearing in the depths of the aisle, an elaborate yawn and stretching of arms, half-concealed smirks spreading across the room. The teacher seemed as blind to this language as the children seemed deaf to his.

"I try to emphasize reading—reading is what keeps them three or four years behind in grade—but they have no attention span." Then for the first time he lowered his voice, half-turning his back to the class, preparing to say something unspeakable. "What do you think the average IQ is in a group like this?" he whispered. "About seventy-five. I mean, that's the *average*, so you can imagine how low they get. You know, seventy-five is the borderline of mentally retarded. Yes, I know the IQ doesn't show everything. But it's a pretty fair indication of what you can *expect*."

On the teacher's desk lay a shaft of two-by-four lumber whittled to a jagged shape. "Some kid brought this to protect himself with," said the teacher, pounding the weapon into his palm, his voice full again. "Naturally, I took it away from him, but now I keep it handy to protect myself. A teacher got bopped again in the rest room this morning. You never know what to *expect*."

Teachers everywhere I went seemed preoccupied with the idea of "what to expect," so seldom with what they might effect. And as Mrs. Stangel, in Milwaukee, had said pointedly, "A child does what's expected of him." Recently a psychologist at the University of North Dakota, Dr. Robert Rosenthal, showed vividly how an expectation becomes a reality. He selected two groups of psychology students and put each in charge of teaching a group of rats to run through a maze. Dr. Rosenthal then told one group its rats were "maze-bright," the other that its rats were "maze-dull." Both these statements were unfounded, but Dr. Rosenthal wanted to give each group of students something to "expect." Sure enough, the students who thought they had "maze-bright" rats got significantly better results than those who had been misled into thinking their rats were dull.

And the schoolteacher's index of what to expect from pupils, of course, is the IQ. Recently, however, Ernest A. Haggard, a psychologist, found he could raise IQs substantially in slum schools by giving children a mere three hours of coaching and practice in how to take the IQ test, by offering small rewards for doing well and by training examiners to convey simple friendliness to the children. While teachers often explain away a child's poor reading by showing his low IQ, Dr. Haggard turned this proposition around. He raised IQs even further by having examiners read test items aloud while children followed them in their test booklets. Their IQs had been depressed *because* they were poor readers.

To convey her contempt for children she has failed to teach, a teacher does not have to be openly hostile. She can do it with condescension and even better with pity. These were the stock in trade of one Chicago principal of an all-white slum school.

She began my tour of her school by pointing out "one of our sweet little Indian girls." Before a class of fidgeting youngsters she drew an attractive child to her side. "Isn't she a darling?" she asked. "We're especially pleased with how clean she is—haven't you noticed?" Turning to the girl she inquired endearingly, "But you aren't a full-blooded Indian, are you, dear?"

Leading me into the library, she announced, "These are our special problem boys, but we do believe in them. Yes, with some the problem may be reading, or it may be other things. Everyone's here to get some little thing doctored. Isn't that right, boys?" The boys, young teen-agers, remained expressionless.

"I wonder if you've noticed," she went on, "what nice haircuts everyone here has. We don't let their being poor stand in the way of their looking presentable. If one of them can't afford the few pennies for a haircut, we have barbers in the neighborhood who cut their hair free. We try to teach our boys pride and self-respect. Everyone is ready to help them."

The school had a feeling not of a place for educational growth, but of a prison with a benign lady warden. Even schoolwork is used as a protective weapon by teachers against "bad" children. "In social studies," a bright 13-year-old girl in seventh grade told me, "we get a chapter a week to read for homework, but nothing to write. Unless we're noisy. Then we get written work for punishment. Twice I had to do a five-hundred-word essay on why I talk so much. If the teacher catches us talking when she's out of the room, we get themes to write. We get themes at other times too, just because she's in a bad mood."

Mrs. Bailey Bishop, teacher of the first grade at Coleman School, an antiquated building in the heart of Chicago's Negro ghetto, looks like neither a continual violator of convention nor one of the most startlingly successful teachers in the world. She is both.

Neither her neighboring teachers nor the powers on high in her school system know that in effect she has fashioned a new kind of education. If her class were "experimental," supported by a foundation, her unusual methods would be the subject of lengthy papers. But hers is an ordinary class of ordinary-class slum kids dealt to her at random. Their IQ scores are low. Their "cultural deprivation" is high. Their families are paralyzed by poverty.

The day I visited Mrs. Bishop's first-grade class, they were reading aloud about space capsules and oxygen. The word "weightlessness" was no trouble to them at all. Why not? Mrs. Bishop had first made them curious about gravity, weight, and finally weightlessness. Once grasping the idea, the children had need for a word to describe the idea. She gave them the word. They treasure its sound, its sight and its correct spelling.

Mrs. Bishop not only ignores IQs but also believes there is no such thing as a first-grade vocabulary. She believes children will learn words they need to know, and their needs depend on the excitement in their minds. To excite their minds Mrs. Bishop almost never teaches. She asks questions—carefully choosing questions the children can answer. She leads them in constructing old information into new ideas; they experience the joys of "finding out," enjoy the feeling of success with every question and every answer.

Since Mrs. Bishop ignores the prescribed first-grade vocabulary, she ignores first-grade textbooks. The room is strewn with books of many levels. During breaks in activity, children go to a "reading table" and choose a book that interests them. If the ideas are interesting, they learn the words. (They seldom choose books that say "Look, Dick, look—Run, Jane, run.")

Mrs. Bishop began her class by chalking words on the blackboard:

I am going to talk to you on the board this morning.

As she wrote, the children read each word aloud, often anticipating the word before she had finished writing it. Their heads strained forward. These were not silly words in a book about strange people. Mrs. Bishop was talking to *them;* if they could make out the words, they'd know what she was trying to say. This was a fascinating game. She wrote:

Things we have to do today.

Hands leaped up. What followed was an exercise in eagerness, planning, organization of time and duty, reading and enunciation of lots of big words that never appeared in a first-grade reader. As Mrs. Bishop recognized each hand raised, the child suggested a duty for the day. Mrs. Bishop listed the duty on the board, the children pronouncing each word without difficulty because it had a meaning for them:

We will do our work papers.
We have to read the bulletin boards.
We must read the chart stories.
We have to fix the thermometer.
We have to take care of the pets.
We have to paint a picture for the mural.

Before one fascinating activity had quite finished, Mrs. Bishop had another under way. Introducing the "new mathematics" to the first grade, Mrs. Bishop drew a strange diagram on the board:

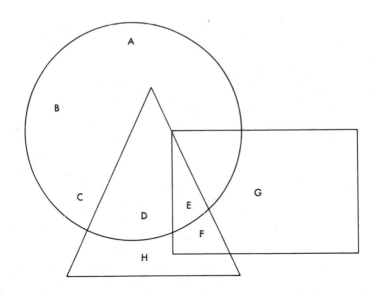

"I am thinking of a letter," she said. "Can you think of three good questions to ask me so you'll know which letter I'm thinking of?"

An explosion of hands. "Is it inside the circle?" . . . "Is it inside the triangle?" . . . "Is it inside the rectangle?" To each of these Mrs. Bishop answered, with rising suspense, "Yes."

One child, hardly able to contain the force of his suspicion, asked, "Is it inside *everything?*"

Mrs. Bishop, eyes agleam, luring him on, nodded yes.

The child triumphantly shouted, "It's *E!*"

She played the game three times. The children, captivated by the pleasures of abstract logic, asked please to play it still another time, then once more again. Finally, putting down her chalk, Mrs. Bishop turned to them and said quietly, "See? If you ask good questions, you can find things out."

The unrelenting excitement in the room, the brightness of the minds, the visible growth of the children's experience, made it easy for one to forget that these were "culturally deprived" children in one of the worst of slum districts. They seemed a class of the especially gifted—which of course they were. They were gifted by a teacher who really liked them; who believed that all children, *including* slum children, *want* to learn whatever appears exciting and useful; and who came to them in the first grade to help mold them instead of in a seventh-grade remedial-reading class, when it was too late.

Dr. Martin Deutsch suspects that even the first grade may be too late for a child's introduction to the ideas, habits and objects of a wordy world. Dr. Deutsch's Institute for Developmental Studies is running four experimental nursery classes for four- and five-year-olds in Harlem school buildings. Carefully trained teachers enliven their children's minds as Mrs. Bishop instinctively does with her Chicago first graders.

A similar experiment is in progress in Baltimore. Both experiments are subsidized by the Ford Foundation, which is also underwriting the special classes in Milwaukee and numerous other large, slum-ridden cities. The most publicized of these experimental projects has been Higher Horizons, a program of "cultural enrichment" given to junior-high-school students in New York City slum areas. In Junior High School No. 43, where the project began in 1956, more than half the students raised their IQs, some an astonishing 40 points. Grades rose impressively; discipline problems were reduced; students did far better in high school than pre-project students; and the number who went on to college multiplied by three and a half times.

New York's Board of Education, confident it had found the formula for educating slum children, rapidly introduced Higher Horizons to 63 schools. Too rapidly. Money for extra remedial-reading teachers and guidance counselors on so large a scale could not be found. Principals and classroom teachers had not been sufficiently trained out of their old habits and ideas. There was some evidence, too, that the sudden exposure to large doses of classical music, art galleries and literature assignments at the junior-high-school level was too much, too late. When expanded to include larger numbers of children, Higher Horizons' spectacular record of results achieved was considerably watered down.

In St. Louis an ex-basketball coach appears to have come closer than anyone to a large-scale enduring success. Samuel Shepard, Jr., superintendent of 23 virtually all-Negro elementary schools, has lifted school attendance of his children from the lowest in the city to the city's average. Their academic abilities rose steadily until June, 1961, when eighth-grade graduates tested at the national norms for reading and arithmetic, and slightly higher than national norms for language skills. This has been accomplished with no significant change in classroom materials or study plans.

Shepard dispatched staff members to teacher after teacher, showing charts of fourth-grade readers reading at second-grade level, seventh graders at fourth-grade level.

"You used to say," Shepard told teachers' meetings, "that you couldn't teach unless your classes were reduced from forty-five to thirty-five. We now have a city-wide average of thirty-five. In this district, because of our special problems, we've won a reduction to thirty-three. If you can't teach better to classes that size, maybe the problem is that you can't teach."

The former basketball coach followed up this challenging locker-room pep talk by requiring teachers to spend after-school time visiting homes of their pupils. Ostensibly these visits were to advise parents on how to help their children do homework by allotting time and study space. Really Shepard wanted his teachers exposed—many for the first time—to the seemingly hopeless home and neighborhood lives of their pupils. He wanted to rid teachers of the middle-class cliché "A teacher can't substitute for the good, wholesome influence of parents." Teachers *must* provide the substitute influence if the new generation is not to be surrendered to old cultural patterns drilled into Negro Americans since slavery—passiveness, dependence, absence of career ambition (made praiseworthy by the white man's phrase. "He knows how to keep his place").

"If the white world could understand," Shepard said to me, "how the nonwhite has had hostility trampled into him for a hundred years, then the white world would begin to understand the problem they have given us to unravel in the lives of these children. Maybe they'd understand how hard it is to convince a kid, in the face of all his home and community influences, that he really belongs in the same world a white man belongs in."

To help tear the children away from the negative influences of home and neighborhood, Shepard enlisted the homes and neighborhoods themselves. Teachers, during visits to homes, urged parents to come to school meetings to learn how to help their children by encouraging study. Parents were taken aback; they had never been asked to school before unless a child was in trouble. Shepard arranged study places in libraries and community buildings, then urged parents of crowded homes to take children there. He distributed homework assignment booklets to children; parents were to sign them each week, affirming that they had inspected the child's homework. Shepard was less concerned with the inspection than with making the parent feel he was participating and needed.

Shepard wrote letters to parents by the hundreds. "I'd find

any excuse to write to them," he says, "anything that would describe a success. These people had never had the simple experience of being told that someone in their family had achieved something. We set up honor rolls for anything we could honor the children for, so that every kid was either on a list or knew someone who was. And I don't mean the suburban kid he knew of whose house gets cleaned by one of our kids' mothers. I mean here.

"We set up an honor roll for high grades, others for perfect attendance, for artwork, for compositions, and one for most improvement—that's usually a list of former hell-raisers who nobody thought could ever be straightened out."

As the academic achievement began to rise, a strange thing happened. Teachers with seniority stopped asking to transfer to "nicer" neighborhoods, as teachers do in almost all slum districts. Instead, Shepard found himself bombarded by applications for transfers into his district at more than five times the rate of vacancies. Just as the pupils and parents hungered for the nourishment of success, so did teachers.

Shepard's big gun is a campaign to convince parents and pupils that a profound change has taken place in the job picture for Negroes. Fifteen years ago, a Negro struggling to earn an engineering degree might be wasting his time; discrimination would bar him from professional jobs. Today the demand for skills is great; jobs are opening up for people of any color— if they are skilled. But the deadly weight of past frustrations has kept the majority of Negroes from training for them.

Shepard and his staff organized a "road show" of 17 young Negroes, each solidly trained, each in a skilled job, but not so advanced that a 12-year-old slum child could not imagine doing the same. The "road show" traveled from school to school, appearing before parents and pupils. One of Shepard's young principals, Ernest Jones, vividly describes the meetings:

"We tell the parents, 'Now, we've been saying that if your child works hard in school, it will pay off in the long run. We're going to try to show you.' The audience is skeptical. Whatever you say, they'll shake their heads for an hour and say, 'Yessir,

that's right,' the same as they've learned to do when white
people talk to them, but you're not communicating. Then we
bring in each of these seventeen people, start interviewing
them before the crowd, and a change takes place.

" 'Where do you work?'

" 'McDonnell Aircraft.'

" 'What do they do?'

" 'They make space capsules.'

"The young fellow illustrates on a blackboard what space
capsules are and how he helps design them. We ask if he needs
any training for such work. He tells about the schooling he had.
Then we ask:

" 'Did you get that kind of job the first time you went somewhere to apply for one?'

"You can almost hear the hall freeze with attention.

"He says, 'No. But I knew I was properly trained and
qualified. I knew there was a place for me somewhere and I
found it at McDonnell.'

"Most of the adults in that hall have never heard a young
Negro from their own neighborhood say anything like that before—because for the most part it was never true before. Next
we bring on a computer programmer who not only has a good job
but recently won an award as the outstanding government
employee in the St. Louis area.

"The one who really shakes the people up is a woman who's
an artist for Pet Milk Company. We ask her, 'How many children were in your family?' She says, 'Nine.' You feel a slight
tremble in the hall from an excuse caving in. Then she adds
she was the oldest and had to look after all the others. Another
excuse hits the ground. She says, 'I remember I had two dresses.
One was to wear while I was washing and drying the other one
for school next day.' You can't imagine the impact on the
people when she tells that. That's the story of every woman in
the hall."

"Our slogan," adds Samuel Shepard, "is 'No excuses.' It's
not an easy slogan to put over after a hundred years of frustration. But we have to face the fact squarely that discrimination
is not only a hindrance to getting a job but can also be used as

an excuse for not expecting to get one. We want to convince people to throw away all the crutches. We want to show that successful people have come from all kinds of undesirable conditions but made it anyhow."

"The greatest joy that you can have in this kind of work," young Ernest Jones concludes, "is seeing a kid get out of high school, his whole world changed from when he went in. I keep thinking of a boy I saw one night at a roller-skating party. He was about seventeen. I hadn't seen him since he got out of my grammar school four years earlier. He was headed, frankly, toward being a bum. No interest. No motivation, no real concern about anything, always out in the street. It's tough when you know a kid's got it but he's not using it. At this skating party I asked the boy how he'd been doing and he said fine, that he was about to graduate from high school. I was surprised he'd stayed in school and I said so. 'Mr. Jones,' he said—he was very polite and lively—'I'm going to keep going to school for a while. I figure if I don't do that, I'm going to wind up just not doing much.' My God—it really got through to him. We work day and night to get through to these kids. Yet it's always a surprise when we run into a kid saying something like that. The job sometimes is so hard that maybe even we don't believe it's possible to get through. Then one kid comes along and tells you all those days and nights have a purpose after all."

"And they need to feel—physically feel—some connection between themselves and words, words, words."

"WHO WOULD
TEACH HERE . . ."*
Marjorie B. Smiley

Here are descriptions of three effective teachers found in inner-city schools, written in this case by a professional educator with considerable experience in the school problems under discussion. Some of the differences in teaching style may be related to the age levels of the children in each case, but even taking this aspect into account, it is clear that the three teachers approach their task in fundamentally different ways. If one considers at the same time the positive models of teaching described in Asbell's article, it is easy to see why it is so difficult to construct a single appropriate role for slum school teaching.

With these descriptions before one, it is instructive to review the issue of teacher role as it was discussed

* From Marjorie B. Smiley, "Who Would Teach Here . . ." *The PTA Magazine,* September 1963, pp. 16–18. Reprinted by permission from *The PTA Magazine,* September 1963.

in the introduction to this section. Do these teachers fit the two qualities that it suggests are crucial? Of the specific characteristics of the effective teachers in both articles, which are probably personality traits that they just happen to have, and which are modifiable by training? Are there any ways in which schools of education might try to produce these characteristics in teachers?

THE TWO classes I visited one day—Mrs. Bannerman's and Mr. Holley's—could hardly have been more difficult, but they were equally memorable. Mrs. Bannerman's ninth-graders were seated in a wide circle, feet twisted around chair legs, heads bent over teacher-made copies of a passage from Chaucer in the original and in two modern versions. Mrs. Bannerman explained that the class had been critical of the sing-song rhythm of the modern *Troilus and Cressida*. "So," she said, "I promised we would compare it with Chaucer's own verse."

Turning to the class, she began the discussion. "Well, what do you think?" What these ninth-graders thought as the hour passed and more and more specific and discriminating comparisons were made of words, word order, metaphor, and rhyme would have done credit to high school seniors or college freshmen.

Classes like this are rather common in junior or senior high schools in communities where there are a number of college-educated families. These families often demand that schools provide cultural advantages for their children. The unusual thing about this class was that it was not in an upper-class suburban school but in the heart of a big city. Young Mrs. Bannerman had chosen to teach in this all-Negro "difficult" school rather than in a "silk stocking" school.

Of course any teacher would be delighted with a class like this. Mrs. Bannerman has only one such class, however. Her full program includes two classes that began the school year several grades behind in reading. "One after another, though, they are getting interested in reading. Most of the boys had never before read a book all the way through."

Mrs. Bannerman was taking part of her lunch hour to show me the "bookstore" that she had set up in an office and was running with her principal's encouragement. Her paperback stock was colorful and varied. Shakespeare's plays and other classics were interspersed with *The Lord of the Flies, The Pearl, The Miracle Worker,* and *Catcher in the Rye.* The paperback collection was started by this teacher, her husband, and some of her friends. It was a small but critically important contribution to a school that, like many underprivileged schools, has no library and a budget that provides for only a few textbooks, often outmoded and inappropriate.

Not all the school's teachers, even its English teachers, use paperbacks in their teaching. Many still prefer the old textbooks, which, they tell you, the children used to like. "I don't know what's come over young people. This used to be a good neighborhood, a good school," one of the older teachers told me at lunch. Among these teachers Mrs. Bannerman's innovations—despite the principal's outspoken approval, and smiles from children not even in her classes—have not won widespread acceptance.

But Mrs. Bannerman seems to find the enthusiasm of the children compensation enough. For the first time books mean something to them. One boy, finishing *Catcher in the Rye* after a diet of comic books, said to her, "Man, that book's got half my life in it!" It is not surprising, then, that Mrs. Bannerman finds deep satisfaction in giving so much of herself to teaching in a slum school. Comparing these children with the ones she had taught in an eastern suburb, she said: "It's true these boys and girls haven't had any advantages. They haven't read, and most of them can't read well. But some of the others had learned to dislike reading. They were against it; it bored them. Here you can help children really discover reading. They're hungry for it—if you can just make a start."

When I reached Mr. Holley's class it was the last period of the school day. Here too the class was seated in a circle. They were all boys—big boys sixteen, seventeen, and eighteen years old. A year or two ago seven out of ten boys like these would not have been in this or any other classroom. They would have dropped out of school, discouraged by classes that made no sense to them and in which they had known a series of failures. The school now offered such boys a program of half classwork, half supervised work at a minimum wage. They had classes in English, arithmetic, and social studies, but what made the difference bewteen leaving and remaining in school, the principal told me, were the chance to earn some money, the self-respect that came from holding a job and improving in it, and, again, a teacher.

Mr. Holley was a tall, solid man probably in his sixties,

though he looked younger. He conducted his class with an old-fashioned, quiet-spoken decorum. He gave every boy a chance to talk about something he knew, and all seemed eager to answer. One boy, who had entered the class late, reviewed the meaning of *custody*. "We take pains," Mr. Holley said, "to learn that there's more to a custodian's work than just cleaning up." He proposed a series of problems, for which the boys eagerly volunteered answers: "What would you do about a stain on a carpet, about a heat ring on a desk, if you smelled smoke that seemed to come from a floor you weren't responsible for, if someone were trespassing in the school building after hours?"

Afterward Mr. Holley asked some of the boys to tell about their work and what use they made of their earnings.

"I save some, but every week my partner and me go downtown Friday night and order us a fancy dinner at some nice place—with tablecloths."

"Some I give to my mother. Most of the rest I'm saving for my graduation expenses."

"I buy my own clothes now. And some I save. Some day I want to have me a little restaurant—a counter one. People'll come, 'cause it'll be nice and clean."

This course, "Maintenance and Custody of Property," may lead to some raised eyebrows. "Is this education?" Whatever name we give it, it helps to keep these boys from the tragic and costly defeat of unemployment and the dead end of drug addiction.

Mr. Holley, who proudly serves as a member of the school's faculty, would cause some raised eyebrows also. As the principal later explained, he is a very special kind of teacher. Formerly the chief custodian of the high school, he grew up in this neighborhood and still lives here. Now, as a result of the principal's administrative ingenuity, he bears the title "field supervisor." A mature and able Negro, he does more than teach the mechanics of buildings and grounds maintenance; he provides a model of a workingman doing his job. For boys like these, often lacking such models at home or even in their immediate neighborhood, Mr. Holley is in a special and important sense an exemplary teacher.

What faith can do.   About a month later in a city several states away I was a guest in Miss Passamanich's third grade "adjustment" class. Here the pupils, a few of them Negro but most of them Spanish speaking, were children damaged by life in an urban slum. Each was too bewildered, too hurt, or too angry to learn or allow other children to learn in the school's regular classes. The school had grouped them together, partly to remove them from other classes but also, I had been told, because "Miss Passamanich can almost always do something even with the worst of them."

During the hour and a half that I sat in the back of her classroom, Miss Passamanich dealt with half a dozen incidents of the kind that cause many teachers to give up teaching entirely, transfer to another school, or suffer the sad transformation from teacher to custodian. In each, her solution was characterized by firmness, belief in the child, and love.

Introducing a small section of the class to dictionary skills, Miss Passamanich explained the magic of dictionaries. "You, and you, and you," she said, putting her hands on both sides of each child's head, "have thousands of words right inside your head—and you can find every word in this book. Try it and see!" When I talked with her later she laughingly agreed that her challenge might have produced some words not in the dictionary. "But it hasn't happened yet," she said. "I know them. I know what they'll say. And they need to feel—physically feel—some connection between themselves and words, words, words."

That morning Miss Passamanich had separated two little girls who had somehow suddenly started hair pulling and biting. She had persuaded Elena, a newcomer to the class, to leave her corner refuge and help another child put away the class crayons. She had held Emilio on her lap while she talked with him about how he tore up his picture because she had looked at another child's work before his. Sometimes there are bruises on her arms and back made by children like Emilio who, desperate for the love they have not found at home, try to claim it by force.

Understandably the principal of this school wishes she had a Miss Passamanich for every class. "She's been here eighteen years, and nothing seems to faze her." In the last three years the school population has come to be predominantly non-English speaking and further depressed economically. As marks of educational deprivation—backwardness in reading and arithmetic—have become more and more apparent, the teaching staff of the school has deteriorated. The principal has found it harder to retain good teachers and recruit new ones. Not a single student teacher has been assigned to the school during the past year. "I've made an appointment with a candidate and seen her drive up to the school, look around at the neighborhood, and drive away."

To recruit, prepare, and retain teachers for "difficult" urban slum schools is a major educational problem. Within the next decade 70 per cent of our population will live in urban areas, one sixth of our total population in the fourteen largest cities alone. By 1970 we may expect every other child in the public schools in these cities to belong to groups described as underprivileged, disadvantaged, or deprived.

We need tens of thousands of new teachers to work constructively with these children. Where will they come from? We cannot count on their arriving by way of the unpredictable natural selection that produced Mrs. Bannerman, Mr. Holley, and Miss Passamanich. Nor can we expect present methods of teacher preparation to provide the understanding, the special knowledge, and the skills required of urban teachers. Yet these skills must be developed if our schools are to fulfill their historic function as gateways to a better life for the less privileged.

"In everybody's style, there are certain strengths. . . ."

THE STRATEGY OF STYLE*

Frank Reissman

This article, by the author of the widely-known book, *The Culturally Deprived Child,* is part of a realistic and promising trend toward an emphasis on a carefully technical approach to teaching in the slum school. The realism lies in its recognition of our inability to do very much that is effective about the social and emotional problems of the children, and in that it meets the practical desires of most teachers for a set of procedures that they can comprehend and use. The piece is valuable also for its explicit and detailed description of the cognitive patterns that one can look for in the classroom as an outgrowth of specific types of early experience.

The approach described clearly demands a considerable amount of time on the part of the teacher for the task of diagnosis and the application of different procedures for individual pupils. Does this make it impractical for the average urban school, with its

* Frank Reissman, "The Strategy of Style," *Teachers College Record,* March, 1964. Reprinted by permission of *Teachers College Record* and the author.

*large classes? Does it suggest the value of changing
the inner-city school to some form of the ungraded
school, in which each child works at his own pace
toward given achievement levels?*

I WOULD LIKE to discuss a concept which I think has been ignored a good deal in teaching and guidance. It is the concept of style—in particular, the style of learning. I believe a crucial element in the development of the individual's learning relates to a careful understanding of the idiosyncratic style elements in the learning process. Students of learning have focused a good deal on rather abstract, molecular concepts of learning derived from pigeons and rats via B. F. Skinner and Clark L. Hull. I am not suggesting that these concepts of learning are not useful, but I think that we have missed the possible value of a more wholistic (molar) or global dimension of learning, operative at the phenomenal level, which I am referring to as style.

AN ILLUSTRATIVE MODEL

One index of style relates to whether you learn things most easily through reading or through hearing or whether you learn through doing things physically, whether you learn things slowly or quickly, whether you learn things in a one-track way or whether you are very flexible in your learning. These examples are not to be conceived as separate from one another. There can be such combinations as a visual-physical learner who learns in a slow, one-track fashion. As a matter of fact, this last pattern is quite characteristic of the disadvantaged child. He learns more slowly; he learns through the physical (that is, by doing things, touching things); he learns visually, and he functions in a rather one-track way in that he doesn't shift easily and is not highly flexible in his learning. This is, of course, an ideal statement—a model.

Let me cite just a few other dimensions of style so that different aspects of it can be seen. For example, some people like to work under pressure; they like a deadline, and they like tests. (Low-income youngsters do not like such conditions.) Some people like to leave a lot of time for their work, enjoying a slow tempo. Some people like to think or even read while walking. Some people like to work in a cold room, some in a warm one. Some people like to work for long periods of times without a break; some people like to shift and take frequent breaks. Some people take a long time to warm up, whereas others get into their work very quickly. Some people like to have all of the facts in front of them before they can do any generalizing, and others prefer to have a few facts. Some people like "props," some people do not.

Typically, people do not know their own style nearly well enough. What I am really concerned about is how one can use this concept to improve one's manner of work—whether it be teaching or guidance, social work or psychiatry. Although I am mainly concerned with working with lower socioeconomic groups, I do not mean to imply that the concept of style must be limited to these social strata.

COGNITION VS. EMOTION

Guidance workers have focused far too much on the categories of emotion, motivation, and personality rather than on the cognitive categories of learning and thinking. There has been much too much emphasis on the emotional approach in attempting to understand why a child doesn't learn. Little careful analysis is given to how the child's learning might improve simply by concentrating on the way that he works and learns, rather than on his affective reasons for not learning. This thesis is almost directly counter to the current view. Today if a child doesn't learn (and if he has intellectual ability), it is quickly assumed that his difficulties must be due to some emotional block or conflict. I am trying to suggest a different way of looking at the problem. He may not be learning because his methods of learning are not suited to his style, and hence he cannot best utilize his power. I would be willing to argue that even where his troubles are, in part, emotional or due to conflict, it still may be possible to ignore this particular focus and concentrate profitably on the specific expression of the difficulty itself—his learning pattern. Even if one rejects my premise that the emotional causes have been overemphasized, one may still give a willing ear to the possibility of dealing with crucial problems of learning in nonemotional, nonpsychodynamic terms. Unfortunately, teachers too often have behaved like psychologists and social workers. It seems to me that they do not sufficiently stress learning processes and styles of learning, apparently preferring motivational categories. One way to build up appropriate prestige in the teaching profession is *not* simply to borrow from psychologists and sociologists, but to concentrate on the development of what education is most concerned with, learning and teaching. When one does borrow from psychology, it may be better to concentrate on learning and cognition rather than personality and motivation.

ANIMALS AND MEN

If we examine the outcomes of teacher-education courses in learning, educational psychology, and the like, we typically are forced to the suspicion that they amount to very little. Borrowing heavily from animal learning experiments (which by itself is not necessarily bad), such courses are victimized by the fact that the particular concepts and formulations developed in the animal literature have not been easily applicable to human learning problems—whether a child learns slowly, whether he is a physical learner, or whether it takes him a long time to warm up. Although these problems are nearer to our subjective experience, the psychological literature and animal experiments have not really helped us very much to deal effectively with them. When educational psychology courses have actually studied human learning, the focus has not been on the significant problems that I think are related to style. When they attempt, for example, to deal with study habits, they are entirely too general. There is a great deal more to study habits than meets the eye of the introductory psychology textbook. The typical suggestions in the chapter on study habits are based upon various experiments which seem to indicate that distributive learning is better, that one should survey material first, etc. But very little is directed toward the *idiosyncratic* factors that are involved.

For example, some people simply can't tolerate surveying a

chapter first. They become so anxious, so disturbed, by being asked to look at the over-all view of the chapter that they can't function. These people want very much to read a chapter atomistically. This is their style. It won't help simply to tell such a person that he is not proceeding in the right way and that he really ought to read the chapter as a whole first. The same is true in terms of the general recommendation that one should have a quiet place to study. Strangely enough, some people study quite well in a noisy place, or with certain kinds of noise, and completely quiet places are not best for them. Some people take a long time to warm up; consequently, a great deal of spacing (or distribution) of learning would not be useful for them. This is their style. But the textbook does not tell you this because, in general, over a large number of cases, spaced learning is best.

The same argument applies to examinations or tests. For some people, a test operates as just the right mild anxiety to stimulate the integration of a great deal of material that needs to be learned. On the other hand, there are large numbers of people for whom tests are terrible because they disorganize them, make them too anxious, and thus prevent them from working. Tests are not conducive to the style of these individuals. When it is argued that tests are educationally undesirable because they produce too much anxiety for learning, the arguments refer to such people. When others argue that tests are marvelous because they aid pupils by providing corrections and criticism, they are referring to persons with a different style. Undoubtedly, tests work happily for some pupils, but there are others who forget their wrong answers on tests because it disturbs them so much to remember them.

As a matter of fact, there is a great deal of controversy in the traditional literature on the very question of whether repression of wrong answers occurs or whether "punishment" for giving the wrong answers on tests helps to produce better recall. I am suggesting that two different kinds of styles are involved here. For some people, the information that they gave wrong answers is extremely useful and challenging. If this information is called to their attention in a definite and stimulating way, it makes the wrong answer the figure in the ground. It draws the incorrect responses productively to their attention. For other people, knowing that they have made a mistake is extremely disturbing, destructive of their morale, and leads to a repressing of this material. Therefore, depending upon one's style and one's way of dealing with these problems, tests may be useful or not useful.

STRATEGIES OF MODIFICATION

My main task is to try to formulate the possible ways in which the strengths of the individual's style can be utilized and its weaknesses reduced or controlled. At this stage in our discussion, I mean the more fundamental, underlying characteristics—for example, the physical style already discussed. This style is laid down early in life and is not subject to fundamental change, although it is possible to *bend* it and to *develop* it. Another aspect of style may be much more malleable and may be more related to habit or set; that is, it may be a derivative or secondary expression of style.

Let us take as an example, what I call the "games" focus of low income youngsters. They like to learn things through games rather than through tests. To put something in the forms of games is an excellent transitional technique for winning their interest. But I do not know how basic a habit this is. It may be much more changeable than the underlying physical style. Such questions are obviously open to further investigation and research. I am simply trying to provide a general framework by means of which to deal with the issue. I am not sure which elements are more or less changeable, but I do believe that some are quite unchangeable and quite basic, whereas some are more susceptible to intervention. A person who likes to learn by listening and speaking (aural style) is unlikely to change completely and become, say, a reader. I am not suggesting that such a pupil will not learn to read and write fluently, but his best learning, the long-lasting, deep learning that gets into his muscles, is more likely to derive from speaking and hearing.

Now let me return to the problem I am essentially trying to deal with—the strategy of style, the strategy of producing basic changes in people through understanding and utilizing their styles. I want to develop the idiosyncratic strengths, find ways of employing the unorthodox, the specific, the unique, and in some ways limit the weaknesses in the person's style. Under certain conditions, one can overcome some of the weak elements of the style pattern through compensatory efforts and through special techniques. I think, however, that weaknesses in learning are more likely to be alleviated when they are at the level of sets and habits.

AWARENESS AND UTILIZATION

In approaching our problem, the first aim is to have the person become aware of the strengths and potentials in his style—because this is going to be the source of his power. Thus, if an individual has a physical style, he has to learn the special attributes of this style and how to use them. The guidance counselor or teacher will have to help him overcome the invidious interpretations of this style that are prevalent in our society.

Let us take an illustration of a different type. A youngster tells us that he sits down to work but cannot concentrate. It is extremely important at this point (and this is crucial in the diagnosis of style) to ascertain as precisely as possible exactly what takes place in this youngster's routine. For example, when does he study? What time does he come home from school? What does he do first when he comes into the house? He may say,

> I come home, throw down my books, and then I start to remember that I have to do some work. So I get out my books. I try to work. I take out the book, but my mind wanders. I look at the book; I look away, I can't get into the work, and after a few minutes of trying this, I begin to feel discouraged; I begin to feel bad. I feel I can't work. I'm not interested. I'm no good. I get very worried, panic builds up, and then I run away from the work.

There are many possibilities operating in this pattern. One possibility is that this youngster has a slow period of warm up. He does not easily get into something new; he does not shift from whatever he's been doing before (whether he's been outside playing ball or inside listening to the radio). This may be due to a number of reasons. He may be a physical learner. If one is a physical learner, one generally must be involved physically in the work process. One has to get one's muscles into it, and this takes time. If this is our student's pattern, then he must come to understand that although he is slow to warm up, this is not necessarily a negative quality; it is simply a different way of approaching work.

As a matter of fact, it may very often be connected to perseverance, once he gets involved! Once he is immersed, he may go deeper and deeper and not be able to shift away from the work easily. The inability to shift doesn't then operate as a negative feature but as a positive element in his style. But the youngster I described here rarely gets to this point. It's not that he doesn't persevere somewhere, in baseball or somewhere else. But in his school work, he's never gotten past the point of the slow warm up. In order to use his pattern effectively, he has to schedule work accordingly. He cannot schedule his time so that he works for one hour. That's no good because it takes him a half hour to warm up. Even if he were to be successful and stick with it for the half hour as a result of a teacher's or guidance worker's support and stimulation, the problem would remain at the end of the half hour of only having a short time left to work. Consequently, he has to plan a larger time period of work and recognize in advance that it will take him about a half hour to warm up. In other words, the person who would help him must give him a definition of his work pattern in order to realize the positive potentialities in it.

STRENGTH OVER WEAKNESS

When this new definition is provided, it is probable that a number of consequences will follow if I'm right about the diagnosis. Over a period of time, the warm-up period will shorten because part of the difficulty in the long warm up is the anxiety that emerges as he tries to get into the work and fails. Thus, by getting into the work, his anxiety decreases, and his interest has a chance, concomitantly, to increase.

Now let us take another example, one in which the person's strengths can be used to deal with his weaknesses. How do you teach a person how to read when reading is not his basic style? Everyone is going to need reading ability and writing ability regardless of his style. In order to teach reading to youngsters for whom it is stylistically uncongenial, one may want to use role-playing, which is more related to the physical style of the individual. He can read about something that he just role-played, or he can read about a trip he has recently taken. While teaching reading under these conditions, the teacher must remember that he is not developing a reading style; he is developing a skill, a *balance* in the pupil's style. He is developing minimal efficiency in an area which is not rooted in the learner's style. In a sense, the teacher is going after his Achilles heel, his weakness, the reading difficulty, by developing it through his strength, whether it be visual, physical, or whatever. This is a basic tactic for defeating or limiting the weakness by connecting it and subjecting it to the strengths.

MINIMAL GOALS

There are some other things one can do in employing the strategy of style. Various transitional techniques can be used, for example, for overcoming some of a pupil's educational weaknesses. Illustratively, low-income youngsters come to the school situation ordinarily with a very poor auditory set. They're not accustomed to listening to people read stories to them. I suggest that this kind of pattern can be limited quite a bit and can be overcome up to a point. I don't think that the school can develop a basic aural style in such children, but effective teachers can teach them to learn through listening even though this isn't their *best* mode of learning. One of the techniques for doing this was developed by a man who worked with schizophrenic children. The technique was simply to make a game out of the auditory problem. He would say, for example, What is six and five? Everybody in the class would have to answer many different times. The pupil cannot fall asleep in such a class. Answering once doesn't leave him free because he may be asked the same question (or somewhat different ones) often. This is an excellent technique for waking up youngsters, and it has been effective with low-income students who are not used to listening. The objective is to bring them up to minimal listening ability, up to grade level. I want to bring low-income youngsters far beyond grade level in most areas, because I think they have considerable creative ability; but in their areas of weakness, I would be happy to bring them simply up to grade level. In areas of weakness, our primary aim should be functioning on a minimal level of adequacy so that weaknesses will not destroy strengths. Techniques of the kind described may be useful in reversing habits and sets which have grown out of the negative aspects of the person's style.

To sum up: In everybody's style, there are certain strengths, and each of us has his own Achilles heel. The issue in developing a powerful change in a person is related to how one gets to the Achilles heel and how one utilizes the strengths. This is the central problem of the strategy of style, especially in its application to the low-income pupils of our urban schools.

"I don't know why I expected to be met by some monster-type people. Could it be that I've grown up with many false images and impressions?"

BRIDGES TO SLUM-GHETTO
CHILDREN*

Among the very large number of projects financed by both the Federal government and private foundations aimed at improving the achievement of slum children, it is surprising to find so few concerned directly with teacher preparation. Project BRIDGE, at Queens College of the City University of New York is one of those few. It operated on the assumption that the most important deterrents to the development of adequate teachers are psychological ones and consequently provided a number of student teachers with intensive experience in tutoring small groups of children in slum schools, supervised by faculty members with a special interest in helping them understand their own reactions and feelings about the children. The following selections from the project report are excerpts from the diaries written

* From Leonard Kornberg, ed., "Bridges to Slum-Ghetto Children: Case Studies in Learning to Become a Teacher (Flushing, New York, Bridge Project, Department of Education, Queens College, 1962), pp. 5–6, 11–13, 21–24, 26–27. Reprinted with permission.

by the student teachers or, in one case, a composition written by one of the children. The parenthetical comments are notes by the editor of the report.

There are many flashes of insight in these diaries, evidence that the project was succeeding in its aims. The group was a small one, however, and the faculty time devoted to the project very expensive. Does the potential payoff for such efforts justify greatly expanding programs like this one, even if it means transferring funds from efforts made to improve the slum school in other directions? Can we hope to develop such a strategy for the application of funds to the problem, and how would one go about doing so?

THE SESSIONS began with the youngsters going to the windows and calling to their teachers and friends who were coming out of the school. Their remarks about their teachers clearly indicated that they are fond of them, but that they consider them to be different from other human beings. They seemed to be awed by the fact that the teachers were running out of the building just as swiftly as the students, in order to get away from the school's atmosphere. If the youngsters happened to see one of the members of the "Bridge Group" on his way home, they called the youngster to my attention and pointed at him with condemnation. I knew that they were waiting for my reaction, but I tried to conceal my feelings in order to show them that their object in attending these sessions shouldn't be to please me, but rather to help themselves.

After the main exodus was over, they continued yelling out the window to passersby until one of them decided that we should get to work. As they got themselves seated, I started an informal conversation by asking them what they were doing in school and what they thought of the latest fads such as the "Twist." At this point, Laverne, one of the more aggressive youngsters, started demonstrating the "Twist," but the others told her to stop so that they could get to work. I told them that we would do something different this time in order to break up the monotony. I explained to them that it was possible to learn algebra even though we would deviate from the normal procedure. They were apprehensive about changing the routine, but I persuaded them that they would have a lot of fun with my new approach and that they would learn algebra at the same time. Finally, they agreed to go along with me.

I then proceeded to explain to them that if they picked a number and didn't tell me what the number was, I could guess the number simply by using the algebraic skills that we had been going over. They doubted that this was possible, so I illustrated my point by asking them each to pick a number and to perform certain arithmetic calculations with the number. They looked puzzled, yet I could see that they were excited to see the outcome. When I finally guessed each of their numbers correctly, they told me that they wanted to know how I did it. I showed them how the number could be guessed by using "x" as the unknown number.

When I saw that they understood my explanation and were enthusiastic about applying their new-found knowledge, I encouraged them to try it out on some of the youngsters who had just walked in. However, many of them weren't successful because they were unable to translate verbal statements into correct algebraic equations, something that they should have learned during their first week in class. Consequently, they became discouraged and their interest began to wane. The few who knew what they were doing were sufficiently enthused and were content to continue, but I thought it would be better for the rest of the group to change the topic.

After a break of about ten minutes in which we ate some cookies that I had brought and I answered some questions about college, four of the girls asked me to go over the topic of graphs. Because I did not want to disappoint them, I reviewed some of the basic information about using and making graphs. However, the other youngsters looked disinterested and fooled around amongst themselves. I tried to enlist their aid in showing the others how they constructed graphs, but they refused to do so. They claimed that they had already gone over graphs in class and that this was so simple that it was a waste of time going over again. I didn't know what to do. Whom should I try to please? If I stopped going over graphs, the four girls who asked me would lose faith and trust in my ability and desire to help them. If I continued helping them, then the others would resent me. Since the other youngsters did not have any suggestions about what to do in the remaining time, I decided it would be more beneficial if I continued helping the four girls with their graph problems. Consequently, the others ran around the room and talked loudly among themselves, despite my request that they quiet down so that everyone could hear me. Luckily, after about ten minutes, it was time to go.

One new understanding for me is that these youngsters are

so intent on making a good impression that they deny to themselves and to me their inability to do algebra. They pretend that they have grasped the material that I have gone over. They say they are bored with it, while in reality, they have no conception of what is going on. From later sessions I have also noticed that these youngsters have an extremely short attention span and that the only way a teacher can hold their attention is by catering to their whims and jumping from one topic to another.

MARIA'S COMPOSITION

(Note: Maria is a 13 year old Puerto Rican girl in an East Harlem Junior High School. Her composition is copied with all its errors and innocence.)

"Stop don't do it" "Please stop them" "Help" She screamed. That was the words she prenounce when I was coming from the store. When I was coming up the stairs I saw blood down the stair and I look up I saw three policeman and two detective and I said what's wrong, were does blood come from? The detective said in a deep voice this blood come from the second floor two neighbors had a fight, and we are waiting for the ambulance. My heart stop for one second, and then I ran up the stairs and I said. "That is where I live". When I came up and saw Mr. Lopez with blood all over his shirt and I kneel down and said "Mr. Lopez what happen" and he said "That no good Luis he" he stop and then I said go on, but the policeman interb and said please goung girl don't try to make him talk, then a policeman and a fat lady the lady was the nurse and she said take this man immediately! to the ambulance he is bleeding to much. The policeman took him to the ambulance. The other she put some bandage around his shoulders and then she said go to your home and report tomorrow at the hospital. Then the nurse call me over and said do you know the man that I sent in the ambulance? Yes nurse. "Then will you answer some questions." Yes. Will you please companion me to the hospital. Yes nurse.

Mr. Lopez die in the ambulance, I call Mrs. Lopez and gave

her the bad news. She started to scream and cry. I came back from the hospital after I answer the question. The first thing that came to my mine was "why" "why" two neighbors fight. "Why" because they maybe don't understand each other or maybe one ask for a advice and the other said why come to me why don't you go to your family.

To be a neighbor is not necessary to be in the neighborhood, it can be country or city or and town anything. For example if you go to a country that you never gone before. All during your travels you would see people staring at your odd clothing, people who would not understand the language you spoke.

Then you would land in a strange country. Everything would be different. You would have to learn a strange language, learn a new trade. Then you try to be kindful and helpful with people. The people will adore you truly. "Why" because you been not only a good neighbor but helpful and friendly with them. This is one of the simple ways to be kind with people, by helping them in anything they need your help today and tomorrow they help you. This composition is for the adolescent to give them an ideal to understand other persons. When a boy or girl comes into a classroom for the first time you try to make a conversation with him or her. Show the boy or girl around the school introduct the boy or girl to your friends so she don't feel lonely. In a way you are helping the boy or girl getting around.

(Note: At the end of this composition, the teacher had written: "too long!")

UNDERSTANDING GROWS

(The following report reveals a moment when the bars are lowered and the youngsters show you a part of their world. Occasionally, the material has a somewhat narrow, middle-class view; but it is nowhere near the bias in the section that follows. It presents a "nether-world" of racial pride and prejudice, of dramatic misconceptions, and of adolescent insecurities. In the final remarks, the observer challenges one with her indignation and hope.)

During our fourth session we somehow began talking about college, and before I knew it, I had told them that I was a French major, which set off an animated discussion of Romance languages. I was amused by their misconception of the term "Romance," because I remember that I remember that I once thought also that it meant, "like when a boy talks to his girl-friend." Most of them are Puerto Rican, thus bilingual, and have a feeling for language. We compared French with Spanish. They were thrilled when I taught them how to count to ten in French. This was their first display of real eagerness to learn something outside the classroom requirements. The one exception is still Jerry, who came in late and found us discussing religion. Despite an invitation to join us, he promptly left, saying, "If we're not doing math, I have to meet my friends and go play basketball." Yet on the day of the Thanksgiving party Jerry walked in one hour late. The party was scheduled for four o'clock and he was dismayed to see us still working at math. Why does he keep coming back, when he is always criticizing, acting bored, and shrugging his shoulders with a grin on his face when I ask him to suggest improvements for the program?

The Thanksgiving party, which all the groups in the school attended, brought to light several interesting characteristics of these adolescents. First of all, they are quite backward and rude in their social behavior. They fought over food that was passed around, and were rowdy and inattentive when one of my colleagues played the guitar for them. I think their behavior might have stemmed from the embarrassment of receiving such a treat. Not to appear flustered, their cover-up manifested itself in a show of bravado and even snickering. Yet when we finally interested them in a song, they forgot their self-consciousness and sang with great enthusiasm. We were partially at fault by trying to teach them American folksongs which were completely alien to them. They would have much preferred Rock-and-Roll.

Another point was hit home to me as a result of the announcement that there was going to be a party. One of my boys asked me whether it would be a "welfare party." When I asked him what he meant, another boy poked him and they both started giggling. The following week, when I complimented one of them on the shirt he was wearing, a boy said, "What's that sticking out from the back of the collar? It looks like a welfare label." Again giggles. But the week after that, one youngster approached me and asked, "You really didn't know what welfare means?" I commented that I had a vague idea, but would they please explain it to me. They spoke very disparagingly of the people who have to receive checks from the Welfare Department. I asked them, "Don't you think that it's wonderful for needy people to be able to get help from the government?" They answered by telling me about a young boy they know who never worked and had no home, but slept on subways and subsisted on the checks. It is because of such people that they are so scornful of welfare.

My last session with them was extremely interesting and enlightening. Before the meeting officially started, David, an exceptionally clever and well-informed youngster, remarked with surprise that my eyes were blue, but black in the middle. This started a scientific discussion about pupils and light rays, as well as an enumerated account of eye color of each person's family and friends. Then a relationship clicked in David's mind and he asked me whether I had heard of the theory of evolution. Those who knew about it explained to those who didn't and then one of the girls indignantly rejected the whole idea as untrue, because "the Bible tells us that Adam was the first man, and God created him, and he didn't come from monkeys:" This set off a heated discussion on religion. They were amazed to find out that I was Jewish, "like those little boys at the dentist with curly sideburns and beanies on their heads." They wanted to know whether I was the only one who wore makeup in my church, whether I danced and went to parties, and whether there were any statues in my church, because they had heard that they weren't allowed. I tried briefly to correct these strange misconceptions, and then got them to talk about their own religions, about which they are extremely well-informed, and in which they have implicit faith. I learned a lot from them and found it heartwarming that they have something to believe in so firmly, and that they accept the discipline and obedience imposed upon them. I was delighted with their animation. There was never a lag in the conversation, which came mostly from them—and I was holding my breath for fear that it would end.

From here, we were led into a discussion about their families. I was upset by the matter-of-factness with which they spoke of circumstances which to me were tragic. David's parents had separated when he was five, placing him in a home for foster children, where he stayed until the age of eleven, when he received foster parents. Now people think that his foster mother is his sister, because she is only twenty-eight and looks so young. Orlando lives here with his mother and sister, but his father is in Puerto Rico, because he is sick. Pat's father is no longer with them, and she has several sisters, with whom she shares many duties at home. She spoke of her neighbor's boy who is in jail now because he shot a boy last summer. And so on. We spoke of dating, clothes, hobbies. They don't like the way people dress in Puerto Rico—"with those baggy pants and big frilly skirts, and all that make-up." They seem to like living here, even under their poor conditions, and show no pride for their native land or desire to return even for a visit. At the end of the period, they were still chattering away, and I was sorry to have to send them off. We did no math that day, but it was by far the most valuable session I have had, and I know they enjoyed it, too.

It was certainly a far cry from our first meeting, and their change in behavior can be exemplified by Orlando, who in the beginning wouldn't raise his eyes to meet yours, and spoke in a whisper. Now he is the life of the party, makes wisecracks, volunteers constantly, and even flirts with girls who wander in. When one young lady stormed in and demanded her scarf, he innocently denied that he had seen it, but when she left he gleefully pulled it out from under his sweater. They seem to have realized that they can trust me and so have let down their guards.

I am still unhappy about the math, though. When I give them problems, they can solve them. But when I offer the slightest deviation, they are stumped because it doesn't quite fit into the rote pattern. Even when I present a puzzle or a game, they are unable to connect or apply it to what they learned in the classroom. When we played a game involving equations, they caught on in a mechanical sense, but I could tell that they saw no relationships to their "work," and soon they asked whether they could do some more examples "from the Book." Their naivete was further brought out to me when David asked me whether I knew how to solve by "T." Puzzled, I asked what he meant. Jerry said to him "Shh, teacher said it's a secret method, and we're not allowed to mention the word." That is why it was referred to by its initial. I finally coaxed out of them that their teacher had taught them a simplification in solving equations—transposing—and that apparently he was not supposed to. Jerry had built up a fantastic notion that if anyone found out the teacher had taught them this, he would be put in jail, because it was used in producing the atom bomb.

In contrast to this astounding display of misconstrued ideas, I have seen moments of great understanding and sensitivity. They seem gratified that I, as a prospective teacher, care about them, and have complained that past teachers just let things slide, and didn't build up their reading levels. They are very conscious of "level," and somehow sense the lack of devotion and even resentment of many teachers, who simply act as police guards because they think they are dealing with hopeless juvenile delinquents. Maybe I have come to know the exceptions rather than the typical youngsters of East Harlem, but even so, I can see that they need more attention, and a classroom situation geared more to learning than to maintaining discipline. Of course, this cannot be brought about easily. Great obstacles must be overcome, and trouble-makers will not just disappear. But I think that by gradually capturing their interest somehow and engaging their trust and faith, a teacher can accomplish

quite a bit. The will to learn is there, as I have seen, but the
youngster is not always conscious of it.

KNIVES JUMPING OUT

(This chapter illustrates what everyone knows: that our values,
our fears, our expectations always shape our image of other
persons. Most of the material in this section, therefore, may
describe better than what he observes. Will it also mirror some
of the readers? The first entry is a segment about attitudes and
fears that are widespread.)

For me, South Jamaica [New York] has always been a neighborhood that I've been afraid to go to—most probably because
it has a reputation of a tough, Negro neighborhood. When I
was assigned to JHS "X" at first, I was very worried. I remember the Tuesday night before I attended the first session—I had
anticipated knives jumping out from the shadows, and big,
rough, rowdy kids. I was so frightened.

Much to my pleasure, when Wednesday finally arrived
(after a very restless night) I met my three girls—Helen, Doris,
and Lotitia. I had expected to be met by a group of ten to
fifteen toughies—maybe even some monsters. But I was so
pleasantly surprised to meet these kids—nice, down-to-earth
adolescents trying to grow up to meet the demands of our
society. I don't know why I expected to be met by some monster-
type-people. Could it be that I've grown up with many false
images and impressions?

A DIFFERENT BREED

(Here we are compared—us and them. See how much nicer,
more obedient and trusting we are. It all goes to show—what?
How much a summer in camp can do for strangers? Or what
life in a slum-ghetto creates?)

I feel that I am getting to know the youngsters a little better
despite their reluctance to discuss personal matters with me.
Although I found that their physical appearances are similar

to middle-class adolescents, I have found that their behavioral traits are completely different. First of all, they are resistant to change and scorn anything new. At the first session they were upset when I was doing problems by a different method than the way that their teacher had previously shown them. Their resistance to change was also evident when they were reluctant to go to the blackboard during the second session. This is directly opposite to the way I would have reacted if I were in their place. I remember that when I was an adolescent I was always interested in knowing the alternate methods for doing a problem, in order to get away from the monotony of routine. Contrary to this, these Negro and Puerto Rican youngsters seem to thrive on routine.

The second way in which these youngsters differ from the adolescent I and my friends were, is that they lack a basic sense of trust. Although they seem to like me, they are still suspicious of everything I do with them and refuse to let me know anything about their personal lives which does not involve school. Again this is completely different from the way middle-class adolescents would react. For instance, my group of adolescents at camp this summer indicated that they trusted me almost immediately after we met, by confiding in me and telling me about their personal problems. Even though I know these Puerto Rican and Negro youngsters for almost four weeks now, their shyness and secrecy reveal that they consider me almost a complete stranger who is not to be "trusted."

THE FIRST SEMESTER IN A
SLUM SCHOOL

The reports that follow move us from the student
teacher to the first semester of teaching in a slum
school and were gathered during the course of another experiment in teacher preparation, this one at
Hunter College. Project TRUE was set up, with
funds from the Office of Juvenile Delinquency
and Youth Development, Welfare Administration,
United States Department of Health, Education and
Welfare, to enable the college to change its own
curriculum in teacher education with a view to making it more relevant to the schools into which Hunter's graduates go to teach. To get a fresh and detailed
view of the immediate problems faced by the graduate, the project drew a reasonably random sample of
those of its June graduates who appeared on Board
of Education assignment lists, and invited the members of the sample to return to the college every
Saturday morning for a semester to report on their
experiences during the week. During that time, each
of them responded to a series of written questions,
recording her answers privately on a tape recorder in
the language laboratory. These selections from the

vast body of material that accumulated as a result of the recording sessions have been made primarily to illustrate the wide range of problems which the beginning teacher faces in the inner-city school, and the inadequacy she often comes to feel about solving them.

It should come as no surprise that members of the faculty responsible for the preparation of these teachers listened to these recordings with a sense of shock. What changes in the normal teacher-training curriculum do these excerpts suggest as desirable?

I AM INTERESTED in Ernest and he is really the only real problem in my class, out of the ordinary as a problem. I have mentioned him, I think, on every recording. He is a child who just does not pay attention. I don't know what it is, I don't know if he is just bored, and I feel that he must be, since he is a holdover. This is his second year in the third grade. I know he must be bored with much of the curriculum, and I can't change it drastically just for him. But I don't know what the nature of his problem is completely. In many of the subject areas he is interested because he does well in these. For instance, he does math pretty well, and he is interested and volunteers and occasionally, not as often as he might, though, not as often as he is able to. When I call on him he never gives me an answer. He just stands there and he seems not to get confused. It's not a willful refusal to answer. He just doesn't seem—well, maybe it's more a confusion. Whatever he is thinking about just sort of slipped away from him. On many occasions it's because, of course, he's not paying attention and he didn't even hear my question. But in many of the areas he does do pretty well, because in social studies he seems to have a very good interest. Reading is his problem. He just doesn't pay attention when we're reading. He just can't seem to be interested. And I get a very strong feeling that he considers all of this very much beneath him. The stories which we read— although the readers have been changed as I mentioned, and the new reader is much better in terms of interest. It has much higher interest levels than the other one did. I think that Ernest was getting very tired of Sally and Puff, and he really seemed to be very much annoyed with them. The new reader introduces a whole new town, with a name which the other series never had, and children with last names which the other series didn't have. It just seems to be a lot more realistic. The stories are more appealing, I think. Also, to children. But in terms of their realism and in terms of situations which are much more frequent than just sitting around in the yard all day—the reader should appeal to him more than the other one did but it doesn't seem to be doing this. I still get the impression, he

80

doesn't know of course that he is reading a first-grade reader, and if he did I think that he would completely give up altogether, but he still thinks that he's reading a third-grade reader. He's much bigger and taller than any of the other children in the class and much more physically mature, and I get the feeling that he just feels out of his element. I have been thinking about what to do about his problem. I did some very brief individual work with him. I really haven't had the time to devote to him. I have been thinking about it very seriously this week; and it really has been troubling me because I really don't know what to do about him and I'm really very concerned.

In our unit on food we had just finished the study of dairy foods last week and this week I had planned to begin them with the study of bread. This is another subtopic within the topic of food which they are concerned with. The social-studies book is a little bit inadequate on this particular topic and although I had no other materials to rely on for the lesson, actually what happened was that the story from the book which I had to read to them, since as I had mentioned before, they are not able to read their social-studies book by themselves. The reading level is quite difficult for them. The story which I read to them, as I was saying, was one which described actually the whole process of bread, the whole process of how the wheat is grown; it described the whole thing from the time the seed is planted to the time the flour goes to the factory to be made into bread, and somehow I think it was a little bit too much in one lesson, although I didn't see any way really to break it up. Perhaps I could have, just reading one or two paragraphs and then discussing it with them and asking them questions about it, but I hadn't done this, and I went through the whole story which meant by the time we got to the end, many of them had forgotten what had . . . what the first steps were in the process. We wrote an experience chart after the reading of it. Well, we had discussed it, of course, stopping here and there along the way to discuss certain things. One of the boys in the class had been to visit his relatives on a farm the previous summer, and he had seen a combine and a tractor and some of the machines which we were discussing, so he was able to tell us a little about these, but most of the children were unfamiliar with this type of machinery, but they could understand, of course, most of the things, most of the events which go into the whole process of growing the wheat and cutting the grain and storing it and the grain elevator, but it seemed to be just a little bit too much to cover in one lesson. However, I had read it, so we did the experience chart and some of the children did remember some of the events, so that we finally we were able to talk again about all of the steps in this process, and one of the difficulties I think in the lesson was that I didn't seem to be able to make a clear distinction between wheat and grain and flour, some of the terms were used, I don't think they quite saw the difference. For example, between the wheat growing in the field and the flour. In other words, what exactly happens to it, to make this change and then understanding again at the end of the story that when the flour is ready, then it has to go to a bread factory where it is made into bread. However, insofar as their reaction to the lesson, they didn't seem to be very interested at all in the lesson. Perhaps because the story, not only being on a reading level a little bit above them, but in terms which were used that they did not understand, and I think since we are not finished with the story of bread by any means we will have to still do some work on what happens at the factory where the bread is made, etc. Perhaps we'll have a chance to go over some of this and to clear up some of these things in their minds and to try to make a more successful impression about the whole topic.

I brought in my own victrola and a record, a Mitch Miller record, which I had used during student teaching, Mitch Miller Sing Along Folk Songs. Many of the songs the children would know, "Pop Goes the Weasel," at least know some of the words, the tune to "Clementine." I used this, took out the victrola and actually, because we had quite a bit of singing previously, I thought that the children perhaps would be ready for this and I didn't spend too much time preparing them for the use of a new term for the class, which, of course, was victrola. This was the main reason why it was a bit of a failure. I took out the victrola and of course the children were very excited. I had them turn around because the victrola was in the back of the room. I told them to sit with their backs of their chairs against their desks and, at listening time, we always say, what kind of a time is it? We point to our ears. It's listening time. It's a time to look and listen but it's not a time to use, and we point to our mouths. It's not the time to use our mouths. I started using it, and of course the tunes are very catchy—songs like "When Johnny Comes Marching Home." Well, within about three minutes the rhythm had just gotten the children and this I should have been aware of. I was aware subconsciously, but I guess I didn't consider the fact that these children, because of their hyperactivity, at least for many of them, it was just impossible for them just to sit and listen to music. They had to be a part of it. Well, of course, people started popping up all over the place, and tried to express themselves to this music and because I had not planned for it, well, we'll listen once and we'll think what we are going to do, then we'll stand up and we'll do it, because I hadn't specifically told the children exactly step by step what we were going to do, mild chaos broke out in the room. There was no fighting or anything of that sort, but while one person was dancing around, another person clapping hands, so that there was no unity in the music at all. We tried to sing the songs but it was more of a movement type music rather than . . . the children didn't exactly want to sing, particularly to "Johnny Comes Marching Home." It was a marching music and they wanted to march. The children did sing "Pop Goes the Weasel" every time we came to the line "Pop Goes the Weasel," but of course at this point the children would pop out of their chairs. We tried to organize this a bit but at this point the children were full of activity so I felt, since it was near recess time, that perhaps the best thing would be to discontinue the use of the record but to continue the activity in the basement through games because the children weren't really gaining anything from the classroom except through unorganized participation in music and I hope, I feel, I did learn one thing, that the children do respond to music . . .

One of my least successful lessons during the week was a science music lesson. I had acquired a record from the music department at P.S. 109 about Creepy, the Crawly Caterpillar. The story was mostly a narration with musical background to express various feelings, the feeling of children who were playing, or birds who were singing, or activity of a creepy crawly caterpillar. And then the story went into the fact that the caterpillar had a secret and the only way we could find out what it is is by making believe that we are caterpillars. And the story goes on that the caterpillar crawls up into a tree and to his warm and woolly cocoon bed and when he comes out he's a butterfly, and that's the secret. I think one reason why the lesson was not successful was that the record player that was being used in my room did not have sufficient volume, so that the entire class could not listen without having to strain to hear, so that I had to stop the recording once we got started and send for another victrola. Luckily the teacher next door had one that I could use, and had much louder volume for the children, so that we had to interrupt once, and several of the children whose attention span is quite short were lost at that point and became quite restless. Some did continue to listen, but of course there was this undercurrent of whispering or trying to do something else, and the children were reminded of . what they were supposed to be doing, how to listen, and our rules for listening. I think that perhaps there was not a realization that a caterpillar does turn into a butterfly. We tried to discuss this after the record but there should probably have been some lead-up discussion to the playing of this record and things to look for. I failed to realize that the children haven't developed their listening abilities to any great extent, so they have to constantly be given things that they have to especially find out.

Every morning they ask: are we going to gym today? And I finally got them to a point where they stop asking because I tell them the more they ask, the less time I'll have to take them to gym, but they are impossible at times in the classroom. How can I reward their behavior? Their bad behavior? By taking them to gym, something they look forward to and enjoy. I don't see how that is possible. If I can't contain them while they are in the classroom, how am I going to contain them walking down three flights of stairs, going through the lunchroom, going through the corridors, walking up the three flights to get to the gym, first of all, and it's just a pathetic situation where the administration tells us we must, must, must, and the individual teachers feel that we can't, and here is another place where we feel we are banging our heads against the stone wall, and I definitely feel that if the class as a whole is all discipline during the day, particularly in the morning because our gym period is in the afternoon, right after lunch, it's just ridiculous to begin with, that they should not be taken to gym as a form of punishment, but obviously the administration disagrees with me and since I'm a new teacher, I have no right to voice my opinion, as I have already been told.

As far as my lessons I can say that I did very little teaching this week. I just found it was impossible to do a lesson. Last week we had a spelling meeting and I had received a spelling inventory test and I gave it on Monday and I could not go on with the rest of it. I could not allow them to study in class. They had to take the stuff home, the words home to study at home. It was just impossible, an impossible week. The children were highstrung. You should look at them in the wrong way and they were very upset, and Michael did not add anything to it at all. There was no lesson I feel that I had taught last week that was successful, and I just can't differentiate between my poor lessons and my least successful lesson because all of them were just the same. They were interrupted; every time I started something they were interrupted by another child in the class or by a group of children in the class who just would not sit and listen. It was just an impossible situation.

I met him right before I was having lunch, and he said to me—how did the rehearsal go? And I said it was terrible. And he said why? And I said because my children may be mature enough to write a play and do a beautiful job on a play—but

I said I have some children in my class who are not mature
enough to be in kindergarten as far as their behavior is concerned. And I told him that I think it's very unfair of you to
require us to put on a play with children who really can't be
controlled. I said I can't have my eyes in thirty-four places at
once. He tried to calm me down. Then he said you're doing a
good job anyway, I'm sure, and would you mind if I observed
a rehearsal? I'd like to see it. He said—when is your next rehearsal? And I said Monday. And he said, would you please
write me a note. I'd very much like to see a rehearsal. So as not
to argue with him again, I said I would do it, and I intend to
do it. I want him to see exactly what happens during rehearsal.
He has no conception of what goes on. Many of these children
do want to put on this play for their class and many of them
are capable of doing it. Of working. They have marvelous suggestions, and there are just those few of them who cannot be
trusted when your back is turned and get into all sorts of mis-
chief and I told Dr. F——— I said to him, I don't think this
play is worth having three accidents per rehearsal, and he said
why, and I said for the simple reason that these are animals
sometimes. They just cannot be trusted alone. I felt terrible for
saying it, but that was exactly how I felt. And as far as rehearsal
is concerned, I will have my children bring their books and
they will be doing work and one boy already told me, Jimmy,
that he refuses to be in this play. So I said, alright, Jimmy, if
that's your choice—it's all right with me and I said you'll be
doing so much work that you won't believe it. So I wrote out
on the report card that he refuses to cooperate in the class
performance of a play of Benjamin Franklin.

Miss G. asked Lydia, she must have asked Lydia to read her
composition and Lydia did, and when she came up, she told
me that Miss G. had asked her why she was sad, and she said
she was sad yesterday when Miss D. started to cry, because on
Thursday I went into a minor hysteria when we were having
our rehearsals and it was horrible, so I turned around and
started writing on the board so the kids wouldn't see me, but
they did see me, and then I got a note from Miss G., who said
that she read the compositions and they were lovely, and if I

please come down to see her on Monday. So this woman is quite a lovely person. I mean, after hearing about the wild escapade in my classroom, of the teacher crying in front of all the kids, she sends up this little note to reassure me that my work is going well because the compositions weren't really great at all, but they were something, and I feel embarrassed, you know, to go down and have to see her and have her know about what happened on Thursday, and I just wonder what's going to happen. And little Lydia told me this so innocently. She told Miss G. about me crying and I wanted to hit her over the head at this very moment and that afternoon, I was about ready to walk down into Miss G.'s office and tell her that it was all over. We had had the fire drill. The kids were acting up, making a lot of noise in the hallway. I saw Miss P. with them and all the crazy things that they were doing when she was in the room and how if you single them out, there were like a hundred in five minutes, not a hundred, that's a little bit of an exaggeration, maybe ninety-nine, in the five minutes she was there, many, many wild things were going on like people calling out and raising hands, kids falling over, teetering over in their chairs and falling over and I thought, this goes on all the time except that I didn't correct it, and it was just a wild afternoon. So I got very upset that afternoon and I was about ready to walk down into Miss G's. office and tell her that I was ready to leave and that I didn't know how to control the children and that I had not wanted to control, so I walked in to Norma and said, Norma, I don't have control in that room, and it was just the talking, to get it out of my system and she told, who knows what she told me because I really wasn't listening, but she was quite sweet. She stayed until 3:30 and then I came in on Friday and everything was just superb, why I had control, and on Friday it amazed me. You know, if I said stop something they'd stop and if I'd, I did a lot of, what do you call those things, finger plays, I think you call them finger plays, but I just stand in front of the room and start acting like a moron and the kids do whatever I do like if I put my hand on my head, I would put my hands on my shoulders and then stretch them out and when I did this, the kids all did it with me which amazed me because half the time, like Thursday, I was standing there and I was sure that as many times during the day, as a matter of fact, we had certain things like, I would just want to see if how many kids were with me and I would say put your finger on your nose, put your finger on your toes, and maybe two kids would do it and those were the two that I had. But Friday, when I do these crazy things, everybody was there. It was very very good. Now I have to find out what I did on Friday that made these kids act like they did because whatever it was, I want to keep it up, and that's the funny thing about it. I can't put my finger on what it is. I know that maybe I was with them more. You're going to wonder what that means. On Thursday, after I saw their behavior in the hallway and how the other children were behaving, of the other two classes, I felt very discouraged and so when I came in, I saw Norma there. I had gone to the ladies' room. Norma was with the class for five minutes, and I saw them doing all the things that I mentioned before and I sort of got very disgusted with them and so I sort of threw myself out halfway in the situation, like, what could I do? I became very negative and after that I had started to cry when we started to rehearse because they were completely wild and on Friday, practically every moment I was there with them. No matter what the activity was, I never got so disgusted that I removed myself even mentally, because I think I did that Thursday, like, just then, I can't stand it, I can't stand it, and I don't care what they do. So I would let things go by, but Friday I was with them all the way and that might be one of the reasons.

I really can't single out one or two other children who gave me a lot of trouble this week. Of course it was the boys. I have eleven boys and except for one or two they can be really impossible. This week they were all obnoxious. They started with spitballs and I just couldn't stop them. I gave them extra homework, and I told them they weren't going to the puppet show on Thursday. I said if this keeps up you won't go to the Christmas party. I had them standing, I had them sitting with their hands folded. I tried everything but wherever my eyes are there's a spitball in the other direction. And them pushing on

line. They line up in the yard before lunch and pretty soon
the whole line is down on the floor. I tell them to straighten
themselves up, so one leans back a little bit and pushes the
whole line down, and it's very hard to see which particular individual it is. Of course, I know one of the boys is very sneaky
and inclined to do this, and this is Robert, and the others of
course are no better once they start. Monkey see, Monkey do.
As far as general confusion this week, Ricky seems to be re-
gressing again, and especially in that he didn't behave and he
was given extra homework, and he did not do it. And as I said,
I want to catch this now, and I'm going to send for his mother
now, so that he will understand that if he doesn't behave, he
must suffer the consequences, and take his punishment. So on
the whole, I don't know why, but this week except for Wednesday and Friday, the kids were pretty crazy and wild and I don't
know what got into them. Right after Thanksgiving, right
before Christmas, change of barometer, I don't know, but the
girls weren't too bad. The boys were really crazy. Some of the
children I've had the least difficulty with during the past week
are maybe all the girls, except for Elena, who has been a little
chatty this week. And maybe one boy, Jose, who is very quiet
and very well behaved, does his work well, conscientiously, good
worker, studies well, does well on tests, and behaves nicely too.
He is the only boy who really knows how to behave in the class.
One boy out of eleven. Their behavior is different from some
of the others in that they just sit quietly and do their work and
they can concentrate, work independently without my being
with them every minute, they can copy say, a social-studies
story, off the blackboard for fifteen minutes without getting up
and walking out of their seats or throwing a spitball or something. They have a longer attention span. They know how to
behave and work independently by themselves. And they don't
get out of their seats for any reason. They don't talk to their
neighbors, they do this occasionally in a whisper so they don't
disturb everyone else. If you tell them to do something, if you
give them extra homework, they do it. They know they did
something wrong, and they do it. In general these girls and
this one boy know how to behave. Their parents have taught

them how, I guess, and they know that if they are punished they accept their punishment and the next time they do it they just won't repeat the behavior that was punished. These children, I have many of them, really, most of them are girls, and they are a pleasure to have. If I could have a class with just my girls with Jose without the other ten boys I would be very happy.

As for the social studies, I am still having trouble making that meaningful and interesting to them, and it is possible that the words in the lesson are as meaningless to them as their conversation is to me, but the whole thing would be probably in establishing some sort of a background, but I am trying to establish the background and this is what they are not interested in. I am going to start taking trips with them in December, and I hope that this will give them some visual background besides what they get in the textbooks and the bulletin boards that I have in school. And maybe give them some actual experience in knowing what the history of New York was all about. And seeing what it was all about. We are going to the New York Historical Society some Friday in December and the Museum of the City of New York in May. I tried to get a trip to that much earlier but they said they were all booked up until May. I am really at my wits' end what to do. I know it's not meaningful, and still it's something that has to be taught and some of them do learn it and are interested and I am not going to drop social studies for the sake of those who cannot get interested in it, so I guess I will just have to go on coping with the discipline problem, and being rewarded by the fact that some of them are learning and are interested, so I will just have to go on like that, and I am going to see if I can get some film strips that will further motivate them to be interested. There are times, such as when we discuss Indian life, that they are interested.

I mimeographed a sheet of all the words in the pre-primers, a total of all the words that he should be knowing and I brought him up to my desk while the other children were having a writing period of something and I went through the list with him and I said, how many words do you know and I found out that of the whole list (there were about sixty words on it) he knew about four. So of course I said to myself, this child should not even be in this reading class, and since I have only the one reading group and I can't put it up to two groups, he has to drag along with the rest of them. Even if I wanted to, I don't have another book to give him to read. So I sent home a list with a note to his mother and I said, Please help Andre with these words. These are the words that are to be studied. I will see how much progress he has made next week. I did not indicate to the parent that the child is weak in reading because I feel that's not the thing the parent wants to hear in a letter. However, if she does come up to school to see me, or if I feel it's necessary to send for her, I will discuss the matter with her then. Now, Julio is a boy who was thrown out of Catholic school in the area. The reason he was thrown out of the school was because he beat up another boy and had a serious fight and the nuns just wouldn't keep him. So you know, that when a child is thrown out of a Catholic school like that, he's dead. So like I said, he talks constantly, and constantly is a sneak. If I look at him he would sit up straight. He didn't know that I could hear him. Now, I heard him and know it was him because he's a Spanish boy and I could detect his accent. I'd say to him, were you talking? He'd look me straight in the eye and say, no. And I don't want to ram a lie down a child's throat . . . I never want to say, you are lying. I don't feel that's right. So I just took Julio away from the table he was sitting at and put him at a desk, in an individual desk. In my room, most of the children sit four at a table, two at each table, two tables together. Now, I have about five individual desks which I had pushed together to make another table. However, I separated these desks and I put Julio at one and since I did that and since I keep severe discipline on him, I am constantly at him, telling him he's not getting away with anything. I don't want him to open up his mouth because he is a bright child and if he would pay attention, I'm sure he would progress lovely, but he's too busy causing trouble, talking, and telling me what other people did when he really did it himself, so I have him sitting now by himself and I find that, I sat him by himself Thursday, and the rest of Thursday and Friday I didn't have any trouble with him except for yesterday afternoon when he came into school and told me he got beat up, but that didn't happen in my classroom so I didn't concern myself with it.

I do think that in teaching them, I will have to oversimplify a lot of materials that I have to present to them. I can't take anything for granted with my class. I know that if the material is presented clearly enough and accurately enough, they will grasp this, but I cannot assume that the class knows this or the class knows that. I have to find out what the class knows and what the class doesn't know, and I can't assume because they knew it on Monday that they are going to know it on Wednesday. If they knew it on Monday, they may very well have forgotten it by Wednesday. Now I didn't think that I would have to be so cautious in the classroom and so keen and observant as to what the children know and what the children don't know. I thought that well, this is the second grade. They should know how to count to twenty, they should know the number story, they should be able to read all the words in this book. I can't believe that I have to be so on guard to find out exactly what they don't know. I must realize that in presenting my material to them I always have to ask them, do you understand? Are you sure that you know this? Who could tell me why such and such a thing happens? Why do we have a fire drill? Because my children don't know that, and ordinarily you would assume that being in the school and having gone through fire drills, they would know the importance of fire drills, but you make no assumptions. You walk into the classroom and you see what the children know and then you go from there, and this is a big problem. Every single day you have to keep watching and watching and watching to see what they know and what they don't know, because if you assume something and you go on the basis of that you are going to have a very big problem because naturally you're going to go on and on and the children will not raise their hands and say, I don't know what you're doing. You have to ask them.

Well, coming back after being out on Monday, the children were wild. First thing, naturally, they ran to tell me how the sub told them how terrible they were and that she would never come back to teach them again. I looked at my anecdotal record book and I saw what she had written. I figured why. The three of them, Michael, Lans, Sammy, and this girl, Dolores, were behaving just terribly and giving a difficult time and it was hard to calm them down when I came back at the end of the week. Once again, this was a week of disciplining the children. When I came back on Wednesday, they were very very noisy and gave me all kinds of compliments. My hair looked beautiful and they were beginning to behave accordingly. Lans was in his glory then, still getting out of his seat; Michael running all over the room; and Sammy running all over the place, and it was just a wild week. In fact, on Thursday they had me so upset that I went home crying and I started to cry in the classroom. They just got me. Usually I would say I'm not going to let it bother me and this and that, and it's just gotten to the point this week that all I had to do was if they did just one more thing I would just have sat down and started to cry. It was all I could do and I was so mad that I slammed the door and I just came out with the statement that if one person got out of his seat I would walk right out of the room and I got my coat on and my boots in that rain and they were sitting with their coats on. I had just gotten to the point that I could leave them in the classroom to walk out and I knew they wouldn't kill the room or something like that. I would just walk out. That's how mad they got me and actually again with all that discipline I naturally had not gotten beyond anything but the basic lesson, reading and arithmetic—we didn't do any art work this week —nothing. I'll show you why I never got to anything else. On Thursday morning we spent a half an hour beginning at about ten to nine—Wednesday I started the reading lesson about five to nine or nine o'clock, and it went along smoothly. It was not so bad, but in the afternoon they were wild. Thursday when I said what book did you read—one would take out the book, one is writing in a notebook, one is doing everything else. Everyone closes their book, and they opened and closed their books until they could all do it at the same time. Not ten minutes later when I start the lesson and I call on a person, they don't have their book out. And this was the type that was Thursday and Friday, and whatever I would say they would stand, one would stand, three were standing, they were going downstairs. This was the end of it. As they progressed they were getting worse. They forgot everything I had taught at the beginning. This never happened—this getting out of seats. I couldn't open the windows. They were stuck. So I would open the door for a few minutes, just to get the room cooled through. The door was opened. Three of them are out of their seats, hanging out the door looking. You can't open the door to the room, you can't leave chalk on the blackboard. They are out of their seats touching everything. I am new to the system and I don't know all the tricks to the trade, as if I was an experienced teacher. One teacher once told me, I don't remember the exact words, but in essence you say the children are bad because the weather is bad if it rains, or they are bad because it is too sunny and warm and they want to go out. In other words, you can never predict how they are going to behave and this is the answer she gives me, and when I ask for help and stand there and say please help me, this is the answer that you get. You don't know what to do. B———— is more helpful. He came down and told me that he sees our problems and that they are quite a bunch, and when they hang over my desk they just want to be near me. They want love and if I ever put my arms around them or something they just loved it. I can't go around hugging twenty-eight children every minute of the day. It's impossible every two minutes to go over and hug someone or put your arms around them and tell them how great they are if they are going to behave. It goes around in a circle and you never get any help. They probably sense that you are young—if I threaten these children they'll behave for about twenty minutes or so. Threatening threatening, threatening is the only thing that penetrates. Would you like me to send a note home? Would you like me to do this? I found out that I am constantly threatening children, and you can't have a sensible lesson. It took me Friday afternoon to do a math lesson. One page took me an hour. Why? Because they don't know how to open their books, they don't know how to do the lesson. They have just become impossible. They talk all day long, and while I'm yelling at them telling them and explaining to them why they mustn't talk, they talk right in front of me unless I go over and pull on their arm or yell, and if I turn around they do it again, and honestly, you just don't know what to do after a while. You can't hit them. And you just don't know what to do with them.

Well, once again comes Lavinia, and I just don't know what to say, really. You must be getting sick and tired of hearing her name; I know I am and everyone is. I am constantly reprimanding her, no matter where or when, or what we are doing. She is always doing the wrong thing, and I just have the feeling and know that it is conscious on her part. She knows exactly what she's doing, and it must be the wrong thing. I guess I'm beginning to put some psychology into it and I think she's just looking for attention. She's doing it by this negative way. I guess the only thing is my problem about handling her. I have tried punishment, in several ways, and punishment doesn't work, and I just can't get myself to do anything else. I praise her when she deserves it for what she does, and she is pretty bright, and she reads nicely, and she generally knows what is going on but I find myself just not—you know—I really feel absolutely at a loss!

On Friday she was again acting up and I said to myself, "I just can't be bothered." I just don't know what to do and I just don't want to keep saying, "Lavinia, Lavinia," when the other kids have something to work with. So I took her and I put her in Miss G———'s room and I said right in front of her in class, "What a bad girl Lavinia is, and she can't have fun with the rest of us." Well, she went in and I made her stand in the corner there, not even sit. And later on Miss G——— came in and she said she felt terrible. Her class was all playing and Lavinia was just standing there. So I said, "Bring her back," and I guess I was getting a little soft. Not that it mattered to Lavinia, I don't think. It might, but I don't know.

Anyway, she came back and she apologized for not behav-

ing and with that she was quite all right for the rest of the day,
which wasn't too long, about twenty minutes.

One thing she did this week also, Friday, was quite puzzling
to me and I believe that something must be wrong with her. I
just don't know. She came up to me at 12:00 o'clock when we
came into the classroom after she hung up her coat and she
handed me a nickel. I said, "Lavinia, what is the nickel for?"
She didn't answer. I said, "I don't want the nickel." She said,
"Here, you take it." She did not say a word. She just kept pushing the nickel towards me. I made her stand next to me, and I
said, "Lavinia, why are you giving me the nickel?" She did not
answer. I said, "Go sit down and take your nickel." This went
on and on and everyone was looking and she just stood there
with this smirk on her face handing me the nickel. I asked her
if she found it on the floor and if she was giving it to me and
she said no. She didn't say no, she shook her head. Finally I
took it and I put it in her little pocket. She took it out and
handed it to me again. I said, "Lavinia, if the nickel is yours,
you take it," and finally she said to me, "No, I want you to buy
candy." I said, "Lavinia, I don't need candy. Thank you very,
very much but you take the nickel and you buy candy," and
with that she walked away laughing. It was very funny. So I
can't figure her out.

I am planning to speak to Mrs. J——— about the problem
with Daniel. It's a problem that I really can't cope with. Any
routine or discipline I have established in the class is virtually
at the point of complete breakdown because of him. It seems
that he just completely sets the other children off their equi-
librium. He's someone—I hate to use the word—vicious, but
that's certainly what he is. I know—on Friday—it's really a
horrible thing—the guidance counsellor had wanted to see him
because—well, he's been in other classrooms before this one,
and the teachers have been having quite a bit of problems with
him and she wanted to meet him. She has more or less stayed
away from him because he was under the care of Northside
center. She didn't want to more or less overstep her limit, but
she did call for him, and she spoke to him, and she sent back a

note that he would try his best and would try more in class
and do better in class. When she finally came back to me after
he had spoken to her, she was quite despondent and told me
the fire was burning low, and this is quite unusual for her, because she really has to be agitated to a very extreme degree to
sound like that, and as soon as I saw Vernon was upset, I knew
that whatever Daniel did was really pretty wretched, but I
just told him to take his seat and sit down, and he got very
indignant, and he refused to take the book out. He took his
coat out of the closet and ran out of the room and was running
up and down the halls.

Then I sent a note into Miss G———— to see if she could
coerce him into the room because I had tried and was quite
unsuccessful with it, and she said that she had gotten him into
her room and she was talking to him and a few minutes later I
had a note saying Daniel ran out and she thinks he's left the
building but fortunately or unfortunately he hadn't, and when
I took my class down before lunch to go to the bathroom, they
were lined up quietly. There was no hubbub; they were fine.
And all of a sudden Daniel was there and spitting and kicking
and hitting, and he had half of them on the floor, and the
children just couldn't take it any more, and what ensued after
that I have never never seen in my class, but I calmed them
down, and Daniel was crying because Moses or one of the other
boys had given him a few good punches. And then he left, but
before he left he said he was going to bring back a knife on
Tuesday and kill Moses and Lewis and one or two others, and
my children really, really, as far as I can see even though there
has been some discipline problems—these things are to be
expected—I have more or less managed to cope with them
either through parental cooperation or sitting down and talking to the child. Sometimes there hasn't been a permanent improvement, but with a reminder or two their behavior has
once again improved. But with Daniel there is—I just can't
cope with him.

I've tried to get him individually, sent him to the guidance
counsellor to see what she can do, and I feel he is . . . I don't
know what it is, really. I can't put my finger on what the

problem is, and I know the children are really out to get him more or less, because they don't want to be punched and smacked and sat upon, and I know neither do I, so I am going to have to speak to Mrs. J——— about this and see what can be done.

I had absolutely no arithmetic supplies. Every time I need a bead board I send across the hall. She's gotten so disgusted with me—not disgusted, really—she's let me keep it already because I guess she doesn't want the interruptions, and I can't blame her. There are still quite a few arithmetic supplies that I still could use. There are quite a few art supplies that I could use and I don't know, it's gotten to the point, since the beginning of the year I've been asking for the alphabet cards to put in front of my room for the children—these are not only penmanship cards, but to see the ABC sequence and the alphabetizing and things like that but I still haven't received it. I requested 9 x 6 yellow lined paper because my supply, my one package, has run out—I still haven't gotten that. So that I really make do with what I have, but in many cases this is pretty difficult. Crayons, things like that that I have asked for time and again haven't been forthcoming, and there's always an excuse for not getting it. It will be here soon. But perhaps by June, May, perhaps even, these things will be coming. So where the lack is I've been forced to borrow—to bring my own —to buy my own and just make do with what I have, and I feel that the program can be enriched far more than it has been had the needed supplies been forthcoming. But since they haven't, I've had to gear myself down more or less.

I know that a lesson that I wanted to do on the thermometer —as far as my math and science go I wanted to show why we use the thermometer—have the three beakers, one with ice water—one with room-temperature water, one with hot water. Your children go out of the room and then they put their hands in either the ice water and then into the room temperature . . . How does it feel? It feels warm—and then from the hot water to the cold water. How does it feel? It feels cold. Well, really, it's a constant thing. How can we tell how cold or warm it really is? I wanted all this by using a thermometer but, of course, I had no thermometer, no beakers to do the experiment with. The beakers I had brought from home in hopes that I would get a thermometer from somewhere but no such luck. So I had to cast that lesson aside.

I mean, there are so many things that I can get on my own. I, too, am limited, so that eventually, after I've been teaching for about two or three years, all these materials will be mine. I have gotten some art supplies; I've gotten envelopes, folders that I requested to keep the children's work in. So maybe slowly but surely these things will be coming in.

Another thing that I requested were enough rulers for the whole class, and when they were delivered to me there was a grand total of twelve. So the work that I had hoped to do with measurements had to be cast aside. But we'll just have to do the best with what we have for the time being and see what evolves.

"An even more important task was defining, understanding, and accepting the role of the person with whom one was to work."

AUXILIARY SCHOOL PERSONNEL: THEIR ROLES, TRAINING, AND INSTITUTIONALIZATION*

Garda W. Bowman and Gordon J. Klopf

An important innovation that holds promise of having a great impact on the future of urban education is the growing use of paraprofessional personnel in the schools of disadvantaged areas. Two important influences have shaped this trend. One was the realization of many leaders in the development of the national poverty program that the poor must be involved in creating and operating programs to help the poor, that "indigenous leaders" could provide crucial insights not available to middle-class professionals. The second was an idea advanced by Pearlman and Reissman in a book called *New Careers for*

* The research reported herein was performed by Bank Street College of Education pursuant to a contract with the office of Economic Opportunity, Washington, D.C.

the Poor, whose thesis was that to break the poverty cycle we must create a host of new jobs at a subprofessional level, for which many of the presently unskilled poor could be trained.

The Head Start program included an early application of these ideas, providing training and jobs for many women who lived in the communities in which the program operated. Some worked directly with early childhood teachers, others with the parents of the children involved in the Head Start centers. The use of auxiliary personnel in the regular school program of many large systems followed shortly. This report on the progress of the idea in fifteen demonstration programs was written on the basis of a study conducted by Bank Street College of Education for the Office of Economic Opportunity.

The major difficulties cited appear to be in general in the realm of human relations and the adjustment of two very different groups of people to one another. How realistic are the recommendations made by the study? If they can be implemented, how probable is it that they will resolve the human conflicts involved?

THE EMPLOYMENT of teacher-aides, teacher-assistants, guidance-aides, health-aides, family workers and other auxiliary personnel in schools increased sharply during the mid-sixties. Often, however, the circumstances under which funds could be secured as well as the urgency of the need required a crash program. The essential component of preparation was therefore lacking—preparation not only of the nonprofessionals themselves but even more importantly, *of the teachers and other professionals with whom they would be working.*

Several convergent forces—social, educational and economic —have contributed to the mushrooming of such employment at a pace which sometimes precluded adequate orientation:

1. The ever changing and expanding needs for school services;

2. Acute shortages of professionals to meet these needs;

3. New dimensions in education, requiring a more complex and demanding role for teachers;

4. Heightened awareness of the special learning needs of disadvantaged children and youth;

5. Recognition of the communication blocks which often exist between middle class professionals and lower class pupils;

6. The plight of undereducated persons unable to compete in an increasingly automated economy;

7. The availability of Federal funds for the employment of low-income nonprofessionals in education, through such sources as O.E.O., M.D.T.A., Title I of the E.S.E.A., and more recently the Nelson-Scheuer Amendment to the Anti-Poverty Act.

The Office of Economic Opportunity, alert to this critical situation, requested Bank Street College of Education to conduct a study of auxiliary personnel in education. This study, exploratory and developmental in nature, has three specific areas of inquiry: role development, training, and institutionalization of auxiliaries in school systems. One component of the Study was the coordination and analysis of 15 demonstration training programs. In these programs professionals and nonprofessionals studied and worked together to increase the effectiveness of auxiliary personnel in various school situations.

The auxiliaries learned specific skills and gained some basic understandings needed to operate in a school setting. The teacher-trainees learned in a reality situation—a practicum—how to utilize and relate to other adults in a classroom.

The auxiliary trainees in the Summer Institutes included Navaho Indians from a reservation; low income whites from Appalachia; Mexican-Americans, Negroes and others in California; predominantly Negroes in Gary, Ind., in Jackson, Mississippi, East St. Louis, Ill. and in Detroit; mothers receiving aid to dependent children in Maine; Puerto Ricans, Negroes and others in East Harlem; Puerto Ricans in disadvantaged sections of Metropolitan San Juan; high school seniors in the lowest academic tracks of the Cardozo H.S. in Washington, D.C.; and a cross-cultural, cross-class group of trainees in Boston.

The varied experiences of the demonstration programs will be described and analyzed in some depth in the final report of the study which is due early in 1967. Meantime, this brochure considers what seems to help or harm effective utilization of auxiliary personnel in education. It offers: (1) rationale for the use of auxiliaries in school systems; (2) some difficulties which might be encountered; and (3) some recommendations for coping with these difficulties, based on the experience thus far in the demonstration training programs.

It is expected that the demonstration programs may have some relevance to other school situations where auxiliary personnel are employed or are about to be employed. Further, this report may elicit comments and counter-suggestions which will contribute to the exploration of a new and promising development in education.

RATIONALE FOR THE UTILIZATION OF AUXILIARY PERSONNEL IN SCHOOL SYSTEMS

The question is often asked: "Should the school system be required to solve all the social problems of our time?" This leads to a second question: "Is the utilization of low income workers as auxiliary school personnel aimed primarily at creating jobs for the poor, at coping with acute manpower shortage, or at helping to meet the needs of pupils?"

To those who conducted demonstration training programs in 1966 the answer appeared to be that the essential criterion of any innovation in education is whether it helps to meet the learning and developmental needs of children and youth. However, they believed that the learning-teaching process can be truly effective only in relation to the totality of the child's experience. The school, like every other institution, operates within a social context, not in isolation.

The sponsors of the demonstration programs believed that even if there were no shortage of teachers, the introduction of more adults into the classroom would enhance the quality of education—adults selected on the basis of their concern for children and their potential as supportive personnel rather than primarily on the basis of previous training. They saw, too, great possibilities in the professional-nonprofessional team in enabling the teacher to differentiate the learning-teaching process to meet the individual needs of pupils, as diagnosed by the teacher. They saw, too, in this multi-level team approach escape from rigid structuring in the classroom—for example, more freedom of movement, more small groupings, more independent activities than would be feasible for one person often operating under difficult teaching conditions. In fact, the teacher might, with this assistance, be able to experiment with innovative techniques which he had long been wanting to inaugurate.

These values are universal—that is to say, they might be realized through the effective utilization of auxiliaries in any classroom regardless of the composition of the school population or the socio-economic background of the auxiliaries. In summary, the multiple benefits which were perceived as possible in *all* school situations were:

1. *To the pupil,* by providing more individualized attention by concerned adults, more mobility in the classroom, and more opportunity for innovation;

2. *To the teacher,* by rendering his role more satisfying in terms of status, and more manageable in terms of teaching conditions;

3. *To the other professionals,* by increasing the scope and effectiveness of their activities;

4. *To the auxiliary,* by providing meaningful employment which contributes at one and the same time to his own development and to the needs of society;

5. *To the school administrator,* by providing some answers to his dilemma of ever increasing needs for school services, coupled with shortage of professionals to meet these needs—*a* solution, not *the* solution, and certainly not a panacea;

6. *To family life,* by giving auxiliaries, many of whom are or may someday become parents, the opportunity to learn child development principles in a reality situation;

7. *To the community at large,* by providing a means through which unemployed and educationally disadvantaged persons may enter the mainstream of productivity.

In addition to these global considerations, there are some specific benefits which may flow from the utilization of indigenous personnel as auxiliaries in schools serving disadvantaged neighborhoods.

The auxiliary who has actually lived in disadvantaged environments often speaks to the disadvantaged child or youth in a way that is neither strange nor threatening. He may help the new pupil to adjust to the unfamiliar world of the school without undue defensiveness; to fill the gaps, if any, in his preparation for learning; and to build upon his strengths, which may have more relevance to the new situation than the child, himself, realizes. This cultural bridge is seen as an asset, in and of itself, even if there were no need to provide jobs for the poor.

Moreover, the low-income auxiliary, having faced up to and overcome some of the difficulties and frustrations the children now face, may serve to motivate the child to further effort. His very presence in a role of some status in the school says to the child: "It can be done; it is worth trying to do; you, too, can succeed here." This has far more meaning than the story of a Ralph Bunche or a Felisa Rincon de Gautier to one who obviously lacks the exceptional ability of these great but remote persons.

Naturally, this message would be imparted more forcefully

if the faculty, too, were mixed in terms of socio-economic background. As work-study programs become increasingly available, economic integration may become more frequent in school faculties. Meantime, the low-income auxiliary sometimes provides incentive to poor pupils which would otherwise be lacking.

Further, the auxiliary from the child's own neighborhood may be able to interpret to the middle class professional some aspects of the behavior of a child who is non-responding in a school situation. The auxiliary may, in turn, interpret the goals of the school and the learning-teaching process to both parent and child. To reach the child for a few hours a day without reaching those who influence his mode of living may be of little avail. The parent who doesn't understand a school official sometimes finds a neighbor serving as a school auxiliary helpful.

However, the fact that low-income auxiliaries may and often do facilitate communication between school and community does not mean that *all* poor people can work effectively with poor pupils and their families. Naturally, any candidate for school employment should be carefully screened for those personal characteristics needed to work with children and youth. However, the demonstration programs have revealed that a flexible and imaginative selection process may discover in poor people potential that has been overlooked thus far—potential which may be developed as an asset in a school setting.

In summary, new dimensions in education call for the utilization of school personnel of various socio-economic backgrounds and at various level of training working together as teams to meet the wide range of pupil needs in changing communities. Since economic, social and educational problems often have some common causal factors, a single solution may have multiple values. It may result in positive pupil outcomes and in socially useful outcomes as well. The utilization of low-income auxiliaries in disadvantaged areas appears to be a case in point. Its possibilities are many. Its real significance is only beginning to be explored.

The study is designed to view these possibilities in terms of several reality situations, and to identify factors which seem to block or facilitate the realization of education values from the utilization of auxiliaries in these specific situations.

DIFFICULTIES WHICH MIGHT ARISE IN THE DEPLOYMENT OF AUXILIARIES IN SCHOOLS

During the pre-planning for the overall study and for the demonstration programs, many professional and administrative concerns were discussed. Some of the anticipated difficulties were actually encountered. Others proved to be mere conjecture, not substantiated by experience. The fact that these possible problems had been considered in advance aided in their solution.

The difficulties anticipated by each of the groups involved in the training programs differed widely. For school administrators they were largely "how to" problems, such as establishing fiscal policies—the whole process of setting up a new hierarchy of positions, with job descriptions, job titles, salaries, increments, role prerogatives, and training requirements for advancement. Another "how to" problem for the superintendent was orienting the principals, who, in turn, were faced with the problem of interpreting the new program to the teachers and other professionals so that they would utilize rather than ignore, reject, or resent their would-be helpers. Theirs was the task to determine who would conduct the training of both professionals and nonprofessionals and how to secure such personnel. Often all this had to be accomplished within and in spite of institutional rigidities. Moreover, the school administrator was responsible for involving local institutions of higher learning, and the indigenous leadership in the planning, and for interpreting the new program to the Board and to the broader community.

The professionals—teachers, supervisors, guidance counselors, *et al.*—were primarily concerned that professional standards should be maintained. They wondered whether the auxiliaries might try to "take over," but they were even more concerned lest the administrators, caught in the bind between increasing enrollment and decreasing availability of professional personnel, might assign functions to the auxiliaries that were essentially professional in nature. The teachers, specifically, believed that teacher-aides might sometimes be assigned to a class without the supervision of a certified professional. Teachers, particularly, questioned whether funds which might have been used to reduce the teaching load would be used instead to employ auxiliaries, while increasing rather than decreasing the size of classes.

Some teachers and other professionals also doubted that adequate time would be set aside during school hours for *planning* and *evaluating* with the auxiliaries assigned to them. Moreover, many professionals were not accustomed to the new leadership function which they were being asked to perform. Some felt threatened by another adult in the classroom. Others could not envision ways in which to use this new source of assistance effectively. Still others anticipated that the auxiliaries might not speak in standard English and hence might undermine their own efforts to improve the pupils' language skills. A few wondered whether the pupils would respond more easily to the auxiliaries than to themselves and that they might therefore lose close, personal contacts with their pupils.

The auxiliaries, themselves, had many trepidations. They, too, appeared to be concerned about the differences in their background, values, and patterns of speech from those prevailing in the school. While the professionals often considered the effects of such factors upon pupils, the auxiliaries tended to become defensive and uncomfortable because of these differences. On the other hand, some auxiliaries were resentful, particularly in pre-school centers, when they observed only the end result of the planning—i.e., what was actually done for pupils and by whom in the classroom. Not understanding the diagnostic skills required of the teacher in designing the program to meet the needs of individual pupils, these auxiliaries were heard to say: "We do the same things as the teachers; why should they be paid more?"

It became evident that the problem of defining and redefining one's own role was only one aspect of the challenge. An even more important task was defining, understanding and accepting the role of the person with whom one was to work. This was equally true of professionals and auxiliaries as they entered into a new, sensitive and complex relationship. In fact, one of the insights gained from the demonstration programs was that many of the doubts and concerns could have been avoided if there had been adequate specification of roles and functions prior to the operation.

In those programs where these possible difficulties were discussed by school administrators, university representatives and community leaders in pre-planning sessions, the problems were either ameliorated or prevented. Usually, only the unexpected proves disastrous.

MAJOR FINDINGS AND RECOMMENDATIONS

The Study was concerned with role development and training of auxiliaries, and with the impact which the utilization of low-income auxiliaries in school settings may have upon (1) pupil learnings, (2) parent-school relations, (3) teacher competence, (4) the development of the auxiliaries, themselves, as workers and persons, and (5) the system or sub-system within which the auxiliaries are institutionalized.

Major Findings

The Study demonstrated that some of the desired outcomes from the training and utilization of low-income workers as auxiliary school personnel could, in fact, be realized under favorable conditions. The programs were analyzed through the use of a uniform questionnaire, through process observations by Visiting Teams, and through interviews with instructional staff and participants. The major findings are summarized below.

1. ROLE DEVELOPMENT AND RELATIONSHIPS

. . . Low-income auxiliaries with minimum education appeared to be capable of assisting with the learning-teaching process in the classroom with benefits to pupils, particularly when the auxiliaries were carefully selected and trained.

. . . This meaningful occupational role for low-income, educationally disadvantaged persons often appeared to have a positive impact upon their familial and community roles, as well as upon their self-concept.

. . . Auxiliaries frequently established communication with pupils and parents of their own background in school situations and helped to reduce home-school alienation.

. . . Auxiliaries often appeared to serve as role models for disadvantaged pupils—which might well be a significant motivational factor in the child's or youth's development.

. . . Many teachers who participated in the programs reported that they perceived their own roles in new perspective after working with aides in the classroom—i.e., as more highly professional with emphasis on diagnosis, planning and coordination, rather than *solely* upon teacher-pupil interaction. This new role was seen as additive rather than as a substitute for teacher-pupil interaction.

. . . There was a high degree of mutuality in the perception of auxiliaries, teacher-trainees, and instructional staff, mutuality of perceptions before and after training, and mutuality of perceptions of the helpfulness and frequency of occurrence of specific functions of auxiliaries. This mutuality of perception appeared to be a positive factor in the demonstration programs.

. . . A salient outcome was that all concerned—administrators, supervisors, teachers, and ancillary personnel (i.e., counselors, curriculum specialists, etc.) had to rethink their roles and relationships when aides were introduced into a school system, in order to develop viable, purposeful teams and integrate all available school services to meet pupil needs.

. . . In essence, the introduction of auxiliaries appeared to serve a catalytic function in the development of all roles in the school system.

2. TRAINING

. . . Training was identified as *the* essential factor in the effective use of auxiliaries. Employment without training appeared to present many problems.

. . . There was no significant correlation between success in the

program and ethnicity or previous training of the auxiliary-
participants, thus reinforcing the proposition that persons
of various backgrounds and levels of academic achievement
can be trained to perform auxiliary roles effectively in a
school setting.

. . . When *both* teachers and auxiliaries participated in demonstration programs as trainees, the effectiveness of training
appeared to be facilitated.

. . . These mutual learnings were even more apparent when the
members of each teacher-auxiliary team had time regularly
scheduled within the school day to review their experiences
of working together in the classroom and to plan as a team
under competent supervision for their future interaction
within the classroom.

. . . Optimum results were obtained when the aide and the
teacher who would be working together during the coming
school year were trained together.

. . . Skill training and basic education, though necessary, seemed
to be inadequate without instruction in the foundations of
human development and without group or individual counseling, as trainees moved into new roles and relationships.

. . . It was clearly evident that opportunities for experiential
learnings were needed to fortify and integrate theory, such
experience to be provided either through a practicum or in
an actual on-the-job work experience, under close and highly
competent supervision.

. . . Inservice training appeared to be the prime desideratum
of auxiliaries as they entered this new era of responsibility.

3. INSTITUTIONALIZATION

. . . A selection process which recognizes potential yet eliminates
those who seem to be incapable of development in the specific role to be filled was seen as a crucial factor.

. . . While employment without training often proved unpro-
ductive, the reverse was equally true: training without employment tended to provoke anxiety and lead to frustration,
since even the most sincere assurance of employment sometimes proved impossible to implement.

. . . Employment *prior to training* so that the trainee was already an incumbent rather than merely a job applicant, appeared to be the ideal situation.

. . . Preservice training of employees sometimes preceded final placement in a given job category so as to provide a probationary period, a practice which school systems found helpful.

. . . Stable employment with opportunity for upward mobility was seen as essential to a successful program.

. . . Training on a work-study basis proved to be a major factor in upward mobility.

Recommendations

In essence, the experience in the 15 demonstration programs which were operating in 1966 seemed to indicate that it is not likely that the desired outcomes from the utilization of auxiliary personnel in a given school situation would be realized unless certain pre-conditions to their use were established, so as to avoid or resolve some of the difficulties which are likely to occur without informed, thoughtful, and cooperative pre-planning.

Specific recommendations are presented below, based on the experiences, thus far, in role development and training demonstrations. The recommendations refer to all types of auxiliaries, not merely to those from low-income groups.

1. ROLE DEFINITION AND DEVELOPMENT

. . . That role specifications of auxiliaries be defined initially, in order to provide a frame of reference for a new set of relationships, thus preventing either *underutilization* by unconvinced professionals or *overutilization* by administrators faced with manpower shortages.

. . . That role *definition*, which indicates "the givens," be balanced with role *development*, which gives variety and scope to the program.

. . . That overemphasis on role differentiation and role prerogatives be avoided, together with their concomitants of rigidity and divisiveness.

. . . That the functions of individual auxiliaries and of the professionals with whom they work be developed reciprocally in terms of the dynamics of each specific situation.

. . . That the whole range of teaching functions be re-examined, so as to differentiate those which may be delegated to non-professionals (such as monitorial, escorting, technical, clerical) from the more important functions directly related to instruction and to home-school relations in which assistance of nonprofessionals may be of value.

. . . That teaching functions be further examined to identify the more complex and highly professional functions which should be performed by a teacher alone, such as diagnosis of the learning needs of pupils, planning programs to meet these needs, and orchestrating other adults, both other professionals and nonprofessionals, in the execution of such programs.

2. TRAINING

a) *Preservice*

. . . That the program be planned cooperatively by school systems, institutions of higher learning, community action agencies, professional staff, and participants.

. . . That there be preservice training of auxiliaries to develop communication skills and other concrete skills as well as some of the basic understandings needed for success during their first work experience, thus bolstering self-confidence and encouraging further effort.

. . . That the training be differentiated to meet the special needs and characteristics of each group, considering such variables as the age of the trainees and the level (elementary, middle, or secondary) at which they are being trained to work.

. . . That there be orientation of both the administrators and the professionals with whom the auxiliaries will be working, including an opportunity for the expression of any doubts or resistance which may exist, and for consideration of the new and challenging leadership role of the professional vis-a-vis the nonprofessionals, and also the new supervisory role of administrators vis-a-vis teacher-auxiliary teams.

. . . That institutes for administrators, teachers, or other professionals and auxiliaries be conducted, where a new concept of team operation can be developed.

. . . That a practicum be included in all preservice training—i.e., a field experience where professionals and nonprofessionals try out and evaluate their team approach, under the close supervision of the training staff.

. . . That training of trainers and supervisors be provided.

. . . That the school system or systems in which the auxiliaries are to work be involved in the planning, thus enabling the trainers to render the program more relevant to the employment situation.

. . . That hiring precede training, wherever possible, so that trainees will be given orientation for an actual job assignment.

. . . That professionals and nonprofessionals who will be working together on the job receive preservice training on a team basis.

b) *Inservice*

. . . That there be a comprehensive, continuing, in-depth program of development and supervision of auxiliaries closely integrated with a long-term program of stable, open-ended employment, so that each level of work responsibility will have comparable training available.

. . . That mechanisms for process observations and feedback be developed with a spirit of openness to suggestion so that dynamic role concepts and relationships may emerge which are relevant to each specific situation.

. . . That both group and individual counseling be available.

. . . That the training of professionals and nonprofessionals on a team basis, started in preservice, be continued and intensified in inservice training, with emphasis upon competent supervision.

c) *Higher Education (on a work-study basis)*

. . . That the cooperation of two-year colleges (both junior colleges and community colleges) be sought in the development of programs for auxiliaries who would move into roles requiring more knowledge and skills than at the entry level; for example, library-aides might have one or two years' training in the objectives and procedures of library operation, and counselor-aides might have special training in guidance principles.

. . . That cooperation of colleges of teacher education and departments of education in institutions of higher learning be sought in two respects: first, by providing educational opportunities for auxiliaries who desire to qualify for advancement to the professional level, and second, in incorporating into their curriculum the expanded role concept of the teacher as one who is able to organize appropriate resources, both human and material, in meeting the needs of children.

Since the demonstration programs conducted for the first phase of the Study in 1966 were primarily for the purposes of role development and training, institutionalization—the focus of the second phase of the Study—was not a significant component of these demonstrations. However, in every training program, the need for institutionalization was stressed by staff and participants alike. They believed that the anticipated benefits had been realized in their training experience, but they also believed that training for jobs that were not stable or were at best "dead-end" would be frustrating to the participants. The following recommendations on institutionalization are, in effect, a look into the future rather than a look backward at the 1966 demonstration programs. They represent the needed developments, as perceived by innovators in the field, for the optimum effectiveness of auxiliary personnel in American education.

3. INSTITUTIONALIZATION

. . . That the first step be a definite commitment by the decision-makers in a given school system to the training and utilization of auxiliary personnel.

. . . That when and if a school system decides to utilize auxiliary personnel, the program be incorporated as an integral part of the school system, not treated as an extraneous and temporary adjunct to the system.

. . . That goals be thought through carefully, stated clearly, and implemented by means of definite procedures.

. . . That there be cooperative planning by the school systems, local institutions of higher learning, and the indigenous leadership of the community served by the schools, both before the program has been inaugurated and after it has been institutionalized.

. . . That each step on the career ladder be specified in terms of job descriptions, salaries, increments, and fringe benefits, moving from routine functions at the entry level to functions which are more responsible and more directly related to the learning-teaching process with appropriate training available at each stage of development on a work-study basis.

. . . That local institutions of higher learning be involved in the inservice training, wherever possible and appropriate.

. . . That professional standards be preserved and that all tasks performed by nonprofessionals be supervised by a professional.

. . . That professionals be asked to volunteer when they are ready to use nonprofessionals, rather than having auxiliary personnel assigned to them without any option on their part.

. . . That encouragement of those who desire to train and qualify for advancement be expressed in such a way that others who prefer to remain at the entry level feel no lack of job satisfaction, status, and recognition of the worth of their services—in other words, that there should be *opportunity* but not *compulsion* for upward mobility.

. . . That time be scheduled during the school day or after school hours with extra compensation[1] for teachers and auxiliaries and other professional-nonprofessional teams to review their team experiences and plan together for the coming day.

---

1. This arrangement would vary according to the pattern established in each school system.

. . . That the purpose and process of staff developments be re-examined in the light of the needs of this program.

. . . That the personal needs and concerns of both professionals and auxiliaries be dealt with in counseling sessions as they adjust to a new and sometimes threatening situation.

. . . That parents be involved in the program both as auxiliaries and as recipients of the services of family workers.

. . . That professional groups and associations be involved in the original conceptualization as well as in the continuing program development.

. . . That a continuing program of interpretation among educators and to the broader community be developed, with emphasis upon feedback as well as imparting information.

. . . That certification be explored fully and that action be deferred pending the results of such exploration.

. . . That an advisory committee of school administrators, supervisors, teachers, auxiliaries, parents, community leaders, and university consultants be established to evaluate and improve the utilization of auxiliaries in each school where such a program is undertaken.

PART II

What Curriculum for the Disadvantaged? Patterns and Issues

Between 1956 and 1967, thousands of special programs for underprivileged children were instituted in the United States as educators and citizens began to recognize the magnitude, the threat, and the inequities of poverty, and to turn, as Americans have traditionally turned, to education as a social equalizer. After the unparalleled federal legislation of the Eighty-eighth and Eighty-ninth Congresses, there were few communities of any size with a substantial group of economically deprived children that did not introduce some school provisions intended to improve the education of these children if they had not already done so. We might expect, because of their number, and because these programs were established during a period of considerable activity in the development of new curricula, in mathematics and in the physical and biological sciences particularly, that many curricular innovations would have appeared in programs for the disadvantaged. In fact, most special programs for the disadvantaged are "special" because of their organizational and administrative features rather than because they offer alienated and underachieving children of the poor a fresh curriculum.

Often additional funds appropriated by state or federal legislation are used to bring slum schools nearer to the standards of class size, full rather than half-day programs, and adequate instructional supplies customary in middle-class schools. More exposure to schooling through after-school tutorial programs, ungraded classes, and an earlier start in school through Head Start, and more exposure to the special services of guidance, social work, and remedial personnel are the most common features of programs for underprivileged children and youth.

It is, of course, possible to view all of these modifications in timing, services, grouping, and class size as a part of the child's curriculum, broadly conceived. If curriculum is defined as "the total effort of the school to bring about desired outcomes in school and out-of-school situations,"[1] then clearly anything the school does in an effort to deal with the needs, problems, and difficulties of underprivileged children and their teachers might properly be discussed here. Indeed, as the final section of this book suggests, the most significant "curriculum" for the socially disadvantaged may be the composition and climate of the total community in which they reside and the student population and climate of the school they attend. But for the purposes of our discussion at this point, curriculum will be somewhat more narrowly conceived as the content of what is intentionally taught by the school, most readily though by no means conclusively revealed in stated objectives, course outlines, and textbooks. "A curriculum consists of the lessons and tasks to be learned and performed by the students."[2] Particular designs

1. J. G. Saylor and W. M. Alexander, *Curriculum Planning for Better Teaching and Learning* (New York: Holt, Rinehart & Winston, 1954), p. 3.
2. J. I. Goodlad, *School Curriculum Reform in the United States*, The Fund for the Advancement of Education, March, 1964, p. 53.

for organizing content, e.g., chronologically or by problems, and specific methods for teaching it, e.g., by teacher exposition or student "discovery" are included in this discussion of curriculum only as they are held by their advocates to be critical in learning a specified content. When the "content" proposed is a way of thinking rather than a body of knowledge, the organization of learning experiences must be viewed as an essential element in the curriculum.

The curriculum modification in many special programs for the disadvantaged is a simplification or slowing down of the traditional curriculum to what educators sometimes call "minimum essentials"; a third-grade reader used in sixth-grade classes, instruction in two of the five or six topics usually taught in social studies or mathematics in a given grade, literary classics "covered" in adaptations or read aloud by the teacher.

Separate courses in reading are probably the one most common curriculum feature in educational programs for underprivileged and underachieving children and youth. Since reading retardation is the most widely recognized characteristic of underachievement, and since this retardation is cumulative as students are moved through the grades, it is understandable that curriculum plans for these students include intensive reading courses, sometimes using programmed reading texts, not only in intermediate school but also in junior and senior high-school programs. In these courses the actual subject matter that traditionally constitutes the reading content of courses in English, social studies, or other subjects, is replaced by content based on exercises intended to develop reading skills that the school failed to teach in the primary grades. Junior and senior high-school students in special programs for the disadvantaged are increasingly scheduled for separate courses in English and in Reading, or in a Reading course only. Reading teachers, as distinct from English teachers, have joined the ranks of professional personnel in most schools in depressed areas, supplementing the Reading Specialists who work with those individual students in slum and suburban schools who do not make expected progress in learning to read.

But the Reading Course as it is found in most programs is

rather an administrative device to schedule time for teaching skill content that is customarily taught within the regular curriculum than it is a new subject or even a new method. The reasons for the paucity of curriculum innovation in these programs, despite the pump-priming of large federal funding, can only be speculated upon. Perhaps the presumption, encountered among educators and laymen, that departures from a common curriculum for special groups of children is somehow undemocratic may be in part responsible for the few efforts to attempt a radically different curriculum for children who have not succeeded with the standard one. Probably an equally important deterrent is the still widespread tendency even among educators to attribute underachievement among the children of the poor to deficits in the child's background and in his and his parents' attitudes that keep him from profiting from a curriculum that is considered essentially sound. From this point of view, of course, it is the child—and his parents, if possible— who should change, and not the curriculum. Finally, our still limited knowledge of whether, and if so, how, the learning processes of economically and socially deprived children differ from those of their more advantaged age mates undoubtedly plays some part in delaying curriculum change.

In this chapter, and in the readings that follow it, therefore, we will be looking for the most part at minor modifications in curriculum, often at curriculum approaches of long standing which are receiving new emphasis in programs for the disadvantaged rather than at striking innovations. Three emphases in curriculum in programs for the disadvantaged are discussed and illustrated: the attempt to vocationalize and to make more "practical" the courses of study offered the underprivileged student; the introduction of content reflecting the ethnic experiences of the minority-group children who constitute so large a proportion of the educationally disadvantaged; and the more radical effort to base a curriculum for these students on a new methodology.

Vocationally oriented curricula, a historic effort to make special curricular provisions for the children of the poor, are still widely advocated and frequently included in programs for the disadvantaged. Dr. James Conant's argument[3] that vocational education would provide safeguards against the "social dynamite" of great and rapidly increasing numbers of rejected and alienated youth, out-of-school and out-of-work, was influential in the drafting of federal legislation supporting education for work as a major weapon in the war against poverty. Unfortunately, the majority of youth most seriously disadvantaged do not reach vocational high schools. The cumulative effects of environmental deprivation, poor teaching, and inappropriate curricula are such that many underprivileged students drop out or are pushed out of school by the end of junior high school because of their own and their teachers' frustrations and discouragement, or because their level of achievement in basic skills is judged too low to warrant admission to vocational high schools.

In recent years recognition of the fact that the vocational high school did not adequately meet the needs of these young people has resulted in modifications in patterns of vocational education which, though not entirely new, are newly endorsed for disadvantaged youth. The most common of these curriculum modifications are the expansion of vocational education to encompass courses incorporating vocational counseling and orientation to working as a desirable goal, and increased use of work experience or even actual employment as a part of the student's school program. Courses in which the content includes topics like these: "Why do we work?" "What kinds of jobs are there in our community?" "Good manners on the job," "Dressing the part," are found in programs for the disadvantaged in junior high-school grades, and again in programs for school dropouts. This curriculum emphasis on attitudes and good job behavior is based on educators' belief that hopelessness and consequent low aspirations common among very poor and minority-group youth must be dealt with before any program of vocational skill training can be expected to "take." The rationale advanced for incorporating work experiences and actual paid employment as a part of vocational education

3. J. B. Conant, *Slums and Suburbs* (New York: McGraw-Hill, 1961).

for teenagers also derives from a realization that such real experiences are needed to persuade the hopeless that hope of regular employment is really for them. In addition to direct work experience and courses in which the content is vocational guidance, vocationally oriented programs for underprivileged youth tend to modify academic subjects so that illustrations and applications are focused on work situations. A recent bulletin of the Board of Education of the City of New York[4] is designed to aid teachers of English, mathematics, social studies, and science in relating their subjects to job and daily life. Such modifications are common to vocational programs generally; in programs for educationally disadvantaged youth they may almost completely supplant traditional academic content. The belief that poor and underachieving children and youth will respond only to subjects that are shown to have immediate practical applicability is widely accepted among curriculum makers. Pronouncements by writers like Sexton and Riessman on the anti-intellectualism and practicalism of the poor are frequently quoted in defense of vocational and practical curriculum emphases: "The most fundamental approach with the deprived person is to show him that ideas and theories have practical merit."[5] Riessman's insistence that this anti-intellectualism should be "combated vigorously" and his recommendation that practical beginnings be developed toward "higher levels of intellectual appreciation,"[6] are less frequently cited.

There are, however, those who take issue with the idea that job training, vocational guidance, and a practical-problems curriculum are the most effective education for the disadvantaged. There are some who believe that the ills of the disadvantaged, the poor concept of self, the sense of alienation in an overpowering, complex, and indifferent world can best be ministered to in a humanistic curriculum. Through literature and

4. Curriculum Resource Materials of Meeting School Retention and Pre-Employment Needs, Board of Education of the City of New York, 1961.

5. F. Reissman, *The Culturally Deprived Child* (New York: Harper & Row, 1962), p. 33.

6. *Ibid.*

the arts, it is argued, poor and disregarded children and youth can learn to understand themselves and to recognize their powers; through the social sciences, anthropology and political science as well as history, they can come to understand the human condition and perceive their capacities to shape their situation. The giant step from powerlessness to power is not, the humanists argue, achieved by the acquisition of a job but by the growth of understanding. Among the special programs funded by recent federal legislation in the war on poverty, the Job Corps and Upward Bound exemplify these two positions on curriculum for the disadvantaged. In the Job Corps the curriculum, whose basic design is mandated in the legislation, is composed of job training and basic subjects in which the content is related to work and to daily life problems. Upward Bound programs, on the other hand, present youth who meet the same federal standards of low income and who are only slightly less retarded in educational achievement with a curriculum that has an essentially humanistic orientation. Fundamentally, the curriculum issue of a practical-vocational versus a humanities emphasis in the education of the disadvantaged parallels the analysis of the nature of their disadvantage. Curriculum priority is given one or the other of these broad alternatives relative to the priority given to lack of skill or to alienation from the dominant culture as the more critical deficit.

The first selections in the readings in this section present arguments for each of these curriculum positions and examples of curriculum modifications of a vocational and practical nature.

The second curriculum modification widely discussed as essential to an improved education for underprivileged students is the inclusion in courses of study and in textbooks of content that is directly related to the cultural backgrounds of those minorities which constitute a disproportionate number of the educationally disadvantaged. American Indians, Negro Americans, Mexican Americans, Americans of Puerto Rican origin, and Americans in the poverty pockets of rural Appalachia are as disregarded in our textbooks as they have been in our economy and in the power and prestige systems of American life. Historically, the Protestant and Anglo-Saxon coloration of the curriculum and texts of United States schools is simply explained. The models for our first schools and textbooks were brought here from England by colonists predominantly Protestant and Anglo-Saxon, and these models were carried across the continent as pioneers from the Eastern Seaboard carried their wares and their institutions westward. Having gained control of earlier Amerindian and Spanish peoples in the Southwest by conquest and economic enterprise, the Anglos instituted schools to teach their language and their ways. In these situations and in response to the subsequent immigration of large numbers of middle Europeans to the United States our unicultural schools were formally rationalized as essential to the Americanization of our pluralistic society. Despite occasional criticism by liberal educators and some religious and ethnic organizations as early as the nineteen-thirties, courses of study and textbooks in the critical fields of literature, language, and the social studies have continued to ignore or stereotype ethnic minorities in our population.

As evidence of the failure of our schools to meet the needs of economically deprived children accumulated in the nineteen-fifties and sixties, the proportion of the very poor who were also members of low-status ethnic minorities received renewed attention. The declaration of the 1954 Supreme Court Decision that segregated education was psychologically damaging to children was soon extended to the proposition that textbooks and courses of study in which Negro children never found themselves portrayed or the contributions of their American or African forebears presented were equally damaging. Since textbooks, together with mass media, provide the chief vicarious models for children, how can the Negro, or Puerto Rican, or American Indian child avoid coming to think himself of little worth when these media show him either no image or denigrating images of himself? Are not these children doomed to low achievement in verbal skills when their own language is so often rejected by teachers who view lower-class dialects and foreignisms as "bad," and who consider it their duty to eradicate "bad English"?

New federal funds supporting special institutes for teachers of disadvantaged children have given these teachers time and the guidance of specialists in cultural anthropology, Negro history, dialectology, and related fields to assist them to make curriculum modifications that will more adequately meet the special needs of their students. An increasing number of communities now offer special courses for newcomers—Southern mountain whites in Chicago, Cubans in Florida, Puerto Ricans in New York—which make a point of recognizing their native culture and speech while assisting them in intepreting their new surroundings. A Merced, California program to teach correct Spanish to Mexican American children also reinforces their pride by study of Hispanic culture. Washington, D.C., Chicago, Detroit, and New York City are among the school systems that have issued special bulletins and offered special courses on Negro History or on Puerto Rican culture with more or less explicit expectations that teachers will include facts, topics, and literature from these cultures in their courses for children. A high school in Fresno, California, recently introduced on the initiative of a single teacher an elective course in American Negro Literature, which has proved extremely popular.

Perhaps the most visible evidence of a trend toward the inclusion of culturally different materials in curricula for the disadvantaged is the marked increase in text and trade books for children that deal with minority-group characters, experiences, and history. Even though a 1966 survey of the treatment of the Negro in history texts shows that only rarely has any text begun to present adequately the extent and character of Negro participation in American life, or to face honestly the inequities forced upon him by the dominant white society, some corrections of fact and attitude do appear in some new texts. Similar observations with respect to Negroes and other cultural minorities in readers and English texts have appeared with increasing frequency in educational literature and the popular press. At the same time, a few new text series have been published that make a conscious effort to include realistic and positive images through literature and through illustrations that reflect our multicultural society. Among the readings that follow this introduction are articles surveying the historical accuracy and ethnic representativeness of history and English textbooks.

As might be expected, these new texts have met with criticism: first, on the part of segregationists and those in positions of power who view criticisms of American institutions as subversive and potentially inflammatory; second, on the part of some who are in sympathy with the aim of correcting the misconceptions of slavery, of Negroes' parts in the abolition movement and the Civil Rigths struggle, and of their and other minorities' contributions to the growth and defense of the United States and who are convinced of the importance of providing minority-group children with positive images of their own cultural group, but who nevertheless view some of these new texts as divisive. Nothing is to be gained, they say, by providing different cultural groups with separate texts that divide them from the mainstream of the culture, even though they may be supportive of the minority's wish to be recognized and valued. These objections, of course, are made by those who object only to the fact that some texts have been designed—as was the case of the Detroit primers—only for Negro children; they tend to endorse texts that incorporate the features of our multicultural world and that are intended for, and supplied to, all children. So with courses, they urge not the separate course or unit in Negro History for Negro students, but the integration of this content into all courses. This position is consonant with that expressed by James Baldwin, who observed that if "one managed to change the curriculum in all the schools so that Negroes learned more about themselves and their real contributions to this culture, you would be liberating not only Negroes, you'd be liberating white people who know nothing about their history."[7] Among the texts sampled in this section

7. James Baldwin, "A Talk to Teachers," *Saturday Review*, December 21, 1963, p. 89.

are some from books dealing entirely with a particular minority and others from books that are integrated and multiethnic.

In some ways the most fundamental curriculum debate on optimum education for the disadvantaged is at the same time the least well known. It centers on the complex question of teaching and learning processes, and implies that the most critical questions of curriculum content are basically questions of method. For purposes of simplification and discussion here, two contending views can be identified. One of these views holds that the core of the curriculum should be a series of highly diversified, emotionally and intellectually stimulating experiences, in which sequence emerges from the interaction of teacher and student engaged in a common quest, and in which the desired outcome is a multiplicity of creative responses on the part of the learners. The other maintains that the curriculum should center on highly restricted, rigidly controlled training exercises in which the function of the teacher is to monitor children's practice, often with programmed materials, and in which the hoped-for outcome is children's acquisition of specific skills, especially in language and quantitative relationships. These two positions, which are here stated in more exaggerated formulations than individual advocates would use, both derive from similar analyses of the source of the underachievement of underprivileged children: that severe early environmental deprivation so retards the deprived child that traditional content and especially traditional methods cannot compensate for his learning handicaps.

Although there are no school programs that fully exemplify the extreme opposing views regarding the most effective cognitive processes curriculum for the disadvantaged, there are evidences of these divergent positions in experimental centers, Head Start programs, and Upward Bound programs. Most descriptions of Head Start programs suggest that the curriculum is planned to include as extensive a series of experiences as possible and to stimulate as much verbal response to these experiences as possible. Teachers endeavor to have these preschool children notice and name everything about them, the toys they play with, the food they eat, their own clothes and appearance, and whatever they see on the trips on which they are taken. Surrounded and stimulated by new objects, and old ones often named for the first time, sung to, read to, exposed to intensive doses of "tender loving care," underprivileged children are expected to blossom into learning readiness. The curriculum in such Head Start Centers, however, is essentially like that of nursery schools and kindergartens previously attended almost exclusively by the children of affluent parents. The assumptions about learning are the same: given enough stimulation and loving rewards, all children will develop their native capacities.

Other Head Start programs endeavor to provide a more structured curriculum: experiences are somewhat more restricted, whereas practice activities are more intensive. Ausubel, whose views on the teaching strategies effective with disadvantaged children concluded the first volume of these readings, urges that each learning task in a given sequence be mastered—overlearned, in fact—before the child is introduced to new ones; he recommends the use of programmed instruction as "particularly well suited to the needs of the culturally deprived child."[8] The curriculum for disadvantaged children in the experimental classes of the Institute for Developmental Studies, directed by Martin Deutsch, is consonant with this view. Children in these classes are introduced to new and varied experiences, but there is a much more systematic emphasis on training in visual, auditory, and oral skills than is generally found in the Head Start programs, which took their inspiration, but not the same rigorous curriculum and method, from Deutsch's experimental classes. It is historically interesting that one of the earliest special programs for children of the poor, instituted in Italy by Maria Montessori at the beginning of this century, specified a curriculum that combined creative activities with intensive training in perception and in quantitative and manual skills. Adaptations of the Montessori curriculum have in

---

8. D. P. Ausubel, "A Teaching Strategy for Culturally Deprived Pupils: Cognitive and Motivational Considerations," quoted in Miller and Smiley, *Education in the Metropolis* (New York: The Free Press, 1967), p. 289.

fact been employed in some preschool programs for the disadvantaged.

Perhaps the most thoroughgoing exponent of training rather than experiential exposure as a curriculum strategy for deprived preschoolers is Carl Bereiter. Dr. Bereiter, who has been conducting an experiment in language training with four-year-old Negro children from the most deprived urban environments in Illinois, believes that programs which feature varied experiences and tender loving care as their major components fail to recognize the severity and urgency of the deficits which these children accumulate in their first few years of life. The enriched curriculum which admirably serves middle-class kindergartners is not sufficient to meet the needs of the seriously disadvantaged child; nor will the aim of stimulating them to achieve average rates of progress in learning suffice. If they are to catch up, Bereiter argues, they must progress at better than average rates. To achieve this acceleration, Bereiter has designed a highly selective curriculum described in the readings that follow, in which "A great many of what we would acknowledge to be desirable preschool experiences have been minimized or left out altogether—such things as arts and crafts, group play, dramatic play, block play, and so on."[9] The curriculum in Bereiter's experimental classes at the University of Illinois provides intensive training in the use of verbal formulations of logical concepts: "this is a book," "this is not a pencil"; "if it isn't long, it must be short," and the like.

Comparable curriculum alternatives may be noted in higher grades, though perhaps in less sharply defined form. Federally supported Upward Bound Programs, whose purpose is to salvage promising but underachieving secondary-school students so that they may earn admission to college, lean toward one or the other of these strategies. In some, the curriculum abstracts chiefly the skills content of traditional English and mathematics courses in order to provide intensive drill in grammar, usage, and mathematical operations. In others the curriculum plunges

9. C. Bereiter, "Academic Instruction and Preschool Children," in *Language Programs for the Disadvantaged: The Report of the NCTE Task Force on Teaching English to the Disadvantaged,* N.C.T.E., 1965, p. 201.

these students into wide exposure to literature, art, and current political issues selected to introduce them to concepts of creativity, reality and illusion, the nature of proof, and the like. The most radical proposal for developing a special curriculum for the disadvantaged follows closely along these lines. The National NDEA Institute for Advanced Study in Teaching Disadvantaged Youth, initiated in 1966 by Ball State University, supported by U.S. Office of Education funds, and managed by the American Association of Colleges for Teacher Education, proposed a series of institutes bringing together curriculum specialists, public-school personnel, and subject specialists to review current curriculum designs for the disadvantaged. It is hoped that out of a series of such institutes, national guidelines can be developed to aid those engaged in planning special programs for educationally disadvantaged children and youth. The statement of purpose for the first of these national institutes calls attention to the fact that schools now organize curricula around basic skills at the elementary level and subsequently around academic disciplines; declaring that curricula so designed have not been effective with disadvantaged children, the proposal suggests as an alternative organizing the curriculum for these students—and possibly for all students—around intellectual concepts which cut across subject lines: e.g., around such germinal ideas as causation, relativism, reality.

As you read the arguments on these three major issues in the debate on what curriculum for the disadvantaged which have been foreshadowed here, and as you examine the textbook samples illustrating some of these approaches you should be considering some even broader questions relating to curriculum. If we accept the general proposition that the purpose of education is to prepare each new generation to function successfully in the culture, we commit ourselves to devising a curriculum that will teach the values and the technological skills which characterize our culture. Anthropologists like Margaret Mead have declared that it is easier to introduce, or teach, new technologies to culturally different groups than to attempt to teach new values. But if, as psychologists and sociologists like Oscar Lewis, Riessman, and Gans declare, the cultural values and realistic expectations of some ethnic or lower-class groups do not provide them with the motivation to learn the tasks set by the schools, is it educationally sound to construct curricula for the disadvantaged that focus primarily on the development of technological skills? On the other hand, are we willing to commit ourselves, despite protestations on the importance in a democracy of maintaining pluralistic values in our pluralistic society, to devise a curriculum that will make a concentrated effort to substitute the values of the middle class for those of lower-class and ethnically different groups? And if we make this commitment, is it educationally realistic to believe that the school can teach disadvantaged children the values, attitudes, behaviors which are denied them in the larger society?

> How does a community decide which value patterns are to be taught in its schools and are to be used as a basis for curricular and instructional decisions? . . . One possible answer is that a pluralistic society wishes for an obvious and open decision never to occur. A struggle of this sort would be divisive, indicating quite clearly to a number of subgroups that their ideas were not being adopted by the society as a whole. Thus a pluralistic society may wish to ignore this question as long as possible in the hope that it will not become too troublesome. Some aspects of our present educational situation suggest that in part we have more or less consciously adopted this answer.[10]

Perhaps our long delayed decision will be precipitated by the urgency of the problem of educating the disadvantaged for a positive role in our world—and theirs.

10. H. B. Dunkel, "Value Decisions and the Public Schools," *School Review*, Summer 1962, Vol. 70, p. 165.

"The essential problem of the alienated group is that they have not found a satisfactory avenue or channel of growth toward adult competence."

NATIONAL POLICY
FOR ALIENATED YOUTH*

*Robert J. Havighurst
and Lindley J. Stiles*

In this early statement of the social problem posed by the increasing numbers of youth whom Conant was to characterize as "social dynamite," the authors' analysis focuses on the disruption of one of the traditional avenues through which young men especially could achieve adult status. As technological changes reduce the opportunities for those who find schooling uncongenial and frustrating to achieve adulthood and economic independence through unskilled and semiskilled work, more and more youth become alienated not only from school but from society.

Reviewing existing patterns of education for work, the authors note that these begin too late and

* Excerpted from Robert J. Havighurst and Lindley J. Stiles, "National Policy for Alienated Youth," *Phi Delta Kappan*, April 1961, Vol. XLII, No. 7, pp. 283–291. Reprinted by permission of the authors and *Phi Delta Kappan*.

have become too competitive to meet the needs of youth whose alienation and school failure have become established before they are old enough for vocational high schools. Provisions for constructing new channels into the adult world of work which would begin before high school and which would include efforts to build positive attitudes toward work are recommended.

How different is the kind of program Havighurst and Stiles envision from traditional programs of vocational education? Although they suggest that content, methods of instruction, and learning materials would need to be adapted for the corollary program they propose, no specific guides for such adaptations are offered. With a particular academic subject in mind, what kinds of adaptations can you suggest?

IF CITIZENS of all occupational, political, and religious affiliations were asked the question, "What should this country do for its young people?," the answer would be unanimous that the United States should give its boys and girls a good chance to grow into productive workers, successful parents, law-abiding citizens, and happy persons—in effect, help them become *competent adults.*

There would of course be some differences of opinion as to how society should provide opportunities suited to the accomplishment of this goal. In addition, disagreement might prevail as to which tasks are appropriate for the schools to do, which are best left to the family, and what contributions should be made by churches and other agencies. Further, there might be some differences of opinion as to the kinds of opportunities that are appropriate for girls as compared with boys, for Negroes in contrast to white youth, or for the mentally dull as compared with gifted children.

General agreement would probably prevail, however, that opportunity is relative. One boy's chance would be another's burden. The circumstances that spell opportunity to a boy or girl depend on the youth's abilities, on what he has been brought up to want from life, and on which openings or positions in the adult society are likely to be available to him.

Satisfactory growth depends upon appropriate opportunity, while appropriate opportunity depends upon the abilities and the personality of the individual.

Some 15 per cent of young people do not grow up in a satisfactory way. This group has been identified in several studies. It has been called by various names—the uneducables, the nonlearners, the hard-to-reach, the alienated. The "alienated" is an appropriate name for this group, because it expresses the fact that they are somehow alien to the larger society in which they live. Such youth have been unsuccessful in meeting the standards set by the society for them—standards of behavior, of learning in school, of performance on a job. By the time they reach adolescence these boys and girls are visible as the misfits in school. Either they are hostile and unruly, or passive and apathetic. They have quit learning and have dropped out of school psychologically two or three years before they can drop out physically.

Most alienated youth come from low income homes; most of them fall in the IQ range 75–90; almost all drop out of school at age 16 or before; they tend to come from broken homes, or homes which are inadequate emotionally and culturally. Yet this is not simply a group low in economic status and IQ; two-thirds of working-class children do satisfactory work in school, as do two-thirds of children with below average IQ's. This is a group whose start in life has been poor because of the disadvantages its members face. Their families have been inadequate. Often their physical health has been poor. Their intellectual skills are usually too marginal to compensate for other deficiencies.

It should be emphasized that alienated youth can be found in all IQ ranges and from middle and upper class homes, although the percentages are higher in the 75–90 IQ bracket and among groups which are culturally and economically disadvantaged. Any child who lacks recognition at home or in school, or who is emotionally insecure, can become alienated.

Within this alienated group are found the majority of juvenile delinquents. Among the girls of this group are found the majority of 16- and 17-year-old brides.

We call them "alienated" because they do not accept the ways of living and achieving that are standard in our society. As younger children they probably accepted the standard ideas of right and wrong, complied with school regulations and tried to succeed, but the combined and repeated frustrations of failure in school and mistreatment at home have turned them either into members of delinquent sub-groups or into defeated, apathetic individuals. The 15 per cent about whom we speak are found in a community which has a normal cross-section of American youth. But in the slum area of a big city the proportion may be doubled. As many as 30 or 40 per cent of the eighth and ninth graders in some of our city schools are alienated youth. On the other hand, this group comprises only a small percentage of youth in the upper middle class suburbs of a metropolitan area.

Members of underprivileged racial or immigrant minorities are likely to be found in the alienated group. Thus Negroes, Mexicans, and Puerto Ricans make up a large proportion of alienated youth in the industrial cities of today, whereas thirty or forty years ago this group would have been composed largely of children of European immigrants. On the other hand, many boys and girls from racial and immigrant minorities are growing up successfully, and these numbers are increasing.

The alienated group seems to be a product of society, its size the resultant of combinations of socio-economic factors, and its particular composition determined by the presence of one or another social group at the bottom of the social scale. Thus in a Midwestern city of 45,000 this group was found to be present to the extent of about 15 per cent; there were no Mexicans or Puerto Ricans in the community, and few Negroes. The boys and girls in the alienated group carried names that reflected English, Scotch, Irish, or German origin. Their families occupied low status in that particular community.

NEED FOR AN ALTERNATIVE PATHWAY TO ADULTHOOD

The essential problem of the alienated group is that they have not found a satisfactory avenue or channel of growth toward adult competence. Since they are failing in school, they cannot grow up by means of the school. They need an alternative pathway to that offered by the school as we now know it.

These boys want the same things in life that are achieved by boys who are growing up successfully. They would like to have money, a job, and as they grow older they want the use of an automobile. They want girl friends, and eventually desire to have a wife and children. Unlike the majority of boys, however, they do not have the combination of family assistance, the intelligence, the social skills, and the good study and work habits necessary to achieve their goal legitimately. Nevertheless, they want to grow up and to have the symbols of manhood, and they become discontented when they do not succeed.

Alienated boys, thwarted in the normal channels, seek illegitimate means to achieve the symbols of manhood. They may turn to the delinquent gang for "moral support" and for instruction in ways to get money, excitement, power, and the feeling of masculinity. These boys, frustrated by the adult society around them, may become hostile and aggressive toward that society. Often they may vent their hostility through such activities as destroying property, burning school buildings, and attacking law-abiding people.

Forty years ago there were many boys who could not grow up through the school system. But at that time there was a clear alternative road to adulthood—the road of work. A boy could quit school at age 14, 15, or 16 and get work on a farm or in a business. In fact, more than half of all boys in 1920 did drop out before graduating from high school; nevertheless, they found work and grew up along the pathway provided by a series of jobs with increasing pay and increasing responsibility. Census records show that in 1920 somewhat more than 50 per cent of boys aged 14 through 17 were employed full-time or part-time. The proportion of 14-year-olds who were out of school and employed full-time was low, but more than half of all boys were out of school by age seventeen and at work. At that time a boy could easily follow a well-traveled highway of work from early adolescence to adulthood.

During the past forty years the number of jobs open to juveniles has been decreasing. Jobs as telegraph messengers, delivery boys, office boys, elevator boys, etc., have grown scarce. The farm population has been reduced greatly and with it the farm as a place where a nonacademic boy could be doing a man's work by the age of 16. The proportion of unskilled and semiskilled jobs in the labor force has also decreased. Employers, faced with an oversupply of adult labor during much of this period, have adopted as a standard for employment the minimum age of 18, or high-school graduation. The 1960 census will show that fewer than 35 per cent of boys aged 14 through 17 were employed at that time, and a large proportion of them have only part-time jobs. The unemployment rate is at least twice as high among boys between 14 and 17 as it is among older boys who are in the labor market. During the latter part of the 1950's, while the overall rate of unemployment in the United States was about 5 per cent, the teen-agers' unemployment rate was 10 per cent, while 16- and 17-year-olds who had dropped out of school had an unemployment rate of 20 per cent.

The employment situation for teen-agers is not likely to improve during the 1960's, for the high birth rate of 1947 and later years will cause the numbers of 16- and 17-year-olds to increase by 1963 to a figure 40 per cent above the numbers in this age bracket in the 1950's.

Thus there is a strong prospect that the road to adulthood through juvenile work which has been narrowing since 1920 will become even more constricted during the coming decade. This road will remain in existence, however. It is being followed with fair success by about half of the 35 to 40 per cent of boys who now drop out of school before finishing a high-school course.

What our society must do is to widen this narrow road once more, through finding or creating more juvenile jobs. With work experience, there is a good chance of bringing many alienated boys back into the mainstream of American youth, where they can grow up with confidence in themselves and in the society.

Since jobs in the American economy, as we now define jobs, are not likely to increase in numbers for boys, it becomes necessary to find ways to provide boys with the *moral equivalent of work,* a kind of work experience that has the growth value of a job, though it is not a job in the narrow sense of the word.

CURRENT PROGRAMS AND PROPOSALS

The fact that work experience is important in the process of growing up has not escaped the attention of educators. For a long time, vocational education has contained work experience as an integral part in many courses. What has been called "cooperative education," which combines a job with study, has been practiced in some engineering schools and technical institutes, as well as in some high schools, for more than thirty years. In 1928 there were seventy-eight cities with 5,682 pupils enrolled in cooperative courses under the Smith-Hughes Act. The government-aided diversified occupations work-study program was started in 1933. Since World War II there has been a substantial growth of work experience programs in schools. In a survey of work experience education programs published by the U.S. Office of Education in 1957, 145 items in the working bibliography of 276 items were produced after 1950. More than 200 articles, books, and research reports on work experience education have been published since 1941.

The following types of work experience are now found in secondary schools:[1]

1. IN-SCHOOL, NONREMUNERATIVE GENERAL EDUCATION WORK EXPERIENCE PROGRAMS.

Experience is provided in the school for students as typists, clerks, parking lot attendants, messengers, multigraph operators, library assistants, motion picture machine operators, locker maintenance workers. Students are not paid except for after-school work. In some cases, credit is given toward graduation.

2. OUT-OF-SCHOOL, NONREMUNERATIVE GENERAL EDUCATION WORK EXPERIENCE PROGRAMS.

a. Community service work in noncommercial organizations: libraries, parks, social agencies, elementary schools.

b. Student-learner assignments in physicians' or dentists' offices, architects' studios, hospitals, city or county offices.

3. REMUNERATIVE GENERAL EDUCATION WORK EXPERIENCE PROGRAMS AT THE JUNIOR HIGH-SCHOOL LEVEL.

This is for youth who are likely to drop out of school at age 16. It is usually provided for 15-year-olds. School credit and

1. DeWitt Hunt, *Work Experience Education Programs in American Secondary Schools*. Washington, D.C.: Department of Health, Education, and Welfare, U.S. Office of Education, Bulletin No. 5, 1957, p. 13.

"going wages" are given. Typical jobs are as bus boys, messengers, waitresses, car washers, printers' helpers, sales clerks.

4. REMUNERATIVE GENERAL EDUCATION WORK EXPERIENCE FOR PUPILS IN SENIOR HIGH SCHOOL.

This type of program is for youth in senior high school who will profit personally and economically from work experience in such a way as to make their schooling more attractive and more successful. Scholastic credit is generally given for work which is coordinated with school studies.

5. REMUNERATIVE VOCATIONAL WORK EXPERIENCE IN SENIOR HIGH SCHOOLS NOT SUBSIDIZED BY FEDERAL VOCATIONAL EDUCATION FUNDS.

A "diversified occupations" type of course is offered, mainly to high-school juniors and seniors over 16 years of age who have good records. Often the course is set up in schools or communities too small to qualify for the federal subsidy. Some of these students will get work experience in selling jobs, some in office assignments, and some in factories. An effort is made to place the student in the field where he is likely to work as an adult.

6. REMUNERATIVE VOCATIONAL WORK EXPERIENCE PROGRAMS IN HIGH SCHOOLS SUBSIDIZED FROM FEDERAL VOCATIONAL EDUCATIONAL FUNDS.

Commencing in 1917 with the Smith-Hughes Act (which was amplified in 1946 by the George-Barden Act), a cooperative part-time education and employment program is available to high-school juniors and seniors. Jobs are in the trades, industrial occupations, and distributive occupations. This is the most highly selective program; it is seldom available to a student who has done poor work in school.

NEEDED: PROGRAMS FOR ALIENATED YOUTH

The most widespread programs are for senior high-school pupils, age 16 or over, who have a good school record. Thus they are not open to alienated youth. They are useful programs; but something more is needed.

The kind of work experience program that will be most useful to alienated youth will have the following characteristics:

1. It will commence at age 13 or 14, and continue to age 18, though many boys will graduate from it a year or two before age 18.

2. It will attempt to teach boys elementary work disciplines: punctuality, ability to take orders from a boss, ability to work cooperatively with others in a team, responsibility on the job.

3. It will lead directly into stable adult jobs.

4. It will be a part of the public school program, with the curriculum adapted to the intellectual level, the interest in practical endeavors, and the work-experience program of alienated youth.

A preventive program of this type must of course rest upon a procedure for identifying the future alienated youth at least by the age of 13 or 14. This can be done and has been done in several researches. The identification process consists of finding those boys who show a combination of aggressive maladjustment with failure in school, plus checking in marginal cases by visiting the home and evaluating the nature of family discipline and help given to the boy.

A work experience program will need to be organized in stages which reflect the boys' level of maturity and responsibility, and which at the same time are geared to prevailing child labor legislation. Probably three stages are indicated.

A. The first stage should be work in groups, under school supervision, completely or partially outside of the labor market. For example, boys might work in groups on parks, school grounds, alleys, beaches, thus contributing to community housekeeping. Alternatively, boys might work in a "sheltered workshop" in the school which would contract for jobs with local business and industry. The workshop might take contracts for stuffing envelopes with advertising matter; simple assembly jobs, such as collecting nuts and bolts into packages for sale; processing material with a simple machine. The difficulty with the sheltered workshop idea for boys is that similar facilities are badly needed for handicapped adults and for old people who need employment.

B. A second stage should be part-time work on an individual basis with employers in private or public business or industry. Here the boy would be more nearly "on his own" in the labor market, but he would still work under close supervision by the school.

C. The final stage would be full-time employment in a stable job, aided by some guidance and supervision on the part of school or employment service personnel.

RESPONSIBILITY OF SOCIETY AS A WHOLE

The corollary school program provided for alienated youth would need to be adapted in content, methods of instruction, and learning materials to the ability and orientation of youth involved. The content would need to be appropriate to the goals of instruction and to the age level of the pupils. At the same time, it would, in most cases, need to be presented in textbook and other learning materials at a lower reading level, and with less abstractness, than is common for high-school courses. Instruction would need to be characterized by practical approaches to problems, shop or laboratory experiences, and an extensive use of audio-visual aids. A close relationship between the program of the school and work experiences would be desirable.

A program of the type just outlined cannot be lodged in the labor force as it is now constituted. There are not nearly enough juvenile jobs, and the trend is toward reduction of juvenile jobs and unskilled jobs. Private business is not in a position to provide all the jobs needed, nor is organized labor in a position to cooperate in a program that might reduce the number of adult jobs in the economy.

Nevertheless, there seems to be good reason for adopting a social policy which guarantees work experience as a part of education to every boy who needs it, just as instruction in mathematics or science or foreign language is guaranteed to youth who need that kind of education. And the society should bear the cost of one kind of education just as it bears the cost of the other kind.

If the provision of juvenile jobs becomes a part of social policy, there are two presently expanding areas of the economy in which jobs for boys may be created fairly easily. One of these areas is that of conservation of natural resources, and the other is that of public service. Assuming that federal, state, and local government funds will be used increasingly on projects for soil and water conservation, and on the maintenance of parks, parkways, beaches, and forest preserves, the respective government agencies might deliberately design work projects in such a way that substantial numbers of boys could be employed on work crews.

A PROGRAM SUPPORTED BY FEDERAL GOVERNMENT

Recently Senator Hubert Humphrey introduced a bill in Congress to set up a Youth Conservation Corps. His proposal was incorporated into the platform of the Democratic Party in 1960. This idea has much in its favor. It might well be developed for boys 16 and over, but if it were limited to work camps, it would not be applicable to boys under 16, where the need is especially great.

Possibly the plan might be developed into a more general Youth Development Program, for boys aged 13 to 20. The program might provide for locally-based work projects in the earlier stages, so that the boys could live at home and go to their regular schools while taking part in a work-study project.

Federal grants might be made to the states for the support of work experience programs meeting certain criteria. The state which received the grant might develop a program with three elements:

1. A program for the big cities, based on elementary or junior high-school units, with a job-creating and job-finding program supported by city-wide civic, business, and labor organizations.

2. A program for the community of 20,000 to 100,000 people, based on a particular junior high school or several elementary schools, and backed by a community commission of business and labor leaders.

3. A program for rural counties and rural sections of urban counties, based on elementary schools or consolidated schools, and developed in collaboration with the county agricultural agent and local community business leaders.

WHAT A WORK-EXPERIENCE PROGRAM WOULD NOT DO

The work experience program suggested in these pages is not a panacea for all youth problems. It is merely one element (but a highly important one) in a complex of arrangements which our society should make in order to reduce the number of alienated youth.

Such a program might be expected to cut down juvenile delinquency by as much as 5 per cent. It could not reduce juvenile delinquency more than this, because a substantial proportion of juvenile delinquency is committed by boys who are not aggressive or are not failing in school, and such boys would not be in the program.

A work-study program needs to be supplemented by community agencies, such as Boys Clubs, Settlement Houses, YMCA, CYO, and other organizations that give boys a chance for wholesome recreation and social life.

Furthermore, a work-study program for adolescent boys may not be needed as much in the future as it is right now. It is likely that the number of boys who fail in school and who become socially maladjusted can be reduced materially by preventive measures taken earlier, when the boys are in kindergarten and first grade.

More work and more effective work needs to be done with these boys and their families when they are five or six years old. A more successful program at this age might cut the numbers of teen-age alienated youth in half, and thus reduce the size of a work-study program.

SUGGESTED STRATEGY
FOR COMMUNITIES

Thus the strategy of attack on the problem of alienated youth appears to have the following phases:

1. Development of a work-study program for alienated 13- and 14-year-old boys.

2. Supplementation of the work-study program by social agencies and community organizations which create and maintain a wholesome social situation for alienated youth.

3. Preventive programs for work with young children in the primary grades and their families to help them make more satisfactory progress in school and thus to reduce the future numbers of alienated youth for whom a work-study program is needed.

This country should be doing all three of these things. If we do, we can look ahead with some confidence to a time, ten or twenty years from now, when the unhappiness and frustration of young people and the danger to society of having a large group of alienated youth will be reduced to less than half their present proportions.

". . . 'disadvantage' has been viewed too narrowly as a deficiency of the child, and education not enough as the enlargement of freedom."

TEACH THEM
THE ARTS OF FREEDOM*
Lawrence C. Howard

The learner's "disadvantaged" status may be a consequence of learning disabilities that stem from the physical and emotional hardships common to families trapped in poverty, as many psychologists declare; or as sociologists aver, it may be a result of a sense of worthlessness and powerlessness that stems from the social discrimination and prejudice to which he is subjected. In either case, Howard argues, the central task of education is to help the disadvantaged to understand themselves and their plight and to see to it that the affluent and powerful re-examine their consciences and their commitment to a democratic way of life. Compensatory programs that focus only on surface deficits in skills and emphasize vocational training and routine methods of drill do not, he

* Excerpted from Lawrence C. Howard, "Teach them the Arts of Freedom," *Saturday Review,* June 18, 1966, pp. 66–67 and 79–80. Reprinted by permission of the author and *Saturday Review.*

declares, meet the basic needs of the poor. A curriculum in which the humanities play a major part and in which methods of inquiry are taught is essential to the liberation of the disadvantaged.

The articles by Havighurst and Stiles and by Howard present widely divergent views on the sources and educational remedies for disadvantage. Which of these two presentations seems to you most convincing? Why? Although the major subject of this article by Howard is the education of the disadvantaged, much of what he has to say has relevance for the education of those who are not socially or economically disadvantaged. What changes would have to be made in education for all students in order to realize Howard's purposes?

TOO LITTLE of the education of the disadvantaged has either the content or the spirit of the humanities. Since the disadvantaged are those who are limited, and the humanities are concerned with liberating man—this void is hard to understand. Part of the problem may be that "disadvantage" has been viewed too narrowly as a deficiency of the child, and education not enough as the enlargement of freedom. This brief review of its nature, history, and current focus suggests the humanities should have a central role in the education of the disadvantaged. And since the humanities are the arts of freedom, such a shift may well permit the disadvantaged to help in the re-education of America.

The child is said to have a cumulative deficit that he must overcome: he's nonverbal, has a limited attention span, poor time perspective, limited response to all stimuli; he is the product of a broken home, reared under a matriarchy, is inadequately guided by adults; few things belong to him, he's under-motivated, and has a negative self-image. This is the conception of the disadvantaged child.

There is a divergent view. It states that disadvantage is a societal problem, a critical flaw in democratic America. The existence of poverty, rather than a problem of the poor, is seen as a weakness in our economic system—much the same as depressions used to be viewed. Persisting discrimination, especially against the Negro, reveals America's underdeveloped morality. Gunnar Myrdal has called this the American dilemma: mouthing words of high ideals and Christian precepts, but acting in relentless patterns of prejudice toward Negroes. "Disadvantage" then becomes the problem of the "advantaged." It reflects the middle-class preoccupation with the material, and insensitivity to the human, the strong taking advantage of the weak, the power structure corrupted by its own power. Archibald MacLeish, commenting about disadvantaged America more recently, said, "There is vulgarity everywhere. There are pockets of ignorance and hatred—not only in the Deep South. Our relations with each other lack richness and tenderness." The very existence of ostracized subcultures reinforces this view, points up our historic insensitivity to certain groups—not just the Negro and the poor—the Indian, Mexican, and Filipino as well.

Those who stress disadvantaged America reject the economic deprivation thesis. While they agree limited income is important, they tend to emphasize the powerlessness of the poor, how they are socially invisible in the eyes of those more affluent. Compared with himself, the Negro economically is better off today than he was ten years ago. Yet Thomas Pettigrew has shown that disadvantage has grown steadily more acute. Relative, not absolute, poverty and isolation are the rub. Similar in relative positions are the continuing conditions of the disadvantaged when compared to the ever-increasing promises of amelioration: antipoverty programs, civil rights reforms, urban renewal projects. Only by comparisons can one know his own inferior position.

To be disadvantaged, concludes this view, is to feel the pain of being labeled disadvantaged. It is defenselessness against compensatory programs hastily assembled by those whose true objective is to preserve white neighborhood schools. It is being ministered *at* by social workers who stigmatize "the clients" and, in fact, increase dependency. When ignoring the moral failures in our history, we demand that the disadvantaged overcome their background by rejecting home and family, the disadvantaged protest, "I cannot so easily put aside my identity."

Discrimination is common ground to both views of "disadvantage." Those who emphasize America's flaw point less to overt bars and more to subtle acts that come from "doing things as usual." The words "de facto segregation" have grown up to describe societal discrimination in housing, jobs, and schools. While not supported by laws, their effect is equally deadly. In this connection the compensatory approach in schools can provide no real solution. Schools remain white-controlled and segregation continues to expand. It thus comes as no surprise that civil rights demonstrations are active where compensatory programs are in greatest prominence. The drive for integration is not a drive to enter white schools, but one to broaden the cultural base of all schools for educational objectives. It is also to make them truly public. Quality education, if our goal is a free society, is not achievable for anyone—Negro or white—without the integration of our schools.

When some are barred and others intolerant, mankind as a whole is the loser. It is this understanding that should turn our attention to the humanities rather than to the more prevalent psychological emphasis which seeks to get the child "undeprived" before he gets any "learning." The humanities embrace all learning and skills which accelerate man in his becoming what he can be. It is because the humanities are fundamentally concerned with the human condition and its betterment that they have such high relevance both to a group stigmatized as "culturally deprived" and to a society with pervasive patterns of inhumane behavior.

The quest to free man, the historical concern of the humanities, is no less the focus today. The forms this takes, according to Richard P. McKeon, are those of increasing man's discovery power, refining his ability to use the past, and bringing men to act when knowledge and power are at hand. Thus, in a sense, the concern with the humanities today remains as with the Greeks: the proper human uses of relevant words and things.

Words grounded in experience illuminate values. And here, too, is relevance, for the disadvantaged are often told to change their values or else to go and get some. The humanities' approach would require that these demands, these moral judgments, rest in understanding. The first step is to weigh the various perspectives on reality including those of the poor and ostracized. No war on poverty, mindful of the humanities, would have delayed so long before including the poor. Judgments of others, in short, should follow, not precede, inquiry. The task of the humanities, and, one would think, of all good education, is to strive to understand what understanding is. Socrates, for one, believed that knowledge of the good would leave man pursuing nothing else.

Values formulated in words and expressed in action are not enough. There must be style, if one would remain true to the humanities. The esthetic dimension is communication so efficient and action so purposeful that elegance is radiated. The discordances have been removed. Is not the unlovely way the disadvantaged are seen much of the problem? To be known as disadvantaged blocks out much of anything else. The label "problem" increases social separation and may itself justify the mistreatment the disadvantaged receive.

Even for those still emphasizing the child's needs, there is a large place for the humanities in our schools. It is to literature that teachers should turn to overcome the poverty of experience. Are not Grimm, Carroll, Graham, Aesop the basic readers, and the lifeless *Dick and Jane* at best for suggested-reading lists? Would not the deportment task of teachers diminish if students had ample opportunities for acting out? Drama, a transliterated Greek word, means a thing done. To live up to this meaning is more than talking literary forms or discussing characters. The fine and performing arts are personalized expressions of conflicts, aspirations, and fears. The tense of drama is current—the present working itself towards destiny. *Hamlet* is a poet's construct; his reality is in the reader's mind. It is we who are Hamlet. "More than any other art," wrote Arthur Miller, "theater calls for relevance. The play must convince that this is the way it is now in human intercourse." Drama is a tool for understanding. It permits telling others who the actors are, as well as letting actors know a world beyond themselves. Much great drama, too, is familial. For those who see family relationships as crucial there is limitless material in *Antigone, Agamemnon,* and virtually all of O'Neill.

Much that is familiar can also be found in poetry, because it is concentrated expression of the human mind in rhythmical language. This should be particularly appropriate for the disadvantaged whose attention spans are said to be short, for those for whom nothing but the existential is of interest. There is even more when poetry is set to music, especially in folk songs, spirituals, the blues, and now the songs of the Civil Rights movement—for they rise out of the disadvantaged themselves.

But more than content, the humanities suggest to teachers attitudes necessary for teaching disadvantaged students. At heart this is belief that freedom is man's proper condition. Carl Rogers's *On Becoming a Person* and Philip Morrison's *Experimenters in the Classroom* draw heavily on this spirit by presenting teaching as the art of liberating the student. Deemphasizing content, they seek not good listeners or good memorizers, but real experimenters, not the empty "why?" but the internalized insight that often comes from manipulation of objects. They see the formulation of questions by students as more important than teacher-supplied answers. Both have high tolerance for the novel. They urge teachers to enter the students' world of feeling and meaning. To see things as the student does requires withholding judgment—the teacher must cultivate openness in himself to see reality in a new way. The attitude of the teacher then becomes one of warmth, interest, respect, and expectation, because the teacher now is learning with the student. The belief that the disadvantaged child has something of value to offer is precisely that attitude of which he is most deprived!

The teacher who would liberate must see student potential at least in equal measure to statistics suggestive of his limitations. Greater use of the humanities would help produce this balance. It would shift the focus—a little—from the failings of the child versus the middle class to the America that could be. In that new emphasis the teacher would see that the disadvantaged have much to teach America, especially about the nature of freedom. It is true that those who have not had freedom are most preoccupied with it. In America the Negro has been concerned with little else. Those with negative thoughts about the disadvantaged should read Frederick Douglas, Henry McNeal Turner, or W. E. B. DuBois; see Martin Duberman's *In White America;* or sing aloud "We Shall Overcome!" The idea that the disadvantaged bring what America long has needed is not new. Alexis de Tocqueville in 1831 visited our prisons and wrote the first reasoned account of democratic government in America. In *De la Démocratie en Amérique* he pointed out America's problem as being born free and therefore perhaps not knowing the real value of freedom.

To continue to deprecate the disadvantaged child, his home

and culture is to prevent the disadvantaged from giving to America what America most needs. The price of this imposed separation, this social ostracism, even—or especially—when accompanied by impersonal compensatory educational and welfare programs, can only bring the social breakdown that Baldwin predicted and Los Angeles now presents in sample form. The approach of the humanities could perhaps turn us away from discordances of guilt and hatred, and toward the harmony of an integrated society.

To be in the learning enterprise with the disadvantaged is in our time an exciting opportunity. The enlargement of freedom is what education is about. So, educators, drink deep from the humanities, the arts of all—even of disadvantaged—mankind.

". . . I hoped that literature might offer other ways of broadening the narrow channels in which they habitually thought."

REACHING THE CULTURALLY
DEPRIVED*

Terry Borton

This personal testament of a young English teacher describes a kind of teaching infrequently recommended and even more rarely practiced in classes for disadvantaged students. Like Howard, Borton affirms the primary importance of bringing to underprivileged and academically slow students perspectives to understand their own feelings and what humanists call the "human condition." He acknowledges that in itself the acquisition of psychological and cultural perspectives will not teach his students to write correctly or to speak an acceptable dialect, but without it, he argues, they will not even care to try to learn those more "practical" skills.

What evidence does Borton present that his students acquired some of the insights he aimed to

* Terry Borton, "Reaching the Culturally Deprived," *Saturday Review,* February 19, 1966, pp. 77–78 and 104–105. Reprinted by permission of the author and *Saturday Review.*

bring them? Do you consider his introduction of explicit discussions of such matters as race, and his encouragement of student expression of their sense of anger against society and the school educationally defensible? To what extent do you think Borton's way of teaching the disadvantaged could be adopted by other teachers?

THE CULTURALLY deprived child has it made. He is Upward Bound from Slum to Suburb, his Horizons Highered, his Youth Unlimited, his Poverty vanquished in a recent War.

Such, at least, is the impression the general public receives when the new crusaders go clanging past. As a teacher of the culturally deprived, I am tremendously encouraged by the genuine interest that lies behind all the slogans. But I am afraid that the new interest may die as the noise dies, and that unless very basic attitudes of public school systems toward these students can be changed, the efforts of a great many intelligent and concerned people may be wasted.

The public school system's attitudes are usually embodied in a detailed curriculum guide, and it was in that form that I first met them when I began teaching high school English two years ago in a large integrated urban school. I could not help being appalled by the reading program for low ability groups. The reading list was made up of easy books that preached "good values," but that made no pretense of adult interest or literary merit. Their titles alone—*Little Britches, Wolf Eye the Bad One*—were enough to tell my most ignorant students that they were children, and would be treated accordingly.

In spite of the fact that the classes I will describe here were "low ability" sections in which the average I.Q. was theoretically about 85, the students were by no means children. Most had already experienced the extremes of hate, love, and fear. Several had had illegitimate children; four or five were on parole; two had been raped by homosexuals in the reformatory. There were others who shut out the evil their classmates knew, and held fast to fundamentalist religion or race pride. And there were some, coming from "bad" backgrounds as well as good, who faced the world openly and had survived relatively unscathed. The one characteristic most of them shared was that they knew too much about too little, and they had run, as one of my students wrote in a poem on loneliness, "to only here." My job was to reach them where they were, and then show them where they could go.

Encouraged by a sympathetic administration, I abandoned

the curriculum guide, though not without many heated arguments with other teachers. I replaced books like *Little Britches* and *Wolf Eye the Bad One* with *Huck Finn, Catcher in the Rye,* and *Lord of the Flies.* Each of the latter books is an exciting story of young people, portrayed in a realistic manner and written in a straightforward style. Each is a book of recognized literary merit with a theme that struck the core of my students' lives. Admittedly the books were hard—all of them had been taught in college—and my eleventh-grade students were only reading at fourth to eighth grade level. Yet I was sure that with help they could handle the material—if they wanted to.

The problem was to get them to want to. I began with *Huck Finn,* and after the initial excitement ("He talk like we does") I met passive resistance. The students did not seem unable to discuss the literature, but they were certainly unwilling. I suspected that the mixed racial composition of the class was behind this reluctance, but the students would not admit it. As I pressed them harder, however, I discovered that racial antagonisms were not only deep, but they could sometimes control most of my students' thinking. I realized that racial tension was one of the things that had made our previous discussions stilted. Stereotypes and fears were so strong that it was impossible to discuss openly even the simplest boy-meets-girl plot. And when students would not even admit that their racial feelings were important to them, *Huck Finn* was dynamite, and they knew it.

To begin discussion I invited to the class an integrated college panel representing integrationists, Black Muslims, and conservatives. They argued about race among themselves, and once my pupils saw that older students could disagree about race and still remain friendly, they began to loosen up. One boy finally spoke his mind, and we were off. (The panel, which was invited for one period, ended up staying all day, with dozens of students pouring into the room during their lunch period. They wanted to continue the discussion, so an Interracial Discussion Group was formed which has been meeting weekly for two years. The members of this group have been instrumental in setting up a series of concerts and lectures, a tutorial project for elementary students, and a Negro Academic Society.)

In order to build upon my students' newly found willingness to talk about race, I tried to relate their reading of *Huck Finn* as closely as possible to their own lives. I divided the class into groups, and asked each to write a short play about a modern racial "incident" in which one race learned something about the other. Each student made up the lines for one character, with whites taking Negro parts, and vice versa. The rough drafts were then revised by the group.

This revision turned out to be the most exciting part of the project, for violent arguments erupted on who would be likely to say what under what circumstances. The clash of stereotypes was deafening, but amid the clamor were the quieter notes of realization ("Nobody'd care much if I married a chink. Then how come . . ."). The plays were finally recorded on tape and analyzed by the class. One group became so involved that all six of them came after school on the day Christmas vacation started to make a better recording of their play.

Vacation was wonderful. I went off to ski and relax, comfortable in the belief that my students were not only understanding good literature, but that what they were understanding was changing their lives, opening realms of thought from which they had previously been excluded. My first class after vacation brought doubts again. It became clear that one Negro student had not understood Huck Finn's use of the word "nigger"—a point I thought I had explained fully. I let the class discuss his objection and explain it to him, but I was upset that such a basic concept had escaped anyone. It was not until I remembered our first discussions of *Huck Finn* that I realized what a tremendous change had occurred. The fear of discussing race was gone; in its place was an open interest. The narrow personal viewpoint was broadened by historical perspective. Toleration was replaced by tolerance. My students were still making mistakes, but they were able to work toward understanding.

My own understanding had been steadily increasing. I soon

began to realize that race was only one of the factors that limited my students' ability to understand themselves and their society. Discussion of race had been an exciting beginning, but I hoped that literature might offer other ways of broadening the narrow channels in which they habitually thought. Yet before I could teach literature successfully, I needed a way to break up the class hour to keep within my students' short attention span. More important, I needed a way to give personal attention to each student every day, and a way to draw out the recalcitrant ones.

I hit upon one relatively simple remedy for these problems when I tried playing tape recordings of the books we were studying. Using a discarded set of fifteen earphones from the language laboratory, I divided the class in half, so that fifteen students listened to the tape recordings for about a quarter of an hour.

The recordings were as dramatic as I could make them, often utilizing the voices of my family and friends, and incorporating a stirring bongo drum accompaniment played by one of my students. They were designed to give the class a sense of how the novel should "sound" to their inner ear. I had noticed that even when my students knew the words they read in short phrases, Dick and Jane fashion, so that they often did not have enough steam to plow through the semicolons of an adult style. Sometimes they took so long to get to the end of a sentence that they had forgotten the beginning. I hoped they could use the recording to help them catch the sweep and flow of English prose, without bogging down on unfamiliar words. To accomplish this I had them read silently while listening to the tape, moving a card down the page so that I knew they were actually at work. With eyes, ears, and hands busy, I had them trapped. They had to learn.

One group wrote while another listened. Then they switched, and the listeners read out loud the same passage they had just heard, using as much expression as possible. Since they had just heard me "reading like you meant it," as one said, they were much less hesitant about trying it themselves and much more willing to take suggestions. After five minutes of reading, we discussed the passage, relating it to the rest of the book. During the third fifteen-minute period of the class hour, the first listeners wrote a short assignment while I discussed the reading with those who had just finished listening to the tape recorder. These discussions were the most exciting I had all year with any class, and several times I left the room with the hair on the back of my neck tingling. For ten minutes at least I had had the public school teacher's dream—a class of fifteen, all of whom had just read the material, were anxious to talk about it, and were thinking hard before they spoke.

I usually related the short writing assignments directly to the taped material, and here again the immediacy of the reading, personal attention, and the flexibility of the situation were major factors in producing good writing. For instance, while the first group was reading *Catcher in the Rye* with the tape, I had the other group writing about the reasons they disliked school. As I circulated through the room, I realized that my question had not led to understanding, but had only intensified the hostility the students felt against school and teachers. They seemed to resent writing on the subject because of a sense that their feelings were not quite legitimate. Because they had not succeeded in school, they felt they were not in a position to condemn it. To help the students understand and explore this feeling I switched assignments for the second group, and taking my cue from a dissected worm which happened to be in the room, I asked them to pretend that they were worms who could see. "What would it be like to be a worm coming up in the middle of a country road? a bustling city? a drag strip?"

I wanted to shock the students out of the clichés into which my first assignment had unintentionally forced their thinking. At the same time I hoped to give them a concrete analogy that could be used to show how Holden's "worm's eye view" was both revealing and yet distorted. While most of the students wrote on the level I expected, one perceived my underlying purpose. Drawing on our discussion of the book's symbolism, he wrote an allegory of *Catcher in the Rye.*

His worm actually represented Holden, disgusted by the dirt, and afraid that society was a ruthless giant that may squash

him, or "can" him in an asylum. In the book, Holden was also
afraid of being "frozen" into society, just as the fish were
frozen into the Central Park pond. But in my student's paper,
the fish—those who survive in society—represented a more immediate threat, one so intensely felt by the class that they
discovered the paper's symbolism at once, and began a hot
discussion on the necessity for responsible social criticism, and
the danger of nonconformity.

> If a worm had eyes he would of seen lots of dirt. The people
> around him would be terrifing giants. He would half to watch
> where he was going 'cause he easy be step on and killed. His
> home might be tore up, and he be taken away and put in a can
> or box. Or the poor worm might be stuck with a hook, and
> drop threw a hole in the ice and be eat up by the fish.

These sudden flashes of brilliance, understanding, and insight were a constant source of bewilderment. Though I hoped
to stimulate them, I never knew what form they would take,
or from whom they would come. One of the most disquieting of
these papers was written in response to an assignment on *Lord
of the Flies*. To prepare the students for the symbolic confrontation between humanity and evil, I asked them to imagine
the conversation between Simon, the lonely mystic, and a rot-
ting pig's head, representative of the evil that had come to
dominate the island. I appropriated a pickled dog's head from
an incredulous biology teacher, set it up in front of the class,
and the students went to work.

The grizzly minded had a field day, and even Fred, the one
kid in the class whom I considered a dolt, was busy scribbling
away. I watched him grip his pencil awkwardly in his fist,
scrawling words that made a jarring descent across the page.
There was scarcely a capital letter or a period on the page and
only a dozen words were spelled correctly. Graded as a conven-
tional essay his paper was a disaster, another failure from a kid
I already knew was stupid. But as I studied his strange hiero-
glyphics, I realized that if the spelling were corrected and the
words re-spaced on the page, his failure became a striking poem.
Dittoed the next day, it startled the class as much as it had me,

and stirred an interest in poetry that led to a comparison of Cassius Clay and Beowulf, and eventually drew the whole class into composing their own poems.

> It was a vine of flies
>   on a monster
>   that hurt my world.
> My friends were Jack and Ralph—
>   a world of loneliness.
> Jack remembered:
>   his world of hatred
>   spears ranged
>   pig's head.
> Ralph remembered:
>   crying for me.
> And then I ran
>   to only here.

I still cannot explain how Fred did it. He never came close to repeating that performance though he often tried. But from then on I knew that behind his mask of stupidity lay a mind with a remarkable ability to condense its experience into a few poignant words. I could not measure it, and I had understood it only once, but I knew it was there.

I believe there are many minds like Fred's. I know at least that many of his classmates were enthusiastic in their response to good literature. They not only bought many of the books themselves—in some cases the first book in the house—but they sought out other books I recommended and brought their own choices for me to read and comment upon. They were willing and able to judge a new book on its merits. As a test case I taught *Mama's Bank Account,* one of the better books recommended by the curriculum guide. The reaction against reading such "kid stuff" was intense. One boy scrawled on his book cover, "The book of nonreading"; another passed in a blank test paper with a big "F" marked on it, and at the bottom a notation, "If you give us another book like this one I will shot you." Discipline problems began to worry me again. There had been almost none for the last several months, in spite of the impressive stack of suspension notices my students had collected elsewhere. All of this evidence confirmed my belief in teaching good literature. However, I discovered that because of the easy material, comprehension test grades were much higher than usual. I asked the students to vote on which they would rather have: good grades or good books? The result was an encouraging vote for culture.

Now, in the middle of my third year of teaching, I feel more confident about the convictions with which I started. I still believe that students who can read anything deserve to read good literature, because good literature speaks about things that are important to them. I do not believe that clothes, or parties, or even cars are the most important things in their lives —all appearances to the contrary. I have seen them weeping for a dead classmate and a dead President. At parties I have been swept up in the joyous and spontaneous rhythms to which they dance. And in the dean's office, I have watched them sulking in anger, desperation, and loneliness. I hope that I have been able to find books that will give perspective to these feelings and help my students understand what they feel.

I believe that such a perspective is the most fundamental aspect of our culture, and is the way we profit from the struggles of our civilization's greatest minds. I am not sure that in itself the study of literature will "humanize"—I have known too many warped and bitter English teachers—but it does offer one way to add breadth to understanding. A good writer's exploration of his theme deals with our most deeply felt convictions, and by knowing his work we get some perspective on our own lives. My students desperately need that perspective, and their lack of it is the cultural deprivation with which I am most concerned.

I know that in itself cultural perspective will not train my students to write standard English, or speak an accepted dialect. But without it, they have no reason to learn these skills, as they believe that they are caught in a system that offers them no future, one that treats them like stupid children. For students in such a position all of life is a nightmare. One of them told me what that nightmare means:

A nightmare is the past, present, and future. I am going to tell you one I had. It was noon and it clouded over and began to snow. The funny thing was the storm came up so suddenly that no one was ready for it. The snow itself was funny looking —a bright red. It kept up for a long time, and the city was buried. When the rescuers came they found people still stuck in their cars.

The frozen people were thawed out and seemed all right, but there was something wrong. It was as though they had lost their minds and had acquired the mind of an animal, like a dog or a cat. Then they found a dog that acted funny when they thawed him out. He started sending Morse code out and told them he was a man, and was alive but could not talk. This was the result of being frozen in the funny snow.

They do not know what made the snow. But if you are ever out and a storm moves in and starts to snow the way this one did, run for cover and stay there until it stops snowing. Otherwise you will end up like me—a dog with a man's brain.

"Poverty exists, but usually only in fairy tales or those set in a foreign land."

LIFE IS FUN IN A SMILING, FAIR-SKINNED WORLD*

Otto Klineberg

This analysis by a social psychologist of readers used in American elementary schools concentrates not on their merit in teaching children to read, but on their presumed effect on children's attitudes toward the peoples and conditions of life in our society. Klineberg's criticisms encompass textbook treatment of minority groups, failure to present a realistic picture of lower-class life, and an anthropomorphic presentation of animals. The total effect of such texts, he asserts, is to indoctrinate children in ethnocentric biases favoring white, Protestant, middle-class culture, which tend to denigrate other ethnic and economic groups. Stories in which animals or inanimate objects talk and act like humans he deplores as retarding children's development of a realistic assessment of nature.

* Otto Klineberg, "Life is Fun in a Smiling, Fair-Skinned World," *Saturday Review*, February 16, 1963, pp. 75–77 and 87. Commissioned by The New World Foundation. Reprinted by permission of the author, *Saturday Review*, and The New World Foundation.

Although Klineberg's general conclusions about these readers are negative, he does note some positive aspects; what are they?

It is sometimes argued that books for children ought to present a "happy" picture of life and ought not to show them the "seamy" side of life. Does Klineberg's plea for realism in children's books adequately deal with such objections?

Try to recall some of the stories that you particularly liked—or disliked—as a child. How do they compare with those Klineberg describes as dominating American readers? If your early education was in another country, you may wish to review some of its readers from Klineberg's point of view.

"*READERS*" *ARE* presumably prepared for the purpose of teaching children to read, adding to their vocabulary, developing the capacity to see the interrelationship of ideas; children are helped to understand the structure of sentences and of grammatical forms, to follow the sequences of events, and to become aware of the manner in which they are united and integrated. One reader speaks of the "steady growth of interpretative powers" which is insured through the content of the stories, and describes the situations and plots as containing a "meaningful interplay of the personality, mood, emotion, and purpose of the characters." (This and the following numbers refer to the books listed in the accompanying box.) The present writer expresses no opinion as to the contribution of these readers to the ability to read, but this analysis of their content raises in his mind, however, some very real questions regarding their contribution to the children's picture of American society, the attitudes and modes of thinking which are presumably developed, and the desire to read further.

First, and perhaps most important, is the picture of American society which is presented. Margaret Mead and Rhoda Metraux have written about "The Study of Culture at a Distance" (University of Chicago Press, 1953), describing the attempts to understand another culture on the basis of its plays or motion pictures, its books, its manuals of child care, etc. Suppose the visitor from Mars or even from Thailand tried to reconstruct American life from the content of these readers, without any other data to guide him. The resultant picture would be approximately as follows:

The American people are almost exclusively white or Caucasian. The only exception discovered in the fifteen readers refers to a visit to a Western ranch, near which lived an American Indian family, who spent most of their time "making beautiful things . . . to sell to the white people who came to the Indian country." The story told is in general friendly and sympathetic to the Indians, except that they are treated as exotic and "different," not really part of the American scene. Their names—"Big Horn," "Shining Star," etc.—strike Jack, the white American boy, as "funny." This incipient ethno-centrism might have been countered by reminding Jack that many proper names may be considered "funny," depending on one's experiences. What about Longfellow or Bacon? Even "old American" names may refer to occupations (Baker, Tinker), or colors (Brown, Green), or places (Hill, Field); some of the most distinguished names in American history, like Roosevelt, Eisenhower, or more recently Shepherd (or its variant Shepard) also refer, as do most American Indian names, to places or occupations. There are other stories of Indians, but mostly of Indian children of a bygone day.

The Americans in these readers are almost exclusively North European in origin and appearance. When any mention of ethnic origin appears, which is rarely, it is English, French (Brittany), or Norwegian. Other peoples and places are visited, including Lapland, Spain, and North Africa, but this is part of travel to foreign lands, and not part of the picture of America. In this particular case, one traveler, on the apparent basis of experience with the North African desert, delivers himself of the following judgment: "A mighty interesting country, Af-rica," as if nothing existed south of the Sahara, and as if Africa were one (Arab) country instead of a great many different ones.

To return to the ethnic picture in the United States, the exceptions to the usual North European appearance and origin are themselves significant. An organ grinder is given an ap-pearance which is stereotypically Italian or Greek, with a red scarf instead of a necktie; he appears in the illustration on the cover, as well as several times in the text. A slightly different version of the same, or similar, organ grinder appears in an-other Reader. There is also an Italian or Greek-looking peddler who carries a big bag on his back. Finally, there is a story of a discontented horse that works for Mr. Polaski, who "sold fruits and vegetables," and who also "looks" very South- or Central-European in the accompanying illustrations. The treatment of these characters is by no means unsympathetic, and the last example occurs in a story which is charmingly written, but one cannot help wondering about the extent to which the stereo-type—South Europeans are organ grinders, peddlers, and fruit and vegetable vendors—may be strengthened by such a presentation.

Americans in these readers are predominantly, almost exclusively, blondes. A check on the illustrations used in three of the readers, found in two of them almost 100 per cent blondes, and another with 75 or 80 per cent. There are occasional references to dark skin, but these usually relate to people far away. Pandas, for example, are found in a distant land (India?) with dark-skinned people; in Lapland there are "small dark men"; and of course the illustrations for these stories about China, India, North Africa, etc., do show dark people. Not in the United States, however, apart from the exceptions noted above. Negroes are nonexistent. One reader has a story called "A Summer in the South," in which a boy and his father go "away down South to see Grandmother." But there are apparently no Negroes even in the South. It is true that Grandmother had a cook whom Paddy liked "almost as well as he liked Grandmother," but even in the case of the cook, there is no indication of what Charlie May looked like. Either there are no Negroes, or they must not be mentioned. Some years ago, H. E. Wilson ("Intergroup Relations in Teaching Materials," Washington, American Council on Education, 1949) pointed out that in American textbooks foreign nationalities, as well as American minority groups, are either placed in an unfavorable light or are treated inadequately. In the readers under review, to speak of "inadequate treatment" of the Negro is an extreme understatement.

Religion, as was to be expected, is rarely mentioned. Only in one reader is there a reference to religious observance, when on Sunday "everyone was going to church" because "this is Sunday, you know." Paddy says, "I always go to church on Sunday, I always do." On a Sunday morning Mr. Carl rolled over in bed until the church bell called, "Come to church! Come to church!" These are the words with which this particular reader closes. No one could argue that in these readers religious (Christian) observance is overemphasized, but again the opportunity might have been taken to give some idea of the range and variety of observance found among the different

religious groups that constitute the American people. There is
no hint of this in any of the readers examined.

Americans in these readers are all quite well-to-do; not
exactly wealth, perhaps, but certainly quite comfortable, to say
the least. The illustrations show, for example, a pleasant home
with good furniture, all the children dressed in clean, attractive
clothes, with talk about buying new dresses; there are all kinds
of toys in the house; the children go out (presumably with their
own pocket money) to buy balloons. Again, they live in pretty
suburban houses, and the children have money in their pockets
with which to go buy toys themselves. The farmer has his own
tractor, and Father brings home a new car, "long and blue and
beautiful." In another reader the family has an attractive home
with a car, a television set, toys, and bicycles. In still another,
the mother buys her girls new coats; or they already have
beautiful clothes and the house a modern, built-in kitchen; or
the family takes a trip on a big and very luxurious ship; or the
boy goes riding on his own pony; or the family lives in "a
pretty white house"; or father takes the children to the circus
and his boys to the ball game; or they take a train out West.
Poverty exists, but usually only in fairy tales or those set in a
foreign environment, and even in those cases everything turns
out right before the end. Occasionally a boy will do some work
in order to earn money, but he then puts away his twenty
pennies in his own "bird bank." Not only is there no poverty,
but work seems to be readily available to everybody, and is on
the whole not only easy, but "fun."

In fact, life in general is fun, filled almost exclusively with
friendly, smiling people, including gentle and understanding
parents, doting grandparents, generous and cooperative neighbors, even warm-hearted strangers. There is an occasional display of anger, but it is usually very transitory. In general, all is
peaceful and happy.

In summary, then, life in the United States as it is portrayed
in these children's readers is in a general way easy and comfortable, frustrations are rare and usually overcome quite easily,
people (all white, mostly blonde, and "North European" in
origin) are almost invariably kind and generous. There are

other kinds of people in the world, but they live in far-off countries or in days gone by; they evidently have no place on the American scene.

When we turn to the attitudes which the content of the readers will develop in the children, we are on less certain ground, since we must depend on inference rather than on direct observation. Certain conclusions can be drawn, however, with a fair degree of probability. There is a great deal of published work which demonstrates that ethnocentric attitudes develop very early in children, and that they are already present at the ages for which these readers are destined. (See for example "Prejudice and Ethnic Relations," by John Harding *et al.*, Chapter 27 in G. Lindzey, editor, "Handbook of Social Psychology," 2 volumes, Addison Wesley, Cambridge, 1954, and K. B. Clark, "Prejudice and Your Child," Beacon Press, Boston, 1955.) Obviously, the responsibility for this cannot all be laid at the door of school experience, since so many other influences make their contribution. Nevertheless, some of that responsibility must be borne by readers which, by what they omit as well as by what they contain, give the impression that the "true" American is of the fair-skinned "North European" variety. Although this was certainly not the aim of the writers concerned, the net effect would almost certainly be to strengthen the ethnocentric attitudes of those children who share these characteristics, and make all others—of Negro, Puerto Rican, South European, possibly also of Jewish origin—feel that they do not quite belong. Since these and other ethnic groups constitute a substantial proportion of the American school population, it would not be surprising if the readers had an alien quality for a great many of the children who come into contact with them. (The writer is reminded of a Brazilian first reader which starts out telling the children that Brazil has three "mothers," one European, white, one Indian, red, and one African, black, and goes on from there to describe how the present Brazilian population has developed.)

In addition to ethnocentrism, the readers also display what might rather clumsily be called a socioeconomic-centrism, a concentration on those who are relatively well-to-do. Here the problem is rather more complicated, because Americans are in general well-to-do, and the amenities described are within the reach of a substantial proportion of the population. For the remaining "one-fourth of a nation" it is part of the American dream that a more comfortable life is attainable. Until it is attained, however, the life portrayed in these readers must represent a very frustrating experience for them. Are no other families as poor as ours? Does everybody else live in a pretty white house? Are there no crowded tenements except where we live? Are we the only ones who can't go out and buy the toys we want? On the other side, is it desirable for the well-to-do children to be unaware that there may be poor people living on the other side of the tracks? Surely a more balanced presentation of American life, both from the ethnic and socio-economic standpoints, would better prepare the children for what they will later encounter and help to correct what would otherwise be a one-sided picture. It may be argued that this will come in time, and that these children are still too young to face that kind of reality. The fact remains that the earliest impressions frequently develop attitudes that persist; it follows that it is never too early to tell children the truth.

There is another striking feature of these readers related to the question of "truth." In addition to the (conceivably factual) accounts of the activities and experiences of children and their families, most of the readers contain a number of stories, which, though fictional in character, deal with animals or with objects such as trains or airplanes which the children have in all probability encountered. These stories are predominantly characterized by anthropomorphism (ascribing human qualities to animals) and animism (ascribing life and thought to inanimate objects). Thus a snowman laughs, animals talk to one another and cooperate in joint enterprises; trains converse, and so do airplanes and helicopters, cars and taxis, and there is even a little red lighthouse, round and fat and "very proud," which carries on a conversation with a new bridge.

There can be no doubt that animistic thinking is widespread among young children, at least in Western society. (J. Piaget, "The Child's Conception of the World," New York, 1929). It has been suggested, however, that this tendency would not be nearly so marked nor so common if it were not for the influence of language (as when we refer to a ship as "she"), the actions of parents and other adults (like spanking the chair that "hurt" the little child), and the stories told as in these particular readers, for example. In any case, animism is a stage through which children pass, through which children must pass if they are to reach a realistic appraisal of the outside world. The present writer feels that the proliferation of anthropomorphism and animism creates an unnecessary barrier to the intellectual development of children, who should rather be encouraged to make, as early as possible, a distinction which is in harmony with the truth. He finds it hard to believe that animistic distortion is necessary in order to attract the attention of even young children. In fact, he has met children of six who would show a pitying smile at each such an insult to their intelligence.

As far as moral attitudes are concerned, the readers appear to be on relatively safe ground. They illustrate, without any overt preaching, the virtues of honesty, fair play, cooperation, family solidarity, work and thrift, friendship, independence, cleanliness, courage and forgiveness. There is even, as has already been indicated, an awareness and acceptance of differences in culture and background, but usually for people far removed in space and time. One could certainly wish for more of this in the case of those nearer home; for these, there are no negative or unfriendly references; they simply do not exist.

In regard to the desire to read further, the editors of these readers, some of whom are personally and favorably known to the present writer, presumably have based their choice of materials on a knowledge of the tastes and interests of children. It is hard to believe, however, that enough is being done to stimulate the curiosity of the children, to make them feel that they would like to know more. The readers do contain a number of well-written stories and some delightful poems, but almost no information. Surely, together with the reading of good prose or verse, a reader could do more to instruct the child.

This report concludes with two specific proposals. The first is that the analysis made of American readers be supplemented by a comparison with readers of other countries (France, the Soviet Union, Brazil, and Sweden, for example) to determine what can be discovered from their experience, and also to see what other children, no brighter than our own, can absorb at an early age. The second is the preparation of sample readers designed to give children a more complete and more adequate picture of American life, and capable at the same time of making important things interesting.

"A Celtic myth or an African one, for example, is both more valid to non-Irish and non-Africans than any truncated and sterile recitation of back-yard or street adventures. The issue is man's heritage, not the black man's or the white man's."

COLOR ME BROWN—
I'M INTEGRATED*
Theodore B. Dolmatch

Although Dolmatch seems to agree with some of Klineberg's criticisms of American textbooks, he recommends rather different correctives. Dolmatch is concerned with the possibility that efforts to rectify the ethnocentrism in existing texts may be exploited by some publishers who hope to capitalize on a new market in large urban school systems having a large proportion of minority-group students. Special books ostensibly designed to meet such "needs," he argues, may further fractionalize our population.

How does the "truth" which Dolmatch urges as a touchstone for judging children's books differ from that proposed by Klineberg?

* Theodore B. Dolmatch, "Color Me Brown—I'm Integrated," *Saturday Review*, September 11, 1965, p. 73. Reprinted by permission of Theodore B. Dolmatch and *Saturday Review*.

*Klineberg's article was written before Dol-
match's, after the publication of the newer textbooks
sampled in the pages that follow this selection. How
do these newer materials appear to relate to these
two opposing views?*

AS A PUBLISHER of textbooks and their accompanying paraphernalia, I have long taken for granted my partnership with teachers in the educational enterprise. I am not alone in my presumptions to professional status; most textbook publishers stress this partnership, and educators are prone to accept publishers as "full-fledged members of the educational fraternity."

But if there is any significance in this publisher-educator relationship, we, as publishers, have a responsibility for producing instructional materials that truly serve the needs of teacher, pupil, and community. Yet, in at least one broad area, I contend, we are failing.

In response to the belated recognition that the American experience is heterogeneous, a growing number of educational authorities are echoing the statement of the Michigan Department of Public Instruction, that: "Education has a responsibility for promoting good inter-group relations and for presenting, from textbooks and curriculum materials, an accurate and unbiased concept of America as the multi-cultural, multi-racial, and multi-religious nation that it is."

Unfortunately, too many of us have read strange meanings into this call for texts that reflect the diversity of American life.

With new eyes, publishers and educators have looked at their older books, only to see blond children and suburban homes, white-collar fathers, and grandparents on farms. On the basis that these are now wrong, they have begun to produce and use what one Negro educator has called "color-me-brown" books, as naïve in their own way as their predecessors. One can ask whether replacing white children with brown ones or replacing country children with children from the city is the answer. In one Harlem classroom, the teacher was most delighted with the new wave of primers that replaced pink complexions with brown ones. She asked her children what was different in these books. They had no immediate answer, so she persisted until one child finally spoke up. "All the children are sunburned," he said, in sad confirmation of Santayana's reflection that the opponents of the ruling orthodoxy merely invert its errors rather than discover new truths.

The immediate response to Anglo-Saxon materials seems to be non-Anglo-Saxon materials. We publishers are urged—nay, told—to provide urban environments, multiracial groups, to stress the "real" as it really is—in the city. Ever eager to please, and with a weather eye out for the market, we do books about Negro heroes instead of books about heroes—Negro and white —and so replace our previous exclusion with separatism. We now seek after the same mythic simplicity, but in a new style, instead of attempting to cope with the increasing complexity of American reality. But that which is truly representative of the American experience is its diversity: We are city *and* suburban, black *and* white (and yellow and red, too, for that matter), blue collar *and* white.

Further, though our ethnic and geographical variety is a key to American life, it cannot be the only rationale for textbooks; they must convey ideas as well. A variety of environments can introduce the child to a world that is wider than either city or suburb alone. The child needs to know that his point of contact with his fellow man is to be found in himself, in the nonenvironmental world of human responses. Conceptual and verbal horizons must be enlarged; this is not achieved merely by changing environments to right old wrongs.

Books can help children develop useful and strengthening concepts of self by stressing the inner reactions which are shared by all children. If education is to expand horizons, the literal environment must be subordinated to the self-evident truths of human experience. A Celtic myth or an African one, for example, is both more valid to non-Irish and non-Africans than any truncated and sterile recitation of backyard or street adventures. The issue is man's heritage, not the black man's or the white man's.

This move to "either-or" books raises yet another issue. By developing different books for specific ethnic or geographic subcultures, we make it too easy to forget that, to quote the president of the American Textbook Publishers Institute: "Textbooks that recognize and respect all kinds of human differences help young people to develop a sense of common destiny." If we produce books that "relate" only to one group, how can the members of that group develop that "common" destiny?

The call for books that, so belatedly, repair old wrongs has not only produced texts that starve the child with a diet as limited in its own way as his previous one. This dictum also tells some publishers only that they must produce—not integrated books—but merely integrated books to parallel existing and continuing segregated ones. Separate but equal, as it were.

I would raise the question, therefore, whether "separate-but-equal" books do not indeed nullify the best efforts of educators. At best, it seems anomalous that texts should be created which pander to the prejudices that we have officially abandoned. At worst, the production of one set of books for segregationists and another for integrationists circumvents moral imperatives, and does so in a particularly unpleasant way. If the President of the United States has suggested that the issue of segregation is moral and not political, when will we decide that it is also not commercial?

There was a day when Darwin was omitted from biology texts destined to be sold in Tennessee, when the Anglo-Saxon heritage was the only American heritage, when separate but equal satisfied too many of us. That day is past, and atavistic texts and opportunistic publishers are particularly out of place.

"To no small degree, the attitude and reaction of many white Americans to the Negroes' struggle for equality now is the consequence of a mythical, as distinguished from an historical, understanding of the American Negro."

BALANCE AND IMBALANCE:
"NEW" HISTORY TEXTS
AND THE NEGRO*
Irving Sloan

This recent survey of history texts follows similar studies that have appeared during the past three decades documenting inadequate or derogatory treatment of American Negroes and other minority groups in our population. Although Sloan's survey still finds much to be desired in the treatment of American Negroes, it does call attention to some new texts that deal more fairly and accurately with this group. His analysis highlights the treatment of those topics and historic periods most crucial to an understanding of the American Negro experience: their African heritage; the conditions of slavery; their par-

* Reprinted with permission from the Fall, 1966, issue of *Changing Education,* published by the American Federation of Teachers, AFL-CIO.

ticipation in major events in American history—the War of Independence, the Civil and subsequent wars; the abolition and freedom movements; their subjection to prejudice and discrimination; distinguished Negro Americans.

What specific changes in attitudes toward the American Negro do you think might follow general use of history texts that meet the criteria suggested by Sloan?

You may wish to examine elementary textbooks in the social studies in the light of Sloan's analysis of secondary texts. Should there be any difference in the topics covered and the treatment of these topics in elementary and secondary texts?

Alternatively, you may wish to examine either secondary or elementary texts in the social studies with respect to their treatment of some other minority group, the American Indians or Spanish American, for example.

THE NUMBER of studies and addresses calling for the improvement of the presentation of the Negro in American history textbooks is legion. "Conspiracy of silence," and "cultural conspiracy," are two of the charges leveled against authors, publishers, and teachers. Nor is this a matter of the recent past provoked by the civil rights movement. Early in the present century, Edward A. Johnson, a leading Negro historian and teacher of his time, wrote that he observed "the sin of omission and commission on the part of white authors, most of whom have written exclusively for white children, and studiously left out the many creditable deeds of the Negro. The general tone of most of the histories taught in our schools," he wrote, "has been that of the inferiority of the Negro, whether actually said in so many words, or left to be implied from the highest laudation of the deeds of one race to the complete exclusion of the other."[1] And, as recently as 1965, another outstanding Negro historian and teacher, Charles H. Wesley, could publish a pamphlet of essays with the revealing title, *Neglected History: Essays in Negro History*, in which he remarks that the views Johnson expressed more than 50 years ago are ". . . historically common in our schools today, although they are decreasing, but with neglect and omission . . . deadly silence and implication."[2]

It is not only Negro historians and teachers who make these damning charges against the writing and teaching about the Negro in our public schools. Only a few years ago a committee of eminent historians—most of them white—representing the history department of the University of California at Berkeley, reviewing the American history textbooks that were most widely used in California from the standpoint of their treatment of Negroes, reported ". . . an unhealthy condition in California education . . . the greatest defect in the textbooks we have examined is the virtual omission of the Negro."[3]

1. Edward A. Johnson, *A School History of the Negro Race in America* (New York: Goldman Co., 1911), p. III.
2. Central State College Press, Wilberforce, Ohio, 1965, p. 24.
3. "The Negro in American History Textbooks," mimeographed report (undated), pp. 1–2.

The truth of the matter is that the account in American history textbooks of what the Negro has meant in American history, as well as his specific contributions to the growth and development /of America, has never been complete or well-balanced.[4] To be sure, there has been marked improvement through the years, however slowly and insufficiently. But only since the civil rights movement in the 1950s has there been a measurable and even dramatic change.

A striking example of this point is presented in the 1966 revised edition of a junior high school text which first appeared in 1959.[5] Professor Levine, in an analysis of the original edition for the University of California report, observed, "Although the book was published in 1959 and mentions events as recent as the launching of American space satellites in 1958, there is not one word about the civil rights movement, the migration of Negroes to the North, the condition of Negroes in the 20th Century, or the Supreme Court's 1954 *Brown* decision. After Reconstruction, the Negro, who was treated vaguely enough until then, becomes wholly invisible."[6]

The present edition, on the other hand, is found to be one of the most complete and admirable treatments of the Negro among those included in this writer's survey of a number of late editions of American history textbooks.[7] There is in the 1966 edition·of this particular text a relatively complete discussion, "An Important Social Revolution Begins," which deals with the civil rights issue. More than that, the authors of the text conclude their discussion with this personal moral judgment: "When each person is willing to give every other person

---

4. For a complete and excellent survey of the changing textbook content from 1826 to 1839 regarding the history of the Negro in the United States see: Marie E. Carpenter, *The Treatment of the Negro in American History School Textbooks* (Privately printed and sponsored by Professor Erling M. Hunt of Columbia University Teachers College, 1941). While Mrs. Carpenter deals with texts used in the South, there is considerable material dealing with historical scholarship as well as textbooks generally.

5. Rebekah R. Liebman, Gertrude A. Young, *The Growth of America* (Englewood Cliffs, N.J.: Prentice-Hall, Inc., 1959; 1966).

6. "The Negro in American History Textbooks," *op. cit.*, pp. 13–15.

7. Irving J. Sloan, *The Negro in Modern American History Textbooks* (Chicago: AFT, 1966).

all the rights he wants for himself, and does so, then all Americans will be truly equal."[8]

In his study, this writer could find no text which, standing alone, encompassed just the right amount of material with just the proper point of view on the topic of the Negro. But it must be recognized that the inherent nature of a textbook imposes limited space for every topic which must be covered. The traditional notion that American history must be "covered" rather than studied in depth in terms of selected topics has given textbook publishers an excuse to be incomplete on this topic.

Nevertheless, the study of the Negro in American history secondary school texts has historically been more neglected and less influenced by historical scholarship than any other topic. To no small degree, the attitude and reaction of many white Americans to the Negroes' struggle for equality now is the consequence of a mythical, as distinguished from an historical, understanding of the American Negro. By omission and commission, the written history of the Negro has helped perpetuate and intensify the pattern of racial discrimination that is, after all, the root of the present "revolution," and as such is the central problem of our society today.

SOME EXTRACTS FROM TEXTS

The purpose of this paper is to highlight some of the material which this writer has gathered in his recent study of a dozen late editions of American history secondary school textbooks as they deal with the role of the Negro in American history. Obviously, what appears here is highly selective. A good many matters have been omitted here but are not overlooked in the original study. Hopefully, the reader can gain at least a notion about the range of strengths and weaknesses of the texts, which still remain the basic source material for both teachers and students in the classrooms of America.

Almost symbolically, only one text looks at Africa histori-

8. Liebman, *op. cit.*, p. 435.

cally and brings to the student a sense of the high degree of civilization which existed prior to the slave trade. "Long before the New World was discovered, a number of African societies—among them the West African kingdoms, or empires, of Ghana, Melle [Mali], and Songhay—had attained a high degree of civilization."[9] Dr. Wesley has commented that the ". . . neglect as to Africa and black folk serves to create an assumption of an inferior history rather than a difference of culture. The hypothesis of the inferiority of achievement becomes the more deeply entrenched in the American mind when the textbooks give little information and there is no teaching concerning the black and brown people in Africa as persons in history. The psychological effect of this neglect upon the minds of youth when they have friends and associates who can speak proudly of their European backgrounds and learn nothing of their African background and heritage has been quite evident."[10] While this omission is crucial in the Negro child's own self-concept, it is equally crucial in terms of the white child's image of the Negro.[11]

NEGROES AS EXPLORERS

In another area, only one text fills a gap in the history of the Negro in America. This is the fact that Negroes were with the Spanish explorers in the 16th Century and so made their first contributions in pre-Columbian America.[12]

INDENTURED SERVANTS

All the other texts teach students that the first Negroes arrived in America in Jamestown in 1619. A few texts com-

9. Lewis Paul Todd, Merle Curti, *The Rise of the American Nation* (New York: Harcourt, Brace & World, Inc., 1966), p. 304.

10. Charles H. Wesley, *Neglected History; Essays in Negro History* (Wilberforce, Ohio: Central State College, 1965), p. 27.

11. See Franklin Patterson (ed.), *Negro Self Concept* (New York: McGraw-Hill Book Co., 1965).

12. Clarence L. Ver Steeg, *The Story of Our Country* (New York: Harper & Row, 1965), p. 75.

pound this error by clinging to the old historical scholarship that this group arrived as slaves.[13] Prevailing historical scholarship holds that these first Negroes who arrived in *English* America were indentured servants who, in the words of one excellent text, were to be compared and likened to the ". . . thousands of men and women from Europe [who] worked as servants for a period of years to pay for their transportation. Once they had repaid the debt, they settled on their own land and worked for themselves."[14] While few of the texts develop the facts in such a way as to give the student this positive view of the Negro, they do at least make the important distinction between slave and indentured servant and indicate that the Negro did not start out as the former, thereby implying a kind of inherently inferior status.

Students may often wonder why the black man and not the white man was brought over to America under duress and by force without any apparent protest, thereby instilling a suspicion about the black man. One text takes the trouble to suggest that the ". . . Negroes, coming from a foreign land, being of different color, and, in the beginning, having no one interested in their welfare, were not able to change their lot."[15]

LIFE AND TREATMENT

The life of the slave and his treatment is given attention by almost all of the texts. The few which omit even this major topic indicate how far some texts do go to play down the historical role and antecedents of the Negro.[16] In any case, textual treatment of slave life ranges from a realistic, but balanced presentation which recognizes that most masters were harsh and only "some planters never punished their slaves and

---

13. Mabel B. Casner, Ralph H. Gabriel, *Story of the American Nation* (New York: Harcourt, Brace & World, Inc., 1962 with 1964 Supplement), p. 72; Leland D. Baldwin, Mary Warring, *History of Our Republic* (Princeton, N.J.: D. Van Nostrand Company, 1965), p. 40.

14. Todd, *op. cit.*, p. 22.

15. Liebman, *op. cit.*, p. 54.

16. See Casner, *op. cit.*, Nathaniel Platt, Muriel Jean Drummond, *Our Nation from Its Creation* (Englewood Cliffs, N.J.: Prentice-Hall, Inc., 1964).

treated them with kindness,"[17] to the majority of texts which put it the other way round, that "by far most" of the masters were good to their slaves.[18] Indeed, the author of this last observation goes on to contend that "strange as it may seem, most slaves had a higher standard of living than that of some whites in United States."[19] Many of the texts offer this argument as one made by Southerners, but not of the authors themselves, as these do so brazenly.

Between the time of the arrival in Jamestown and the discussion of the lot of the slave in the South in the early 19th Century, all of the texts manage to omit any reference to the Negro during the Revolutionary period of American history except for mentioning that the first victim to fall in the Boston Massacre was Crispus Attucks, a Negro. None of the texts mentions such outstanding personalities as Phillis Wheatley, the poetess, or Benjamin Banneker, the mathematician. A number of texts, however, do deal with different aspects of the situation of the Negro during this era. One, for example, discusses manumission—an expression which comes up in no other text.[20] A few texts consider the apprehensions of Patrick Henry, Jefferson, Washington, and some of the other "founding fathers." At least two texts quote Jefferson's compelling remark, "I cannot justify it (slavery) . . . I tremble for my country when I reflect that God is just; that his justice cannot sleep forever."[21] Another text has the guts to note Jefferson did not act on his beliefs.[22]

At least one text deals with Lord Dunmore's declaration inviting Negroes to join the British, and his establishment of a Negro regiment during the Revolutionary War.[23] This text is among the few which make the student aware that the orig-

17. John W. Caughey, John Hope Franklin, Ernest R. May, *Land of the Free* (New York: Benziger Bros., 1966), p. 251.

18. Baldwin, *op. cit.,* p. 297.

19. *Loc. cit.*

20. Henry F. Graff, John A. Krout, *The Adventure of the American People* (Chicago: Rand McNally & Co., 1965), p. 247.

21. See Drummond, *op. cit.,* p. 346; Graff, *op. cit.,* p. 247.

22. Todd, *op. cit.,* p. 349.

23. Caughey, *op. cit.,* pp. 141–142.

inal draft of the Declaration of Independence included a charge against George III for protecting and continuing the slave trade. This grievance was struck out at the objections of "slave-owning South Carolina and slave-trading Rhode Island. . . . On this issue, thus, the Declaration of Independence was a compromise."[24]

VIEWING ABOLITIONISM

The work of the abolitionists is a major topic which all the texts consider in a variety of ways. For the most part, the abolitionists in the North are portrayed as fanatics and their motives are unsympathetically described. One text states, "Abolition efforts seemed to thrive on opposition and persecution."[25] The Underground Railroad is quickly dismissed as "the most dramatic activity of the abolitionists."[26] As in most of the texts, Negro participation in this movement, reflecting self-advancement in the struggle for freedom, is omitted. Indeed, this is a text which managed not to name a single Negro personality up to this point, not even Crispus Attucks in its detailed description of the Boston Massacre!

While Garrison is always noted as the best-known abolitionist in many texts, one author typically observes that "many others were equally devoted if less fanatical."[27]

Another text does not even mention the Underground Railroad in its brief discussion of abolitionist activities.[28] Two paragraphs comprise the entire discussion of this topic in one text.[29] The authors of another text assure the student that this movement had little support in the North. "Most Northerners believed that the Negro race was inferior. They dreaded only less than Southerners what might happen if the slaves were

24. *Ibid.,* p. 145.

25. Leon H. Canfield, Howard B. Wilder, *Making of Modern America* (Boston: Houghton Mifflin Company, 1966), p. 247.

26. *Loc. cit.*

27. Ruth W. Gavian, William A. Hamm, Frank Freidel, *United States History* (Boston: D. C. Heath & Company, 1965), p. 319.

28. Ver Steeg, *op. cit.*

29. Casner, *op. cit.,* p. 310.

freed."[30] Consistent with this tone, Garrison is described as being "so domineering that most abolitionists tried to steer clear of him."[31] It is, however, gratifying to note that a few texts do mention a few Negro abolitionists, including Frederick Douglass and Harriet Tubman.[32]

Only one text emphasizes the high moral ideals which generally prevailed among the abolitionists:[33] "They believed that they were conducting a holy crusade against the world's worst evil, and they insisted that the future of the country depended on the end of slavery."[34]

SLAVE UPRISINGS

A few texts briefly mention the slave uprisings led by Turner, Prosser, and Denmark, so that students get a further sense of the slaves' discontent with their status. However, none of the texts indicates that actually there were hundreds of such violent rebellions, thus conveying the fact that these three incidents were not as isolated and incidental as they appear to be.

THE CIVIL WAR

A large number of the texts make no mention at all of any Negro participation in the Civil War. Those few which do offer nothing more than a sentence or two stating the number of Negroes who fought in the Northern army. One text, however, does offer a full page "feature" on the 54th Regiment describing the heroism of this Negro regiment in the Battle of Fort Wagner.[35] It should also be noted that another text contains a topical heading, "The Negro Takes Part," begin-

30. Baldwin, *op. cit.*, p. 298.
31. *Loc. cit.*
32. See *Our American Republic: Rise of the American Nation; Land of the Free; Growth of America*. This writer found four out of 23 teachers had heard of Frederick Douglass when the question was raised in an in-service course he conducted recently; three of these four were Negroes, the remainder of the group was white.
33. See Caughey, *op. cit.*, p. 309.
34. *Loc. cit.*
35. Todd, *op. cit.*, p. 384.

ning with a question everywhere else greatly overlooked, "What part did Negroes play in the war which freed them from slavery?" The authors go so far as to point out that, "Even before the war began, many of the free Negroes were abolitionists and were willing to give their lives for the freedom of all Negroes." The section then goes on to review further the activities of Negro abolitionists and the flight of Negroes to freedom because "they would no longer live as slaves."[36] Unfortunately, however, this presentation is almost unique among those surveyed in this study.

The subject of the free Negroes during the period before the Civil War is one that is generally overlooked. A number of texts do, however, deal with this topic to varying degrees. One text gives a particularly strong account. "There was a handful of exceptional free Negroes who were able to achieve recognition for their attainments in the arts and in business despite their obvious handicaps."[37] The concluding statement that ". . . in general the life of the free Negro was a hard one, and they lived in fear of being kidnapped and sold into slavery again," is accurate.[38]

DURING RECONSTRUCTION

Mark Krug has pointed out that of all the topics in American history which have been the victim of historical scholarship, the Reconstruction has suffered the most.[39] And it is here where the image of the Negro in American history has suffered the worst. Professor Krug has also correctly observed that the treatment of such a vast and complicated topic as Reconstruction is particularly vulnerable to the limitations of space in a secondary school textbook as well as limitations placed on the scholarship of textbook authors.

Under the circumstances, the textbook treatment of this major topic invites our considerable attention. Here, more

36. Liebman, *op. cit.,* pp. 288–289.
37. Graff, *op. cit.,* p. 251.
38. *Loc. cit.*
39. "On Rewriting of the Story of Reconstruction in the United States History Textbooks," *Journal of Negro History* (1961), p. 133.

than anywhere else in our survey, we find the greatest range
of strengths and weaknesses as well as the greatest opportunities to do good or ill to the minds of students.

Some texts give a very precise account of the events of this
period and thereby reflect the current scholarship and materials concerning it. Dealing with the controversial view of
the motives of the Radicals, one text draws a rather balanced
conclusion that "sorting out the motives of men is a fascinating
undertaking, but the answers are uncertain. The South considered the Radicals to be madmen taking pleasure in tor-
menting their defeated brethren; Northerners friendly to the
Radicals considered them heroic defenders of the true principles in the Declaration of Independence."[40] Another balanced
text observes that "it is not easy to characterize the Reconstruction governments in the Southern states because they varied
so greatly in complexion and character."[41] A final paragraph
in this section then goes on to describe the "record of constructive work" of these governments.

A text reflecting the best historical scholarship recognizes,
for example, that not all the Northerners who moved South
came to exploit the section. "Some of them came to teach and
uplift the Negroes. Some came to invest and help the South
recover. Some came as money-hungry adventurers." It is clearly
pointed out that "Negroes were never in control of any
Southern government."[42] Many of the leading Negro statesmen
of the period are described, and, for most students, this will
prove eye-opening. It pulverizes the commonly-held notion
that illiterate, money-grasping ex-slaves ran the South during
this period. The authors of this text do concede that there
were "lapses from good behavior," and give examples. "But
as compared to the scandals in the federal government in the
1870s and in New York City, these errors were small."[43]

Another text, after giving credit to the achievements of the
Reconstruction governments, concludes that, "These changes

40. Graff, *op. cit.,* p. 329.
41. Arthur S. Link, David S. Muzzey, *Our American Republic* (Boston: Ginn
& Co., 1966), p. 366.
42. Caughey, *op. cit.,* p. 366.
43. *Loc. cit.*

made the South less feudalistic and more democratic than it had ever been."[44]

On the other side of the coin, a good number of the most widely used texts offer many of the myths of the older and largely Southern scholarship. Usually the approach is made with a negative and critical view of the Freedmen's Bureau, the agency which more than any other assisted the Negroes after the Civil War. One text charges that its work was ". . . hindered both by scoundrels and impractical dreamers among its administrators."[45] The authors then go on to picture the Radical Republicans as villains who were out to "control . . . Congress and destroy the powers of the States."[46] At another point, Thaddeus Stevens and Charles Sumner are said to have made "strong efforts . . . to take the land of 'rebels.' " A photograph of Stevens describes him as "the vindictive Thaddeus Stevens."[47] The Union League "horsewhipped Negroes who did not vote Republican."[48] But, according to the notion of these authors, "The *planters* were on the whole concerned with aiding and advising the freedmen in the serious business of adjusting to freedom."[49] The authors do acknowledge, however, that the "Carpetbaggers did much to modernize the Southern state governments and to undo the damage of war . . . Strange as it may seem, the Carpetbagger state constitutions were so plainly suited to the new day that they remained in force after the Southern Democrats came to power."[50] Note the constant use of the emotionally-charged word "carpetbagger" over and over again.

Another text pursues the subject this way: "The Congressional Reconstruction plan put scalawags and carpetbaggers in power and kept them there. Once the plan went into operation, scalawags and carpetbaggers held most of the high offices in

44. Gavian, *op. cit.*, p. 400.
45. Baldwin, *op. cit.*, p. 384.
46. *Ibid.*, p. 385.
47. *Ibid.*, p. 387.
48. *Ibid.*, p. 390.
49. *Loc. cit.*
50. *Ibid.*, p. 391.

the Southern states. Negro voters elected them, along with former slaves."[51] There is a statement that "Some good laws were passed during the Reconstruction period."[52]

Putting it bluntly, one text explains that the Radical Republicans "wanted to punish the Southerners," and thus instituted policies which protected the Negroes.[53] No room is allowed for suspecting that, to some extent at least, the Negroes needed and deserved this protection, and that some Radical Republicans were motivated for such reasons. An example of patently distorting the facts is the heading "Reconstruction governments spend public funds."[54] The incredible criticism is made that since the legislators as individuals "owned little property and paid few taxes," they were guilty of improper conduct in voting appropriations of public funds![55] These authors make no mention of the Negroes' contribution during this period. They do point out that "in South Carolina . . . about two-thirds of the members of the lower house were ex-slaves."[56] This is an apparent attempt to give the impression that Negroes dominated the Southern state governments throughout the South.

Another text refers to the Reconstruction governments throughout the discussion as "Carpetbagger governments."[57] The opening passage describes a "governor" who saved a half million dollars on an $8,000 salary after four years. "When criticized, he answered: 'Corruption is the fashion. I do not pretend to be honest.' This governor was not the only dishonest politician in the Southern state governments set up as a result of the Reconstruction Acts."[58] After acknowledging some constructive conduct on the part of some Negro legislators, the authors conclude that, "In spite of these achieve-

---

51. Casner, *op. cit.*, p. 427.
52. *Loc. cit.*
53. Canfield, *op. cit.*, p. 322.
54. *Ibid.*, p. 328.
55. *Loc. cit.*
56. *Loc. cit.*
57. Drummond, *op. cit.*, pp. 414–416.
58. *Ibid.*, pp. 414–415.

ments, the period of carpetbagger governments was a most disgraceful period in American history."[59]

Finally, there is even one text which does not deal at all with the Reconstruction governments.[60]

THE KLAN APPEARS

Almost invariably, the topic which follows the Reconstruction era in most textbook accounts is the rise of the Ku Klux Klan as a Southern response. In this connection the "moral objectivity" of almost all of the text writers presents itself most obviously. These writers almost imply a moral justification for the Klan, suggesting that the "moderate whites" had no choice. "Some Southern whites, unable to improve conditions in a lawful and orderly way, decided to go outside the law."[61] What Professor Levine wrote in connection with the overall tone of one 1959 text is applicable here to all of the texts: "It should be mentioned that the authors are not morally obtuse or unwilling to take a stand on every issue. Thus they criticize the manner in which the Mormons were treated and describe their hardships; they describe the often inhuman conditions of early factories, the plight of the workers and justify the rise of labor unions; the American Indians are treated sympathetically and the treatment accorded them by the white settlers is criticized; the immigrants are treated with a bit less sympathy but at least their plight is described."[62] In short, authors are not inhibited about moral judgments in areas outside the subject of the Negro.

At the conclusion of the Reconstruction era, the Negro gets only the most minimal attention in the texts for the next few hundred pages, until after World War II. Several of the texts manage to go by without a single reference to a Negro personality or an event involving Negroes.[63] One text contains a few paragraphs mentioning the founding of the NAACP and

---

59. *Ibid.*, p. 416.
60. Ver Steeg, *op. cit.*
61. Canfield, *op. cit.*, p. 328.
62. "Negro in American History Textbooks," *op. cit.*, p. 15.
63. Liebman; Graff, *op. cit.*

the Urban League, and gives a summary statement that "Many Negroes worked to make their lives better and to help build a stronger America. In time, Negroes became important teachers, doctors, scientists, athletes, musicians, and lawyers."[64] Another text passes through some 400 pages with but two brief references to the participation of Negroes in education programs [segregated] as examples of their "progress."[65]

One text provides a photograph of George Washington Carver, a summary paragraph dealing with the shift of the Negro from the South to the Northern cities, and a final paragraph stating that the "Negroes had great obstacles to overcome." As evidence, however, that the position had improved, Jackie Robinson's admission to major league baseball is cited. Furthermore, "In recent Olympic Games, Negro athletes have won many points for the American teams." Finally, a listing of more impressive and more varied Negroes in the arts, sciences, and statecraft is given.[66] In one text, a mention of Booker T. Washington is the only reference made to a Negro in 250 pages of material between Reconstruction and World War II.[67] Another text also includes a portrait of Booker T. Washington, but also adds a comment on the philosophical differences between him and W. E. B. DuBois. It is the only reference to Negroes during this "stretch."[68] Again, Booker T. Washington appears as the only Negro reference in a text, but here the passage is longer than those already cited and it presents Washington as the exemplary Negro working for self-improvement.[69] These references indicate that a number of texts seek to play it "safe" with a figure like Booker T. Washington.

On the other hand, at least one text gives an impressive treatment of Negroes during this period.[70] In this text there is a section dealing with the development of the "New South," giving a good summary account of the pattern of segregation

64. Ver Steeg, *op. cit.*, p. 275.
65. Drummond, *op. cit.*, pp. 423, 566.
66. Canfield, *op. cit.*, pp. 590–591.
67. Casner, *op. cit.*, p. 428.
68. Baldwin, *op. cit.*, p. 501.
69. Gavian, *op. cit.*, p. 446.
70. Todd, *op. cit.*

which was beginning to take shape. The authors sum up this situation by noting that, "Northerners who, on the whole, had lost interest in the Negro cause, did not raise any serious protests against these developments. In fact, as the years passed, Negroes in Northern cities also faced increasing discrimination, particularly in employment and housing."[71] Here, too, the philosophies of Washington and DuBois are discussed. There is also a full account of the disfranchisement of Negroes which took place during the period. This makes the later discussion of the civil rights movement come as a natural consequence rather than as a shock. On the other hand, 150 pages of text passes with no mention of the Negro in units discussing the West and American industrial society, although there is discussion of the new problems encountered by the Negroes as a result of the growth of industry during World War I and the 1920s. While a number of individual Negroes who achieved success during this period are cited, the authors note that, while there were achievements by individuals, ". . . in 1930 many doors of opportunity still remained closed to Negroes."[72] On the whole, this text stands out among the other texts in handling the period of time under discussion.

THE FREEDOM MOVEMENT

The treatment of the civil rights revolution in the texts surveyed in this study reflects the strengths and weaknesses which are inevitable in a textbook. It is a topic so charged with available material, in view of its timeliness as well as its central importance in contemporary affairs, that the problem of what to include and what to exclude is formidable. A reasonable approach to an analysis is to emphasize the quality of the material offered rather than the quantity of it. While this position is certainly applicable to the other topics as well as to this one, the point is that past history is less known and less available, so that it may be more important to include as much possible relevant material about the past. Much current material comes to students from a variety of sources available

71. *Ibid.*, p. 419.
72. *Ibid.*, p. 652.

to them daily, including table-talk at home as well as from the table TV set.

In any case, most of the texts do a better job in their presentation of contemporary events dealing with the Negro than they do with the historical antecedents leading up to them, especially after the Reconstruction era. Yet, one high school text, which does a particularly good job with some of the early history dealing with the Negro, falls down considerably in its handling of the civil rights movement.[73] This fact points up an earlier comment that it is quite impossible to find a single text with a completely even quality throughout. Nevertheless, another of the high school texts nearly achieves this consistency by offering the longest and most detailed account of the movement among all the texts included in this study.[74] First, there is a review of the roots of the problem with a summary discussion of the way the 13th, 14th, and 15th Amendments have been violated by the South since Reconstruction. "As a result of these developments, American Negroes entered the 1900s handicapped by problems they had not anticipated during the first hopeful years of freedom."[75] Postwar advances are discussed in a series of paragraphs dealing with voting, education, public facilities, housing, and employment. Each topic is given detailed treatment.[76] The March on Washington and the Civil Rights Act of 1964 are given individual analysis and treatment in separate passages.[77]

Another text deals with the violence of the Negro revolt in a well-balanced passage: ". . . Negroes had conducted their campaign for equal rights with a notable sense of restraint . . . violence in the spring of 1963 came to the surface. . . . Most of it was directed at Negroes and whites demonstrating in a nonviolent manner."[78] However, there is a passage later on dealing with "Kennedy's efforts" on behalf of the Negro which contains a possible indication of the author's attitude when he observes that, "Not the least disheartening feature of the

73. Link, *op. cit.*
74. Todd, *op. cit.*
75. *Ibid.*, p. 804.
76. *Ibid.*, pp. 804–806.
77. *Ibid.*, p. 807.
78. Baldwin, *op. cit.*, p. 767.

situation [the Negro's call for equality] was the way in which the world, always prone to criticize the United States, was more inclined to emphasize the hypocrisy of white attitudes and the long roll of injustices to the Negro than to recognize that Kennedy had gone further than any President in history in his efforts to rectify them. This, moreover, was the attitude of many of the newly militant Negroes as they refused to accept anything short of full equality now."[79] Here is another example of the inconsistencies which can be found within the same text. The *attitude* of the author reflected by this last comment may have more influence on the student's thinking than the earlier praised statements of *facts*.

The California report's statement about the importance of the civil rights revolution in the American history text is worth quoting in full as an appropriate closing for this topical treatment:

"This civil rights revolution" it states, "seems to us to be one of the major historical events of the mid-20th Century and to demand full treatment in any American history textbook. The gains that have been made should be described realistically and not as an ode to the inevitable justice and progress of the democratic system. It should be made clear that the outcome of the civil rights struggle is still in doubt, and that the inequalities are so great as to defy quick remedy by even the most vigorous effort."[80] To suggest that current texts have achieved the goal described here would be overstating the case. But it is fair to say that for the most part most of the texts are moving in this direction.

Clearly, some texts are "more unequal" than others in terms of offering students a truthful and adequate treatment of the Negro in American history. What is equally clear from this study is, however, that that subject has gained great ground in the very recent past and there is no reason to predict anything less than that these gains will be broadened. Someday they may help instill in every student a sense of what Negroes have contributed to America.

79. *Ibid.*, p. 769.
80. "Negro in American History Textbooks," *op. cit.*, p. 5.

". . . right-wingers charge that the textbook teaches children 'guilt and shame' about America's past . . ."

THE NEGRO IN HISTORY:
NEW TEXTBOOKS
ARE TARGETS OF BACKLASH*
Gerald Grant

This news report about reactions in California,
Ohio, and the South to one of the texts praised in
the preceding selection and to a supplementary
social-studies series on minorities suggests some of
the difficulties in introducing historically sound and
unbiased materials into the schools.

> *What do you think might be the motives of those
> individuals and groups that oppose the use of these
> texts? How would you respond to the charge that
> they teach "shame and guilt"?*

* From *World Journal Tribune,* Tuesday, December 13, 1966, p. 53. © 1966
The Washington Post Co. Reprinted by permission.

Washington—A drastic change in the portrayal of Negroes and other minority groups in many American history school textbooks has spurred a strong right-wing backlash in some parts of the country.

Many American youngsters are reading for the first time this year about the 14 Negro soldiers who won the Congressional Medal of Honor for heroism in battle during the Civil War. Or about the Japanese-Americans who were forced to leave their homes and go to detention camps in World War II.

Many texts no longer gloss over the accomplishments of Negroes or the unpleasantness about treatment of minority groups, practices that had been common in order to sell textbooks in the South and to squeamish school officials.

STORY OF DOCTOR

Illustrative of the sweep of the change is a textbook account of the Negro physician Charles R. Drew in pioneering the development of plasma blood banks in the 1940s. Noting that the American Red Cross later widely copied Dr. Drew's methods, the textbook concludes:

"In the light of what this distinguished Negro doctor contributed, it is hard to believe, but true, that the Red Cross then had a ruling that Negro and white blood used for plasma had to be segregated and so labeled."

John Hope Franklin, a co-author of the textbook, "Land of the Free," now used in nearly 100 school systems, told an interviewer of the "vicious vendetta" being carried out against the book and its authors.

"You have no idea how much money is being spent in this vilification campaign," said Franklin, the noted Negro historian who is a professor at the University of Chicago.

TARGET OF ATTACK

Vincent D. Murphy, a vice president of Benziger Bros. Inc., which published Franklin textbook last January, said the book is a target of a "Let Freedom Ring" attack on Columbus, Ohio. Telephone callers are told by a recorded voice that the book is unpatriotic and Communist-inspired because one of the authors, now a professor at the University of California, once refused to take an academic loyalty oath.

The most virulent campaign has been waged in California, where "Land of the Free" committees have been formed to keep the book out of public schools. Pamphlets and film-strips reviling the book have been distributed by a Pasadena group called Publius Publications.

Murphy said the right-wingers charge that the textbook teaches children "guilt and shame" about America's past and find it unthinkable that the book has no picture of Betsy Ross sewing the American Flag.

ATTENDED CONFERENCE

The book was originally placed on the approved textbook list in California but has been held up.

Franklin spoke at a weekend Washington conference on "Racism in Education . . . Correcting America's Image of its Past." Among the 2,000 participants were many of the publishers of history textbooks that have been revised to give "proper emphasis" to minority contributions.

Loretta A. Barrett, editor of a new series of books published by Doubleday Co., said that "Worth Fighting For," a book about the Negro's role in the Civil War, produced a sharp reaction in those parts of the South where teachers were brave enough to use it.

A teacher in Florida had her automobile tires slashed and windows soaped with warnings because she used the book, Miss Barrett said.

Some southerners are particularly incensed because the book's cover shows Negro riflemen firing on southern whites. Until very recently, textbooks implied that Negroes carried only slop pails during the Civil War.

The book points out that more than 200,000 Negroes fought in the conflict, many winning battle citations and others assuming leadership positions.

Miss Barrett said the series, which also includes "A Guide to African History" by the British author Basil Davidson, has been purchased by nearly every big city school system in the North and some in the South.

CHANGED IMAGE

Many of the revised texts sweep aside the myth of the happy well-cared-for slave and show frankly the brutal side of slavery. They give a more balanced view of the Reconstruction era, reflecting new scholarship that shows many Negroes performed admirably in the Reconstruction government and that graft and corruption was no worse in the South than it was in many parts of the United States at that time.

But a significant number of texts continue with the old stereotypes, and if some right-wing groups have their say, this practice will continue.

TEXTBOOKS FOR
INNER-CITY CHILDREN

The facsimile pages from twelve textbooks for inner-city children that follow illustrate some of the responses by publishers to criticisms of existing texts and to recommendations for curriculum modification to meet the needs of underprivileged and underachieving students. You will be able to identify such modifications as these: text and illustrations reflecting the ethnic diversity of our population; consideration of such social deficits in American democracy as slavery and the contemporary struggle for full civil rights; literature depicting the struggles of the poor; reading materials written to deal with such practical concerns of alienated and academically unsuccessful youth as relationships with the law, or job applications and interviews; and inclusion of juvenile slang and street talk as part of the study of language. English language arts and social-studies texts have been selected to illustrate these newer texts, because it is in these fields that most modifications have been made.

Can you explain why publishers of English and social-studies texts have been particularly responsive to demands for change to meet the needs of the underprivileged? In general terms the intent of these newer texts is to interest underprivileged and alienated children and youth and to improve their conceptions of themselves. To what extent do these texts seem to fulfill these purposes? How widely should texts of this nature be used? Are they equally important for children in affluent, predominantly white, Anglo-Saxon schools? Why? Consider these texts in the light of the views of the authors of the preceding articles. How do you think each would react? You may wish to compare the full text of one of the books sampled here with a comparable book not designed to answer the charges of ethnocentrism leveled by many reviewers at current texts.

"You can push the cart.

Push it to me.

Do you have the money?"

"I have my money.

It is in here.

I will get it out."

23

From *Chandler Language-Experience Readers, Supermarket* (Book 5),
Baugh & Pulsifer, p. 23. Reprinted by permission of the Chandler Publishing Company.

Come, Mother, come.

Come and see.

Come and see Father.

From *Fun with David* by Writers Committee of the Great Cities School Improvement Program of the Detroit Public Schools. © 1962 by the

Look, look, Jimmy.

See Father.

See Kitty.

See Father and Kitty.

People

11

Houses are in the city.

Streets are in the city.

People are in the city.

14

24

Excerpt from ''A Place of My Own'' reprinted by permission from *The Hidden Lookout, Skyline Series, Book B,* by Virginia Brown, Billie Phillips,

A Place of My Own

This is Rosita.

She lives in a house full of people. She has a big sister, a big brother, and a little brother. And they all live together in one apartment.

Sometimes Rosita likes her big sister and her big brother. She even likes her little brother, but not very often.

25

The storekeeper had so many things to sell
   he put it all outside.

The store was too small.

You can buy bobby pins, hair spray, and soap there.

The girl and her mother
   are going to buy some hair spray.

The big sign says:
   "This is the place to change your underwear."

That's funny! I think it means
   that you can take your old underwear there
   and exchange it.

I think it means that when your underwear gets old
   you can buy new underwear.

I was baffled. My mother was telling me to fight, a thing that she had never done before.

"But I'm scared," I said.

"Don't you come into this house until you've gotten those groceries," she said.

"They'll beat me; they'll beat me," I said.

"Then stay in the streets; don't come back here!"

I ran up the steps and tried to force my way past her into the house. A stinging slap came on my jaw. I stood on the sidewalk, crying.

"Please, let me wait until tomorrow," I begged.

"No," she said. "Go now! If you come back into this house without those groceries, I'll whip you!"

15

Reproduced with permission from The Macmillan Company from *Coping* by Marjorie B. Smiley et al., part of The Gateway English Program. Copyright © The Macmillan Company, 1967. Text from *Black Boy* by Richard Wright, New York: Harper Brothers, 1945. Reprinted by permission of Harper & Row, Publishers, and Paul R. Reynolds, Inc. Picture by Douglas Paddock. Used by permission.

Chorus: As long as the moon shall rise,
        As long as the rivers flow,
        As long as the sun will shine,
        As long as the grass shall grow.

On the Seneca Reservation, there is much sadness now,
Washington's treaty has been broken, there is no hope, no how.
All across the Allegheny River, they're throwing up a dam,
It will flood the Indian country, a sad day for Uncle Sam.
It has broken the ancient treaty, with a politician's grin,
It will drown the Indians' graveyards, Cornplanter, can you
    swim?
The earth is mother to the Senecas, they're trampling sacred
    ground,
Change the mint green earth to black mud flats,
As honor hobbles down.

    [*Chorus*]

Too Late

On Wednesday after school, Elaine went to the beauty parlor where her mother worked. She was going to speak to Mrs. Carter, the owner of the shop, about the receptionist's job for the summer. When she came into the shop, the girl sitting at the receptionist's desk asked Elaine if she could help her. Elaine told the girl her name and said that she'd like to talk to Mrs. Carter.

The girl went to the back of the shop to get Mrs. Carter. After she'd gone, Elaine took a quick look at herself in a mirror. After being in school all day, her dress was rumpled. Elaine wondered why she hadn't thought of going home first and putting on a clean dress. She also noticed that her hair needed combing. Suddenly she remembered that she had a run in one of her stockings. She'd gotten it at school.

"I'm not ready for an interview for a job," Elaine thought. "I should have taken time to do something about the way I look."

When Mrs. Carter came out, Elaine introduced herself. Mrs. Carter was pleased to see her. They sat down and Mrs. Carter started to explain to Elaine what the duties of a receptionist were. As Mrs. Carter began to talk, Elaine saw her glance at the run in her stocking.

"If I don't get this job," Elaine said to herself, "I'll have only myself to blame. Ma did everything she could to get me the job. But I just didn't care enough to make sure that I looked right. Now I do care, and it's too late!"

HIRING PEOPLE

If you were the owner of a store and had to hire a clerk, would you know whom to hire? If you were interviewing people for the clerk's job, and during the interview they did the things that are listed below, would you hire them? If you would, write *yes*. If you wouldn't, write *no*.

_____ 1. Chewed gum during the interview.

_____ 2. Arrived late for the interview.

_____ 3. Was friendly and alert.

_____ 4. Talked about himself constantly.

_____ 5. Said very little during the interview.

_____ 6. Answered your questions carefully.

_____ 7. Bragged too much about what a good worker he was.

_____ 8. Seemed eager to get the job.

_____ 9. Had a very good appearance.

_____ 10. Was sloppily dressed.

_____ 11. Seemed to be too friendly.

_____ 12. Had good references.

_____ 13. Looked at his watch while you were talking.

_____ 14. Had lots of self-control.

_____ 15. Bit his nails while you were talking.

From *The Jobs You Get* by Richard H. Turner. *(The Turner-Livingston Reading Series)*. © 1962 by Richard H. Turner. Used by permission of

Draw a line under the correct answer to each question.
1. How did Elaine's dress look?
    dirty   rumpled   starched   torn
2. Where did the receptionist go to get Mrs. Carter?
    drugstore   cellar   back of shop   basement
3. What did Elaine suddenly remember?
    hair wasn't combed   fingernails were dirty   run in a stocking
4. What did Elaine see Mrs. Carter glance at?
    her watch   run in stocking   the desk   a notebook
5. To whom did Elaine introduce herself?
    receptionist   customer   owner of the shop   her mother
6. What did Mrs. Carter start to explain to Elaine?
    salary   hours   advantages   duties
7. If Elaine didn't get the job, whom would she have to blame?
    herself   her mother   the owner   the receptionist
8. Elaine felt she would have looked right for the interview if she had done what?
    been on time   cared more   had more sleep   not gone to school
9. Where did Elaine's mother work?
    factory   drugstore   beauty parlor   restaurant
10. How did Mrs. Carter feel when she saw Elaine?
    pleased   unhappy   tired   disappointed

JOB DUTIES

Every job has certain duties. See if you can sort out the duties in the list below and put them into the correct columns.

1. dye hair	7. make appointments	13. clean stables	19. answer telephone
2. make beds	8. clean windshields	14. mix batter	20. check oil
3. plant seeds	9. give alcohol rubs	15. type letters	21. sift flour
4. open mail	10. fill gas tanks	16. take temperatures	22. change bandages
5. plow earth	11. frost cakes	17. put air into tires	23. milk cows
6. pluck eyebrows	12. give facials	18. give manicures	24. bake bread

RECEPTIONIST	BAKER	NURSE

GAS STATION ATTENDANT	BEAUTICIAN	FARMER

Follett Publishing Co.

This book is about hip words. Not everyone agrees about what is hip and what is not hip, so you and someone else using this book might not agree either. This is good. It is good because the book is supposed to be about YOUR vocabulary—the words YOU use and the way YOU use them.

You are the judge. If a word with its meaning is hip to you, leave it alone. If it is not quite right, change it so it is right. Do whatever you have to do so it's your kind of word. If a word is strange altogether—if, as far as you know, you've never heard it before—just cross it out with a big heavy mark. It is NOT your word.

Everyone should work through the book together. Think about the words out loud, say them in sentences, act them out, find some way to give them meaning, argue about them—then do the writing in the book.

5

From *Play It Cool in English* by Frank Riesman and John Dawkins.

one ☐1 Some of the pictures show hip meanings for words and some do not. Draw a big cross (X) through each picture that does NOT show a hip meaning.

ax

cabbage

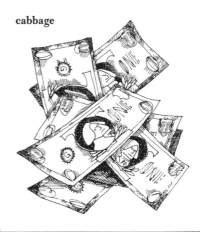

crib

lid

6

BECAUSE HE WOULDN'T GIVE UP

Jose was afraid. He was alone in the strange city of New York without friends or family. How long could he last on the few pennies he had in his pocket? He had to find a place to live and he had to find a job. This would not be easy. At home his English had sounded wonderful. But New York City was not Puerto Rico. Would people understand him? At the age of twenty-two, Jose still had two more years of high school to complete. And at the age of twenty-two, Jose still had his dream.

Jose Saez was born in Puerto Rico in 1903. He was very much like all the other children in his small village except for one thing: Jose wanted to be a doctor. It did not matter that he had never even seen a doctor. As a young child, he often heard people talking about doctors. He knew that they helped people. He spent many of his days playing "hospital." He practiced on everyone. Even his pet cat learned that it was safer to stay away from Jose.

There were no medical schools in Puerto Rico at that time, so when he was old enough, Jose decided to go to New York to study. In 1925 he left his home and took a first step toward his dream. The idea of going to a strange land frightened Jose. But he kept remembering why he was going. Jose Saez had decided to be the finest doctor in all of New York.

Jose found a friend in New York. This friend let Jose stay with him until he found a job. Soon Jose began to work in a grocery store and to think about school. He went to Washington Irving High School at night and worked during the day. Two years later Jose received his high school diploma.

28

dventures in Negro History

Part I

usic up and under

RRATOR:

America has truly been blessed with bountiful resources, stretching from the Atlantic to the Pacific. Today, America is blessed with great industrial and agricultural developments which provide its citizens a standard of living unequalled by any other nation in the world.

But how did this come to be? Was it by miracle or some sudden streak of luck? The obvious answer is no! America is a world leader because of the contributions and sacrifices made by Americans since the beginning of our glorious history. And who were these people who endeavored to build America? Well, they were all kinds of people—rich, poor, adventurous, and brave. And all races and nationalities—Italians, Englishmen, Mexicans, Germans, Poles, Indians, Chinese, Norwegians, Frenchmen, Japanese, Russians, Spaniards, and many, many more. Truly a melting pot of humanity!

usic out

ICE:

But what of the Negro's role and contributions in American history?

RRATOR:

The Negro's role in the history of America? A good question! Perhaps we can briefly try to answer this for you.

Let us turn back the pages of history and start from the very beginning.

(Pause)

usic in
usic up and under

RRATOR:

Let us consider the era when the New World was first being explored by European nations. Let us not forget that it took tremendous courage to venture into new and uncharted lands. Pedro Alonzo Niño, a Negro, was a pilot for one of the brave ships which sailed on and on to fame and glory with Christopher Columbus. And there were many other exploration parties, and among these adventurous men were many Negroes.

ST VOICE:

Yes, there were many of us. We came to the New World with the conquistadors and explorers of the sixteenth century.

und of ocean surf up and under

COND VOICE:

Thirty of us were with Balboa on that glorious day in 1513 when the Pacific Ocean was discovered. What an awesome sight it was to gaze upon the mighty waters of the largest ocean in the world!

und of surf out

From *A Glorious Age in Africa: The Story of Three Great African Empires* by Daniel Chu and Elliott Skinner. Copyright © 1965 by Doubleday &

Such was the glamour and splendor of the first great empire in West Africa, a wealthy and mighty Negro empire that came to be known as Ghana. In its own time the fame and glory of Ghana spread far beyond its own borders.

The King of Ghana conducting the daily affairs of his mighty empire.

Slaves for sale

Trouble I've Seen" and "Let My People Go" are examples. "Everybody Talkin' 'bout Heaven Ain't Goin' There" implies a rebuke to their masters.

Most of the slaves endured what they had to. If they loafed on the job, it was often a form of protest. Slaves pretended to be ill and unable to work. Sometimes they destroyed tools or other property or damaged the crops. A few slaves were so desperate that they cut off their own hands or committed suicide.

In a few instances, an aroused slave killed a hated overseer or his master. The southern whites lived in dread of a slave uprising. Led by Gabriel Prosser, a thousand slaves in Virginia prepared for such an uprising in 1800. A violent storm and betrayal by two informers ended their attempt. In 1822 the slaves of Charleston planned a revolt under the leadership of Denmark Vesey. The word leaked out, and the plot was put down, but

the whites were terrified to discover how massive an uprising had been planned.

In 1831 a Negro revolt led by Nat Turner in Southampton County, Virginia, was almost successful. On the first day, the slaves killed sixty whites, but soon they were overpowered by state and federal troops. More than a hundred slaves, including Turner, were captured and executed. There were other attempts to revolt, but none was successful.

"Follow the Drinkin' Gourd"

A more hopeful but still desperate move was for a slave to run away. In the South, he might be able to pass himself off as a free Negro. It would not be easy. In southern states, a strange free Negro was looked upon with suspicion. If he did not have papers or someone to vouch for him, he might be seized and returned to slavery.

306

From *Land of the Free* by John Caughey, John H. Franklin, Ernest R. May and Laree Caughey. New York: Benziger Brothers, Inc., 1966.

Trying to make it to freedom

The better plan for the runaway slave was to hurry into free territory. This he might be able to do if he lived in the upper South. Anywhere in the South, a person who helped a runaway slave was taking the chance of heavy penalty. In parts of the North, also, local opinion did not sympathize with runaways.

Yet there was help. Individuals were willing to lend a hand. Levi Coffin of Indiana organized friends of the Negro into a network to shelter runaways. Because his network had stations and conductors and because it was secret, it was called the Underground Railroad. Other such systems were organized.

Agents of the Underground Railroad sometimes went into the South to help slaves escape. The most famous agent was Harriet Tubman, an escaped slave herself, who returned south time and again and brought out more than three hundred slaves.

At first, the Underground ran only into Indiana or Ohio or Pennsylvania. In the 1850's, because of a tightened fugitive slave law, it was necessary to take the "passengers" all the way to Canada if they were to be safe.

The Underground, hated by the southern slaveholders, is the theme of the haunting ballad "Follow the Drinkin' Gourd." The song has a double meaning. The drinking gourd is the Big Dipper, pointing to the North Star, which gave direction to the runaway slave. Along the Underground, it was the practice to hang out a drinking gourd as a sign to runaways of houses where they could count on help.

"Follow, follow the drinkin' gourd,
Follow, follow the drinkin' gourd,
For the Old Man is a-waitin'
For to carry you to freedom,
Follow the drinkin' gourd."

307

"They use the same grammar, but they do not use the potentials of language, and their vocabulary and usage are different."

A SUSTAINED PROGRAM
OF LANGUAGE LEARNING*
Walter Loban

Walter Loban, who has done some of the most significant research on the language of lower-class children, reviews the major differences between their usage and that of children from middle-class homes and suggests a sequence of language instruction for disadvantaged students. Contrary to the beliefs and practices of many teachers of English and speech, Loban urges that children be encouraged to speak in whatever dialect is native to them. Participation in activities that call for language to be used in many ways—naming, describing, asking questions, role-playing, as well as responding to the questions of the teacher—should have priority over efforts to change

* Walter Loban, "A Sustained Program of Language Learning," *Language Programs for the Disadvantaged: Report of the NCTE Task Force on Teaching English to the Disadvantaged,* © 1965 by the National Council of Teachers of English, pp. 221–229. Reprinted with the permission of the National Council of Teachers of English and Walter Loban.

children's speech to conform to the prestige dialect of the community. Ultimately, Loban would have teachers assist children to acquire a socially acceptable dialect; such efforts, he warns, should be preceded by exposure to a variety of regional and social-class dialects presented in a nonjudgmental fashion and should lead to practice in a nonthreatening climate.

To what extent does the program Loban recommends conform to your own recollection or current observations of classroom practices? How serious a handicap do you think lower-class dialects present to students' academic success? To their acceptance in the job market? Which features of lower-class English do you think constitute the major handicaps in these situations: pronunciation? intonation? syntax?

PUPILS NEED to learn standard English in addition to the social class dialect they know, Cajun, Appalachian, or whatever it may be. (We are not here concerned with *regional variations* of English but with *social class variations.*) If such pupils do not learn a second kind of dialect, standard English, they will be forever prevented from access to economic opportunity and social acceptance. We can learn to grant full dignity to the child and to the language spoken in his home. At the same time, we must help him to acquire the established standard language so he can operate in society as fully as he may wish. He would, of course, be free to make the choice of not using his second dialect.

The research of Basil Bernstein in England and my own research on language development are pertinent here. The Cockney and the upper middle class British speaker have the same basic language, the same grammar. The difference lies, according to Bernstein,[1] in the extent to which Cockney fails to use the potential of the language. This is exactly what I found in my research in the Oakland, California, schools. In kindergarten and in subsequent years, the same grammar operated in the language of all the youngsters. But subjects from the lower socioeconomic groups do not use language with as full a range of potential as those from more favored groups. They can use the full potential, but if they are in the lower socioeconomic group they do not do so very often. By full potential, I mean using such syntactical devices as coordination or subordination to express a complex idea or using an appositive to reinforce or to extend the listener's understanding of what is being communicated. They do not use infinitives—not so much the infinitive alone as the infinitive phrase, the elaborated infinitive phrase, a much neater device

1. Basil Bernstein, "Language and Social Class," *British Journal of Sociology,* XI (1960), 271–276.
———, "Some Sociological Determinants of Perception," *British Journal of Sociology,* IX (1958), 159–174.
———, "Social Class and Linguistic Development: A Theory of Social Learning," *Education, Economy, and Society,* ed. A. H. Halsey, Jean Floud, and C. Arnold Anderson (New York: Macmillan [Free Press of Glencoe], 1961).

than dependent, subordinate clauses for tightly coiling ideas. Gerund phrases, participial phrases, and infinitive phrases are usually indicative of a much tighter kind of thinking than is the long dependent clause. For instance, in the two sentences which follow the first version is better than the second:

Concepts evoked by the total situation may be relevant.
Concepts that are evoked by the total situation may be relevant.

Instead of, "The sparrows urged that Peter exert himself," the skilled speaker says, "The sparrows urged Peter to exert himself." In language research, various devices of subordination prove to be the mark of a person with the best control of the English sentence, the one who has the most to say and the skill to say it in skillfully compact forms.

People who live in the lower socioeconomic disadvantaged groups use language primarily for immediate concrete situations. For that reason, they are able to use many partial sentences. The tired father says to the older boy, "My slippers." He means, "Go get my soft shoes." The mother says to the daughter, "The table." She means, "It is time now for you to set the table." Children are making a lot of noise outside. The middle class mother would say, "Now you children know that Mrs. Jones has rheumatic spells every once in a while. She has pains in her shoulders, and at such times she's very unhappy and easily upset. When children are running around making a lot of noise, it makes her even worse. Now children, how would you feel if you were Mrs. Jones? So, then, what must we do, children?" The lower class mother says, "Quiet!" She may be just as kind and just as loving to her children as the middle class mother who has used the greater amount of language.

These less favored people do not often use language to examine the future. To cope with the present is enough of a problem for them. They do not go back to re-examine the past to see what lessons might be learned in the light of the past to foresee consequences of the future. Therefore, they have less occasion to use infinitives, appositives, gerunds, participles, and dependent clauses for amplification, embroidering, and extension of the subject-predicate relationships. They use short, brief sentences or partial sentences. Furthermore, they are not in the habit of expressing subjective emotions and feelings, a very important possibility of language. It is not part of their culture to look at feelings and talk about them extensively. They indicate their feelings visually with shrugs, hands, bodies, eyes, and facial expressions much more than do middle class or upper class persons. And they are not frequently engaged in examining the nuances of ideas, looking at the very delicate possibilities or ramifications of an idea. Their lives are focused on the immediate, the concrete, the practical, the necessary. They use the same grammar, but they do not use the potentials of language, and their vocabulary and usage are different. In my own research,[2] the most important finding is not that disadvantaged children use the same basic grammatical patterns as others. Rather the significant difference is that those who have the greatest control and power over language have the largest repertoire of linguistic skills to extend and embroider and amplify their basic sentence patterns. These understandings provide necessary background to understand what should be done to enable people like the Cajun- or the pidgin-speaking child to use the full potential of language, including the established dialect.

In a sequential program, all disadvantaged children would begin earlier than others with experiences selected by virtue of their necessity for learning concepts and for amplifying the language (dialect) they already use. In preschool and kindergarten these disadvantaged children would have experiences in which they would talk as much as possible, using the living, oral language. The purpose of this talk would be quite clearly to extend the length of the sentences they use. Much of it would occur in what the kindergarten teacher calls "unstructured activity," but I would like the teacher to know *why* she is having it. Children picking up magnets in schools become excited and talk

2. Walter Loban, *The Language of Elementary School Children: A Study of the Use and Control of Language Effectiveness in Communication, and the Relations among Speaking, Reading, Writing, and Listening* (Champaign, Ill.: National Council of Teachers of English, 1963).

a great deal. Children go out to see the baby sheep that have just been born; they talk tremendously! Or a boy says, "If he bes mah frien', ah don't meddle him." This is an "if-then" construction. Wonderful! Don't worry now about usage! Not this early in school.

What we want is to persuade disadvantaged pupils at this early age to talk as much as possible. Through grappling with ideas and the kinds of questions the preschool and kindergarten teacher asks, the child will begin to amplify and embroider in order to foresee consequences, to examine ideas, and to say, "if-then." In fact, the teacher *asks* questions, "What if we did this? Then what?" One teacher took the children to a dairy. At first she asked the usual perception questions, but then she began to maneuver more purposefully. "Mr. Johansen gave each one of us a free glass of milk. If he gave everybody a free glass of milk what would happen?" It is the "why" kind of question that will get the children to talk most fully. This means, of course, that we must educate the teachers, both in service and in preservice, as to the true nature of language. Many teachers still have an understanding of language equivalent to the medical knowledge possessed by a quack doctor. They worry about "may" and "can" and make the small child self-conscious about his indigenous language.

Now we face a critical problem: the children speak a social class dialect. In the kindergarten and in the earliest years of school, the emphasis should be upon the child's using *whatever dialect of the language he already speaks* as the means of thinking and exploring and imagining. Language is also more than a tool of thought. It is a way of expressing emotions and feelings. It is a way of adjusting to other people, of expressing solidarity with the human race. Language has many purposes among which one of the most important, and certainly the most important to the teacher, is the use of language as a means of developing the powers of reason. But it is not the only one. If the child speaks a dialect and says, "Them magnet's pickin' up the nails," we do not need to worry about "them magnet's" at this point. Let him say, "them magnet's." That usage will not interfere with the crucial cognitive processes. If we do not first encourage the child to use his own language in its full range, we may diminish his desire to use language in school. First of all, orally, he must develop and amplify sentences until he is using the full range of his mental and linguistic potential. It is much easier for him to do that in the dialect he already uses. (Do not worry that we intend to let him do this forever in school.) The preschool stage and kindergarten are much too early to press him to use standard dialect. Such teaching only confuses children, causing them to speak much less frequently in school.

However, if children do not soon begin to practice all of the phonemes in the English language, eventually they will not be able to make some of the phonemes as, for instance, Yugoslavs cannot make our "v" or "w" and North Americans have great difficulty with the Spanish "r." Children must practice early. So in primary school, perhaps beginning with the first, second, and third grades (I am using grades only roughly; I am not concerned with grade placement; I would even hope that this could be in a nongraded school) when a child is six, seven, and eight, we should introduce a great many listening experiences which the pupil is to imitate. These would be taped, short little skits repeated twice, once in the dialect with which the child is familiar and once in the standard English. The purpose is to focus his attention upon *differences;* otherwise he will not hear them. They sound to him just as he says them; he must learn they are not exactly the same. One of the major tasks of the linguistically trained elementary school teacher is to focus the child's attention upon the linguistic distinctions presented in these skits, using language of both the established and the nonestablished dialects.

During grades 4, 5, and 6, we should introduce a barrage of language in different dialects, so pupils may become accustomed to the fact that there are many dialects they can imitate. Even small children imitate skillfully; this is why they pick up foreign language so quickly. They should listen to Scotch, Australian, and New Zealand dialects, to pidgin, to Cajun, even to the Beatles. They should sing songs, recite rhymes, and engage in choral speaking in their own dialect and in the established dialect, trying to become flexible with all the many dialects that are possible, always with the idea that one should be able to imitate many different kinds of sounds.

In grades 4, 5, and 6, then, there would be an emphasis upon imitation and upon playing out short skits, drama, and creative dramatics. Drama is thus tremendously important in the theory of this articulated, sequential program. Often the drama would require puppets because children project themselves into puppets very easily. Simple little hand puppets presented on a stage made from cardboard boxes borrowed from the grocery store provide an incentive for children to write their own brief skits. Then they practice them, standing behind the stage. Thus they carry out the puppetry while someone reads the parts. Throughout all this they would be imitating different dialects, but always with an increasing emphasis on the established standard English—one more tongue to imitate in the same way that Scotch or Irish dialects are imitated.

Never at any time throughout this elementary school period would we indicate to the child that there is the slightest thing wrong with his dialect, because we would not, in our own hearts, believe this. We need teachers who know that such dialects are essentially respectable and good, although the teachers realize these children must learn the dialect accepted by convention. There would never be any invidious comparisons, any criticism, at the preschool and primary school stage of the child's education.

However, before it is too late, teachers should begin to work on some of the more crucial items of usage by means of oral training. This would involve emphasis on usage *through the ear*. If "Him a good dog" exemplifies a crucial usage, the teacher in about grade 4 begins to say, "He is a good dog," and drills orally on case of pronouns—but does *not* employ grammatical analysis. Sometimes the teacher reads ten sentences aloud, explaining first which is standard dialect and which is not. The children listen to hear if the teacher expresses the usage in the established dialect. Often the pupils number from one to ten on a sheet and put a "plus" down if the teacher says an expression appropriately and a "zero" if the expression is not standard dialect. "See if the teacher can get every one in

standard!" "I will try." Then I read: "(1) *He is a good dog.*
(2) *She is my friend.* (3) *Him a happy fellow.*" and so forth
up to 10 and the pupils listen to hear if I can handle the dialect
(that is, standard dialect) correctly. But never would I indicate
that there is anything bad about saying, "Him a good dog," or
any other valid dialectal expression.

But the time comes when we face these pupils with the facts
of social distinctions, and that time, to my way of thinking, is
usually grade 5, 6, or 7. Teachers differ on the age for introducing this idea, but I see no point in telling children this
earlier. Before they can really see the value of learning standard
English, pupils need to understand the social consequences the
world will exact of them if they cannot handle the established
dialect. Grade 5, 6, or 7, therefore, would be the point at which
I would select most carefully the teachers who had no snobbish
attitudes about language, the scholar-linguist-humanists whom
I could most safely entrust with the important task of explaining the sociological truth to these children. "Although the language your father uses is a perfectly good language and we have
used it in this class, it is not the only way of speaking English.
Have you ever noticed that the textbooks are printed in only
one kind of dialect?" the teacher would say. "The day we went
down to visit the juvenile court, the judges and lawyers all
talked that standard language. When we had that speaker in
assembly the other day and she told us about her work as a
judge in the courts, even though she belongs to our same ethnic
and racial group, she was using the same kind of standard English dialect you hear television announcers use. Now, here is
something you need to know. Unless you can use that standard
dialect as well as the one you speak, you will not be able to get
certain kinds of jobs; that is the way the world is. Many business and professional people and many people who hire teachers
and architects and clerks and stenographers just will not hire
people who do not speak standard. And so, we must begin to
handle this special standard dialect much better than we have
been able to so far. We'll have to begin to work on it much
more." Then from grades 6 through 12 I would try to eliminate
as far as possible the use of social class dialect *in school.* The

aim in school during these secondary years would be to help young people acquire this very important kind of dialect, this second language they need.

In acquiring the standard dialect, pupils must continue to amplify, embroider, and extend sentences. Thus, they should begin in grades 4, 5, and 6 a special kinesthetic method of sentence study. The teacher gives some of the children individual words printed on cards. These pupils come up to the front of the room where they arrange and rearrange themselves, determining how many possible ways they can make sentences with the words they are carrying. Then those not in front of the room practice saying the sentences aloud, using intonation patterns: Where do you drop the voice? Where do you pause? What words should we stress? Teachers may have other children waiting with extra cards, ready to come up in front to extend the sentences, to see how long they can make them, and then again how short they can make a sentence and still make sense: "What's wrong when we just have, *The great white horse.* . . . ? What's wrong with that? What do we have to do? More words, more words! What kind of words? All right—add them!" After they have done this, the next step is to provide smaller cards for seatwork; everybody rearranges his cards and work out different solutions and problems as a game. Next the pupils write compositions and with the opaque projector or some other projector, the teacher throws on the wall some of the papers for discussion. At other times a group of children may suggest better sentences as they work with each other's papers. Always, the teacher relates the study to the spoken language, to oral intonation, to pause, juncture, and all verbal signalling. From grade 7 on the activity would be in the established dialect, but in the early years we would accept "Him a good dog." We would be interested in seeing if the child could say, "Him a good dog *but with three fleas.*" We would be interested in amplification.

In addition to these strategies there should be much oral reading—by the teacher, through tapes and records and television, and by the pupils. We should restore the oral tradition to English instruction. In grades 7 through 12, I would use drill tapes and language laboratories in order to accomplish ear training that would alternate with dramatics, literature, discussion, and writing. The tapes would focus on usage, pronunciation, vocabulary, and idiom. Through the ear all of us learned to speak before we came to school. Only through the ear will any of us ever change our usage or pronunciation.

Today these disadvantaged people are demanding the rights and privileges other people have, and it is just and right that they should have them. If they are not belligerent and do not demand them, there is indeed something wrong about them. Their craven acquiescence would worry me much more than any justified belligerence. This change in our society has to happen if our society is to be healthy.

". . . time is against the disadvantaged child. . . . The disadvantaged four-year-old, happily shoveling sand at a sand table, gives the impression that he will be four years old forever. But for the teacher to act as if this were true is disastrous. She should be constantly aware that the first grade is hurtling toward the child like an express train, and that the child's fate may well depend on what she as a teacher is able to do and how quickly."

ACADEMIC INSTRUCTION
AND PRESCHOOL CHILDREN*

Carl Bereiter

Bereiter's view of the way to compensate for disadvantaged children's limitations in language, was presented at the same conference as that of the preceding author. Bereiter sees the cumulative nature of lower-class children's difficulties with the logical and abstract functions of language as requiring extreme measures. Where Loban recommends following the child's normal developmental progress in language

* Carl Bereiter, "Academic Instruction and Preschool Children," *Language Programs for the Disadvantaged: Report of the NCTE Task Force on Teaching English to the Disadvantaged,* © 1965 by the National Council of Teachers of English, pp. 195–205. Reprinted with the permission of the National Council of Teachers of English and Carl Bereiter.

but providing numerous and varied experiences to heighten language activities, Bereiter proposes a much narrower, rigidly controlled and intensive training in specific language patterns basic to logical thought and expression. Those who approve Loban's analysis and program are likely to consider Bereiter's proposal inhumane; Bereiter's advocates would score Loban's recommendations as time-wasting and irresponsibly romantic. It should be noted, however, that Bereiter's four-year-old subjects are younger and apparently more severely deprived than the elementary children in Loban's lower-class category.

Which of these views seems to you to present more persuasive evidence and argument? Why? What do you think might be the effects of eliminating from a preschool program, as Bereiter suggests, arts and crafts, dramatic play, block play, and the like? Which of these two approaches are now more common in preschool programs? For which type of program does your own program in teacher education prepare you?

IT IS A TRUISM of academic life that a scholar will magnify the importance of whatever he devotes his life to studying. It is not surprising, then, that a person studying the feet comes to believe that the feet are the most important part of the body. I therefore find it somewhat incongruous to be telling a group of people whose primary interest is in language that they do not seem to appreciate its full importance, but this is the distinct impression I have received both from the reports delivered and from the conversation at this meeting. There seem to be two reasons for this unusual state of affairs. One is a basic lack of realization of the gravity of the whole problem of cultural disadvantage, and the other is a somewhat limited conception of the language problems of disadvantaged children.

We have heard it said at this conference that disadvantaged children are not culturally deprived, but only culturally different, and that there are intelligent and capable children in every disadvantaged group. Charitable as these comments may be, they nevertheless serve to divert our attention from the fundamental problems. Let me summarize for you several facts which in my opinion no reasonable educator, whatever his particular interest may be in disadvantaged children, can in good conscience ignore:

1. By the time they are five years old, disadvantaged children of almost every kind are typically one to two years retarded in language development. This is supported by virtually any index of language development one cares to look at.

2. Half a century of studies on the prediction of school success clearly establishes that verbal abilities are the best single predictors of achievement in a wide variety of school subjects. Thus the child who enters school markedly behind in the development of verbal abilities enters with a severe handicap.

3. School failure is the expected rather than the occasional fate of disadvantaged children. From the evidence I have seen, half the children in the many low income area schools repeat one or more grades during elementary school, though this fact is sometimes hidden behind administrative labels for special classes. This proportion of failure does not include the children

designated as mentally retarded and assigned to special classes. Lower class areas produce at least twice the average number of children labeled mentally retarded as middle and upper class areas. We are all familiar with the high dropout rate among lower class children and with the fact that most of these children are hopelessly behind in school when they drop out. What is less commonly known is the miserable level of attainment that characterizes even those disadvantaged children who remain in school. I do not have solid data on this point, but the estimate given me by people who have studied the matter closely is that in the most disadvantaged segments of our society, such as the southern Negroes, the average terminal level of achievement reached by high school graduates is around seventh grade. The fact that an occasional disadvantaged child goes on to achieve high academic excellence should not blind us to the fact that all the odds are against it. Recent statistics on high school seniors reaching the final round of the National Merit Scholarship screening process indicate that a child from a prosperous family has from four to thirty times the chance that a child from a poor family does, depending on the state. This is one among many possible indexes of the extent to which disadvantaged children, if not deprived of the culture content necessary to the formal educational process, are at least deprived of the opportunities which educational attainment can provide in this country.

4. If a child who starts out behind is to catch up, he has to progress at a faster than normal rate. This is not an empirical fact but a logical one. It follows, therefore, that any educational program that claims to be helping children overcome their environmental handicaps must be able to show not just a normal rate of progress but a superior rate. I have the impression from the reports of Task Force members that little attention was given to rate of progress at all, and that in many cases a program that looked good in other respects may have been producing progress at a slower rate than is normal for children of the age involved.

5. It is too much to expect that programs can be accelerated above the normal level in all areas of development at once. If this is true, it follows that educational programs for disad-

vantaged children must be selective in their goals, striving for maximum progress in those things that are judged to be most crucial for later success in school. It is therefore necessary, in evaluating an educational program, to look not only at the rate of progress but at its content and to ask whether five minutes devoted to one kind of learning might not better have been devoted to some other kind.

If these facts are taken to heart, they give the whole problem of education for disadvantaged children a tremendous urgency. One is forced to recognize that time is against the disadvantaged child, and one becomes impatient with any teacher who wastes that precious time. The disadvantaged four-year-old, happily shoveling sand at a sand table, gives the impression that he will be four years old forever. But for the teacher to act as if this were true is disastrous. She should be constantly aware that the first grade is hurtling toward that child like an express train, and that the child's fate may well depend on what she as a teacher is able to do and how quickly.

The Task Force members have reported observing enthusiasm, optimism, and dedication among the teachers of disadvantaged children, but none of this sense of urgency. I must report that I find it lacking in this group as well. One reason, in addition to a natural tendency to look on the bright side, may be that you have selected as your major concern the problem of teaching a standard English dialect to children whose native dialect is of some other sort. Though this is one of the problems of disadvantaged children that deserves attention, it is atypical in that no great urgency attends it. Some time during his schooling the child should master the standard English dialect, but it does not much matter when, and thus nothing is wrong with a gradual, drawn-out approach to teaching it. This is not true of the more fundamental language skills because these are instrumental to the whole process of education. Reading provides the clearest example of this point. If reading were only of value once the child gets out into the world, it would not matter if he did not learn to read until his last year of school. But because reading is instrumental to school learning, because progress in most other academic areas is held down to the rate at which children progress in reading, it is important that the child learn to read as early as possible in his school career. The child who falls behind in reading is held back in all other areas.

In the same way, oral language may be conceived of as an instrument of learning and thinking, and it is from this point of view that the problem of retarded language development in disadvantaged children becomes an urgent one, requiring the quickest and most powerful remedies.

The paper that I have been circulating by Siegfried Engelmann is an attempt to identify those specific weaknesses in the language of preschool disadvantaged children that seem on logical grounds to be crucial from the point of view of academic learning.[1] On the basis of this kind of analysis we have constructed a preschool program that tries, through direct and intensive teaching, to remedy these lacks. We have not been very much concerned with many of those aspects of language which serve mainly social or expressive purposes—standard vocabulary, idiomatic expressions, intonation, niceties of agreement and the like. It has not bothered us so much that a child may not know the word *sheep* as that he does not know the word *not,* for while in the former case a child might encounter an occasional difficulty, in the latter case he is deprived of one of the most powerful logical tools our language provides—a tool, moreover, which it is assumed in school work that a child possesses from the very beginning. In our program, we have been less concerned with the child's lack of empirical knowledge than with his lack of ability to derive knowledge from statements. It seems to us far less serious that a child might not know that milk comes from cows than that he might not be able to tell you where milk came from after he had been told.

The children we have worked with have for the most part been four-year-old Negro children from the most disadvantaged stratum of the lowest income urban Negro group in the state of Illinois. I can perhaps accomplish two things at once by listing for you some of the specific performance goals of the lan-

---

1. S. E. Englemann, *Cultural Deprivation—Description and Remedy* (Urbana, Ill.: University of Illinois Institute for Research on Exceptional Children). Mimeographed.

guage program we employed. This list will serve first of all to indicate the nature and severity of these children's language handicaps, for I can state that not one child of the fifteen we worked with was able initially to meet a single one of these criteria. The list will also serve as one indication of the effectiveness of the program, for after eight months of instruction, all but one of the children were able to meet all of criteria, the one exception being a definitely retarded child who has not come close to any of the goals. The goals are as follows:

1. Ability to use both affirmative and "not" statements in reply to the question, "What is this?": "This is a ball. This is not a book."

2. Ability to handle polar opposites ("If it is not ————, it must be ————.") for at least four concept pairs: big-little, up-down, long-short, fat-skinny.

3. Ability to use the following prepositions correctly in statements describing arrangements of objects: *on, in, under, over, between*. Example: "Where is the pencil?" "The pencil is under the book."

4. Ability to name positive and negative instances for at least four classes, such as tools, weapons, pieces of furniture, wild animals, farm animals, and vehicles. Example: "Tell me something that is a weapon." "A gun is a weapon." "Tell me something that is not a weapon." "A cow is not a weapon."

5. Ability to perform simple "if-then" deductions. Example: The child is presented a diagram containing big squares and little squares. All the big squares are red, but the little squares are of various other colors. "If the square is big, what do you know about it?" "It's red." (This use of *if* should not be confused with the antecedent-consequent use that appears in such expressions as, "If you do that again, I'm going to hit you," and which the child may already be able to understand.)

6. Ability to use "not" in deductions: "If the square is little, what else can you say about it?" "It is not red."

7. Ability to use *or* in simple deductions: "If the square is little, then it is not red. What else can you say about it?" "It's blue or yellow."

This list, of course, is not exhaustive. Many of the children have gone far beyond these goals. But they have proved to be focal points of difficulty and progress in many different kinds of learning of these basic tools. Although I cannot elaborate on the matter here, it should not be difficult to see how important these language operations are for understanding concepts of all kinds and for logical thinking and problem solving. If it seems premature to worry about logic at the preschool level, one has only to consider that middle class children are typically able to handle all of these operations at this age and that a great deal of what they learn from their parents and teachers and even from each other is made possible because of this. Disadvantaged children would learn them in time also, but the longer it is delayed the more retarded would be their whole conceptual development.

In teaching these logical statement patterns we have placed strong emphasis on learning to produce them and not merely respond to them. We have made continual use of pattern drills not unlike those used in the teaching of foreign languages to college students. Initially the children could not even repeat statements of the kind illustrated, let alone produce ones appropriate to the situation. But the drills have been used to teach new language operations rather than to replace old patterns, and thus we have avoided the conflicts that arise when children have already learned to express the same thoughts in nonstandard ways. This has also made motivation easier, because the children are not merely learning a way of expressing themselves that is more acceptable to the teacher but are acquiring tools that enable them to do things intellectually that they had not been able to do before.

In keeping with the principle enunciated previously, we have been highly selective as to what went into the program in order to produce maximum learning in the areas chosen as most important. A great many of what we would acknowledge to be desirable preschool experiences have been minimized or left out altogether—such things as arts and crafts, group play, dramatic play, block play, and so on. Singing has been included, but with songs specially composed to supplement the instructional program. What has knowingly been left out has been left out for one or both of two reasons: because it seemed less important than what took its place or because it seemed that out-of-class experience adequately made up for the lack. (Unlike some of our more relativistic colleagues we do not regard the disadvantaged child's home environment as a void.) We cannot claim infallibility, however, and so we always welcome observations on the important things that have been left out of our program. What we do insist, however, is that some things must be left out if an above-average rate of progress is to be maintained. Thus, any suggested addition must be justified as worthy of replacing something already in the program—unless, as is sometimes possible, additions can be made without additional use of time.

It may seem to you that the approach we are taking to language places it within the realm of logic or psychology and outside the range of interests of English and language arts teachers. To this I can only say that if English and language arts teachers do not assume the responsibility for teaching disadvantaged children the cognitive uses of language, I don't know who will. Except for a few experimental projects such as ours, there are no logicians or cognitive psychologists in the schools, but there are plenty of teachers who are supposed to be concerned with teaching language. It seems to me inexcusable that they should decline an interest in one of language's most important functions. If it is language as an instrument of social communication that separates man from apes, it is language as a tool of thought that separates civilized men from barbarians. It is this latter use of language which, if I read my history correctly, was the legacy of ancient Greece. If the term "cultural deprivation" has any legitimate meaning, then it means to me that two thousand years later millions of people in our society have yet to receive their full share of this legacy.

DISCUSSION

Conference participants discussed the extent to which generalizations for other situations could be derived exclusively from the preschool experiment which Mr. Bereiter is directing at the University of Illinois. Although the apparent increases in intelligence as indicated on tests were admittedly impressive, Task Force members thought them predictable because of the heavy emphasis placed in such tests on verbal symbolism and the corresponding emphasis on verbal learning in Mr. Bereiter's program. The concentration throughout the experimentation on specific behaviors related to success in school offers valuable suggestions for the limited problem of his project. Many conferees, however, felt that larger generalizations about the linguistic behavior of boys and girls in other environments could not be based on such data without additional supporting evidence. For example, conversations of children in informal discussion might be compared with their language behavior in more structured situations.

Task Force members objected to Mr. Bereiter's assumption that they failed to recognize the urgency of the educational problems facing the disadvantaged. They pointed to their willingness to interrupt spring and summer plans to join the Task Force. The discussion indicated that the comments on urgency were directed less at the attitudes of Task Force members to the total problem than at the reluctance of many to sense the urgent need to accelerate crucial learning in programs for the disadvantaged.

Task Force members discussed the language spoken by the parents of disadvantaged children. Mr. Bereiter said that the parents of his children often use better language than their children are able to absorb. Such a family condition may or may not be characteristic of other disadvantaged children, but it suggests the importance to educators and social workers of finding ways to help parents help their own children.

Discussants were interested in the discovery that the children whom Mr. Bereiter studied do not seem in all ways to reveal the same language tendencies as do children of similar ages in other studies. Walter Loban suggested that linguistic deprivation takes many forms, that some children may be disadvantaged in dialect, some in vocabulary, others in cognitive processes and logic. He also urged that Mr. Bereiter's program be linked to experience designed to serve as a base for using language for thinking effectively and powerfully. Mr. Bereiter's experiments offer valuable insights to elementary teachers who mean to give direction to language. Naturally, teachers, unlike experimenters, will wish to integrate Mr. Bereiter's performance goals with the larger global elements of elementary curriculum. Some participants suggested that normative data, systematically collected, were needed to indicate the actual language behavior of the children before firm generalizations could be advanced.

Despite reservations about the applicability of some of the findings and methods of Mr. Bereiter's work to the normal preschool situation for disadvantaged children, conferees saw much value in specific experiments of this kind assisting educators to identify characteristics of disadvantaged children and approaches which provide remediation critical to success in school. The conferees felt that such projects seem less to provide model programs for emulation than ways of advancing general knowledge about the characteristics of disadvantaged learners of preschool age.

"A methodology is a compassionate human being in action. A curriculum is the interaction of student needs and teacher strengths."

CONFLICT AND REFORM*

Douglas Pedersen

The conviction that the alienation of economically and educationally disadvantaged students can only be reconstituted into motivation to learn and belief in self through direct and unconventional efforts to reach the student on a completely personal level is the thesis of the following selection. Douglas Pedersen's detailed description of his experiences conducting an art studio class for a group of underprivileged high-school boys in a summer Upward Bound program on a college campus is of particular interest because it details the reactions of several individual students. His approach represents an extreme example of open planning, of intentionally unstructured "curriculum." "Aside from an initiating exercise to help the students get started painting there were no lesson plans, no assignments, no specified goals." Pedersen, viewing the failure of these students as

* Excerpts from Douglas Pedersen, "Conflict and Reform," from *The Disadvantaged Student: A Conflict of Cultures in the School*, pp. 6–8 (pamphlet, 1966), by Douglas Pedersen. Reprinted by permission of the author.

stemming more from the unresponsive and hence
stultifying effects of the school rather than from students' "deficits," designed a learning environment as
different as possible from the traditional school.

> *What did Pedersen's students learn? The teaching
> approach was a highly unconventional one; did the
> students' behavior change in the direction of more
> or less conventional norms? Do you think this ap-
> proach could be applied in other subjects? Pedersen
> made a point of engaging professional artists for
> this program; how might the attitudes of these
> professionals toward their students differ from the
> attitudes of most teachers?*

MUCH, AND in some cases all, of the formal school experience for the alienated student has been humiliating, frustrating and unpleasant—in short, painful. Because of this the student is conditioned, in a behavioral sense, to respond negatively to the conditions of school. To protect himself the student withdraws, seals himself off from further injury. In the vernacular he "tunes-out." Therefore, *rapprochement* can only happen if this negative response is alleviated.

Hence, all formal practices—the way in which schools and teachers present their subject matter and themselves to the students—must be examined for their effect on a learning environment that is viewed negatively by the student. This argues for many changes in and some elimination of elements of formal school behavior.

To break through the wall of protection each alienated student has erected (in the vernacular, "to turn him on") the school must involve the student in the learning process; i.e., the school must overcome student passivity. Instead of allowing the alienated student to be a spectator of the educational task, the school must find a way to entice him to *participate* actively and fully in the learning process. An existential description for this: *rapprochement* is a function of *engagement*.

Engagement, involvement, results in part from recognition. The school must convince each alienated student that it sees him as a separate and special person, that his individuality counts and will be acknowledged.

Knowing—in the fullest sense of discovering and believing and acting responsibly with respect to what is known—can never result solely from intellective processes, but must include neural, emotional responses.

Extreme verbalization—a curriculum and methodology that depend on written and spoken words only—can merely approximate experience, and often it can falsify experience. Such negation of actuality, of what is, is an affront to the perceptions, many of them subliminal, of the alienated student.

Therefore, the curriculum and methodology must include experiential components, must provide for inductive and undirected discovery.

As long as the student is merely confronted with an unfamiliar object or idea (story, poem, painting, equation, formula, concept, judgment, etc.) he is an observer, a spectator, an outsider. Not until he tries to make, shape, conceive-of, formulate or create an object or idea is he truly and fully a participant. Therefore, confronting the alienated student with an unknown object or idea can only reinforce his sense of alienation and inadequacy. And the more incomprehensible or foreign the object or idea, the greater the reinforcement.

Since feelings of alienation and inadequacy are basic attitudes to overcome in establishing *rapprochement* initial learning exercises should concentrate on the production by students of their own ideas and objects.

On the other hand, if the teacher presents himself and his subject matter in such a way as to enable the alienated student to interpret what the teacher's desires are (i.e., as long as the student can perceive the teacher's goals) then the student can respond in purely cerebral, totally disengaged fashion. The student can assimilate enough information to "get by" without participating, without becoming involved—*sans engagement.*

Uninvolved response is *fake.* Being permitted to "fake it" enables the alienated student to avoid knowing, believing. If the student is never made to confront himself, so that in this confrontation he begins to understand, accept and become responsible for himself, the student will not find realization in the educational process or personal fulfillment through intellectual development and growth. He will never become fully productive with respect to his potentiality for productivity.

Production—the externalized, objectified, tangible and communicable form of an idea, attitude, feeling, percept, concept, etc., that is within the capacity of the student to originate at any given time—is what must inform the school of each student's strength and weakness, interest and need. Only with this kind of information can the school truly relate to and be relevant for the student. This information must form the basis for curriculum and methodology reform.

Increasingly sophisticated production must be the aim of education. Too frequently *faking* is the only result. By predetermining and imposing external goals and by evaluating students by their ability to approximate them, schools deny students the possibility of realizing and expressing their own uniqueness. Conformity of this kind contradicts the greater meaning of education.

Grades reinforce feelings of alienation and inadequacy. Grades are based usually on tests and tests place a premium on speed and memory. The alienated student who frequently feels he is going nowhere is not habituated to hurry, nor is the mind of the alienated student often habituated to memory, for this student has lived a life he would rather forget.

In the classroom the teacher is absolute authority. Powerless in such circumstances the student easily develops hostile attitudes. These attitudes prevent positive, healthy interaction of student and teacher.

Two existential addenda for the learning situation: *A methodology is a compassionate human being in action. A curriculum is the interaction of student needs and teacher strengths.*

The class. While the use of studio art as an educational force is not new, it does have particular potency with respect to the alienated student. Painting demands involvement and can be undertaken without any restrictions or without requiring any former experience. The therapeutic effects of painting are well known, but the essence of this approach to the alienated student lies in its tremendous *rapprochement* potential.

As a non-verbal language capable of expressing psychic, emotional and intellectual attitudes, painting is a way of communicating with the individual despite repression, suspicion and doubt, and is a way of off-setting the nearly total verbal emphasis of the school curriculum—an emphasis that unjustly restricts the achievement of the alienated student.

This cycle of restricted achievement with its resulting feelings of inadequacy and loss of aspiration can be broken rapidly with a success in art, for the act of painting, in addition to being rewarding in itself, leads to immediate results that are gratifying to the student and capable of being approved of by the teacher. Each subsequent production reinforces the positive accomplishments of the student, and thus impels him forward with greater confidence toward more sophisticated achievement. He learns to trust the learning environment by feeling its approval and experiencing the immediacy of its rewards. As confidence grows with each production, *rapprochement* becomes more firmly established and in short time the student can be approached in a more formal way and the dialogue of the school can begin.

The following is a generalized report of a particular art studio program designed to satisfy the needs of the alienated student as previously discussed.

In addition to the abiding concern to accommodate the alienated student, the painting studio emphasized several aesthetic principles that are common to many forms of production, not just visual ones, and therefore the studio may be said to have had an intrinsically valuable intellectual content. Students were encouraged to:

organize pictorial components with respect to harmony, balance, unity, vitality and effectiveness of expression;
question their initial perceptions and try to see directly, to see things as they are and not as they had learned, consciously or unconsciously, to interpret them;
analyze objects and ideas for their formal as well as ideational content, and for their consonance to things as they are and to feelings that are genuine.

Each scheduled session of the painting studio was two hours long. However, students could come earlier if they cared to and stay longer if they desired. Some did. Also, the studio was open evenings and weekends and was used at those unscheduled times.

In selecting the studio site great care was taken to find the largest space available and to find a space that could be used and even physically abused. If painting is engaged in with spontaneity, vigor and true breadth of expression, large spaces for large canvases and ample elbow room are necessary, and paint quite inevitably splashes on floors and walls. The robust style of the student requires this physical freedom. Physical limitations reinforce frustrations, while their absence alleviates them.

All media and all kinds of painting surfaces were available in the studio. Students were allowed to experiment freely, to select at random the sizes, shapes and surfaces and particular media they wished to use. Creation presupposes destruction and therefore waste. No attention was given to legitimate waste and students were encouraged to abandon obvious errors.

Instructors in the painting studio were selected for their commitment to painting as professionals, as much as for their experience as teachers. This was a fundamental choice developing from a desire to encourage student production and to minimize routine approaches to the practice of art. Innovation, a creative approach to both students and the act of painting, and a progressive attitude about contemporary art, confidence as artists based on continuing production of paintings, and an extremely flexible attitude with respect to student behavior and student achievement were considered valuable instructorial assets.

Selection of instructors by these criteria led to a high degree of working compatibility in the studio. No competition whatsoever existed between instructors, and each possessed complementary skills that proved invaluable in handling the numerous problems presented by a group of students quite varied in interest, skill, experience and attitude.

The instructors painted throughout the duration of the program, and did so for several purposes. They wanted to demonstrate that hard and sustained work was involved in productivity. They wanted students to observe what professional painters in action, in fact, do. And they painted in a variety of styles so that students would have models to compensate for any lack of awareness of the variety of paintings and the various styles possible. They used the same materials as the students, for obvious reasons.

The program in the painting studio was quite simple and direct. Aside from an initiating exercise to help the students get started painting there were no lesson plans, no assignments, no specified goals.

The initiating exercise was conceived to help students through the frequently self-conscious period during which they are reluctant to paint for the simple reason that they do not want to display their inadequacy, lack of skill and experience and possible ignorance to the other students. The initiating exercise, then, was designed to move the students into an involvement with the materials of painting before they could experience embarrassment and other inhibitions.

The group was divided into teams of five students each. The teams were given a common theme to paint, *Man's Struggle for Freedom*. Each team was furnished with a 4′ x 8′ Masonite panel and reinforcing materials, and the group was subtly challenged with the fact that when they finished their panels they would be given an opportunity to display them publicly.

Although each team was told that they should try to discuss their theme and work-up sketches prior to painting, they were started at work with what was essentially an exercise in carpentry. They reinforced the edges of their Masonite panels with strips of lumber, attached plywood triangles at the corners, and sized the panels with white paint. This meant that each team had an investment of labor in their panel, and to protect that investment they had to go ahead and complete the painting. Also, they gained a feeling for each other as a team before they faced the exigencies and initial frustrations of painting as one. While the panels were drying the teams worked on sketches, all of which were essentially approved of, since the execution would force the necessary alterations that would ultimately transform initial concepts into actual paintings.

At this time the social studies teachers were invited into the studio to probe the students' attitudes about their personal involvement in the theme. Also, at this time, the resources of the community were exploited thoroughly to broaden as quickly as possible each student's experience of art. The group was taken to the Metropolitan Museum of Art to see an exhibition of contemporary American painting. No attempt was made to lecture or otherwise prepare in advance their perceptions. The students were instructed to look at what other painters had produced in terms of size, style, imagery, etc. The group was given complete freedom to explore the exhibit and other areas of the museum.

Several days later the students were given two brief slide demonstrations, one dealing with expression of social themes in art and the other with a short history of the European backgrounds of modern American painting.

The local print club was asked to arrange a modest exhibit of paintings and sculpture by artists throughout the entire range of art history who had dealt in one way or another with the theme of man's struggle for freedom.

By this time, the teams were involved with their murals and the instructors spent all of their time during scheduled meetings of the painting studio moving from group to group, need to need, probing, questioning, and generally buoying spirits and encouraging efforts.

Naturally, some students defected from their teams and started working on personal solutions to the given theme, or else on paintings dealing with other matters. No effort was made to force a student to remain with his team if he chose not to. The only requirement was that each student become somehow productively engaged in the act of painting, and the only disciplinary instruction was that no student could interfere with another's involvement.

The following list of changes in student behavior as observed in the studio indicates a change in the attitude of the students toward the painting program, and this change in attitude seemed entirely consistent with the increasing productivity in the studio and compatible with the needs of a more general learning situation.

Students arrived for the painting session wearing clean, well-pressed clothing. This in itself presented a serious obstacle to involvement. At this point, the instructors were aware that students had no working garments. They had come dressed for "college." The instructors took off their shirts at that point and worked that way the rest of the summer. At first students were reluctant to take off their shirts to protect them from paint, but by the end of the program many students did. An added benefit from this was that it removed one more reminder of the usual school climate. And this freedom within responsibility, reflected in many student actions, indicated their growing trust and ease.

This freedom and naturalness was further reflected in the speech and conduct of the students. Several students made tentative use of the instructors' first names. Conversation grew open and frank as trust and mutual respect was attained. There was joking and fun in addition to serious effort.

Initially, there was a great deal of prodding and cajoling necessary to get students started painting at the beginning of each studio session. Also, the general habit was to arrive a few minutes late and leave a few minutes early. As involvement grew more sustained and productivity increased students arrived early and left late. They assumed responsibility for their materials and became self-starting.

Students availed themselves of the studio facilities at many unscheduled hours.

After the exhibition of paintings was hung, the students began to congregate in the exhibit area. They gathered there before and after meals, while previously it had been an uninhabited space. Students were frequently observed looking at the paintings, not just their own. They were interested in and proud of their own productivity and that of the class.

Several students questioned the instructors about career possibilities in art.

The noise level in the studio remained about the same, but the source of noise changed from disparate fooling around to excited involvement. Conduct in the studio was increasingly more disciplined, but the source of discipline was in each student and his involvement, not external.

The studio was left cleaner, again the result of interest focused on productive activity.

The individual. The following anecdotal material is intended to illustrate the varieties of individual student behavior and responses to the art studio.

A's attention span was apparently five or six minutes. After that duration, he would lay down his brush and smoke, seeking conversation with whomever was nearby. Failing to become involved, he would move through the studio, and if he could not divert a fellow student's energies legitimately he would resort to splashing paint or scribbling on another's painting. *A* depended for his own sense of being on the attention of others, even if that meant angering them. This was his game, and once he involved a teacher in playing it with him. The teacher had accused him, once too often, of annoying another student. The conversation ended in the student's turning angrily away. Later the instructor carefully explained to him why he could not be allowed to divert productively-involved students. After this he was asked to do slight favors for the instructor from time to time, and slowly developed a kind of confidence and trust. Eventually he responded to the production around him and started to design a symbolic painting, the execution of which depended upon skill at controlling the brush. One instructor aided him in the completion of the painting and both praised his concept. Each instructor had a lengthy discussion with him about its meaning and origin. *A* was observed at the exhibition pointing out his painting to his parents. His requirements led the instructor to coin the phrase "tough-loving-care."

B was a sleeper, in the literal sense. In his own words, "I didn't like art, now I have a different opinion." It was probably for this reason that when he entered the studio he invariably sat down and frequently went to sleep. The teachers interpreted this as an act of defiance. *B* wore a moustache and his face usually held that subtly challenging, indifferent, nearly implacable expression characteristic of "center-city" coolness. *B* was allowed to sleep. Once his team got started he participated, but only desultorily. At one juncture in the execution of their mural when the painting seemed to lack any zip *B* was asked if he didn't think a lively color would improve it. He responded by mixing a bright purple. This was immediately praised and he was told about several famous artists who had founded reputations as colorists. After this *B* arrived promptly and stayed beyond the scheduled two hours. He assumed a major share of the responsibility for developing the largest (17' x 8') painting and *B's* purple became prominent in the studio.

Several times he was asked to demonstrate how it was mixed. These are *B's* own words at the end of the program, "I like mixing paint to form different colors . . . here you do what you want. You don't get any marks or a report card."

C was a shy, muscular bright young man, but constricted. He couldn't seem to "cut loose." He and his teammates doggedly pursued the end of their mural, and *C* carried the major share of the burden of seeing it through. It was touch and go all the way and the instructors never knew if the project would be abandoned or not. Each false start was painstakingly approved of but critically examined so as to avert the certain disaster the team invariably seemed headed for. Finally *C's* team started moving toward a resolution and with persistence completed the job. After that *C* was willing to try something else. One instructor set up two canvases side by side and both *C* and the instructor painted on one of them. Efforts were made to unfreeze or unlock his tight, rigid manipulation of the brush and pigment. One instructor demonstrated for him the Pollock technique of throwing rather than brushing paint. This was a further step in the unlocking process. The painting turned out successfully, displaying a remarkable freedom and verve. In commenting about this painting at the exhibit, *C* told the instructor that he never thought he would do anything like that, but that he liked it very much. In a written statement he said, "The art program has taught me that being an artist does not mean being a Michaelangelo. You can draw fairly well with just large areas of color. You are encouraged to draw because you won't be punished for not being greater."

D was just the kind of student who needed the fullest realization of the goals set for the painting studio, but he opted out at the first chance. He was therefore assigned "back" to the studio to work. (Each student in the program was given a chance to hold a job one hour every day to earn spending money.) His employer sent him to the studio to paint a picture to decorate the administrative office. While *D* had fled from this new learning experience in painting it did not occur to him to question painting as a job. He produced several sketches of an abstract design, was allowed to pick out his own painting surface, given tubes of paint and left pretty much alone. The instructor passed by his easel once or twice an hour to comment on how good it seemed to be going. *D* worked diligently, set

up and cleaned up his painting station each day and progressed slowly but surely to the achievement of producing a
painting. On completion he attached hooks and eyes to it
and carried it off to his employer. Several days later he was
asked if his painting could be borrowed for the exhibit. For
the first time visible traces of a smile passed into that usually
urgent and somewhat sad face.

E drifted through the first days in the studio, his participation
in the team mural neither assertive nor sustained. About two-
thirds of the way along, however, he entered the studio one
day, picked up a large painting surface, found an easel and
without conversation, questions or flourish began developing
an intricate and challenging design. He worked devotedly on
this painting, and near the end, as the time for the exhibit
approached, appeared at odd hours in the studio to continue
his work. Although he completed his painting after the exhibit
was hung, a space was found for it and it was hung up while
still wet. What forces were at work here will probably never
be completely known. It is safe to assume that E developed a
growing sense of security in the studio environment and a
desire to produce, as so many of his peers were doing. He was,
in other words, carried along and stimulated by the momentum
and climate of the painting studio. It is no doubt difficult to
maintain self-respect and a non-productive stance in an environment where energies are directed toward production and
where the tangible rewards of such effort are continually being
realized. E's painting was unique in form and color and disclosed a precise and determined intellect quite like his personality.

F was the surprise success of the painting studio. His emerg-
ence as a confident and competent artist was remarkable. A
thoughtful, silent student, F can be characterized as one who
works with extreme concentration, true simplicity, directly and
with quiet authority. Prior to the summer he had taken one
course in commercial art.

At the outset of the program he and his team experienced the
greatest difficulty in starting their mural in any meaningful
way. After several blind efforts to get going, their frustrations
mounted to a height that all but immobilized them. At this
time F broke away and started a sketch. The instructor sug-

gested that he try painting this sketch and he did so immediately, finishing the painting in one sitting. With this success under his belt he returned to his team and started them on the mural again, improvising a variation of his first painting for its imagery. The result was outstanding. Their work as a team progressed smoothly after that, they came earlier and stayed later than the scheduled time, their interest mounting as their efforts payed off. Frequently they could be seen painting as a group, three of them absolutely concentrating as individuals but their efforts flowing harmoniously. Division of labor according to skill took place, as it did in most other teams. After their mural was finished the entire team, joined by six others from the group started a gigantic 17' x 8' mural. At one point the instructor counted nine students absorbed in this project, the ones who could draw, drawing, the ones who could color, coloring and not once were there instances of competition or quarreling about what should be done, or how, or by whom. After the large mural was well under way visitors came to the studio one day. *F* asked one of them to pose for him and he started and completed in one two-hour sitting an 8' x 4' figure painting.

F said he had a good time and learned a great deal about how to express himself in art. This example demonstrates something (magnified certainly in his case because his talents were obviously greater than many of his peers, though by no means greater than some of the others) characteristic of the alienated students. Once they can feel secure in a situation, unthreatened and supported in whatever efforts they decided to make, and rewarded for them, they will plunge into any challenge no matter how large, and almost invariably they will meet this challenge with success. *F* progressed to successively larger and more personally meaningful challenges, without any hesitation whatsoever and with increasing competence. His production in a short period of time was inordinately large and his growth during this period was tremendous.

This experience was, in varying degrees, true of many of the students in the painting studio. They shifted from their team-work to personal work easily, accepted larger responsibilities and met these growing challenges with greater involvement and certainly increasing self-satisfaction.

The art studio: A summary. The paintings produced by the students demonstrated a directness of expression, a willingness to explore the materials of painting and to experiment in search of significant forms. That these valuable qualities, essential to the creative artist and rare enough among artists considerably more experienced, should appear with the great frequency they do among student painters is a tribute to the innate and not infrequently powerful talents of the students themselves.

The release and support of such talent was, of course, a fundamental aim of the art studio. In itself, the conception, execution and completion of a work of art proved to be an exhilarating and immediately rewarding experience. This is important in the academic setting where rewards and gratification are necessarily deferred until such a time as skills and ideas can mature and be tested, for immediate gratification can be a vital stimulus to students striving to realize long-range intellectual goals. Students were supported and encouraged in their examination of ideas and in their exploration of the painting materials to express them. The discovery of satisfying techniques and relevant images was stressed, not the initial mastery of technical skills—drawing, color, composition—which often frustrates the beginning student. Every individual effort, regardless of how rudimentary, was recognized with approval as well as criticism. Special care was taken to help each student find appropriate personal solutions for any technical and expressive problems he might encounter.

In this way skills were developed internally and experimentally through doing and discovering and not imposed externally in arbitrary and uniform fashion. Because of the absence of absolute standards for the evaluation of student effort, students were free to innovate and try new approaches and seek unique solutions without fear or penalty for failure. An experimental studio atmosphere is liberating and encourages individuality rather than conformity, and it enables every student to be at least relatively successful.

Art, in these ways, is a strong ally of intellectual attainment and a powerful impetus to individual effort. It offers a success experience to each student which can become a strong motivating factor in the realization of further success. It can help reconstruct damaged egos, it can invigorate despairing self-concepts and it can build a bridge between alienated students and inimicable school.

As one student said about the art exhibit, "Wait until the ———— teachers see this." When asked why, he replied, "Because they don't think we can do anything."

". . . the curriculum itself needs to be reorganized at the
elementary level in particular so that it combats the
myths which surround poor and segregated children,
and gives them the tools with which they can organize
knowledge for themselves."

A CONCEPT-CENTERED
CURRICULUM FOR THE
DISADVANTAGED*
Virginia Frank

The following position paper was prepared for a national conference of educators active in programs for
the disadvantaged. The author starts, as does Pedersen, with the failure of the school to educate lower-
class children; unlike him she suggests that the
corrective is not in personalizing the teacher-student
relationship but in reorganizing the curriculum. The
organizing principle suggested in this paper is concept development; the curriculum envisioned would
not focus on subject fields as such or on "real-life

* Mrs. Virginia Frank, Southern Education Foundation, Atlanta, Georgia.
Prepared as background material for a conference of the National Institute
for Advanced Study in Teaching Disadvantaged Youth, Washington, D.C., June
19, 1967.

problems," but rather on key concepts in Western culture. Concepts like causation, appearance and reality, or relativism would be explored through carefully planned activities and instructional materials drawn from various disciplines in this curriculum.

Why is a curriculum organized on this basis suggested as particularly important for underprivileged children? Which of the other authors in this section of the book do you think might be most in sympathy with this approach? Why? What drawbacks, if any, do you see in this plan? Can you suggest one or more activities under any of the concepts listed that would further develop the concept? What additional fundamental concepts can you suggest that you think should be incorporated in such a curriculum? What changes in teacher education would be required for teachers in such a curriculum?

WITHIN THE past decade a major thrust in American education has been the concern with curriculum reform, with new materials, and with modernizing the structure and content of individual fields and groups of fields. A large number of projects, national and local in scope, embrace the natural and social sciences and the humanities. Most of these projects are geared to the needs of the college-bound youth who resides in middle-class suburbia.

The National Institute feels that there is inadequate attention placed on the problem of curriculum as related to the poor and in turn to the values and objectives of the majority.

We are therefore issuing an invitation to a number of selected national curriculum makers, some possessing insight and experience with the problem, some who have not yet directed their attention to it, to participate in a national workshop dealing with the issues of new materials and the teaching of the disadvantaged. This workshop is conceived as the initial step in a process that will hopefully see the attention of many major curriculum makers turned to one of the major educational issues of our time.

There are thousands of children in this country for whom the schools represent a foreign world, another culture. For some of those children the school is part of the enemy—an institution, like the police force, which seeks to control and exploit them. For many others it is simply a futile exercise, leading to no tangible improvement in their situation and unconnected to the real concerns of daily life.

Some of these children begin school with enthusiasm, if only because it may promise escape from an uncomfortable and unhappy home. Or the value of education may have been conveyed to them; a natural sense of adventure and curiosity can operate.

But it is not long before most of these children become discouraged; poor children do not measure up to the grade level achievement standards set by more affluent school populations, and poor minority children remain even further behind. As these children grow older the school becomes less and less meaningful.

The children of the middle class know that application and at least average intelligence in a school setting provide the only real access to the occupations and comforts of their parents; they recognize that they must pass through the same process to achieve the same results.

But the poor and segregated children soon see clearly that the same aspirations are not expected of them. They learn the hierarchy of school values that says they do not need and cannot achieve a mastery of all the material there offered. And since few of the ways in which they expect to spend their lives seem connected to the school curriculum in any case, they accept that judgment. The weight of determinism settles over the student. As they learn that they do not much matter in the wider education setting, they react either with passive acquiescence to the low expectations, or active rejection and hostility.

The schools of course cannot be expected to reach all of these children with sensitive repair of the whole damage. But within the school context it is not too much to expect that children should learn to understand themselves and their world more accurately, and gain a realistic set of expectations and exposures. The classic American definition of education is, after all, that it leads away from poverty, isolation and discrimination. We have only seriously considered how schools might tackle this problem over the last decade; reshaping our ideas about how to serve these children will take many more years.

There are many areas in which this examination is now being carried forward with great hope. One of the most important is in teacher training. Changing the homogenous character of school populations also promises to increase the ability of disadvantaged children to gain confidence and knowledge. Another arena of new discovery is related to learning theory, better understanding of why children do and do not learn certain things. The organization of the schools themselves is beginning to get attention and criticism.

But among all these is another field that requires attention: the instructional content, or curriculum of the schools. We have not yet learned how to arrange and apply the subject matter of the school room so that it will have relevance to the life concerns of the children of poverty. We are now learning to cast the material so that children can discover knowledge for themselves and thus make it an effective part of their mental equipment, but we have not yet solved the prior problem of how to make that material have meaning to their own problems and concerns.

Alternative Ways to Organize Curriculum

The temptation is to consider the disadvantaged child as an unexposed and empty vessel, whose environment has not provided him with the experience he needs in order to take advantage of academic education. In fact, he is full of concerns, experiences, values, questions; the fact that some of them are negative and self-defeating rather than responsive to the idea of learning means that we must do more than "get him ready" to learn. We must organize the curriculum so that it answers his questions; if we hope to transmit to a child certain values and views we must deal simultaneously with his own values and views.

If we think of education as a process of getting into more education (college) or of getting a job, we cannot arrange it in a way which is relevant to a child who is sure that college and good jobs are not in his scheme of things in any case. If we are anxious to produce children who have a realistic estimate of who they are, why they matter, what is important and possible in life, then we must organize the earliest years of school to deal with those matters.

We are not seeking to help them adjust. Nor are we precluding the pursuit of knowledge for its own sake and for pleasure. The debate is not bland exposure vs. intellectual rigor. Rather the task is to undergird investigation of the disciplines with a structure related to the human concerns of these children.

This requires more than a peripheral effort to "motivate" children back into the structure that has demonstrably failed them, by telling them that to play the game and survive will pay off. We should instead take more seriously the lesson of the original rejection, which tells us that we have been designing instruction to meet the needs of children who already have certain assumptions and perceptions; who seek certain goals and are prepared to face certain pressures. If we intend to provide education for all children, we need to accept alternative estimates of needs and goals, without putting a lower value on them. This means reorganizing academic instruction into meaningful patterns, which will relate to the lives of the children.

Along with the lack of verbal skills that characterizes many disadvantaged children, comes a kind of attitudinal starvation. Their diet is deficient in perceptions of reality about themselves and the world that can make motivation to learn and achieve possible, that can stimulate them to acquire those skills which are universally helpful, that can enable them to choose a working set of positive values.

There are many values of our society that the schools attempt to transmit to the children. A national group need not make any judgment about relative merit among these values to see quite clearly that there are some which are uniquely and severely absent among disadvantaged children and whose absence makes impossible an appreciation of academic instruction. Our failure to transmit some of these values, or perceptions of the world, at an early age means that the pursuit of academic knowledge becomes increasingly irrelevant. Schools now organize curricula around acquisition of basic skills first, and later around academic disciplines as ends in themselves. They tend to ignore the inaccurate or distorted perceptions that children often bring to school; in fact the schools frequently intensify and promote these inaccuracies.

If disadvantaged children are to be taught how to learn and make use of knowledge, the curriculum itself needs to be reorganized at the elementary level in particular so that it combats the myths that surround poor and segregated children and gives them the tools with which they can organize knowledge for themselves.

A National Curriculum Workshop

Some units around which a curriculum might be organized have been selected for the purposes of a national workshop. They are not meant to be definitive, and the purpose of the workshop will not be to argue their merits for this or other purposes. They have rather been selected, with some care, as examples of the kind of organizing principles that would speak directly and overtly to the needs of poor and segregated children, and would at the same time be sufficiently universal not to single out one population group or another for special or artificial constructs. They have also been selected as examples of units that could include a wide variety of material selected from all the disciplines, coordinated into meaningful ideas for young children.

It is the belief of the conveners of the workshop that many teachers and administrators in disadvantaged schools are searching for such tools to work with, and would welcome an opportunity to test and explore such new curricular ideas.

There are now available new funds, both public and private, for curriculum development. Systematic evaluation of the instructional content of schools in depressed areas is underway in many places.

This national workshop proposes to examine a relatively new approach to curricular organization, to discuss it intensively over a period of a few days and to reach conclusions about its value for further development. The workshop will bring together many individuals who have thought about this problem extensively, some of whom have already been engaged in efforts to write relevant curriculum units for the disadvantaged.

The suggested units are listed in the following draft. In addition to an opportunity for some general discussions, participants will be asked to meet in separate small groups to examine one of these units in relation to one kind of disadvantaged population. By working through the implications of this kind of content organization in various specific settings, the workshop should provide useful guidelines for the future.

SUGGESTED ORGANIZING CONCEPTS

Creation and Manipulation

"Man differs from the animals in that he can create material and spiritual things and can control his natural environment."

Rationale. This is a fairly obvious attempt to get at the negative feeling that "nothing I do matters," to create a sense of control of environment, to erase the feeling of immutable forces and a world of "givens." Things do change; our country is in fact built on the conviction that man can shape his world to his own needs. Creation of something new can be simply arranging things in new ways; things can be arranged for the purpose of beauty, for communication, for comfort, for protection, for pleasure, etc. The sense of manipulating the environment for specific purposes is a simple but necessary idea for young children.

Relativism

"There is more than one valid way of seeing everything and of responding."

Rationale. Here is an overall need to get rid of the "right answer" syndrome, an attempt to make an instinctive relativism part of every child's equipment. For every problem there is more than one solution, usually raising more problems. The specific application to disadvantaged children will be a perception that there is more than one way to accomplish a goal, that their values and options are not "wrong" as opposed to somebody else's "right." Cultural relativism is a more positive notion than assimilation. The study of polarization should lead to a realization that life is not either-or, but a series of connected options to make relative changes (not nihilism vs. capitulation to Mr. Charlie, not following exactly the way of our fathers vs. rejecting it entirely, not "making it" vs. giving up). Tolerance for relativism, and for ambiguity, and for un-certainty depends on a secure self-image and self-confidence.

Causation

"Everything has a cause; past experience governs present action. Some of these causes are man-made, some natural."

Rationale. Here again the concept of control is vital: children are taught to distinguish between what they can in-fluence and what they cannot. They naturally question how much of themselves is subject to manipulation, how much given. They increasingly realize that just as what others do and say affects them, so what they do and say affects others. The disadvantaged child needs to know that there is no magic order of things governing his affairs; life situations have causes that can be understood and influenced by individuals. He can thus deal with the idea that although his options may be more limited, there are always areas open to influence by personal action.

Expectations

"What we expect of ourselves and of others is based on learning and experience, and is not always accurate."

Rationale. Like the concept of relativism, the concept of expectations will help children to be more skeptical and discriminating about things around them. They can learn to have more realistic expectations about themselves, to take rational chances, to develop internal expectations that may differ from the norm. As they understand that their expecta-tions about things and about people are governed by external appearances and past experience—and are sometimes deceptive or inaccurate—they will discover that the way they see them-selves is also influenced by the expectations of others.

PART III

Redressing the Imbalance
of the Urban School

The New York Times of June 16, 1966, carried a front-page story headlined, "Segregation Up In Schools Here." The article quoted a New York Board of Education report that, although the number of predominantly white schools decreased substantially and the system's "mid-range" schools, those with "better-integration," showed a marked increase, there was a sharp rise in recent years of *"de facto* Negro and Puerto Rican segregated schools." The accompanying school census figures indicated that in 1960, 118 out of 782 schools were predominantly Negro and Puerto Rican; in 1964, 187 out of 811 were in that category; and in 1965, 201 of the system's 829 schools were segregated.

Several days later, on June 9, the *Times* quoted extensively from a speech by a national figure on the general significance of these and other like data countryside. He said, in part:

We have, to be sure, gotten a fair amount of newspaper space and published enough committee reports on the inequalities of segregated education to build a paper Tower of Babel. Nothing is safer these days than denouncing bigotry. But I find myself puzzling over which is worse, honest bigotry or well-intentioned timidity.

While we have gone on urging moderation, sweet reason, and bigger and better panel discussions, the schools throughout the nation remain almost as segregated today as they were in 1954 when the Supreme Court decided that racially segregated education was illegal.

The facts today are that a Negro youngster in an American elementary school has on the national average not much more than 15 per cent of his classmates from the majority white groups; in the Southern states the figure is nearer 5 per cent.

Our words have urged the nation to desegregate its schools. But our reluctance to act has said even louder, "Not yet." Somehow we seem to have been lulled into a blind faith in gradualism, a mindless confidence that some morning, some year, a suddenly transformed electorate will spontaneously and joyously decide that this is the day to integrate America.

Well, it's not going to happen. . . . Gradualism, no matter what we call it, has failed, and I think it fair to say that those who continue to espouse it are fooling themselves and, in many ways, failing our nation. It seems to me time for school officials to form a third front for racial equality in the United States. . . .

There is no such thing as a perfect way to achieve school de-segregation. We must simply bore ahead with the tools we have, and it won't be pleasant and it won't be quiet, and it would be much nicer if someone else would share this work. . . . The load we must carry is that of irritating a fair percentage of our white constituents, of embarrassing some governors and mayors, of alarming some newspaper publishers and of enraging suburban taxpayers, who in proportion to the means, are not paying as much for their good schools as paupers in the city are paying for their bad ones.

Words so impatient and blunt might well have come from one of the civil rights militants, but they are part of an address by United States Education Commissioner Harold Howe, Jr., to a meeting of educators and school administrators, cosponsored by the National Urban League and Teachers College of Columbia University. It is significant, however, that the public official speaking is at the Federal level; so positive a statement has yet to be heard from any large city Board of Education or Superintendent of Education.

The reasons why we are unlikely to hear it from these sources are obvious from the news stories included in this section, which form a connected case study of one of the most turbulent of conflicts over *de facto* segregation in any of the Northern cities. Omitted from the series of events are the accompanying stories of sit-downs, pupil strikes, parent strikes, and other forms of pressure on both sides, which everyone will recall from those years. The selection has been made primarily to highlight the reasons given for their positions by the people and groups involved in the struggle, and it is to an analysis of those positions that this introduction is devoted.

Although the Supreme Court argued, in its 1954 decision that began the current situation, that segregation is inherently unequal because separation, itself, produced feelings of inferiority in the Negro child and consequently lowered his motivation to learn, it restricted its ruling to the cases before it of state-imposed segregation. Although many Northern city boards of education were reasonably sympathetic to an effort to integrate their schools which were segregated only as a result of existing housing patterns, it is by no means yet clear that they are compelled by law to do so. Nor is it clear, in a number of specific instances, how, with the best will, they can succeed in integrating without tearing everything down and starting all over. One cannot help feeling some sympathy for the harassed city educator, faced with prolonged pressures from civil rights groups, who exasperatedly suggested that the demonstrators come up with a workable plan for integration, if they thought it was so easy.

In the modern metropolis, in which the inner city has become increasingly dominated by a variety of ethnic groups subject to discrimination and the suburban ring by the white middle class and upper working class, few of the technical

SIX METHODS OF DESEGREGATION

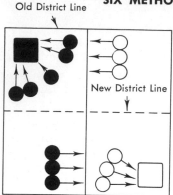

Redistricting

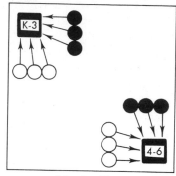

Princeton Plan

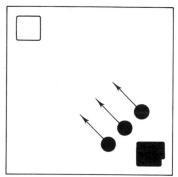

Open Enrollment

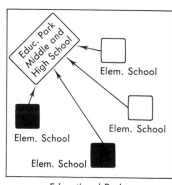

Educational Park

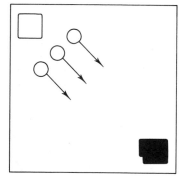

Open Enrollment
"in Reverse"

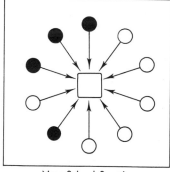

New School Spotting

devices available for school integration are very useful in more than one or two kinds of situation. The review of the major types below suggests why this is so:

1. *Redistricting.* Elementary school district lines, particularly, were often drawn originally with the intention of having a school service a homogeneous neighborhood, and it is possible, in these cases, to redefine the district in such a way as to automatically integrate the school by drawing its population from several ethnically different neighborhoods. The well-known case of District 6, Manhattan, is a good example. The district was an excessively long, narrow rectangle, extending along the east side of New York's Central Park, a strip in which large numbers of upper-middle professionals and executives live. If it had been wider by a block or two, it would have run through a neighborhood of East European working-class flavor, as well as the very lowest reaches of East Harlem. The school was widely known as a "silk stocking" one, and many people moved into its high-rent district just to take advantage of its presence there. The city has recently redrawn the lines, however, in a shape a little closer to a square, thus providing a more heterogeneous social-class mixture in the school, though the move did not greatly improve the ethnic balance.

2. *Open enrollment.* The most common, and most widely useful, of integration devices is also the most fiercely attacked, that of bussing groups of children from a school of heavy ethnic concentration into one that is mainly white. Cities throughout the country have tried several forms of open enrollment; a voluntary system, under which parents in ghetto areas may choose to send their child to any school in the city that is declared "open," that is, that has room; and bussing systems, in which the schools make arrangements to transport groups of children to schools designated as "receiving schools." Voluntarism has proved generally disappointing because, as one might expect, only parents who are already socially mobile have the time, energy, and interest to take advantage of the scheme. Most current open enrollment plans are of the second type.

3. *Reverse open enrollment.* In this seldom-tried expedient, white middle-class children are bussed into schools of

heavy ethnic concentration, a specter that haunts the suburban white parent, and possibly accounts for much of the enraged opposition to all bussing. It has also been the butt of one of Art Buchwald's satirical newspaper columns, in which he describes the plight of a Negro family that worked hard to save money, finally overcame discrimination and succeeded in buying a house in a middle-class suburb with a good school for their children. All went well until the school decided to bus their children back to the school in the same ghetto they had managed to leave.

4. *Pairing.* Widely known as "the Princeton Plan," this device can be employed only where two neighborhoods, one white and the other Negro or Puerto Rican, share a common boundary. The elementary school in each district is reorganized by assigning only kindergarten through third grade to one, and grades four to six to the other (sometimes kindergarten is retained in both schools). All children in the lower grades in both neighborhoods attend one school, all upper graders in both areas the other, thus automatically integrating both schools. The advantages of the plan are many, but obviously it is inapplicable to the large ghetto areas common to most urban centers.

5. *New school spotting.* As boards of education build new schools to accommodate a rapidly increasing population, it is suggested that they deliberately seek sites for them in areas where the population they draw will be an integrated one. An obvious difficulty is that, in the length of time that most cities take to build a school (New York, for example, somehow needs five years from appropriation to completion), the ethnic composition of the area is quite likely to have changed.

6. *Educational parks.* Although the idea for such parks is of little use in the immediate future, it offers great promise for a long-run attack on *de facto* segregation. The proposal is to place large school campuses at strategic points in the city, where the core city meets the first of the outer city rings, for example, and construct on them buildings to house the whole range of normal public schooling: a number of elementary schools, several junior high schools or middle schools, and a comprehensive high school. Such a complex would afford a number of

advantages aside from racial integration; it would be feasible to provide expensive services such as film libraries or closed-circuit television that all the schools on the campus could use in common, for instance. New York is actively seeking a site on which to experiment with the idea; its difficulty in finding a large enough piece of land to do so is indicative of a major drawback to the plan for many very large cities of the crowded east.

Whether one finds any or all of these integration schemes urgently necessary or even palatable, however, depends on where one stands generally in regard to integrating the urban schools. The selections that follow illustrate a wide range of positions on the issue, both community and professional; for discussion purposes, it is possible to consider them as three major positions, for each of which one could find fairly widespread support: the militant; the conservative; and the negative.

Mr. Howe's speech, quoted earlier, surely puts him in the militant camp, and further examples may be found in the news stories about the Reverend Milton Galamison of Brooklyn. The militants argue that school integration is so vitally necessary that it must be achieved as immediately as possible, at whatever the cost. Mr. Howe, at the close of his address, tells his school administrator audience that they must be willing to risk their jobs by taking unpopular steps toward integration; Negro civil rights leaders have not hesitated to persuade their people to take children out of school for long periods of time to protest segregation in their schools. The militants agree that immediate steps toward integration will require very large sums of money and a considerable amount of disruption, but they justify the demand for these costs by moral, legal, and educational appeals.

The moral appeal is based on several grounds. A major one may be found in Mr. Young's argument for overcompensation for the Negro in the readings. The nation as a whole owes recompense to the Negro for centuries of brutal inequity, which has left them, as a people, with a disintegrated family structure, heir to an implacable system of social and job discrimination that prevents them from effectively participating as equals in the society. As applied to the schools, this argument joins with an assertion of the democratic ethic, for few would deny that most segregated schools are poor schools and that attendance at one almost guarantees inequality of educational opportunities. Furthermore, from the point of view of the democratic order, segregation does harm to the white child also, for it reinforces the barriers between important groups in the society to the detriment of free communication and understanding.

The militants stand most consistently on this moral argument, and properly so, because it is powerfully persuasive to anyone with even a vestigial social conscience who is committed to the Judaeo-Christian ethical tradition and twentieth-century democratic ideals. To deny its force is to hedge on both of them, a not very popular public position to take. Nor can anyone familiar with the schools of the inner city deny the factual basis for the inequality complaint, despite the pieties of public relations statements by various city boards of education.

The other major bases of militancy are less unambiguous. Legally, the application of the 1954 decision to northern *de facto* segregation is cloudy, as a reading of the local and state court decisions shows. Some courts have demanded proof that the particular condition of segregation results from a deliberate act of the responsible community officials before they will act on it. On the other hand, some education officials are themselves taking stronger stands; Commissioner Allen of New York State has insisted that local school systems must find ways of integrating whether or not existing school segregation is accidental, and the courts seem so far disposed to back up such actions. The Supreme Court will, no doubt, sooner or later make national sense out of the welter of lower-court decisions, but if its past actions are any guide, it will probably be later.

As for the educational basis strongly advanced here in the article by Jencks, the host of technical questions raised by its most important assumptions detract from its force. The belief that Negro youngsters will "catch" an achievement orientation from white middle-class classmates has little evidence to support it; Jencks just seems to accept it on face value. The review of evidence on integrated situations by Katz casts some doubt on the principle, and certainly at least suggests that the integrated classroom must have some very special features if it is to become a favorable environment for the Negro child.

It is in part the uncertainty about the real effect on the learning levels of the child which underlies the conservative position. On this issue, those who take a conservative stand favor integration wherever it can reasonably be brought about, but would prefer to put large-scale effort and funds into the task of improving the slum school itself. The educational justification offered is likely to be that it is far from helpful to the average lower-class Negro child to put him in a classroom where he must enter a competition under terms which mean inevitable failure. If, in an effort to avoid this type of situation, one retains the practice of grouping in the receiving or paired school, the end result is a classroom just as segregated as the one the child left. The alternative of bussing only the academically most competent children out into middle-class schools not only defeats the purposes of integration, in the educational sense, but deprives the slum school of those children who might provide useful models.

As the moral argument is the strongest part of the militant position, so these realities of the educational process constitute the most persuasive part of the conservatives'. In answer to political pressures, there is no doubt that many boards of education have engaged in hasty and ill-conceived integration schemes, with little thought of what was going to happen to the children in the new setting. In this respect, the Greenburgh School District 8 experience reported in this section is a rare exception to the common practice. Teachers report numerous examples of bussed children facing administrative indifference in receiving schools, not to mention faculty hostility and segregation.

Conservatives also make the point that there are too many practical obstacles to immediate integration on a large scale to consider seriously the possibility of a general solution to the problem. The only valid immediate response to the segregated schools in the large ghetto areas of northern cities is bussing most of the children out of them. Conant, in particular, has viewed with dismay the chaos he envisages as thousands of school busses join the morning traffic jams already endemic in the urban centers. One occasionally hears too, a note of tender concern for the poor children who must endure long, tiring rides morning and afternoon.

One might suppose, in examining the practical arguments of the conservative position, that driving children to school by bus is not a common practice in this country. Of course it has always been such, and still is in the small towns and country areas of the country, as those of us who have been caught behind a school bus on a narrow road can attest. City traffic does pose special problems, but in this case the busses move, for the most part, in a direction opposite to the morning rush-hour traffic, and, in any event, as a technical problem for competent city planners, it hardly seems a significant enough issue to justify the attention it often receives.

On a considerably more fundamental level, however, the conservatives justify their position more persuasively by an appeal to a specific view of the school's role. If one perceives that the social order rests on a division of labor among the institutions which comprise it, then it is important to determine the special task which the school must perform, and prevent it from dissipating its energies doing the job of other institutions. The position of many in the conservative camp rests on the belief that the school's role, as distinct from that of the family, the church, the government, etc., is the transmission of knowledge and the development of intellectual skills. Racial integration, however desirable and necessary, is the concern of other institutions in the community, and to disrupt the instructional process by attempts to provide integrated schools in a segregated metropolis is an overextension of the school's role, and takes its attention from the task which only it is set up to do.

The argument is valid, of course, only if one agrees with this view of the school as separated from the vital concerns of the society. But, for the school as an institution to deny its involvement in those concerns, and its share of responsibility for the problem, can only further alienate it from those of its pupils with whom it fails most dramatically already in its instructional role.

A third group includes those who take a generally negative position on school integration in the North, and who have fought it in the courts and in many specific schools where it has been put into effect. Because most of the members of the negative camp are so clearly acting on the basis of social bias and their own economic self-interest as they perceive it, it is tempting to dismiss, *ad hominem,* whatever arguments they advance against integration as mere rationalizations. In the face of many denials of this assumption, however, it is necessary to look at the arguments for the position, which are of two general kinds: legal and educational.

As the news story sequence indicates, the major legal issue raised by the negatives is that of reverse discrimination. This is already moot, as several courts have refused to accept it, but it is interesting to examine for its curious logic. To require a white child, in a school pairing situation, to attend a school other than his neighborhood school, the argument runs, is to discriminate against him on the basis of his race; it is a violation of the principle that "each person shall be treated without regard to race, religion, or national origin," as a dissenting judge put it. The consequences of this argument, of course, would be that no historically established situation in which a dominant majority wrongs a minority one could ever be corrected, because the dominant race could always argue that steps taken to right the wrong inevitably discriminate against them by disrupting the patterns they themselves had set up. A complaint of discrimination by those who live in neighborhoods that carefully maintain a lily-white character is not only historically and sociologically specious, but absurd.

The educational arguments are a little more substantial. One is that parents often move to neighborhoods in which there are good schools, and pay an economic premium for having the school available. If the school is paired, they might be compelled to send their children to an entirely different and inferior school. If children are bussed in, the pupils from the slum schools bring bad influences with them, or in any event, depress the standards of the school. It is, in the first place, hard to know how much justice there is in the complaints themselves. In the most bitterly fought school-pairing battle in New York City, the Board promised the parents that the predominantly Negro school in the pair would be brought up to the same level of quality as the white school, and most observers agree that they did so.

But, even if we accept the facts alleged as true, the anti-integration forces are asking us to consider the relatively minor harm caused them by the situation as worse than the infinitely greater harm done to the Negro slum child, which may be an excusable demand from a position of pure self-interest, but hardly acceptable from a more general social viewpoint. We sympathize with a friend who has a bad head cold, but are not inclined to feel that he is worse off than someone who has an incurable cancer.

The same considerations apply to the arguments for the neighborhood school as a principle. There is, in the first instance, no such principle; it is a mere traditional convenience. Nor do the burdens added to the life of a middle-class mother whose child must go a few extra blocks to elementary school seem intolerable. If the child falls ill, she cannot reach him as easily; she loses the close contact with her child's teacher; if she has two children, they may be compelled to go to different schools; and so on. Making all possible allowances for the parental anxieties so marked among the middle class during this generation, it is difficult to regard these reasons as more than snivelling.

This particular analysis appears to point to a crucial dilemma, involving two considerations that hold up most strongly among all those we have examined: the moral urgency of school integration as a signification of equality, if nothing else; and the educational doubts about its effectiveness for school achievement unless very complex steps are taken to make it effective. It is difficult to come to any conclusion that does not include the desirability of as much integration as we can possibly manage, and a willingness to pay the often considerable cost. But we need to couple that demand with a far greater awareness than is now evident that school officials must do far more than put various schemes of integration into effect; they must do something about making the resulting experience a positive one for all the children involved in it.

". . . the quality of education depends largely on the spontaneous interplay of habits, interests and ideals which each group of classmates brings from its homes . . ."

SLUMS AND SCHOOLS*

Christopher Jencks

In this series of articles from *The New Republic,* Jencks takes a militant stand on school integration, insisting that improvement of the occupational position of the children of the poor is unlikely to come about except by providing them with peer models in the classroom. He also reviews a number of possible general methods for integrating the schools, and pessimistically concludes that those who hold power in American communities are unlikely to permit any of them. As do many militants in the war against poverty, he ends by arguing that only mass political pressure from the poor can do much to change the situation. Jencks has suggested, in a more recent article, that another, and even more radical, answer to the integration problem in northern cities is to do away with public schools as an institution; if

* Christopher Jencks, "Slums and Schools," *The New Republic,* September 10–17, 1962. Reprinted by permission of *The New Republic.* © 1962, Harrison-Blaine of New Jersey, Inc.

parents are given money to educate their children, good private schools will spring up to fill educational needs efficiently and creatively.

The crux of his argument is in his belief that the disadvantaged slum child will acquire middle-class values from his classmates. What questions can one raise about this assumption? What kinds of evidence would one have to gather to prove or disprove it?

FOR MORE than a century the rural poor have been pouring into American cities. Up to World War I they came mainly from the overpopulated European countryside to cities which needed unskilled industrial labor. Since World War II they have come from the now-overpopulated American countryside to cities so mechanized and even automated that unskilled labor has little market value. But still they came—Negroes and Puerto Ricans in the East, Spanish Americans and Indians in the West, marginal farmers and hillbillies everywhere, all trying to jump in a single generation from the Eighteenth Century to the Twentieth. Often they fall short. Unable to adapt themselves to the requirements of a post-industrial economy which mainly values the bureaucratic virtues, they fill the jails and mental hospitals, crowd the unemployment offices and relief rolls, blight housing and recreation facilities. Not only do they threaten to bankrupt the metropolis, but they (and their children and grandchildren) make it uninhabitable—for themselves as well as for the middle classes which originally shaped it.

Nor do the slums in question show very many signs of disappearing, or even diminishing. Urban renewal may move them away from the commercial center of the city—from the West Side to Newark and from the East Side to Queens. Public housing may even change the physical face of the slum beyond recognition. But the impoverishment and disorder which are the essence of a slum seem to remain. They can only be eliminated when the slum dweller himself changes.

Some would disagree, but it appears to me that the urban poor change only when they acquire respectable and responsible jobs. So long as they spend eight or ten hours a day in repetitive, soul-destroying work they have neither the courage nor the energy to fight the loneliness, the squalor, and the impulsive hedonism which make the slum so appalling—and so vibrant. Fortunately the number of jobs a man can do without losing touch with himself is steadily increasing, and the number which turn their occupants into automatons decreasing. In the years ahead we will need more teachers, and fewer charwomen, more chemists and fewer miners, more auto salesmen and fewer auto workers, more IBM executives and fewer filing clerks.

The only difficulty is that while the economy is changing in a way which makes the eventual liquidation of the slums at least conceivable, young people are not seizing the opportunities this change presents. Too many are dropping out of school before graduation (more than half in many slums); too few are going to college (less than twenty percent in many areas). As a result there are serious shortages of teachers, nurses, doctors, technicians, and scientifically trained executives, but 4.5 million unemployables.

What is the trouble? Fundamentally, it is that the technologists are transforming work faster than educators can transform workers. The slum school is now being asked to do in one generation what it formerly did in three, and it can't do it. Instead of making the first generation off the farm into literate but unskilled factory workers, making their children into craftsmen, office employees, and small businessmen, and their grandchildren into professional and managerial experts, the slum school must complete the whole cycle at once.

There are no tested formulae for meeting this challenge. But I will outline two tentative approaches: in this first article I will discuss some fairly obvious improvements in existing slum schools; in a second I will suggest just how such slum schools might be supplemented or replaced with radically different ones.

How big is the problem? In recent years an average of 1.5 million people a year have been leaving the farm. Some of them, of course, are the children of commercial farmers, and head for the cities with a good deal of formal education and with the predominantly small-business mentality of their parents. But the majority of the emigrants from the farm come from subsistence farms, and theirs is the outlook of the peasant rather than the entrepreneur. They are usually jacks of all trades (a little carpentry, a little plumbing, a little auto mechanics), but have neither the formal education nor the cultural agility needed to fit into the highly specialized urban job market. When they arrive in the city they join others equally unprepared for urban life in the slums—a milieu which is in many ways utterly dissociated from the rest of America. Often this milieu is self-perpetuating. I have been unable to find any statistics on how many of these migrants' children and grandchildren have become middle-class, but it is probably not too inaccurate to estimate that about 30 million people live in urban slums, and that about half are second generation residents.

The incoming DP's from the farm are rarely realistic about what they want from the city. They hope, of course, to make more money—to afford meat for dinner or a beer while watching TV, to pay for a roof that doesn't leak and medicine when they are sick. But while they want to consume the goods in the newspaper and TV advertisements, they are less ready to adopt the job-oriented "all American" style which makes this standard of living possible—both for individuals and for the nation. They rarely come to the city with any religious or ideological commitment to the middle-class virtues. Even (perhaps especially) in the Bible Belt, the rural poor are seldom Calvinist apostles of work, saving, self-help and self-discipline.

Neither before nor after their coming to the city is the world of the poor one in which foresight and the long view pay off. It leads to little but despair. In the city they live often from one spouse to another and always from one eviction notice and repossession order to another; from day to day and hand to mouth, at temporary jobs on hourly pay, in basements washing dishes and in backrooms sorting laundry. Perhaps because they dislike the thought that these jobs will be permanent, they create no unions to protect themselves. As a result their working conditions remain appalling, their job security slight, and their pay scale desperate.

Conversely, these immigrants to the city feel no obligation to their employers. Some habitually miss work after a bad night on the town. Others ignore those parts of their job which they find confusing, tiring or pointless. So employers decide that it would be cheaper and less worrisome to have a machine doing the job. The machine cannot be sullen and cantankerous. It cannot sabotage its employer by doing shoddy work when he

is rude. It has no personal problems and few neurotic tendencies. Its back is stronger and its patience longer than that of
even the most docile illiterate. So the poor grow poorer, more
resentful, and still more unemployable.

UPPER-MIDDLE- VS.
LOWER-MIDDLE-CLASS SCHOOLS

For those educated in the small, provincial and impoverished rural school, where even literacy is an achievement
(one American adult in thirteen is believed to be functionally
illiterate), the chances of reversing this vicious cycle are small.
But need the sins of the fathers be visited on their children?
Cannot the slum school do what the rural school cannot: show
its pupils how to live within the highly organized corporations
and professions which increasingly dominate America?

For better or worse the school is, almost by its very nature,
just such an organization. It provides the lower-class child of
limited experience with almost his only image of middle-class
"work." Unfortunately, it often shows such work at its worst
rather than its best. His experience at school, and especially his
observation of his teachers, often makes the slum child think
that middle-class work is in essence clerical, not professional.
The child comes to believe that success in the "respectable"
world depends only on doing an infinite succession of meaningless jobs, which he has no part in planning. He assumes, in
many cases correctly, that the only difference between school
work and adult work is that at the latter one is given adding
machines to abet the boredom, and filing cabinets to put the
"homework" in. In both cases the reason for doing the job is
not the hope of personal satisfaction from its completion but
the necessity of earning a wage of grades, credits, and promo-
tions.

When this is the essence of slum education, and of the
menial white collar world to which it seems to lead, it is hardly
surprising that many slum children rebel. Why should they be
on time to work when there is no urgency, or even apparent
consequence, in getting the work done? Why should they be

orderly when the order has no connection with the pattern of their life? Why should they repress their anger at the person at the next desk when they are tied to him not by a real working relationship or sense of colleagueship but simply by physical proximity? Most of all, why should they make themselves the tools of other people's ambitions? ("I will not be at the beck and call of every man with three cents," William Faulkner is reported to have said on quitting a post office job.)

In theory, of course, the schools can offer more than this. Teachers may be civil servants, but they do not have to appear to their students as clerks whose every action is controlled and checked by the "front office." They could be autonomous professionals who largely controlled their own day to day activities. If they were, the slum child would see that the middle-class world included at least some jobs in which a man (or woman) was largely his own master. And surely if the school presented this face it would make the respectable adult world seem more attractive to many of the talented, ambitious and creative rebels who now see only self-inhibition, goody-goody-ism, and the squares.

Let me emphasize here that I am not equating education with adjustment to middle-class life, either of the upper-middle or the lower-middle variety. I doubt that any genuinely educated man can live fully within the limits of the bourgeois world. But the limits of the proletarian world seem to my largely middle-class eye even more narrowly circumscribed, and even less compatible with the good life. So while I would urge every school to encourage rebellion against the prevailing middle-class orthodoxies, I would also urge it to recognize that some forms of rebellion are more creative than others. In particular, it seems to me clear that the rebel who begins with some comprehension of middle-class mores is likely to fare better, at least in America, than one who begins without this grasp of his world. Unless the school furnishes its pupils with this grasp, their rebellion is likely to be self-defeating and futile. Instead of creating a new order for themselves or for the world they will fall back into the disorder which lies at both the psychological and sociological heart of slumdom. In-

stead of becoming revolutionaries they will become delinquents; instead of transcending America they will be defeated
by it.

THE SCHOOL VS. THE HOME

If the school is to familiarize its pupils with the main
stream of American culture it must provide the slum child
with an alternative to the self-defeating style of his family and
neighbors. It must be a home away from home. This is no easy
task, for the regular school calendar provides that the ghetto
shall have exclusive jurisdiction over the child during the first
five formative years of life, and that even after that the child
shall spend an annual average of only one waking hour out of
six in school. Rarely is this enough. Big cities ought to have
nursery schools and kindergartens—perhaps compulsory—to
give the three, four or five year old some bulwark against his
often loveless and mindless home. Perhaps too a six day week,
similar to many European schools, and a longer school year
would help the child who really wants to get away from the
crowded rooms and squabbling relatives which are his home.
After-school programs, both of study and of recreation, would
also help—especially for those who have nowhere at home to
study, even if they want to.

Clearly, however, it takes more than physical facilities to
pry the slum child loose from his streetcorner. The teachers
must be able to stand *in loco parentis*. They must be warm
enough and clever enough (and have time enough) to help the
child with the crises that inevitably accompany breaking with
home. They must also be strong enough and admirable enough
so that the child can, at least in part, try to become like them.
The importance of this cannot be overemphasized. Viscerally,
though not usually intellectually, the slum child often senses
that his family is incapable of coping with the urban bureaucratic world into which it has drifted from the farm. Since these
children participate in America's worship of competence, they
tend to view their family, and by implication themselves, with
contempt. Yet most of these children see no better alternative.

Their parents may be afraid of the middle-class world and especially of the school and its authorities, but their teachers (especially the women who are almost universal at the elementary level) are equally afraid of the slums and of lower-class life (especially its sexual side). In such a setting the young are likely to be taken in by the apparent bravado of their slightly older schoolmates, and to adopt the streetcorner gang as their ersatz family circle.

If teachers are to replace parents as mentors of the young slum child, the teachers will have to be better than they now are. The recruitment problem is, however, in large measure a circular one. Unless substantial numbers of lower-class children respond enthusiastically to the slum schools, decide to go on to college, and emerge into the adult world with one foot in the slum and the other in suburbia, an adequate supply of good teachers will be hard to come by. And those who do enter slum teaching will not stay if their school principal treats them as irresponsible clods who must be constantly forced into a prescribed pattern lest they do something stupid. (The principal who thinks this way is, of course, often right. But unless he takes more chances he will never get better staff who more deserve his confidence.)

Beyond this general problem the special difficulties of slum work must be recognized, both by hardship pay and by special training. If this is not done talented teachers will continue to transfer to middle-class parts of town, new jobs in the suburbs, and new careers with better pay. Classes in slum schools must also be reorganized, so that those who are in open rebellion against education are not allowed to obstruct the teacher's efforts to instruct the rest. It is all very well to have heterogeneous classes in a suburban school where the norm is to do assigned work and pass prescribed exams. Then the bright students help educate the dullards and curb the delinquents. But in a slum school the heterogeneous class has exactly the opposite effect: the dullards and delinquents form a majority and help suppress any eccentric who wants to hear what the teacher says or try to master the work she assigns. No child, no matter how ambitious, can learn much in a classroom with 40 pupils when five are seriously disturbed, 25 are indifferent, and the noise level never drops low enough so that you can hear the teacher from the back of the room.

Of course most teachers deny that a student can be properly educated in a class as large as 40, even if it is homogeneous. In the slums, according to an excellent pamphlet ("Education and the Disadvantaged American") recently drafted for the NEA's Educational Policies Commission, 20 is probably the optimal size. Yet research has never provided much empirical support for this claim. At least on exams, children taught in large classes usually do about as well as those taught in small. Before spending the billion-odd dollars it would cost to cut slum classes to 20, it would be worthwhile setting up a number of experimental slum schools, similar to others in all but this respect, and seeing if the innovation made any perceptible long-term difference to either teachers or students. (My guess is it would, at least to staff morale.)

Indeed if any single expenditure could make a decisive long-term difference in the education of the lower classes, it would probably be the establishment, either by a foundation or by a federal agency, of perhaps a dozen experimental schools in slum areas. Each could then take an unselected cross section of the local slum population and try out various administrative and pedagogic schemes for improving the over-all educational climate. One could test whether specially trained and carefully selected teachers produce perceptibly different students over the years. Another might demonstrate whether adequate staffs of school psychiatrists and social workers, and programs providing for direct contact between teachers and parents of "difficult" or "unmotivated" children, make a difference. Still another might try to show that making the curriculum either more or less "achievement oriented" has some measurable long-term effect on slum students. The Ford Foundation is now sponsoring a variety of valuable pilot programs along with some of these lines, but few of these are research-oriented, i.e., few use control groups.

In all of the foregoing discussion I have assumed that the school must be an adequate microcosm of the possibilities of American life. In my observation children will rarely work hard in school merely to get rewards after graduation. They succeed only where, at least covertly, they enjoy the ritual of the classroom, the library, the laboratory, and the exam room. But while the school should be a microcosm of the middle class adult world, it should also systematically introduce its pupils to that world. Unless they acquire some grasp of the corporate and professional organizations in which intelligence and knowledge are valued, students are likely to assume that the school is conning them when it tries to develop these qualities. Many have never heard a concert or seen a play, much less met a man (especially a man of their own ethnic group) who held an important job of which he was proud. This kind of exposure is important—partly to convince the child that school is not a dead-end but mostly to give him a firmer hold on the world to which his text books, his teachers, and even (with conspicuous and intriguing exceptions) his language, refer.

WHO PAYS THE BILL?

The reforms and experiments discussed above—the school calendar, the recruitment and training of teachers, classroom organization and size, broader adult contacts—could easily mean doubling the $300–400 per student which most cities now spend in the slums. Does such an expenditure make economic sense? Will it increase the productivity of the schools' graduates sufficiently to justify itself? Or decrease the vast sums now spent for public welfare?

Nobody can be sure. But this uncertainty is not the principal obstacle to making the experiment. Even if we had thoroughly documented studies showing that investment in slum schools paid off, the capital would probably be very hard to raise. For the slums are an underdeveloped country. They have little capital, and less sense of how to invest it productively. The poor make no strong political demand for better schools.

In principle, perhaps, the middle classes ought to be interested in slum schools, on the ground that better education would provide a bigger tax base and less public welfare taxation. But few taxpayers see that far ahead. Even if they did, they would see that the child who goes to a slum school and becomes a junior executive will move as quickly as possible to suburbia, and pay his taxes there. He will be replaced by a new relief applicant from Georgia or the Ozarks. So long as there is a backlog of rural poverty to be liquidated, money spent on trying to eliminate the slums will seem like money down the drain from the viewpoint of local businessmen who control local school budgets.

The same logic applies to manpower problems. So long as schools are locally controlled, a kind of Gresham's law of education seems to operate, in which every taxpaying business tries to keep the cost of local education down while bidding up the price of highly trained workers educated elsewhere. If education were nationally controlled this might change. Businessmen might find it attractive to pay more taxes for education and create skilled manpower surpluses which would keep their labor costs down. But that is not just around the corner.

So long as the origins of the slums lie in the countryside, while the symptoms lie in the cities, local action is unlikely to meet the problem. To date the states have been singularly indifferent to the problems of the really poor, either rural or urban. The federal government has been mainly interested in the popular short-term paliatives like public housing and unemployment insurance, not long-term ventures like education.

The main obstacle to Federal action is the conviction that it is politically impossible to concentrate aid in the slums at the expense of suburbs, small towns and everybody else. (General aid to all schools on the $10–$20 per pupil now contemplated would hardly make a dent in the slum school's problems.) Then too, Congress is understandably reluctant to go on record either for or against aid to parochial schools. This may make the situation hopeless. But I will outline some rather unorthodox programs which might simultaneously allow Congressmen to help the slum child and avoid cutting their political throats.

I have argued that America is not devoting enough of its resources to educating the poor, and that as a result we are likely to have a growing number of unemployables, with all the personal and social troubles that implies. The main problem, I suggested, is that the slum schools have neither the time, the facilities, the ideology, nor most important of all the teachers to wean their pupils from slum life and provide them with a home away from home. I also outlined a series of reforms, many of which already have the support of educators, which would be comparatively easy to implement if Congress were to take an urgent interest in educating the poor and spend several billion dollars a year on it.

But suppose for a moment that we had nursery schools and kindergartens, that primary schools were open six days a week, 40 to 45 weeks a year, and that after-school programs (and perhaps even dormitories) were available for those whose families weren't interested or sympathetic enough to continue a child's education at home. Suppose too that we had special psychiatric and sociological training programs, along with hardship pay, to get suitable teachers into the slum schools, and that with smaller classes, more preparation periods, and more freedom from bureaucratic supervision we could persuade teachers to stay in slums. Finally, suppose that we made an elaborate effort to show the slum child the real possibilities of middle-class adult life and to persuade him he had a chance to "make it" in this life. What then? Would we sharply reduce the number of students who drop out before graduating? Would we persuade hundreds of thousands more youngsters to seek college scholarships and prepare for the managerial and professional occupations which seem likely to survive automation? I am not sure. More fundamental reforms may be required.

In my observation the most important single factor in shaping an alumnus of a school is neither the physical facilities, the content of the curriculum, the erudition or imagination of the teachers, nor the size of the classes, but the habits and values of the pupil's classmates. Students learn most of what they know informally rather than formally, and they learn from one another rather than from their elders. Their lives are organized not by the official administrative machinery but by the ebb and flow of what sociologists call "the student culture."

If, as often happens in the slums, the school is dominated by the "hoods," it doesn't seem to matter how small the classes are: the most ambitious and often the most gifted students will concentrate their attention on learning how to jump the wires on a car rather than on learning the theory of electromagnetism. If, as may happen in the small town, the school football team is the focus of the whole community's chauvinism —its patriotic representative in competition with neighboring towns—the most talented students will become athletes no matter how many Ph.D.'s the school board hires. And if, as increasingly happens in prosperous suburbs, attending school is mainly a way of getting into a competitive big-name college, the ambitious pupil will become something of an intellectual no matter how dim most of his teachers may be. (Of course every school has individual pupils who defy its norms, who go to Harvard despite attending a "football school." Some conclude from this fact that the school itself makes no difference; that good pupils survive dreary schools and that dreary pupils will be dreary even after leaving a lively school. There is some truth in this "either-or" argument, but not much. Carried to its logical conclusion it suggests that schools should all be abolished, since the clever will educate themselves and the foolish are uneducable.)

If I am right about the importance of the student culture, the quality of education depends largely on the spontaneous interplay of habits, interests and ideals which each group of classmates brings from its homes, partly on the ingenuity of teachers and administrators in controlling this interplay, and hardly at all on the quality of the formal instruction offered by the teachers. It seems to follow, moreover, that if you want to improve the education available to a child from the slums the most important thing to improve is the attitude of his classmates toward adults, toward "brains," and toward work generally.

Slum children come to school with a pattern of habits and values of which even the most tolerant teacher can hardly approve. They are usually obsessed with physical prowess, contemptuous of ideas and books. They are also likely to be infatuated with the outward symbols of success—money, ostentation, and publicity—without any apparent respect for the technical skill and craftsmanship which makes success possible for most people. Perhaps because their parents live up neither to lower-class ideals of strength and loyalty nor to middle-class standards of respectability, most slum children regard not only their parents but all adults as knaves and fools.

The only way to keep such a child from growing up into another of the unloveable and unemployable adults he scorns is to make him change in fundamental ways. He will not do this simply because his teachers urge him to do so. The teacher's approval isn't that important to most slum children. The thing that counts—that makes his day-to-day life either tolerable or intolerable—is the opinion of his classmates, and more especially of the popular and omnicompetent children who are the cynosure of all eyes. In effect these children are the teacher's unofficial self-appointed deputies. Even in the best cases, where they have been brought up to share most of her future-oriented "bourgeois" values, they short-circuit many of her efforts. When these young taste-makers and opinion-molders are hostile to the school and the teacher, her hope of converting lower-class pupils to her sedate values is almost nil. To put it another way, a lower-class pupil is unlikely to become middle-class unless he has potential middle-class friends in his class; friends who will support him when his streetcorner playmates make fun of his new respectability.

If I am right about the importance of middle-class students as models, genuine reform of the slum school seems to require radical changes in the school system—and indeed in society itself. Instead of sending thousands of college-trained teachers into the slums as evangelists for middle-class values, we ought presumably to be sending millions of college-bound middle-class students. For by the time the suburban child has grown up and become a teacher it is too late for him (or more often her) to affect the life of a slum child. No amount of formal pedagogic training can compensate for age differences.

Needless to say, very few middle-class parents are radical enough to send their children to slum schools, even as a *sub rosa* "Peace Corps." Most parents have relatively little confidence in their children's capacity to look after themselves, much less to influence others. They certainly are not prepared to believe that their child could have an effect on slum children good enough to offset the bad effect the slum children would have on them. The overt sensuality and violence of America's lower class sub-culture apparently strikes these parents as so appealing (at least to the child within us all) that they assume it will dominate any school in which lower-class and middle-class pupils mix.

All the available evidence suggests that such parents are fundamentally wrong. In socially heterogeneous small town high schools the leaders are, as James Conant discovered to his surprise, almost invariably middle-class children. It is only when the school is almost entirely lower class that the leaders become lower class, and even then, as James Coleman has shown in his brilliant if unreadable book *The Adolescent Society,* middle-class pupils exercise an influence out of proportion to their numbers.

Still, it would be foolish to claim that sending 200 Scarsdale children to a 500-pupil Brooklyn slum school would leave the Scarsdalites untouched. The academic and social tone of the school might become largely suburban, but the native Brooklynites would have some effect, and probably not an effect which most Scarsdale parents would approve. After all, many of them moved from Brooklyn to Scarsdale primarily so their children could attend school in an upper-middle-class community free from the "corrupting" influence of slum children. Even those Scarsdalites who are genuinely public spirited, willing to pay higher taxes and often even to give their leisure time to helping the poor, draw the line at sacrificing their children.

THE POLITICS OF SOCIAL INTEGRATION

From a political viewpoint we must admit that social integration will never be achieved by sending middle-class children to previously lower-class schools. What about sending lower-class children to previously middle-class schools?

There are two approaches to integration of this sort. The first is to ignore the suburbs and simply try to improve the social balance of schools within the big urban school districts. A first step is to rescind the rule that children must attend school in their own neighborhood. Instead, children can be allowed to attend any school in the city. The ambitious slum child can then commute to a predominantly middle-class area which offers a good academic program. Since only the proto-respectable child takes advantage of this opportunity, the academic standards and essentially middle-class character of the better schools are not threatened.

Many cities already allow this kind of city-wide choice at the high school level. But this still means that the slum child must spend eight or nine years in neighborhood schools with other slum children. After this experience he is usually so hostile to education that he picks the nearest (and worst) high school and drops out at 16. Serious efforts to eliminate the slum school must therefore include elementary schools. This is politically difficult, but not impossible.

Open registration would, of course, be a great asset to the minority of slum children and parents who know they want to enter the middle-class world, and see that the schools are the gateway. But what of the majority who are not interested enough in education to commute half an hour a day to another neighborhood, or who fear (often rightly) that they would be out of place and miserable in a middle-class school? Under open registration such children will continue to attend nearby schools—stagnant backwaters which ultimately drain back into the reservoir of misery from which they arise, rather than into the main stream of American life. If a real assault is to be made on the slums, these schools must surely be eliminated, either by redrawing neighborhood lines so that every school is socially heterogeneous or, where this is impossible, by simply closing down slum schools and sending their pupils by bus to other neighborhoods.

The difficulty in this scheme, over the long run, is that it may simply accelerate the flight of the middle classes to suburbia. Thus in New York the NAACP found that some white neighborhoods were so decimated that they actually had empty classrooms. Since Negro slums were desperately overcrowded, the NAACP urged that Negro pupils be reassigned to the white schools. This was done, and no immediate trouble was reported. But may not the ultimate result be to drive even more white parents to suburbia, creating what is in effect a Negro school in a white neighborhood?

If city-wide integration is going to have this effect, the only answer is to open suburban schools to slum children. Given the present distribution of political power this cannot be done on a compulsory basis. But much might be done voluntarily. The big problem is who will pay the bills.

In the days when Evanston High School admitted Chicago students, for example, Chicago parents naturally had to pay a substantial tuition charge in lieu of taxes, and this kept out all children from really bad neighborhoods. The Chicago School Board could not possibly have offered scholarships to support slum children at Evanston, because this would have been an official confession of what everybody knew but nobody admitted, namely that it was next to impossible to get a decent education in the Chicago public schools. The state legislature could perhaps have provided the scholarships without risking its political neck, but in Illinois as elsewhere the state legislature is predominantly rural and has little interest in a scheme which would barely touch the countryside. The only way to finance poor applicants would therefore have been for the Federal government to provide the scholarships.

Yet what if the Congress had voted such scholarships? Would anybody have used them? How many youngsters would be willing or able to adapt themselves to Evanston High School after a South Side elementary school? And even if real guts were put in the scheme by opening elementary schools to outsiders too, how many children from lower-class homes would be adaptable, even at the age of six? Nobody knows. But a pilot program, with scholarships financed by a big foundation in cooperation with a few forward-looking suburbs might be worthwhile.

Still another way to help poor children get a decent education is to work through the private rather than the public system. To those who see private schools merely as exclusive clubs which segregate the rich from the rest, this will seem an incredible suggestion. But the fact is that in many cities private schools are more classless than their public competitors. This is because most private schools are run by the Catholic Church— one of the few organizations in America which cuts across class lines. (Of course the class heterogeneity of the parochial school is a matter of logistics as well as ideology: except in heavily Catholic areas the parochial school must, in order to reach an efficient size, include a wide variety of neighborhoods.)

There is no good reason why the Catholics should be the only private group interested in educating the poor. The Ford Foundation has been spending millions of dollars a year to support experiments in public slum schools. Yet none of the schools being helped by the Ford program is in any genuine sense a comprehensive school. None has what seems to me the most essential ingredient of education: a leaven of middle-class children from education-conscious homes. Would it not be worthwhile to establish at least one school, outside the public system, which tried to attract both middle-class and lower-class children?

But suppose the experiment worked. No private foundation can afford to provide scholarships to the millions of children who ought to be gotten out of the slums. Such scholarships would have to come from public funds, and for the political reasons already mentioned in connection with subsidizing children who want to attend suburban schools, public funds in this case would have to mean federal funds. Could Congress be persuaded to promote private education at the expense of public? Today the answer is certainly "No." The free public school is a sacred cow in America, and anything which threatens it is regarded as somehow undemocratic. This is true despite the fact that we are nominally committed to private enterprise, competition, and pluralism.

ARE PUBLIC SCHOOLS "DEMOCRATIC"?

In the years ahead, however, there may be a growing recognition that the traditional arguments for public and against private schools have become irrelevant. We no longer live in small towns, where the free public school embraced the children of rich and poor alike and became an important (if often only partially effective) egalitarian force. Today we live in big cities and suburbs, where the neighborhood school is as much a bastion of ethnic and economic privilege as most private schools. A school which recruits only from Lincoln, Mass., Bronxville, N.Y., or Oak Park, Ill., is in many respects less democratic than one which, like Phillips Andover, recruits from every neighborhood where it can arouse interest in a scholarship.

Yet even if Congress accepted these arguments, how could it help poor parents pay private school tuition without getting involved in an explosive church-state dispute? Just before resigning from the Department of Health, Education and Welfare, Secretary Abraham Ribicoff suggested that Congress might provide tax credits to parents paying private school tuition. Since tax deductions for gifts to private schools (and churches) are already legal, the tax credit would raise no new constitutional issues. As Ribicoff envisioned the scheme, Congress would vote a $10 or $20 per pupil annual subsidy to the states for public education, and would give every parent paying private tuition a $10 or $20 rebate on his income tax, If, as seems likely, $10 or $20 per pupil expanded over the years to $100 or $200, private schools would get a real boost. If state legislatures followed the Federal example, private enrollment would undoubtedly skyrocket.

But these gains would be almost exclusively among the middle classes. Few slum residents understand taxes, and even fewer pay enough to finance private education out of rebates. If slum children are to attend private schools they must be given scholarships which pay the full cost of their education. Indeed, if any substantial number are to attend private schools (or even quasi-public suburban schools), scholarships will have to cover not only tuition but $10 or $20 a month for books, clothes, and entertainment. Without such money the slum child will be unwilling to venture into the affluent middle-class world. Such scholarships, if based on need rather than on the religious affiliation (or lack of it) of the school at which they were used, would not appear to create an "establishment of religion."

THE TRAGEDY OF THE SLUMS

I have outlined four approaches to providing slum children with the middle-class friends they must have if they are to acquire middle-class mores and join the prosperous American majority. We could send middle-class children to slum schools; we could abolish slum schools and distribute their pupils among middle-class schools in the city; we could open suburban schools to outsiders and provide scholarships to pay the bills; or we could set up private schools with generous scholarship funds. Are we likely to do any of these things? No realist, familiar with the mood of either Congress or the country, can really think we will. The haves are far too complacent, and the have-nots far too wretched, for radical educational reform to appear likely.

What is really likely to happen? My guess is that in the short run things will go on about the way they have since 1945. The rural poor will keep pouring into the cities for at least another generation, by the end of which time most subsistence farmers will probably have disappeared. Meanwhile, the slum schools will siphon off the more educable children into the suburbs, while the majority remain untouched. This majority will become increasingly unemployable, and will live more and more by the grace of public agencies. Unemployment and relief benefits will expand as politicians bid for restless votes, and so too will subsidized public housing and public hospitals. The time may even come when, from a physical viewpoint, people can live fairly tolerably without being employed.

But psychologically the situation will grow more and more intolerable. The unemployed will be more and more alienated from society, not only because they feel useless but because they will be unable to participate in an increasingly middle-brow culture shaped by the fact that more and more people hold complex professional and managerial jobs. One of the ironies of automation and bureaucratization is that while many people become unemployable, the rest devote more and more of their time and interest to their work. As jobs become increasingly professionalized, occupation may even supersede religion, income and ethnic ties as the chief shaper of an American's subculture. The man who has no occupation, or who moves rapidly from one to another, may become a man without an identity.

What will happen to these literal "non-entities"? Conservatives like James Conant speak of "social dynamite" building up in the slums. But despite Marxist hopes this probably does not mean that the slums contain the seeds of revolution. The violence and resentment of the poor, unlike that of people living outwardly respectable lives, is easily directed against their children and neighbors. As a result they tend to remain apolitical. Radicals of the Left and Right, who urge the destruction of either the existing American social order or of alleged foreign enemies, seem to arouse little enthusiasm in the slums. So long as this continues—so long as the poor vent their spleen mainly on one another rather than on the rich—they will remain a threat only to middle-class consciences, not to the economic and social fabric of middle-class life.

Is there any way out? Not if we wait for middle-class social critics and do-gooders like myself to solve the problem. In the last analysis the poor, like everyone else, must solve their own problems. The poor today have only one source of power: the voting machine. The critical problem is therefore to devise a political program which will at once bring the poor to the polls and yet, when implemented, keep them off the streets.

"I have found it difficult to discover support for proposals for massive shifting of Negro and white children
out of their own districts. . . ."

THE NEGRO AS AN AMERICAN*

Joseph P. Lyford

The paper is adapted from a talk given by Mr.
Lyford in Chicago, later distributed by the Center
for the Study of Democratic Institutions. It is a preliminary report on a study of Manhattan's West Side,
which deals with an area roughly sixty square blocks,
from streets in the low Eighties to those in the
low Hundreds, between Riverside Drive and Central
Park West. The area's population of about 100,000
includes a large minority of Puerto Ricans and a
smaller minority of Negroes. Lyford's perception of
the views of the inhabitants of this section provides a
very different picture than one ordinarily gets from
the newspaper headlines that chiefly describe the actions of the civil rights militants.

*It has been suggested that Lyford's interviewers
got "correct" and less than frank answers to their*

* "The Negro as an American" by Lyndon B. Johnson, Robert C. Weaver,
Joseph P. Lyford, and John Cogley. Published by the Center for the Study of
Democratic Institutions, Santa Barbara, California.

questions about the desirability of school integration. Similar surveys, however, consistently find Negro slum parents ranking school integration very low on their list of priorities, though they put "quality education" very high. If he correctly describes the attitudes of the poor as indifferent to the question of school integration, what conclusion can one come to as a result? That the demand for integrated schools is a leadership demand only, and therefore to be reasonably disregarded? Or, that the less-educated and more deprived masses are not capable of seeing the real interests of their children?

ACCORDING TO my census, there must be about three dozen small children who live on West 105th Street between Central Park and Manhattan Avenue. In June they take over the block, and for the rest of the summer they spend most of their time racing up and down looking for something to do. Since they have no equipment for the usual games, they invent their own, which is a misfortune for the city. The major emphasis is on breakage, with the result that all through July and August the sidewalks glitter with broken glass. Experiments with fire and water are also popular. These include setting trash cans afire after sunset, the generation of small explosions, and the opening of hydrants. Since these episodes frequently bring fire trucks and policemen around, the hot months are fairly lively in our neighborhood.

With all their rushing, the children rarely venture beyond the four corners of the block. Whatever travels they take are imaginary ones inside the hulk of an abandoned car that periodically turns up along the curb. I don't recall ever seeing a child leave 105th Street to climb the big rocks that loom up on the edge of the park a few hundred feet to the east. The children cling to their island as if each moment in the neighborhood were their last. Eventually such a moment does arrive, when their families are forced to move out of the way of some civic improvement or housing accommodation designed for other people's tastes and incomes. Then the children are taken, along with the furniture, to some other temporary encampment on a similar street where they will help fill up another ancient tenement and another school. This is the way childhood ordinarily proceeds for most of the Negro boys and girls who come and go on 105th Street. It is also likely that this is the way things will develop, in turn, for their children.

Our neighborhood is one of several West Side "communities," as they are sometimes called. Negroes averaging about $3,000 annual income live in all of them in greater numbers the farther north one goes above 86th Street. About 11 per cent of them are unemployed, as against a 7.3 per cent average for whites. The Negroes are intermingled with Puerto Ricans, who earn even less as a rule and who have even greater difficulty getting employment. Since the two minority groups are poor, pay higher rents on the average than whites, are frequently on welfare, and are jammed into housing which is generally in the last stages of decay, they tend to be transients who have no opportunity to ripen into full-fledged inhabitants of any area. Their individual arrivals and departures go unnoticed. The established residents are only aware of the fact that there seem to be more or less of them this year than last.

Many parts of the West Side, especially the crosstown streets, have the atmosphere of vertical waiting rooms built above transportation systems from the South, from the city's lower East Side, and from as far away as San Juan or Hong Kong. Of those families which find themselves in the path of the vast urban renewal program between 87th and 96th Streets the lucky ones escape to a housing project. It is difficult to discover what happens to most of the other D.P.'s and impossible to trace the single males or females who drift into the area and live in $20-a-week apertures off rotting hallways until the buildings are pulled down around their ears. Since 1945, Western civilization has not allowed people to be buried in the rubble of their homes; therefore they are required to go somewhere else. In recent months the city's Department of Relocation has announced plans for humane transportation of these subject peoples. Meanwhile, the Negro and Puerto Rican are shunted from place to place, because, being unemployed or poor, they have to make way for those who are not.

Many white people concerned about this state of affairs have made efforts to draw the Negro and Puerto Rican into some part of their community life. Some of the parent-teacher associations have tried to get more Negro and Puerto Rican mothers to their meetings, but the efforts usually peter out and the white parents continue to dominate the P.T.A.'s while the Negroes and Puerto Ricans work during the day, if they have jobs, and try to tie up the family's loose ends at night. The reform Democratic political clubs in the area began life with a strongly social service cast to their activities, but they could not attract members from the low-income groups; now more and more of the clubs' time is devoted to organizational politics.

The churches' efforts to bring more Negroes to Sunday service and Church membership have also been a disappointment. While the Catholic parishes have managed to replace their original Irish constituency with the Spanish population, other local institutions seem to have found no way of convincing the Negroes that there is any point to community activity.

What is there really to talk about? The Negro inhabits a Malthusian world of subsistence living, enforced idleness— either partial or total—acute physical discomforts, and an abundance of disillusionment. This is not to say the world of the unemployed and unemployable is a totally black one in New York City. The Negro shares it not only with his Puerto Rican neighbors, but also with a substantial minority of whites. His preoccupations are sufficiently remote from those of a middle-class family on Central Park West to prevent any regular communication even where there is a desire for contact. A family able to take hot water and a comfortable income for granted can plunge very easily into political affairs, books, peace movements, and the trials of getting a child into Bronx High School of Science and Columbia or Harvard; on the black side streets a broken toilet can precipitate a crisis that will disrupt a family's life for weeks. A multiplication of such disasters can reduce families to the point where they become insensible to the outside world.

The name slots in hallways off a street like West 93rd are usually empty or carry the almost obliterated names of people who moved away years ago. Since the buzzers, like the occupants, generally do not work, the insertion of new names would seem to be superfluous. Some of the occupants are so isolated that the only mail they receive is a welfare check or an eviction notice.

To find some hope in the situation, one always returns to the public schools. Unfortunately, there is no way of letting more than a fraction of a worried public look through the classroom doors of one of the better, integrated elementary schools on the West Side. The unrehearsed activity inside might rid even a childless taxpayer of his suspicions. Most of the teachers I have observed show an ability to sustain the instinctive urge of children to group themselves without regard to color and even to uncover common interests between children with pronounced differences in learning capacity and family background. The informality and freedom are symbolized by the irregular clusters of movable desks in which the slower child or the new arrival gets some unofficial help and encouragement from children who have already picked up the pace. Sister Mary Francilda, head of the girls' branch of Holy Name School, is trying to further this type of pupil-to-pupil assistance by discarding the old system of grouping classes according to speed of learning and introducing classes, after the second grade, where the bright and slow children are mixed together. This seasoning experiment has worked pretty well so far, Sister Francilda reports, and the nuns seem to like the idea.

Hopeful developments in even an ideal school can be quickly extinguished by the swelling of class sizes, the inability of the city to provide proper teaching materials, and the instability that besets most Negro and Puerto Rican children in almost every phase of their life outside school. Next year, because of family reasons, hundreds of them will move to other schools in very different parts of the city, where they will be looking at new teachers and struggling with new versions of the customary privations. The dislocations occur so rapidly that some teachers lose their pupils almost as soon as they begin to understand their personalities and educational aptitudes. Some of the children are frequently transferred two or three times a year; others will average a new school every year all the way through elementary and junior high school.

A child has been known to go to unbelievable lengths to hang onto a particular school or teacher. His family may conceal a change of address in order to avoid the child's transfer. One youngster, whose family moved to Yonkers, commutes to Junior High School 44; officially, he "lives" with an aunt in Manhattan. Principals are aware that such skulduggery takes place, and teachers are instructed to question children periodically about their current address. But in cases where the child is a good student he has little to fear; the teacher will join in the conspiracy.

Although Negro parents rarely show up at school functions, they have absorbed some of their children's enthusiasm to the point where they express a generalized but favorable opinion of the local school based largely on what their children have to say about it. This is true particularly of Negroes who have recently arrived from the South and whose children display the effects of a shockingly inadequate schooling, often being nearly illiterate after several years of "separate but equal" education. If these children improve in their school work and show signs of ambition, there is a tendency for the parents to transfer their hopes to their children and to look to education as the only way out of an eternal labyrinth of family frustration. Their concern is whether the child is learning to read and write, whether he has a teacher who likes him and has taken the trouble to acquire some knowledge about his family. The tremendous but unspecific ambitions of many Negro parents for their children sometimes frighten the teachers. A large percentage of children will drop out, others will not be able to keep up the pace after high school, and most who would be qualified for college will not get there because of a myriad of misfortunes. What will happen inside the family, teachers ask, to children who fail to measure up to their parents' expectations?

There is also fear for the child who manages to compete successfully only to find himself trapped by an economic system in which jobs are disappearing as people increase and in a society which, despite everything that has been said and done recently about equality, has institutionalized its prejudices beyond the possibility of immediate repeal. Even when law or other pressure has brought racial discrimination under some effective control, the probability has to be faced that technological changes will soon make it impossible for 50 per cent of our high school graduates, white or black, to find employment of any kind. The young people who take at face value current propaganda about the need for an education and are thus disappointed can hardly be expected to take the education of their own future children very seriously.

In view of the civil rights organizations' preoccupation with education it is of some interest that the question of racial percentages in the local schools was never brought up by the Negro and Puerto Rican parents whom I interviewed. When I introduced the subject, it evoked little interest. I found no feeling that school authorities were, either through intent or through neglect, maintaining school districts to keep certain schools predominantly white or non-white, or that the teachers in the so-called "difficult" schools were incompetent or biased in their attitudes—charges that have been made overtly or privately by some integration "spokesmen."

It was the middle-class white families that often displayed an extreme sensitiveness to the matter of racial percentages. Explanations for this sensitivity can be contradictory. For instance, some white parents with children in mixed schools become highly agitated when other white children are withdrawn, but it is generally impossible to find out whether they react this way because they believe strongly in integration or because they are upset that the school is becoming more and more non-white. One white parent I know proclaims the value of racially mixed schools, but privately says he would take his child out of school if the boy were to be removed from an all-white IGC (intellectually gifted children) class and put into a regular one where there is a much higher proportion of Puerto Rican and Negro children.

Another type of white parent who irritates principals is the "school shopper." This individual insists on making a cellar-to-ceiling investigation of the school in his district and on subjecting the principal to a careful inquisition prior to deciding whether to send his child there or to a private school. In view of the constant criticism which seems to be the public school's daily ration in New York City, the school shopper has some justification for his misgivings; it is also understandable, however, that the principal and staff thus being investigated are highly irritated by such inspectional tours. To them the school shopper is a by-product of the attacks on public education.

These types of apprehensive white parents do not ordinarily have their counterpart among the Negroes and Puerto Ricans, who seem to assume the schools are doing as well as they can unless there is proof to the contrary. To some Negro leaders such an attitude is regarded as the result of deplorable ignorance or as the kind of over-adjustment to segregation considered characteristic of many Southern Negroes. Whatever his reasons, the low-income Negro on the West Side is not as quick as some of his spokesmen to assume that the quality of his child's school is directly related to the extent to which it is white.

I have found it difficult to discover support for proposals for a massive shifting of Negro and white children out of their own districts in order to bring about some sort of racial parity in the various sending and receiving schools. The reasons are not difficult to find. It is apparent that almost all parents are determined to keep their children as near home as possible, especially when they live in such a turbulent area as the upper West Side, where narcotics peddlers, alcoholics, prostitutes, and other varieties of sick and criminally inclined people abound. There is also the customary distaste for distant neighborhoods based on all sorts of folk tales and rumors about the terrible people who live in them. Whatever possibilities might exist for closer parent-teacher contacts are practically eliminated for those who do participate in the open enrollment program. Also, the child who has a long route home by bus from a distant school has less chance to participate in local after-school activities sponsored by the city and by the settlement houses.

Another comment I have heard from white parents and school staffs is that the children who are bussed to another school under this program tend to be the better students and their parents the more sophisticated in their community; thus, the sending school loses its better students and the local community is deprived of its best prospects for Negro leadership.

These points are not introduced as an argument against the purpose of the open enrollment program but to explain why it has worked out disappointingly. Had the sponsors of open enrollment questioned the intended beneficiaries of the matter thoroughly they would have discovered, for example, that most West Side Negro and Puerto Rican families want to stay in

Manhattan, preferably where they are if their housing can be improved or if they can get into a nearby housing project. They do not like the prospect of moving to Queens, Brooklyn, or the Bronx even if housing projects are available. It is therefore even less likely that they want to ship their children to these boroughs for long hours of schooling and transportation to and from.

The extent to which the official pronouncements on education by the Urban League and the NAACP are familiar to most Negro families is negligible. It is doubtful that even if these opinions were made widely known they would be taken seriously, for they seem to have almost no relevance. One example, is the view expressed by the director of the Urban League, Whitney Young, that public schools henceforth compensate Negro children for past deprivations by discriminating educationally in their favor, presumably at the expense of the Spanish children and "others" (the Board of Education euphemism for "white") in the same classrooms. I doubt that any such proposal could be voiced by someone who had seen very many West Side classrooms or who had an elementary understanding of the teaching profession. Educational experiences are not customarily parceled out in doses or in various-sized pills, the larger being automatically distributed to special ethnic or racial groups.

With the inevitable exceptions, most of the teachers I have observed deal with their children from moment to moment and day to day as needs make themselves apparent, and they try to group their children in such a way that they can get the most out of their experience. It seems preposterous to request a self-respecting teacher to build some sort of discriminatory bias into her attitude about her children. It is obvious that some children gain more of their teachers' attention than others, but this happens because the teacher had made her own estimate, partly intuitive and partly by testing, of the need, and not because she has indexed the need according to the pigmentation of the child. As things work out, notably in the "Special Service" schools, the presence of large numbers of Negro and

Puerto Rican children critically affects the direction of the school program, but this is a natural result of intelligent educational policy. All that recommendations like Mr. Young's accomplish is to build up the disquieting idea among some white parents that their children are not getting their share of attention, an idea that can be depended upon to accelerate the withdrawal of white children from the schools and to encourage the departure of white families for the suburbs.

The lack of rapport between the low-income Negro families and the NAACP and Urban League prevails in other areas. Frequently I asked families what individual or agency they felt they could turn to if they needed help with a housing, health, financial, or personal problem. The civil rights organizations were never mentioned. When a respondent did hazard an opinion, he gave the name of a person on the block who was supposed to have "influence with the city," of the Strycker's Bay Neighborhood Council (with forty-five member organizations), the family welfare investigator, a social worker from the settlement house, or the like. Most seemed to feel that there was no one who could or would help them in their difficulties. The civil rights groups were not the only ones ignored as a source of assistance. The churches (except for the local Catholic parishes which are closely tied to the Puerto Ricans), political parties, office-holders, and even local city agencies—if my respondents think about them at all—seem to have been invented for other people in other worlds.

Such a lack of faith in official institutions and leadership is obviously not peculiar to the impoverished families of the West Side. In fact, their attitudes would seem to be mild compared to the contempt and cynicism of the suburbanite for politicians and institutions in general. And it should be said that at least some politicians, notably the district's ebullient and energetic congressman, William Fitts Ryan, deserve credit for trying to do something about the depression and disorder that darken life on the side streets.

The NAACP has some justification for its failure to involve itself directly in West Side problems. Percy Sutton, former head of the Manhattan NAACP, says, "We are a volunteer group; and we can't do everything at once. We have to pick the worst situations and the places where we can get the most volunteers. That place is Harlem." I doubt that the Urban League, which has a paid staff of some size and has publicly represented itself for many years as working with racial minority problems on the community level, can offer the same justification.

The third of the "big three" groups now acting as "spokesmen" for the Negro, CORE, would seem to be the most remote from the every-day interest of the West Side Negro. Although the organization has been successful in attracting public attention by its demonstrations at City Hall and its frequent press statements attacking discrimination, it has shown little disposition to work on the neighborhood level at the day-to-day business of helping Negro and Puerto Rican families figure out practical ways of dealing with their immediate health, housing, and educational problems. In the field of education CORE's troops seem to be concentrated solely at the top, in the publicity department. I have found no evidence that its official representatives are taking an active part in local efforts to learn more about neighborhood schools and their special problems and to provide concrete suggestions for improvement. It may seem extraordinary that an organization which lays so heavy an emphasis on education has not taken the trouble to conduct a school visiting program or solicit the views of principals and teachers, yet this is exactly the case on the West Side. Perhaps this failure in the field accounts for CORE's preoccupation with balancing racial percentages of pupil population to the point where more urgent educational needs are given no emphasis whatsoever.

The recent prominence of CORE's Rev. Gardner Taylor of Brooklyn as a fiery speaker on such subjects as education and employment opportunities for Negroes has provoked a number of wry comments from educators who remember him as a member of a notoriously ineffective city Board of Education that was finally asked in 1961 to resign en masse by Mayor Wagner because it could not face up to a crisis of overcrowded classes and underpaid teachers—issues of direct concern to every West Side parent.

Another example of the discrepancy between the preoccupations of Negro "spokesmen" and the low-income Negro occurs in the field of housing, where segregation begins. Although housing is the chief concern of low-income West Side families, especially of the Negroes and Puerto Ricans who are subjected to special discrimination and exploitation and end up in the worst accommodations, neither the NAACP nor the Urban League has made any real effort to attack the problem in the area. In fact, it was not until the summer of 1963 that the Urban League reconstituted its housing division after a lapse of several years.

When hearings were held on the city's vast urban renewal program, affecting twenty blocks in the West Side area populated by low-income Negroes and Puerto Ricans, the Urban League did not even present testimony, and the NAACP's national office formally supported the final city plan providing only 1,500 units of low-cost housing, despite the fact that most of the people being displaced could hardly afford to live in low-cost housing much less in the alternative middle-income housing. It remained for an unparalleled coalition of a minority of the local Democratic reform club, several members of Strycker's Bay Neighborhood Council, the Americans for Democratic Action, the leadership of the two Catholic parishes in the renewal area, various Puerto Rican leaders, Theodore Weiss, the local City Councilman, and Congressman Ryan to fight the city plan and to force changes for more low-income housing. Today the plan, as finally revised, provides for 2,500 units of low-cost public housing. One Puerto Rican leader, commenting on the history of the urban renewal fight, declares bitterly, "The other minority group leaders not only didn't help us, they were on the other side opposing us." A local clergyman who supported revision of the city plan says the national NAACP and the Urban League behaved as they did because "they are part of the establishment."[1]

The effective work—and it seems pitifully inadequate to meet the swelling need—for low-income families of all descrip-

1. Unanimity on such issues as housing does not exist even within the NAACP. Mr. Sutton, representing the Manhattan branch, supported over 2,000 low-cost housing units in contrast to the policy of the national office.

tions is being done rather quietly by people and organizations that have their roots in the area. One of them is Fred Johnson, a bony-faced social worker from the Goddard-Riverside Settlement House who, with his group of four assistants, works with the street gangs (or "clubs" as they are now called), visits hard-pressed tenants, advises them of their rights, helps them fill out the forms, organizes recreation activities for their children, and refers them to the agencies that can help with their problems.

Two other troublesome defenders of the less privileged are Father Henry J. Browne of St. Gregory's Church, who has been president of Strycker's Bay Neighborhood Council, and the Council's executive secretary, Esta Kransdorf. They have represented the neighborhood's interests in repeated engagements with the city's hydra-headed bureaucracy. There are school teachers like Nancy Brigham, who spends her spare time checking up on cheating landlords as head of the Council's housing committee, and unaffiliated individuals like Aramis Gomez, a jeweler, who got into politics to protect his home and who has been representing his fellow Puerto Ricans ever since. There are Ralph Acosta, the house detective of the Hotel Endicott, who helped found a recreation center, and the Irish nuns of the parochial schools of the neighborhood, who have come to feel that teaching Puerto Rican children (their school populations are 80 per cent Spanish) is the most rewarding educational experience they have ever had.

So far the constructive forces at work in the area only suggest how to deal with its difficulties. The enormity of the poverty and frustration which spin out their tragedies every day of the year is too much for such efforts unaided by something else. Nor will things be changed very much by angry demands for city officials to "do something quick." The tragedy of the poor in this West Side "community" is the hopelessness of their position because society still will not face the fact that it has exiled the poor from national and local life. As far as the Negro of the city is concerned, the achievement of every remaining civil right will not solve the fundamental misery that is the white man's special gift to him. The fact is that the republic has little use for the people whom, through design or neglect, it has prevented from getting a decent education. The Negro has joined a new and integrated race of Americans, the race of the poor. In some ways this affiliation is of more importance than the fact that he is black.

There is a final fact to be faced. Our troubles with each other are not likely to end with the signing of a compact between the white and Negro American that simply guarantees coexistence in the same nation with equal protection of the laws, each in his own world. The doctrine of "separate but equal" applied to race is as full of future disorder and tragedy as it was when speciously applied to our system of public education. Simply to know that other human beings can vote, pray, and exercise every other constitutional right as freely as ourselves is not enough. If a free society is founded on the proposition that people shall learn from each other and share in each others' trials, it seems reasonable that we must reach a state where it will be natural and desirable to engage in a social relationship embracing every aspect of human existence.

". . . these expressions lead me to believe that racial
balance in our public schools is not constitutionally
mandated."

LEGAL DECISIONS AFFECTING
SCHOOL DESEGREGATION*

Lee O. Garber

The following summaries of court cases relating to
de facto segregation deserve careful reading, for the
issue is likely to be ultimately settled by the courts.
The tendency of these decisions, as Garber points
out, is toward demanding some proof of deliberate
segregation by officials before legally approving desegregation plans. It is interesting, however, that
only in the middlewestern *Bell* case is there any
judicial approval of the principle of the neighborhood school, and the news reports of later cases included in this section further reinforce the conclusion
that the eastern courts are disinclined to give weight
to the principle.

*If the issue is finally officially resolved by judicial
action, in favor of desegregation in the schools,*

* From Lee O. Garber, 1964 *Yearbook of School Law* (Danville, Ill.: The
Interstate Printers and Publishers Inc., 1964) pp. 192–199. Copyright 1964 by
Lee O. Garber, reprinted by permission of the author.

are we likely to face a situation similar to that in the South where, twelve years after the historic Supreme Court decision only a small percentage of the schools are integrated? If the courts decide to permit local officials to desegregate if they wish to, but do not compel them to, what is likely to result?

DE FACTO SEGREGATION

DURING THE PAST year at least four cases were decided which have implications for *de facto* segregation.[1] It should be noted that, while the term *de facto* segregation is reserved for that type of segregation which is not intentional or deliberate in most cases, it is, however, real segregation. It is segregation that results from the manner in which attendance-area boundary lines are drawn. It is generally the result of patterns of racial housing, rather than any intent on the part of the school board to create segregated schools. Because of the current interest in this type of segregation, the four cases mentioned will be reported in turn.

In New York. In New York, an action was brought for an injunction to restrain a school board from continuing to maintain allegedly racially segregated public schools.[2] Likewise, plaintiffs asked for an injunction against a projected referendum and bond issue that had for its purpose the obtaining of funds to provide for the enlargement of two predominantly Negro schools. Defendants contended that any segregation that existed was not "by any design, pattern of conduct, or contrivance created or maintained" for that purpose, but that it was the sole result of the residential pattern—that the school boundaries were not "gerrymandered." The district had a population of about 25,000. In May, 1961, approximately 47 per cent of the children in the district were Negroes and 53 per cent were white. Until 1949 there had been no officially adopted school zone boundaries. In that year an appeal was taken to the Commissioner of Education regarding the boundaries of the one school that was predominantly Negro in character, and which, it was contended, was racially segregated. As a result of that appeal, the board redrew the school zone boundaries for that one school, and the Commissioner approved its

1. *Bell* v. *School City of Gary,* 213 F. Supp. 819 (originating in Ind.); *Branche* v. *Board of Education,* 204 F. Supp. 150 (originating in N.Y.); *McNeese* v. *Board of Education,* 305 F. (2d) 783 (originating in Ill.); and *Shepard* v. *Board of Education,* 207 F. Supp. 341 (originating in N.J.).
2. *Branche* v. *Board of Education,* 204 F. Supp. 150 (originating in N.Y.).

action. At the time of the zoning the board adopted a resolution requiring all children to attend the school located in the zone of their residence. The court held that the facts presented by the defendants did not authorize summary judgments in their favor. In so doing it said: "Segregated education is inadequate and when that inadequacy is attributable to state action it is a deprivation of constitutional right." Further, it held that the fact that segregation was not the result of coercion by direct action of an arm of the state and was not, in and of itself, decisive of the issue of whether or not a child had been deprived of his constitutional rights. The educational system, according to the court, that is public in character "must deal with the inadequacy arising from adventitious segregation; it cannot accept and indurate segregation on the ground that it is not coerced or planned but accepted." The court also stated that "failure to deal with a condition as really inflicts it as does any grosser imposition of it." It reasoned that it was not enough to show that segregation grew out of residence alone. It appeared to reason that it was the job of the board to mitigate, whenever possible, the conditions that grew out of housing patterns, and failure to do so could have serious repercussions. Thus it is seen that this decision is similar to the one handed down earlier by a federal court in New York under somewhat similar circumstances.[3]

In New Jersey.   In New Jersey, several pupils brought an action to enjoin a school board from maintaining a public elementary school system, alleged to be racial in character, for the City of Englewood.[4] Plaintiffs, who were Negroes, alleged that the board of education, in assigning children to schools, "pursued what is commonly known as the 'neighborhood school policy.'" The use of this policy, it contended, resulted in racially segregated schools, which it was alleged were unconstitutional. The Attorney General moved to have the action dismissed, on the ground that plaintiffs failed to exhaust the

3. *Taylor* v. *Board of Education*, 191 F. Supp. 181 (originating in N.Y.). (See *Yearbook of School Law 1962*, p. 158, and *Yearbook of School Law 1963*, pp. 177–178.)
    4. *Shepard* v. *Board of Education*, 207 F. Supp. 341 (originating in N.J.).

available state administrative remedies. Consequently, the main question before the court was whether plaintiffs must exhaust their administrative remedies before resorting to the courts, rather than whether the schools were actually segregated schools. The statutes of New Jersey provided that the Commissioner of Education should decide all questions arising under the school laws, and that his decision should be binding until a decision thereon had been rendered by the state board of education. Under this statute, the court held that the Commissioner appeared to have the jurisdiction to decide disputes involving racial discrimination.

Because the remedy provided by the statute in this case was judicial rather than administrative in nature, plaintiffs argued that the doctrine of exhaustion of administrative remedies did not apply. They argued that "where a person asserts the violation of a federal constitutional right or privilege he need not first exhaust the *judicial* remedies provided by state law before resorting to a federal court." The court was not convinced that the remedy was judicial rather than administrative and that the Commissioner was without authority to decide the matter originally. Likewise, it was not convinced of the plaintiffs' contention that to ask for such a decision would be futile. With respect to *de facto* segregation the court did have the following to say: "Of course, a determination of the manner in which the 'neighborhood school policy' operates in any particular community requires a consideration and evaluation of a multitude of factors." On the ground that the Commissioner was specially well qualified, by reason of his expertise in a specialized field, to make these factual determinations, the court held that plaintiffs, who claimed that the city's neighborhood school policy was unconstitutional, must first exhaust the administrative remedies given them by statute before seeking judicial relief.

In Illinois. A very similar question to that which was raised in New Jersey regarding *de facto* segregation was also raised in Illinois.[5] Here, an action for "redress of alleged deprivation . . . of their rights to non-segregated public educational facilities" was brought by plaintiffs, who were elemen-

5. *McNeese* v. *Board of Education,* 305 F. (2d) 783 (originating in Ill.).

tary-school students in St. Clair County, Illinois. The lower court—a federal district court—dismissed the case on the ground that plaintiffs " 'failed to comply in the remotest manner with' their administrative remedy under the Illinois School Code." Plaintiffs contended that they were not required to resort to the administrative remedy and that, in any case, the remedy was not administrative but judicial, and was inadequate. The court, however, held otherwise and upheld the act of the trial court. In so doing, it held that, because the amended complaint did not contain an allegation to the effect that the policies of the board were unconstitutional in themselves, the plaintiffs were required to resort to the administrative remedy, which required that a complaint first be made to the Superintendent of Public Instruction. In commenting on the effect of such a complaint the court said:

> The Superintendent of Public Instruction in Illinois has no judicial power and his finding of fact as to whether segregation on account of race or color is being practiced in a school district is not binding in a suit at law or in equity; a complaint before him 'may cause an adjustment' if there is substance to the allegations in that complaint; and his decision, when made, merely ripens the controversy for judicial action if needed.

In Indiana. By far the most significant case regarding *de facto* segregation that was decided during the past year was one decided by a federal district court in Indiana.[6] This case had its origin in Gary, where it was contended the schools were racially segregated. Gary, Indiana, a rapidly growing city, increased its population by about one-third in the decade between 1950 and 1960. While this was happening, its Negro population almost doubled. In 1951–52, 37 per cent of the student population in Gary was Negro. Ten years later the school population had almost doubled, and at that time the Negro pupil population was 53 per cent of the total enrollment. In 1961–62, approximately 10,000 students attended 14 schools which were 100 per cent white. Sixteen thousand attended 12 schools which were populated by 99 to 100 per cent Negroes. Slightly over 4,000 pupils attended four schools that had a range of

6. *Bell* v. *School City of Gary,* 213 F. Supp. 819 (originating in Ind.).

Negro population from 13 to 37 per cent, and approximately 5,000 attended five schools which had a Negro population from 1 to 5 per cent. It is significant that, while the Negro population of Gary was increasing, it became concentrated in one general area, referred to as the "Central District." Gary, a comparatively new city, was organized in 1906. At that time the school district of the City of Gary was divided into eight attendance areas, each served by one large school which provided educational facilities for all children, kindergarten through high school. As the pupil population increased, expanded elementary schools became necessary. These generally served children from kindergarten through grade 6. Some served children from only one of the original eight districts, while others provided accommodations for pupils residing in two or even three such districts. As new elementary schools were built, new attendance areas were created. Likewise, new junior high schools were constructed, with new attendance areas.

Prior to 1949, Gary segregated its schools, as it was entitled to do by statute. In that year, however, the separate-but-equal statute was repealed by the legislature, and a new act expressly prohibiting segregation was enacted. Gary complied with the act and ostensibly abolished its segregated schools. Plaintiffs here, however, contend that the defendant purposely and intentionally maintained its segregated school system, because of the manner in which it drew its attendance-area boundary lines. The defendant district denied this contention and insisted that the board and the staff were color-blind so far as races were concerned. For the most part, evidence indicated that the boundary lines were the same as they had been for a number of years and that changes that had been wrought were only those that became necessary in order to accommodate increased enrollments. These changes, it was contended, did not involve questions of race. The board had adopted a policy of total integration of its staff "from the administrative level on down." In this connection it is significant to note that one of three assistant superintendents was a Negro. The Coordinator of Secondary Education was also a Negro, as was the Supervisor of Special Education, the consultant in charge of mathematics programs in secondary schools, a coordinator in the food services department, an elementary supervisor, and a member of the special services department who devoted a large part of his time to the problem of drawing proper boundary lines for attendance areas. Of 61 principals, 18 were Negroes; and the teaching staff consisted of 833–½ white teachers, 798–½ Negro teachers, and 3 Orientals. With respect to transfer between attendance areas, the board frowned upon it, except where such was necessary to alleviate overcrowded conditions. Otherwise, any transfer of students was handled on a purely individual basis. After considering all the evidence, the court concluded there was no reason to hold that the board of education had deliberately or purposely segregated Gary's schools according to race. It stated that, in its opinion, the problem was "not one of segregated schools but rather one of segregated housing." To the plaintiffs' contention that instruction in the predominantly Negro schools was of an inferior quality, as was also the curriculum, the court ruled that all evidence regarding the existence of discrimination was unimpressive and lacked conviction. With respect to the neighborhood school, the court said:

> It has many social, cultural and administrative advantages which are apparent without enumeration. With the use of the neighborhood school districts in any school system with a large and expanding percentage of Negro population, it is almost inevitable that a racial imbalance will result in certain schools. Nevertheless, I have seen nothing in the many cases dealing with the segregation problem which leads me to believe that the law requires that a school system developed on the neighborhood school plan, honestly and conscientiously constructed with no intention or purpose to segregate the races, must be destroyed or abandoned because the resulting effect is to have a racial imbalance in certain schools where the district is populated almost entirely by Negroes or whites. On the other hand, there are many expressions to the contrary, and these expressions lead me to believe that racial balance in our public schools is not constitutionally mandated.

In answering plaintiffs' contentions relating to segregation, the court stated that "the fact that certain schools are completely or predominantly Negro does not mean that the defendant maintains a segregated school system" and, in support of this, relied upon a statement from the *Brown* decision (349 U.S. 294) which declared segregation unconstitutional, where that court said: ". . . a school is not segregated because it is attended by all Negro students if the district is inhabited entirely by Negroes and they are compelled to attend the schools in the district in which they live." The court took the position that the *Brown* case forbade discrimination but did not compel integration.

In rendering this decision the court took judicial cognizance of the *Taylor* case in New York in which it was held that *de facto* segregation was unconstitutional and that neighborhood schools were, in reality, illegal.[7] It pointed out the difference between cases, however, and stated that in the *Taylor* case the court was dealing with a situation where, it concluded, the school board had deliberately segregated the schools. It interpreted the *Taylor* case as a mandate that the school board undo what it had illegally done.

Finally, it may be stated that the *Taylor* case in New York and the *Bell* case in Indiana are not too far apart. Here the court gave judicial sanction to *de facto* segregation that resulted from a housing pattern and was not intentional on the part of the administrative officers of the district. In the *Taylor* case it frowned upon *de facto* segregation that resulted from a deliberate board policy. It might be stated that in this case, unlike the New York case, the court did not require that the board show it had done everything possible to remedy the situation, and in this connection made the following significant statement:

> . . . requiring certain students to leave their neighborhood and friends and be transferred to another school miles away, while other students, similarly situated, remained in the neighborhood school, simply for the purpose of balancing the races in the various schools would in my opinion be indeed a violation of the equal protection clause of the Fourteenth Amendment.

7. *Taylor* v. *Board of Education*, 191 F. Supp. 181 (originating in N.Y.). See *Yearbook of School Law 1962*, p. 158, and *Yearbook of School Law 1963*, pp. 177–178.)

". . . I see no basis to draw a distinction, legal or moral, between segregation established by the formality of a dual system of education, as in Brown, and that created by gerrymandering . . ."

THE NEW ROCHELLE DECISION*

This decision, written by Judge Irving R. Kaufman of the Federal District Court, is included in full as an example of the tendency of many courts to compel integration where any evidence of deliberate intent to segregate is available, and of their unwillingness to accept the neighborhood-school concept as a barrier to integration. In addition to its vigorous style, it is further instructive for the weight it gives to the testimony of social scientists, which recalls the citation by the Supreme Court, in the *Brown* case, of similar evidence to support their major finding on the effects of segregation.

Is it possible, from the evidence of Board actions cited here, to come to a conclusion other than the one reached, that is, that the Board deliberately maintained segregation? Could not one say that "the Board of Education has adhered too rigidly to established district lines" about the Gary case as well, and, if so, does this leave us with any alternative than to test each case individually in the courts?

* Taylor et al. v. New Rochelle Board of Education. S.D.N.Y. 1961.

333

IT IS admitted by the defendant that approximately 94 percent of the pupils at Lincoln are Negroes. Plaintiffs contend that the Board has deliberately and intentionally created and maintained Lincoln School as a racially segregated school and thus has violated the Fourteenth Amendment and the principles enunciated in Brown v. Board of Education, 347 U.S. 483 (1954).

The Board operates the elementary school system in New Rochelle by means of the neighborhood school plan. Under this plan, as it functions in New Rochelle, the city is divided into twelve districts, each of which is served by a centrally located school. Pupils residing within a particular district are required to attend the school within that district, and permission to transfer to other schools is granted by the school authorities only in exceptional circumstances. Thus, as a result of this policy, the plaintiffs have been compelled to attend the Lincoln School. At the start of the 1960 school term, they sought to register in other elementary schools in the city having a more heterogeneous racial composition; permission to so register was uniformly denied, and this action then followed. During the pendency of this action, plaintiffs have withdrawn from the Lincoln School and are receiving private tutoring.

In the fall of 1959, after much public agitation against the racial imbalance in the Lincoln School, the Board proposed to replace the present Lincoln School building with a modern facility on the same site to serve the same neighborhood.

Financing for this proposal was approved in a referendum held on May 24, 1960. The plaintiffs view this decision by the Board as the culmination of a course of conduct designed to maintain Lincoln as a racially segregated school. They thus seek an injunction restraining the defendant from proceeding with the construction of the new school. They also seek to enjoin the Board from refusing to allow them to register in schools other than Lincoln which are not racially segregated, and from requiring them to register in the Lincoln School.

The defendant Board vigorously contends that the charge of racial segregation is absurd. Its position is that no child is compelled to attend any school in the City of New Rochelle solely on the basis of race or color.

Lincoln School was built in 1898; there is no evidence as to the Negro population, if any, at that time. Marylynn G. Pierce, a member of the Board of Education testified that there has been a tradition of a Negro school in New Rochelle for approximately one hundred years, but she did not indicate how this tradition had been inherited by the Lincoln School. Events occurring subsequent to 1930 indicate that by that time the majority of the Negro population of the city was being served by the Lincoln School. In 1930, according to the uncontradicted testimony of Bertha O. White, corroborated in part by the testimony of Mrs. Pierce, and also by official school maps, a policy of gerrymandering was instituted which led to the confining of Negroes within the Lincoln School district by redrawing the district lines to coincide with Negro population movements.

In addition to this gerrymandering, the Board instituted further policies to assure that the Lincoln School District would remain Negro, and to relieve white children of the burden of attending a predominantly Negro school. Thus, up until 1949, white children remaining in the Lincoln district were allowed to transfer to other elementary schools.

This policy produced the anomaly, testified to by Mrs. White, of children living in adjoining houses attending different schools solely on the basis of their race.

Further, it appears, for example, that white children living south of the Lincoln School were assigned to Mayflower School, approximately half a mile north of Lincoln. Thus, they apparently had to pass Lincoln each day on their way to school. The inevitable result of this transfer policy, when combined with the earlier gerrymandering was that by January of 1949, Lincoln had become a 100 percent Negro school.

By 1949, the segregated condition at Lincoln had come to the public attention, and numerous civic groups exerted pressure on the Board to alleviate it. As a result of this agitation, the Board passed a resolution on Jan. 11, 1949, ending the policy of transferring white children out of the Lincoln School and indicating that readjustment of district lines would be considered.

At that time, however, the Board did not redistrict in any way nor has it done so until the present day. Thus, it has done nothing to eliminate the effects of this gerrymandering undertaken previously. Rather it has chosen to maintain the status quo, imposing, in effect, a freeze on the artificially created boundaries of the Lincoln district. When it determined to maintain the status quo, the Board could hardly have been unaware that this would necessarily perpetuate Lincoln as a predominantly Negro school.

The Board has steadfastly refused to alter the rigid neighborhood school policy with the result that the Lincoln School has continued to be a predominantly Negro school. Today, it contains approximately 94 percent Negroes.

The years between 1949 and 1960 have been eleven years of agitation for New Rochelle. For eleven years, responsible civic-minded organizations and groups have urged that something be done to correct the Lincoln situation: for eleven years the Board has discussed the problem, hired experts, made surveys, and constantly reiterated its belief in racial equality and the necessity for equal opportunities. But, in these eleven years, it has taken no action whatsoever to alter the racial imbalance in the Lincoln School. It has met the problem with mere words, barren of meaning, for they were never followed by deeds.

In 1954, the Supreme Court rendered its opinion in Brown v. Board of Education, supra.

This decision heralded a new epoch in the quest for equality of the individual. It called for responsible public officials throughout the country to re-appraise their thinking and policies, and to make every effort to afford Negroes the more meaningful equality guaranteed to them by the Constitution. The Brown decision, in short, was a lesson in democracy, directed to the public at large and more particularly to those responsible for the operation of the schools. It imposed a legal and moral obligation upon officials who had created or maintained segregated schools to undo the damage which they had fostered. And, compliance with the Supreme Court's edict was not to be less forthright in the North than in the South; no double standard was to be tolerated.

DODSON REPORT

The Board hired a distinguished group of educators, psychologists and sociologists, headed by Dr. Dan Dodson, one of the country's foremost experts on the problems of integration.

In December of 1957, this group after an exhaustive study, delivered its report, entitled "Racial Imbalance in Public Education in New Rochelle, New York" (popularly known as the Dodson Report). This report concluded that the Board had been derelict in its duties, and remiss in its attitudes. Moreover, Dr. Dodson testified that his initial proposed report had been even more severe in its criticism of the Board, but that the final report submitted had been toned down so as to make it more acceptable. The Dodson Report framed the essential issue involved as follows:

"Specifically, if the Board of Education in the past, operating in a different social setting, encouraged or permitted the present situation to develop, does the present Board of Education have the obligation to undo any damages which may have accrued under previous decisions of its predecessors? Does the present Board have an obligation to eradicate the imbalance of races in the Lincoln School which was permitted to develop under previous Boards?"

The report pointed out that:

"It is basically through the mechanism of the public school that members of a group occupying an inferior position in our society can achieve equal opportunities. Help in breaking down economic, social and cultural barriers should begin with the public schools."

Comparing the situation to that involved in the Brown case, the report said:

"It seems that morally the situation is little different than the situation which the United States Supreme Court in 1954 found to generate 'a feeling of inferiority as to their status in the community that may affect their hearts and minds in a way unlikely ever to be undone.' "

Dodson pointed out that change in New Rochelle was necessary; new facilities were required. Thus, the Board was faced with the necessity of dealing with the racial problem at once. Procrastination had to give way to action.

"The Board must realize that any building or utilization plan it adopts will implicitly make this decision. It is not possible to avoid the question of whether racial imbalance is going to be alleviated or encouraged. To do nothing about it is to encourage racial imbalance. To do nothing about it is a decision just as powerful and as important as a decision to try to do something about the imbalance."

The report pointed out that the Board of Education is in a position to eliminate de facto segregation in schools by its decision on a matter which has to be resolved—namely how to accommodate the increasing numbers of students in the public schools of New Rochelle. Obviously the racial imbalance in the school is related to the housing patterns. The housing patterns, however, cannot be changed overnight. The school district boundaries can.

The Dodson Report discussed the concern for "status" of various schools which has apparently been a strong motivating factor in the Board's conduct through the years.

"The panel was puzzled that in a city as dynamic as New Rochelle, in a decade, with insignificant exceptions, few children from the outside have ever been sent into the three schools located in the low socio-economic status neighborhoods."

Dodson commented on "What seems to be a lack of willingness on the part of the Board to move district lines" and found that "Acquiescence has heightened concern as to the 'status' of one school as against another with the result that there is almost a 'phobia' about the district lines in several of the schools surrounding Washington, Lincoln and Columbus."

The experts found, as a result of the survey, that the Board had been largely responsible for the situation.

"The panel believes the Board of Education has adhered

too rigidly to established district lines for elementary schools. It has tended to make under-use of some facilities at the expense of over-crowding in others. This policy has reinforced the 'status appeal' of some schools and depreciated others. It has helped fragment the community into neighborhoods identified by school attended and made more provincial the experience of all children."

With respect to the rebuilding of Lincoln School, Dodson said:

"To do so would further reinforce the segregation of Negroes. It would leave two schools in the same neighborhood (Washington and Columbus) only partially used and it would reinforce community fragmentation."

Subsequently the Board made it clear that it saw only one course of action: rebuild the Lincoln School on its present site. This, as Dodson made clear, could mean only the continuing of segregation at Lincoln.

This, then, completes the picture of Board intransigence and refusal to act through the years. The "freeze" placed by the Board in 1949 on the already gerrymandered boundaries of the Lincoln district remained unchanged, despite eleven years of public agitation, pleas and advice from distinguished educators and sociologists. And, what is more the Board has not evidenced any intention to change its policies in the future.

THE LAW

Any discussion of the applicable law must begin with the case of Brown v. Board of Education, supra. Principles long accepted by psychologists and sociologists were given the stature of the law of the land. The Supreme Court made it clear that in the field of public education separate but equal was inherently unequal, and hence violation of the Constitution. Thus, the operation of separate schools for whites and Negroes was proscribed. Those school authorities throughout the country which had operated such schools were instructed to implement desegregation, in good faith, "with all deliberate speed."

I hold that the Board of Education of New Rochelle by its

conduct in the years prior to 1949, created and established the Lincoln School as a segregated, Negro school. Thus formulated, the present case falls squarely within the plain meaning of the Brown decision.

The Board contends that since Lincoln School is not in form a component of a dual system of education for whites and Negroes such as was invalidated by Brown, and since the school contains 94% Negroes rather than 100 percent Negroes, there can be no violation of the Fourteenth Amendment or of the Brown principles.

But, this contention misconstrues the underlying premise of the Brown rationale. That opinion, while dealing with a state-maintained dual system of education was premised on the factual conclusion that a segregated education created and maintained by official acts had a detrimental and deleterious effect on the educational and mental development of the minority-group children. The unanimous Court, speaking through Chief Justice Warren, declared that segregation of Negro children especially in their formative years "generates a feeling of inferiority as to their status in the community that may affect their hearts and minds in a way unlikely ever to be undone." 347 U.S. at 494. The Court further emphasized the necessity of giving these minority-group children the opportunity for extensive contact with other children at an early stage in their educational experience, finding such contact to be indispensable if children of all races and creeds were to become inculcated with a meaningful understanding of the essentials of our democratic way of life. That the benefits inherent in an integrated education are essential to the proper development of all children has been reiterated time and again by the many witnesses in the present case, including those called by the defendant.

With these principles clear in mind, I see no basis to draw a distinction, legal or moral, between segregation established by the formality of a dual system of education, as in Brown, and that created by gerrymandering of school district lines and transferring of white children as in the instant case. The result is the same in each case: the conduct of responsible school officials has operated to deny to Negro children the opportunities for a full and meaningful educational experience guaranteed to them by the Fourteenth Amendment. Further, the fact that the Lincoln School contains approximately 6% whites, surely cannot divest Lincoln of its segregated character. In a community such as New Rochelle, the presence of some 29 white children certainly does not afford the 454 Negro children in the school the educational and social contacts and interaction envisioned by Brown.

Having created a segregated school, the Constitution imposed upon the Board the duty to end segregation, in good faith, and with all deliberate speed. It is patently clear that this obligation has not been fulfilled.

The Board argues that the study which it has given to the problem, and the surveys which it has requested, conclusively indicate its good faith. But, history is made, and Constitutional rights vindicated, by deeds, not by talk, resolutions, and fine phrases. As already indicated, the Board has discussed the problem, hired experts, made surveys, and constantly reiterated verbally its belief in racial equality and the necessity for equal opportunities. But the fact remains that, in eleven years, not one single act was taken to implement these expressed principles. And, the Board's attitude, as indicated by its overt conduct, has been one of negation; it has publicly disclaimed all responsibility for the Lincoln problem. . . .

I cannot accept the proposition that in this relatively small community in the north, men of good will, wisdom and ingenuity could not have devised a plan for the orderly desegregation of the Lincoln School.

If the school boards could satisfy their obligations under the Fourteenth Amendment merely by waiting complacently until an "ideal" solution presented itself, the Brown decision, and the advances in the area of individual equality which it represents, would be a virtual nullity. Brown, if it meant anything, meant much more than this. Necessarily implied in its proscription of segregation was the positive obligation of eliminating it. This obligation requires both good faith, and action with dispatch, and I am compelled to the conclusion that the Board of Education of New Rochelle has complied with neither of these requirements in the present case. . . .

I also conclude that if a Board of Education enters into a course of conduct motivated by a purposeful desire to perpetuate and maintain a segregated school, the constitutional rights of those confined within this segregated establishment have been violated.

If a Board of Education selects a school site, or otherwise operates its schools, with a purposeful desire to segregate, or to maintain segregation, the Constitution has been violated.

If such motivation is present, it makes no meaningful difference whether the segregation involved is maintained directly or through formal separation, or indirectly, through over-rigid adherence to artificially created boundary lines as in the present case.

Similarly it is of no moment whether the segregation is labelled by the defendant as "de jure" or "de facto," as long as the Board, by its conduct, is responsible for its maintenance.

The defendant argues, however, that the neighborhood school policy is a reasonable and educationally sound one, and thus that it is not violating the Constitution in adhering to it. But, this argument ignores the essential nature of the plaintiffs' position. They are not attacking the concept of the neighborhood school as an abstract proposition. They are, rather, attacking its application so as to deny opportunities guaranteed to them by the Constitution. It is a legal truism that "acts generally lawful may become unlawful when done to accomplish an unlawful end."

Moreover, as Justice Frankfurter succinctly noted: "Local customs, however hardened by time, are not decreed in heaven."

The neighborhood school policy certainly is not sacrosanct. It is valid only insofar as it is operated within the confines established by the Constitution. It cannot be used as an instrument to confine Negroes within an area artificially delineated in the first instance by official acts. If it is so used, the Constitution has been violated and court must intervene.

The court thus indicated that it would not permit the school authorities to confine integration to a bare token under the guise of a neighborhood school plan. The Evans decision clearly answers the Board's contention that since Negroes are free to move to other districts, they are not being required to attend a segregated school. Moreover, the Board indicates a naivete in not recognizing the difficulties inherent in changing long established residential patterns.

The Board raises several other contentions in an attempt to justify its conduct. With respect to its refusal to institute permissive zoning . . . the Board argues that it would be violative of the law to accord Negroes special privileges not allowed to other minority groups. It points to the fact that several other elementary schools in New Rochelle have student compositions which are primarily of one religious or national-origin group. . . . There are instances where it is not only justified, but necessary, to provide for such allegedly "unequal treatment" in order to achieve the equality guaranteed by the Constitution.

The Lincoln School was established as an all-Negro school by the gerrymandering of district lines, and by the transfer of white children residing in the district to schools outside the district. The Board of Education of the City of New Rochelle was responsible for both of these policies. Subsequent to 1949, the Board by its arbitrary rejection of all proposals for change has purposefully maintained Lincoln as a segregated school. This decision is rendered on the facts in this case and holds that, in the instant situation, Constitutional rights have been violated.

In conclusion, the words of Justice Frankfurter bear repetition:

"That the responsibility of those who exercise power in a democratic government is not to reflect inflamed public feeling but to help form its understanding, is especially true when they are confronted with a problem like a racially discriminating public school system. This is the lesson to be drawn from the heartening experience in ending enforced racial segregation in the public schools in cities with Negro populations of large proportions. Compliance with decisions of this Court, as the constitutional organ of the supreme law of the land, has often, throughout our history, depended on active support by state and local authorities: it presupposes such support. To withhold it, and indeed to use political power to try to paralyze the supreme law, precludes the maintenance of our federal system as we have known and cherished it for one hundred and seventy years."

Litigation is an unsatisfactory way to resolve issues such as have been presented here. . . . Men of good will, such as the individual members of the Board submit they are, could have solved and still can solve the problem by exercising the judgment and understanding for which they presumably were chosen. The School Board is a public body charged with a public responsibility. This responsibility must be exercised solely in the best interests of the children attending the schools. The Board cannot relieve itself of this responsibility by giving the community whatever result might gratify the impulse of the moment. Nothing can be permitted to conflict with the Board's moral and legal obligation.

THE DECREE

In determining the manner in which the Negro children residing within the Lincoln district are to be afforded the opportunities guaranteed by the Constitution, I will follow the procedure authorized by the Supreme Court in Brown v. Board of Education, 349 U.S. 294 (1955), and utilized by many district courts in implementing the Brown principles. Thus, I deem it unnecessary at this time to determine the extent to which each of the items of relief requested by plaintiffs will be afforded. Instead, the Board is hereby ordered to present to this Court, on or before April 14, 1961, a plan for desegregation in accordance with this Opinion, said desegregation to begin no later than the start of the 1961–62 school year. This court will retain jurisdiction of this action until such plan has been presented, approved by the court, and then implemented.

The foregoing Opinion will constitute the court's findings of fact and conclusions of law.

Dated: New York, N.Y.

January 24, 1961

IRVING R. KAUFMAN
U.S.D.J.

"Principals Deny Bias in Schools . . . Say Intemperate
Criticism is Undermining Morale."

SCHOOL INTEGRATION:
A CASE STUDY*

The following selections from *The New York Times*
follow the dramatic story of school integration in
New York from 1963 to 1966, as it unfolded. A
review of the opening paragraph of the introduction
to this section provides a pessimistic ending to the
story, because all the pressures and court actions described here seem to have made little difference in
the actual racial composition of New York schools.

*A reading of these news stories, which include
statements from people representing a wide spec-
trum of public opinion, is a good test for the analysis presented in the Part introduction. Are there
points of view not adequately represented there?
Could the analysis be reformulated into a different
structure?*

* Selected articles from *The New York Times*, © 1963, 1964 and 1965 by
The New York Times Company. Reprinted by permission.

PUPIL TRANSFERS TO DIVIDE RACES VOIDED BY COURT

By Anthony Lewis

SPECIAL TO THE NEW YORK TIMES

Washington, June 3—The Supreme Court held unconstitutional today a school desegregation plan that allows pupils to transfer out of schools where their race is in the minority.

Justice Tom C. Clark said that the plan was invalid because it based transfers "solely on racial factors" and led to "perpetuation of segregation." He spoke for a unanimous Court. . . .

Justice Clark's opinion emphasized what he called this "one-way" transfer system.

"The right of transfer," Justice Clark said, "which operates solely on the basis of a racial classification, is a one-way ticket leading to but one destination, i.e., the majority race of the transferee and continued segregation."

Racial classifications for purposes of school transfer, he said, are as inherently "invidious" as others the Court has struck down. He listed cases condemning segregation in parks, courtrooms and many other areas.

The Court's reliance on the inherently invalid nature of racial classifications seemed to some observers to raise questions about Northern plans that deliberately arrange school transfers to promote integration.

Negroes have been strongly advocating, for example, transfers from all-Negro schools in and around New York as a way to end "de facto segregation" based on housing patterns. New Jersey authorities have just ruled that such transfers should be made.

It could be argued that these transfers are explicitly based on race and thus are also unconstitutional under the reasoning of today's decision. On the other hand, the transfers there would be a step to decrease, not return to, segregation.

The Court's treatment of the pupil-transfer issue illustrated how time might alter its outlook on a problem.

June 25, 1963

CITY STUDY GROUP URGES SENDING
OF WHITE PUPILS TO NEGRO AREAS

The Board of Education was urged yesterday to consider transporting white children to schools in Negro neighborhoods to help achieve better racial balances in the city school system.

At the same time, Mayor Wagner was urged to establish a top-level committee on school integration to coordinate the activities of all city agencies and the school board.

The proposals were contained in a report made by a group of school and community leaders who took part in a recent conference on integration in the city's public schools. Copies of the report were sent on Friday to Dr. Calvin E. Gross, Superintendent of Schools, and Max J. Rubin, president of the Board of Education. The conference was sponsored by the school board, the City Commission on Human Rights, seven teacher-training institutions and a number of other organizations, including the Urban League of Greater New York and the National Association for the Advancement of Colored People.

The group said that "new approaches" should be introduced to promote school integration. Its report urged the consideration of "reverse open enrollment (two-way bussing)."

ASSIGNMENTS POSSIBLE

"Open enrollment" is the term used by the school system to identify a program under which children from predominantly Negro and Puerto Rican schools are given the option of transferring to under-utilized schools in other areas.

"Reverse open enrollment" means that white pupils would replace the transferred Negroes and Puerto Ricans.

Asked to amplify the recommendation, Dr. Gordon Klopf, associate professor of education at Teachers College, Columbia University, and conference co-chairman, said that initially white parents could be requested to send their children to schools outside their neighborhoods for the purpose of integration. But, he added, if this did not work, assignments might be made.

The proposal's backers contend that this is the only way to assure integration in all-Negro areas such as Harlem.

Another recommendation was the "development of conclaves of schools on all levels in educational centers in park-like areas of the community, serving large numbers of children from various sections of the city."

Other resolutions called upon the board to do the following:

¶Intensify its efforts "to obtain the massive financial resources required for effective integrated education."

¶Extend its program for educating school personnel in human development and social relations.

¶Allocate a substantial part of its budget for a more comprehensive program of research and experimentation in guidance and instruction for pupils of varying cultural backgrounds and to develop effective approaches to integroup education.

A conference statement asserted that the improvement of segregated schools "while currently valuable and necessary" was not "a substitute for integrated education."

The statement called for "a commitment to the concept of complete integration" throughout the city.

August 2, 1963

SUIT FOR WHITE PUPILS
CHARGES DISCRIMINATION

By Leonard Buder

The Board of Education has been accused of racial discrimination against white children in a suit brought by four white parents in State Supreme Court in Brooklyn.

The suit charged that the constitutional rights of white parents and their children were violated and that Negro parents and children were granted "superior" privileges by the school system.

The court action seeks to restrain the board from assigning white pupils from East Flatbush to a new junior high school in Brownsville on the basis of a racial "quota system." Under the board's zoning plan, which the parents are trying to upset, the new school would open in the fall with 35.2 per cent Negroes, 33.6 per cent Puerto Ricans and 31.2 per cent "others."

According to school officials, the suit is probably the first ever brought against the city system on the ground that white children were being discriminated against because of their race and color. Previous suits have charged discrimination against Negroes and Puerto Ricans. . . .

In their petition, the two white couples charged that the zoning plan—a modification of one originally proposed by the assistant superintendent in the area—ignored traditional neighborhood lines, traffic conditions, topographical barriers and other factors.

They said that their children and others from East Flatbush would normally have attended Junior High School 285 at Beverly Road and Ralph Avenue. To take the place of the whites who will go to the Brownsville school, the petition said, the board would have to take Negro children to East Flatbush by bus.

The parents charged that the board's quota system was based "upon unreasonable, unconstitutional ethnic and racial considerations."

They added that the action deprived the white children of "the right to associate with their friends and to attend a public school in their neighborhood."

August 8, 1963

PUPILS IN IMBALANCED SCHOOLS ARE FOUND DECLINING TRANSFERS

By Robert H. Terte

Pupils from 30 predominantly Negro and Puerto Rican elementary schools have for the most part chosen to attend sixth grade at their neighboring junior high schools rather than transfer to better-integrated elementary schools further away from home.

The choice was offered to the parents of 3,374 children who were scheduled to move out of their present schools to provide added space for pre-school and kindergarten programs and to reduce short-time instruction.

Only 942 requested assignment to selected elementary schools with space available and better racial balance, while 2,204 chose to enter sixth-grade classes being formed in the junior high schools that they would otherwise have entered as seventh graders.

No racial breakdown was given on the children requesting transfers.

Space is being created in the junior high schools by sending ninth-grade students to 36 designated senior high schools where they will attend integrated classes. The junior highs involved are predominantly Negro and Puerto Rican.

Jacob Landers, assistant superintendent of schools for integration, pointed out that more students—nearly 25 per cent—had requested transfers than under other voluntary transfer programs, which have averaged 5 per cent or less.

The board's original plan to send all of the sixth graders from the 30 schools into the junior high schools was changed when civil rights groups charged that the move would not improve integration.

Mr. Landers said that most of the children involved in the transfers had had opportunities to attend other schools under the board's open enrollment or free choice plans. The sixth grade children currently requesting transfer will not receive bus transportation but will travel free on public transportation, he added.

August 26, 1963

CITY WILL PERMIT PUPIL TRANSFERS
FOR INTEGRATION

The Board of Education reported yesterday that it planned to waive the neighborhood school policy for large numbers of Negro and Puerto Rican children to allow them to attend schools outside their districts.

The plan was disclosed in a report to the State Education Commissioner on the board's immediate and long-range program to achieve better integration. The program, which will cost $10,000,000 in the coming school year, includes both desegregation and improvement in the quality of instruction.

Schools that receive pupils transferring from areas where de facto segregation exists in housing will be given additional teachers. Educational opportunities will be increased through a wide range of activities including after-school tutoring and improved guidance in gaining admission to college and in getting jobs.

The report was submitted to comply with an order issued to all school districts on June 14 by the State Education Commissioner, Dr. James E. Allen Jr.

PLAN IS HAILED

Dr. Calvin E. Gross, the city's Superintendent of Schools, called the plan "the most comprehensive effort to achieve maximum integration, both on the basis of past performance and future commitment, of any city school system in the country."

He said it would permit the city schools to "move toward complete ethnic integration to the limit permitted by feasibility and sound educational practice."

The plan represents "all possible steps we have been able to devise, short of the compulsory interchange of Negro and white students between distant communities," he said.

The board insists it will not yield to integrationist pressures to transport white children involuntarily to schools that, because of de facto housing segregation, are predominantly Negro or Puerto Rican.

September 7, 1963

SCHOOL REZONING IS RULED ILLEGAL

By Homer Bigart

A Board of Education plan to achieve racial balance in a Brooklyn school by altering the zoning was upset in court yesterday.

The ruling appeared to compromise an important part of the board's program for achieving school integration.

State Supreme Court Justice Edward G. Baker said the Brooklyn plan violated the State Education Law, which provides that "no person shall be refused admission into or excluded from any public school in the state of New York on account of race, creed, color or national origin."

Justice Baker ruled in a case involving two white pupils who were to be transferred from East Flatbush to a new junior high school in Brownsville, which is predominantly Negro and Puerto Rican.

He found that a compelling factor in the board's rezoning of the new school district was to attain a student body that would be approximately one-third white, one-third Negro and one-third Puerto Rican.

Justice Baker ruled specifically on the plan for the new Junior High School 275, at Lincoln Boulevard and Rockaway Avenue.

In a protest over zoning policies, East Flatbush parents kept 7,000 children out of 13 neighborhood schools last March to protest plans to transport children to the new school, which is scheduled to open Monday. On June 15 a second "sit-out" demonstration was held, this one involving 3,600 children.

The Board of Education, which is involved in 11th-hour negotiations to avert a teachers' strike, declined immediate comment on yesterday's ruling. A spokesman said the board would need time to study it.

The Rev. Milton A. Galamison, chairman of the City-wide Committee for Integrated Schools, said last night that the ruling "defies the letter and spirit of the law."

Mr. Galamison, noting that the decision "was based on a part of the law to the effect that no persons shall be assigned to school on the basis of race, religion and national origin," said:

"This law was designed to prevent segregation. In the decision, the law is being used to prevent integration. It is being used to make segregation inevitable."

QUOTES SCHOOL OFFICIALS

In his ruling, Justice Baker quoted from two school officials who had made it clear that there was a deliberate design to achieve a racial balance at the Brownsville school.

It was this evidence of deliberate intent to take race and ethnic origin into consideration that made the board's action illegal, the justice said.

October 3, 1963

NEW GROUP FIGHTS MASS PUPIL SHIFTS

By Peter Kihss

A citywide civic council to resist involuntary mass transfers of public school pupils and to insist on the neighborhood school concept was reported yesterday to have been formed.

The formation was reported by Bernard Kessler, counsel to the Parents and Taxpayers of Jackson Heights, which was started three weeks ago to oppose integration proposals currently under study for two Queens schools.

The coordinating council was said to have at least 15 affiliates. Mr. Kessler said these included both old and new organizations with claimed memberships of 275,000 to 300,000.

Their plans, Mr. Kessler said, call for mutual support in legal action and, if necessary, picketing, boycotts, strikes and even undergoing arrest. He said the groups would work together to defeat legislators supporting transfer proposals.

Mr. Kessler contended transfers based on race would violate anti-discrimination provisions of the 14th Amendment to the Constitution. . . .

Mrs. Gloria Gold, president of the Parents Association of Public School 149, said the proposals had been evolved and unanimously endorsed by the executive boards of her group and of the Parent Teacher Association of Public School 92. . . .

The proposal, Mrs. Gold said, was evolved after school officials last July pointed out state and city policies seeking greater racial balance. All kindergarten through third-grade classes would be assigned to P.S. 149, and all fourth-grade through sixth-grade classes to P.S. 92. This is the so-called Princeton plan.

This proposal was linked to plans for maximum class sizes of 28 pupils, junior guidance classes and other special services. The Board of Education is studying the proposals.

Since the opposition developed, a Citizens Committee for Balanced Schools has sprung up to support the integration effort.

Councilman Edward L. Sadowsky, a Democrat, who has two children in P.S. 149, said yesterday that both law and morals required doing "something to end de facto segregation." But he emphasized that he was "personally opposed to mandatory bussing of children all over the community."

The Parents and Taxpayers of Jackson Heights (known as PAT), in a circular, said it opposed "segregated schools" but was also "vehemently opposed to block-busting tactics of any kind."

It says it welcomed Negroes at Public School 149 when the district was rezoned several years ago.

PETITION SPONSORED

Mr. Kessler said PAT had sponsored a petition with 1,400 signatures sent to the Board of Education. Some of the signers, he said, were Negroes.

In his own circular to parents, Mr. Kessler asserted that "children are not chattels of the state." In this, he objected to hardships and the risks of travel outside neighborhoods, the "tremendous expense of forcible transfers" and damage to "large investments in real property" if prospective purchasers' children had to attend distant schools.

October 4, 1963

NEW PARENT UNIT ORGANIZED HERE

Spreading controversy over moves to increase integration in the city's public schools has led to the formation of a city-wide Interracial Parents Committee to work for "school integration and quality education for all."

The new group, headed by Mrs. Lemoine Callender, chairman of the schools committee of the Harlem Neighborhood Association, said it had rejected "the Board of Education's recently stated free-choice-transfer policy since this plan permits the board to abrogate its responsibility for integration, shifting it to the individual parent." . . .

Mrs. Ellen Lurie, a member of a twelve-member coordinating committee for the Interracial Parents Committee, said that group had not agreed on specific alternatives to the free-choice-transfer policy, which it has called only a token.

But it has criticized the free-choice policy as merely shifting overcrowding to other schools "without concomitant services and traveling aids, without retraining of teachers, re-education of administrative staff or revaluation of curriculum."

It has promised "to mobilize citywide support in both the Negro and white communities for integrated quality education in all New York City schools."

December 9, 1963

HARLEM CATHOLIC SCHOOLS
COOL TO TRANSFERS

By Gene Currivan

Roman Catholic elementary schools in the heart of Harlem where enrollments are almost totally Negro, have made no attempt to alter the racial balance and there has been no insistent demand for it by parents or civil rights groups.

Non-Catholic as well as Catholic Negro parents voluntarily send their children to these schools and pay for the privilege.

While there is general agreement among Catholic spokesmen that a racial balance is preferable to de facto segregation if it can be accomplished without serious dislocation, the hierarchy feels that shifting or transporting elementary school pupils in Harlem is not the solution. Parents appear to agree.

Instead, the parochial elementary schools regard "segregation" as a condition thrust upon them. They are retaining the neighborhood concept in Central Harlem, determined to educate whatever children come along. And in Central Harlem those youngsters are Negroes.

These schools operate in the ghetto, have classes almost double the size of many public schools and provide few of the luxuries associated with private schools. No voices have been raised in protest from the civil rights organizations, which feel that this is a private affair.

'SINS OF OMISSION'

From within, there is some self-criticism, such as from a teaching nun who said: "We are not practicing what we preach when we perpetuate segregration," and from a priest who complained about the "sins of omission" in textbooks and social studies that fail properly to evaluate the Negro and his heritage or acknowledge his equality.

He referred to the often-heard criticism that the Negro is invariably portrayed in textbooks at a menial level, while the typical middle-class person is shown as a prosperous caucasian. These complaints, however, are heard in both public and private schools.

The eight Catholic schools of Central Harlem, which are almost wholly Negro, are relatively small institutions with from 200 to about 500 pupils each. They are constructed and financed by their parishes but are under the general supervision of the New York Archdiocese, which prescribes curriculum and standards.

SUPERINTENDENT GIVES VIEW

The position taken in regard to de facto segregation was summed up by Msgr. John Paul Haverty, superintendent of the archdiocesan schools. He said:

"There is no legal requirement that compels Catholic parents of the parishes in central Harlem to enroll their boys and girls in our neighborhood Catholic elementary schools. This decision to have their children attend these schools is voluntarily made.

"It certainly gives strong proof of the earnest desire of these parents that their boys and girls have solid moral training together with the benefits of intellectual stimulation in a wholesome religious environment.

"Evidently this concern overrides and takes precedence over the wish for education in schools with a racially balanced enrollment. I am convinced that if we had the teachers and the facilities we could easily double our present enrollment in the parish elementary schools of Central Harlem."

The present enrollment in the eight predominantly Negro schools is 3,269, including about 20 per cent of non-Catholics. St. Mark the Evangelist, at 55 West 138th Street, for example, has about one third non-Catholics.

Catholics, whose numbers have been dwindling in recent years as a result of migration to other parts of the metropolitan area, are given first choice. Then the doors are opened to others. With all its seats filled, St. Marks has a waiting list of 50.

It has been estimated that there are 1.1 million Negroes in the city with about 500,000 in Harlem. While no official figures are available, the number of Negro Catholics in the city has been placed at between 70,000 and 80,000.

The reasons that non-Catholic Negro parents send their children to a parochial school where they have to pay and where the youngsters study a religious doctrine other than their own are varied.

Leander Jones of 36 West 138th Street, a Baptist who has four daughters at St. Mark's, put it this way: "They teach moral principles and values and do a job 10 times better than the public schools. My daughter who is in the fourth grade can do the same work as the kid next door who is in sixth grade in public school."

As to segregation, he said: "Here they are trying to do something about it like teaching about the Negro's accomplishments. But the public schools give only lip service. Sure, I want integration but I also want my kids going to school near home."

CHILD PUT BACK YEAR

Mrs. Rubie Parker of 21 West 137th Street, an Episcopalian, has two sons in the school, Charles, 6 years old, and Michael, 8. Last week she took Michael out of Public School 100, down the street at Fifth Avenue, where he was in third grade. The move cost Michael a year because St. Mark's put him back to second grade after studying the results of his entrance test.

"It's all right with me," Mrs. Parker said. "I'd rather have him get a firm educational foundation now than have him passed along from grade to grade. It seems to me that the public schools spend too much time disciplining."

Mrs. Enid Brann Henry, an Episcopalian of 1850 Lexington Avenue who has three girls in the school, said that even though there was "segregation" there was "no feeling of segregation."

"What I mean," she explained, "is that the boys and girls seem different than a lot of others because they learn respect and how to be little ladies and gentlemen. Somehow there is a sense of difference going to a private Catholic school."

Another parent, with two girls in the school, Mrs. Verdelle Francis of 2101 Madison Avenue, is a recent convert who had been a Baptist.

'THEY LEARN FASTER'

"I would certainly like to see some integration," she said, "but meanwhile the children are away from public school split sessions, they learn faster, read better and they are better behaved. Maybe the occasional spankings have something to do with it, but they need it."

Rice High School at Lenox Avenue and 124th Street is deep in the Negro area. Yet this school, operated by the Christian Brothers of Ireland, has an enrollment of 855 boys, of whom 75 per cent are white.

Half come from Manhattan and the Bronx and the other half travel from Brooklyn and Queens. As in the case of other high schools that draw their enrollments from widespread areas, Rice, unlike the elementary schools, is not adaptable to the neighborhood concept.

Here is integration in the heart of Harlem, although no intentional effort was made to bring it about. After passing the diocesan tests for high school entrance the boys were permitted to list four high school preferences throughout the city. They were accepted wherever there was room.

The low percentage of Negroes at Rice appears to indicate,

according to some observers, that the other Negroes in the neighborhood who were eligible to attend either could not afford the cost ($20 a month and about $25 a year for books) or were anxious for the opportunity to escape from Harlem and attend schools outside.

According to Brother Francis K. Fish, superintendent at Rice, Negro students have been winning a third of the available prizes and the second and third students in the senior class this year are Negroes. He added that 60 per cent of the Negro graduates went on to college in the last two years.

WHITES ASKED WHY

Several white students who were asked why they travelled long distances to a school in the midst of Harlem said the area was of little consequence to them since they walked only a block to either subway or bus. To them it was "a good school," and most of the students would have to travel to high school in any event.

While no move has been made to bus parochial elementary school pupils either into or out of Harlem, a break with the neighborhood tradition has been tried in several other localities. This transfer of pupils from one neighborhood to another is known in official circles as "school utilization" and not integration or open enrollment as the public schools define it.

It is a program of transporting pupils from overcrowded schools to under-utilized ones. Integration resulted in one case where 142 pupils, mostly Negro and Puerto Rican, travel each day between southeast Bronx and Yorkville.

They come from St. Athanasius parish school, 880 Fox Street the Bronx, to St. Catherine of Siena, 420 East 69th Street. All but the seventh and eighth graders, who go by subway, travel by bus.

PARISH IN TRANSITION

Until this experiment was tried in the fall of 1961, St. Catherine's School, which is in an upper-middle-class neighborhood near Cornell Medical College, was almost completely white. In recent years the parish has lost a large part of its Catholic population.

Of its 425 pupils about half now are from the parish. The new residents who displaced the old families are either non-Catholics or have few or no children.

As to the reaction of the mothers to the new arrivals from the southeast Bronx, Sister Bernardita, the Mother Superior, said she had heard there was some resentment "but they don't tell me about it."

One of the mothers, who declined to be identified, said: "What can we do about it? We were told it was a temporary arrangement and now whether it is temporary or not we are used to them and—well, maybe it's better all around. But I feel sorry for them because they are herded into buses after school without a chance to play with the other kids. What kind of integration is that?"

Transportation for the youngsters is provided by the Board of Education, which is reimbursed by the state. The sending school pays the tuition which is $5 a family a month plus $15 a year for books. Uniforms cost about $14 for girls and half that for the boys.

In Harlem, where racial balance is not attempted, there appear to be two reasons why the current acceptance of de facto segregation is working out. The first is the cooperation of uncomplaining parents who are periodically consulted as to academic and disciplinary matters. The other is the choice of religious teaching orders, which has demonstrated an interest in racial education.

As in all private institutions, the authorities have no obligation to retain unruly children. Unlike the public schools, the parochial schools reserve the right of expulsion for any cause whatever. Parents who value the prestige of a private school and its spiritual training manage to impress upon the children the need to toe the line. This cooperation, according to school authorities, represents the difference between success and failure.

The schools themselves are similar to small public schools, except for the teaching of religious doctrine and the limited amount of modern equipment.

At St. Mark's, which is typical, French is taught in the

seventh and eighth grades and will later be extended to lower grades. There are no elaborate language laboratories such as are seen in many public schools, but there are teaching machines, programmed learning, audio-visual aids especially for remedial reading and a modified version of the Higher Horizons program.

CULTURAL OPPORTUNITIES

This program, which is used in many New York City public schools, offers a variety of cultural opportunities such as visits to museums, concerts and other places of interest that ordinarily would not be available to the children.

Some of the classes run as high as 55 pupils compared with 30 or 35 in similar public school classes. But according to both parents and authorities the disciplinary problems are minimal.

The most prominent of the teaching orders in the Central Harlem area is the Sisters of the Blessed Sacrament for Indians and Colored People. It was founded in Pittsburgh in 1891 by Rev. Mother Katherine, who was the daughter of Francis Anthony Drexel, a Philadelphia banker and partner of J. P. Morgan. There are now 64 schools in 21 states.

The New York chapter, headed by Mother Loyola at St. Mark's, where it began teaching in 1912, is now also at St. Charles Borromeo and St. Joseph's, 168 Morningside Avenue; All Saints, 50 East 130th Street, and St. Thomas Apostle, 155 St. Nicholas Avenue.

CONTRARY TO CHURCH TEACHING

Mother Loyola strongly believes that segregation is contrary to the teaching of the church, although in some cases, such as in Harlem's ghetto, it has to be temporarily accepted until some other way is found.

"We try to impress on these young boys and girls that there is really no difference between them and us," Mother Loyola said. "That is what Christ taught. We show them through religious training, whether they are Catholics or not, that they are part of the Mystical Body of Christ—that they are the same as we are."

Mother Loyola said segregation invariably brought a feeling of inferiority in the children.

The sisters try to counteract this by bringing back to the school on occasion those graduates who have gone on to high school and college. This helps provide motivation and a sense of identification as the graduates bring back tales of the world beyond the ghetto.

January 11, 1964

SCHOOL REZONING FOR INTEGRATION BARRED BY COURT

By John Sibley

SPECIAL TO THE NEW YORK TIMES

Albany, Jan. 10—Efforts to bring about racial balance in public schools by redrawing district lines suffered a new setback today.

Ruling in a Malverne, L.I., case, State Supreme Court Justice Isadore Brookstein said that whether their intentions were good or not, school authorities had no right to consider racial or ethnic factors in drawing school zones.

His decision invalidated an order issued last June 17 by Education Commissioner James E. Allen Jr. that would have shuffled pupils in the Malverne-Lakeview school district.

The Commissioner had directed that pupils from kindergarten through third grade be assigned to either the Davison Avenue or Lindner Place school, each of which has an enrollment about 14 per cent Negro, and that all fourth-grade and fifth-grade pupils attend the Woodfield Road School, which has an enrollment that is 75 per cent Negro.

ALLEN'S POSITION

Dr. Allen's order had been stayed pending today's decision by Justice Bookstein.

Charles Brind, counsel for the State Education Department, had declared when the case was argued before Justice Bookstein that Commissioner Allen's order was based on educational considerations. He contended that the racial imbalance was harmful to education.

Mason Hampton, lawyer for parents challenging the order, insisted that redistricting to achieve racial balance was illegal whatever the motivation. It was this contention that Justice Bookstein upheld today.

His ruling reinforced a decision handed down in an almost identical case last September by Supreme Court Justice Edward G. Baker in Brooklyn.

Justice Baker held in that case that the New York City Board of Education could not legally alter school district lines in the Brownsville and East Flatbush sections to remedy de facto racial segregation there.

Justice Baker's ruling is currently on appeal before the Appellate Division of State Supreme Court in Brooklyn. Both the Brooklyn and Malverne cases hinged on Section 3201 of the State Education Law, which declares:

"No person shall be refused admission into or be excluded from any public school in the State of New York on account of race, creed, color or national origin."

Justice Bookstein's decision noted:

"While the United States Constitution forbids segregation by law in the public schools, it neither forbids racial imbalance nor compels racial balance."

FEDERAL RULING NOTED

In support of the principle, he cited the decision of a Federal District Court in Indiana (Bell vs. City of Gary, Ind.). This decision subsequently upheld by a Federal Court of Appeals, held that a neighborhood school plan set up with no intention of segregating races, need not be revised if it results in racial imbalance because a district happens to be populated predominantly by one race or another.

At the same time, Justice Bookstein's decision contained several references to court rulings declaring it unconstitutional to gerrymander, or manipulate, school district lines to maintain racial segregation.

Justice Bookstein made no reference to Justice Baker's decision, although the Brooklyn case had been cited frequently during argument of the Malverne case.

Justice Bookstein said that Commissioner Allen himself, in a situation that arose in 1956, had subscribed to the principles set forth in today's court decision. He quoted the Commissioner as saying at that time:

"Because of the incidence of location, the mere fact that the preponderance of the children who would normally attend the neighborhood school happened to be white or Negro, of Polish, Irish, Scotch, Swedish, Italian or English descent or otherwise, or who espouse one religion or another, does not require a board to attempt to gerrymander the lines, to assign but a certain percentage to a particular school. This would constitute as much discrimination as a gerrymandered line to accomplish the opposite effect."

The State Education Department said today there would be no immediate decision on whether to appeal Justice Bookstein's ruling. . . .

N.A.A.C.P. TO APPEAL

Robert L. Carter, general counsel of the National Association for the Advancement of Colored People, announced that the organization would appeal the decision.

He said that Justice Bookstein's ruling was more far-reaching than the earlier decision by Justice Baker, because "it affects every school district in the state."

Asserting that Justice Bookstein's analysis did not meet the basic issue posed by this and other cases involving the constitutionality of de facto school segregation, Mr. Carter declared:

"If segregated education is inferior education constitutionally, as the United States Supreme Court has held in the Brown case, there must be a constitutional requirement imposed on school authorities to take action to eliminate the segregated school."

Miss June Shagaloff, the organization's special assistant for education, added:

"In view of the intense concern of Negro parents and the clear and continuing damage to their children in segregated schools, it is inevitable that Negro parents will increasingly feel that they must rely upon nonjudicial approaches such as political persuasion and direct action in order to make their case and bring about meaningful school desegregation. The N.A.A.C.P. will certainly continue to provide leadership and support in these efforts."

March 6, 1964

PRINCIPALS DENY BIAS IN SCHOOLS

By Leonard Buder

City high school principals struck back yesterday at charges that the school system discriminated against Negro pupils.

The principals denied that schools in low-income areas were inferior, that teachers expected less from Negro pupils and shunted them into programs that doomed them "to menial status or unemployment" and that less money was spent on schools attended by minority-group children.

"Intemperate criticism is undermining the morale of our teachers and supervisors," the school administrators asserted. "It is contributing to the polarization of our community."

The defense of the schools was made by the High School Principals Association, which is comprised of the heads of the system's 57 academic high schools. Abraham H. Lass of Abraham Lincoln High School, president of the organization, said that the association's stand had been unanimously approved.

The association declared in a strongly worded statement that the "attacks have been made on the basis of superficial examination by individuals and groups who appear to be using the public school as a whipping boy for unresolved social and economic problems."

'TORRENT OF CRITICISM'

The principals did not identify the sources of "the recent torrent of unfair criticism," but it was clear that they were referring to charges made by some civil rights leaders and parents' spokesmen in the school integration controversy.

May 5, 1964

CIVIL RIGHTS SUIT OVER
IMBALANCE IN SCHOOLS FAILS

Supreme Court Bars Review of Ruling Against Forcing
Local Boards to Act

BUS-PLAN FOES BUOYED

No Legal Basis Is Found for Halting Inequity
Due Only to Pattern in Housing

By Anthony Lewis

SPECIAL TO THE NEW YORK TIMES

Washington, May 4—The Supreme Court left standing today a decision that school boards have no constitutional duty to end racial imbalance resulting from housing patterns.

The action was a major set-back for civil rights forces attacking what they call de facto segregation in Northern cities. This is the situation in which neighborhood public schools are all, or predominantly, Negro or white.

The Supreme Court did not itself pass on the merits of the problem today. It simply declined, in a brief and unexplained order, to review the lower court ruling.

Nevertheless, those who oppose moving pupils by bus to end racial imbalance will doubtless take comfort from the Supreme Court's refusal to consider the contention that such action is constitutionally required.

The case came from Gary, Ind. According to the Negro plaintiffs, 97 per cent of that city's Negro public-school pupils are in predominantly Negro schools.

The Court of Appeals for the Seventh Circuit, in deciding the case last October, found that the school imbalance did not result from any official policy. The court said that school districts had been drawn originally on non-racial lines and that their racial characteristics had changed with population shifts.

In taking the case to the Supreme Court, the complainants did not challenge these findings. They did not argue that the Gary school board had deliberately caused the racial division of its schools.

The argument was, rather, that it is unconstitutional for a school board to "acquiesce" in such de facto segregation. The petition to the Supreme Court suggested that the Constitution's bar against racial discrimination required the school board to take affirmative action.

Such affirmative action could presumably be a redrawing of school zones to improve racial imbalance. It could be forced busing of pupils to distant schools. It could be pairing of schools, the so-called Princeton plan.

Nothing in the case ended today puts any legal roadblock in the way of such moves by local school boards. They may act to diminish racial imbalance. But the Constitution does not require them to, according to the decision of the Appeals Court.

Thus the way remains open for civil rights groups to press through political means and protests for better racial balance in northern schools. It also remains open for opposition by groups that have arisen to defend "neighborhood schools."

May 8, 1964

WHITE PARENTS LOSE CASE
AGAINST SCHOOL REZONING

By Fred M. Hechinger

The Court of Appeals ruled yesterday that the Board of Education had the right to consider better racial integration as a factor in selecting school sites. The state's highest court thus upheld, in a 6-to-1 decision, a ruling by the Appellate Division in Brooklyn that school authorities could rezone a district, provided all pupils were still permitted to attend the school nearest their homes.

Chief Judge Charles S. Desmond, in the majority opinion, said that the question whether there was an "affirmative constitutional obligation to take action to reduce de facto segregation is simply not in this case."

The ruling on behalf of the board's action therefore was based solely on the fact that "it excludes no one from any school and has no tendency to foster or produce racial segregation."

Associate Judge John Van Voorhis, in a dissenting opinion, said that race was the "dominant factor and controlling consideration" in the rezoning of the schools. He called that "the reverse of anti-discrimination" and thus a violation of the principle that "each person shall be treated without regard to race, religion or national origin." He declared that "if a person can be legally admitted to a school for racial or religious reasons, he can be excluded for the same reasons."

The suit was brought by a group of white parents in East Flatbush, Brooklyn, who contended that their children were being ordered out of their neighborhood and forced to attend a school elsewhere to bring about racial integration.

The court, however, held that the board's zoning had not been "arbitrary, capricious or unreasonable." It pointed out that none of the children, who had not attended junior high school before, were actually being transferred from a school in which they had been enrolled.

The decision constituted the second defeat for the white parents who charged that their children were being assigned against their will to a school outside their neighborhood. However, the ruling represented a more limited victory for the proponents of integration than they had won from the Appellate Division's.

While the Appellate Division said that a school board, under decisions of the Supreme Court of the United States was responsible for the zoning of new schools to "prevent the creation of a segregated public school," yesterday's ruling limited its concern to the question: "May (not must) the schools correct racial imbalance?"

The court held that the board had this right, provided that no child would have to travel further to the new school than to get to his "neighborhood" school. It found that in the Brooklyn case the children's rights were fully protected.

A spokesman for the Brooklyn parents expressed disappointment over the decision. He said the case would be taken to the Supreme Court.

The parents contended that their children were being assigned to Junior High School 275 in Brownsville solely on the basis of race to achieve better integration among the pupils. Brownsville is largely Negro and Puerto Rican. The school to which they ordinarily would have been assigned, Junior High 285, is in East Flatbush.

QUOTA SYSTEM CHARGED

The parents had charged that by assigning their children to a school outside the East Flatbush neighborhood to bring about an enrollment of equal numbers of Negro, Puerto Rican and white students violated their rights and established a racial quota system.

The white parents won the first round when Supreme Court Justice Edward G. Baker ruled last September that the proposed rezoning was illegal. He cited Section 3201 of the State Education Law that holds that "no person shall be refused admission into or be excluded from any public school in the State of New York on account of race, creed, color or national origin."

In the second round, however, the Appellate Division said that section of the law had been introduced specifically to do away with actual segregation. It held that, if the law were now to be used as an instrument of segregation it would be unconstitutional under the 1954 Supreme Court ruling.

While upholding the neighborhood school as the nearest school to a child's home, the Appeals Court ruled that such terms as East Flatbush or Brownsville were "purely artificial" and did not constitute a neighborhood in terms of school zoning.

Both the Appellate Division and the Court of Appeals made special efforts, however, to limit the impact of their rulings and to state specifically that their decisions did not imply that the board was required to bring about racial balance through rezoning in all schools. Yesterday's decision made it explicit that it was concerned only with "newly instituted" schools.

While the ruling thus may bring about integration in a specific school, it could serve as a precedent to prevent integration in any case that required pupils to go to a rezoned school further from their home.

Nevertheless, James Farmer, national director of the Congress of Racial Equality, said: "New York State's highest court has issued a very significant ruling. At long last, New York State has judicial clearance on reassigning pupils to break up racial imbalance."

Isidore Balaban of Brooklyn, one of the parents who brought the suit, on the other hand, said: "We feel that the Court of Appeals based the decision on geography rather than racial quotas, which was what the original suit was based on." He declared that "the final say" would be up to the Supreme Court.

Judge Van Voorhis, in a long dissent, said that "it would be hopeless for any school board or other governing body to try to assemble an ideal amalgam by admitting the right quotas." He also referred to the refusal of the Supreme Court last Monday to review the Gary, Ind., case in which Negro groups charged that school zones had been drawn so as to maintain segregation.

May 13, 1964

STATE BIDS CITY RECAST SCHOOLS
FOR INTEGRATION

By David Anderson

Integration leaders offered conflicting opinions yesterday about the state advisory committee's report on racial imbalance in the city schools.

The report drew criticism from a spokesman for a largely white group that wants to keep the neighborhood-school system.

Miss June Shagaloff, special assistant for education for the National Association for the Advancement of Colored People, said: "It really is an excellent report. No one has ever attempted so comprehensive a plan for desegregation and good schools. It is a model for every Northern city."

Miss Shagaloff and Frederick Jones, state education chairman of the N.A.A.C.P., urged the Board of Education and the school system's administration to implement the report's proposals without delay.

The Rev. Milton A. Galamison, chairman of the Citywide Committee for Integrated Schools and a leader of the two school boycotts this year, said the report was "a forceful, extremely imaginative approach, a giant step in the right direction."

"It is far and away the best thing we have had from this kind of quarter," he added.

However, the report's contention that segregation could never be wholly eliminated in the city schools met with an objection from Alexander J. Allen, executive director of the Urban League.

REJECTS 'NEGATIVE' VIEW

"I definitely could not go along with so negative an approach," he said. "We can do anything we want to do."

Mr. Allen also said the proposal to "equalize" schools would provide only the minimum desirable level of education. Deprived schools, he argued, must get special attention to overcome past shortcomings, regardless of the racial composition of such schools.

The Urban League also indicated concern over the committee's concept of what is "possible."

The report, while declaring that total desegregation of the city schools is impossible, called for a major reorganization of the school system, including prekindergarten-to-fourth-grade neighborhood schools and middle-grade schools, with racially balanced enrollments, situated in educational parks.

"How integrated would those middle schools be?" the league asked.

Bernard Kessler, policy committee chairman of the Parents and Taxpayers Citywide Coordinating Council, an organization consisting predominantly of white parents, was critical of the report. Mr. Kessler's group is the one that picketed City Hall to protest plans for pairing schools.

WILL OPPOSE TRANSFERS

"We will oppose most strenuously the creation of educational parks and will also oppose the elimination of neighborhood junior high schools or the forcible transfer of students presently in the fifth and sixth grades," he said.

Mr. Galamison, however, praised the committee's plan, saying it would make segregation above the fourth grade "extremely difficult."

"One would hope that with educational parks desegregation would be even more widespread," he said.

The report also won approval from Frederick C. McLaughlin, director of the Public Education Association, who said it contained "some of the most drastic and far-reaching recommendations within recent memory."

Norman Hill, national program director of the Congress of Racial Equality, said last night that the reaction in the organization generally had been positive.

May 13, 1964

EXCERPTS FROM REPORT
ON SCHOOL INTEGRATION IN CITY

Following are excerpts from the report on "Desegregating the Public Schools of New York City," prepared by the State Education Commissioner's Advisory Committee on Human Relations and Community Tensions:

FROM COMMITTEE LETTER

The problems of desegregating and improving the schools of New York City can be dealt with only when they are seen against the broader objective of making and keeping New York City a community in which intelligent, discerning, and responsible parents will choose to raise their families. This cannot be done, however, without a number of changes in the schools of which the first and most important is to provide first-rate teaching for every child in every section of the city.

In addition, the need is urgent to expand and improve the supporting services that undergird and supplement the teacher's work. School plants must be built in larger numbers and more rapidly than in the past. Teaching materials must be improved and furnished more promptly and flexibly. As earlier studies have repeatedly pointed out, the administration of the New York City schools must be decentralized if initiative, originality, and imagination are to be encouraged on as wide a scale as is necessary to cope with the complex and varied tasks the schools face. Decentralization should not, however, become the means to erect regional barriers separating segments of the city. It should not, for example, be used as an excuse to keep children in one administrative unit from entering another if there are good educational and social reasons to warrant such transfers.

The changes we have proposed do not in every case require additional funds, but many do and the additions will have to be substantial. If the New York City schools are to be as good as they must become, the average expenditure per pupil may have to be raised a third or more over present levels. In the absence of more realistic budgets most of the good things the schools need will either be impossible or will have to be so meagerly done as to produce virtually no effect upon the City as a whole.

The money problems of the New York City schools must be faced squarely and responsibly by city, state, and national leaders. Because New York City is so important to the entire country the national aspect of its problems must be viewed as in part a Federal responsibility. At issue here is far more than how to build a few schools or raise teachers' salaries another notch. The whole question of New York City's future as a place to live is now being answered.

The challenge of finding the ways and means to finance the public schools properly must be accepted not only by the appropriate governmental officers but equally by those leaders of the business community and other segments of city life whose influence so often stimulates and ratifies the major decisions of government. It would be a disgraceful commentary on the values by which we live if the financial capital of the free world should find itself unable to marshal the talents, the money, and the foresight to underwrite the development of its own most precious and promising resources . . .

Faithfully yours,
Judah Cahn
Kenneth B. Clark
John H. Fischer, Chairman

SUMMARY OF REPORT

A. Findings:

1. Puerto Rican, Negro and other students in public schools in New York City, suffer extensive and serious ethnic segregation.

2. This segregation increased between 1958 and 1963, and will continue to increase over the next 10 to 15 years, unless deliberate policies are introduced to reduce current levels and prevent future increases in segregation.

3. The Board of Education has made efforts between 1954 and the present which were intended to reduce segregation. These efforts have had no measurable effect upon the overall number of students attending segregated schools or upon the number of segregated schools in the system.

4. Early in 1954, the Board of Education introduced new proposals intended to aid in desegregating the public schools. The new proposals, considered singly and in combination, would not reduce current levels of school segregation or prevent future increases.

5. Ethnic segregation cannot be wholly eliminated from the schools of New York City in the foreseeable future, but the adoption of wise and intelligent policies can reduce segregation substantially. The basic requirement is a deep and sustained commitment on the part of the Board and its staff to the purpose of reducing segregation throughout the city at the earliest time and at the fastest possible rate.

6. The adopted building program of the board does not treat desegregation as a main factor in choosing sites, although this factor could be utilized.

7. Wise and intelligent policies to foster desegregation must include intensified efforts to raise the quality of school program and teaching in New York City schools to the highest level, which is to say a degree of excellence second to none in the United States. The purposes of desegregation and increased excellence must be pursued simultaneously. They are absolutely interdependent.

8. The real accomplishment of both objectives is a complicated, costly, and difficult undertaking. It is far beyond what many advocates of change have seemed willing to recognize or acknowledge. Basic changes in the present organization of the school grades and the revision of construction programs are essential to desegregation and improvement, as are new concepts of recruitment, faculty involvement, curriculum design, pupil services, administrative operation, plant use, and interschool communication.

B. Recommendations:

1. Comprehensive four-year high schools should be built at points well outside existing ethnic ghettoes, to be attended by commuting youths from points all over the city as by local residents.

2. Fifth through eighth-grade middle schools should replace junior high schools ultimately in the entire system. The purpose of these units should be to furnish improved instruction for older children. They should be so located as to provide for as many children as possible an experience in an integrated school. Shuttle buses should be used to reach these middle schools.

3. Primary units extending from pre-kindergarten classes through the fourth grade should replace existing elementary schools. These units would still be neighborhood schools, but they would be organized differently and would feed into the middle schools. Many existing elementary schools could be reorganized to contain two or more primary units.

4. Educational complexes should be formed, consisting of from two to six primary units clustered around the middle schools. These should be managed by a single administrator, with assistant administrators in the separate unit buildings. The complexes should integrate educational activities, improve the distribution of facilities and resources, and promote communication between faculties, parents, and students from diverse ethnic backgrounds. The complexes should have a high degree of organizational autonomy over their programs.

5. Eventually, educational parks housed in newly developed structures on cleared sites should replace single middle schools with their educational complexes.

6. Facilities should be equalized in every way, so that mainly Puerto Rican and Negro schools in the city will not continue to be older, more overcrowded, and in greater need of installation of essential facilities than other schools.

7. The new organization of the system should be utilized to stabilize and improve the staffing of the schools. The middle schools and clustered primary units with their new autonomy should be used to attract and retain the best teachers and administrators.

8. Board programs to improve recruitment and advancement of minority group teachers and other personnel should be extended and intensified. As part of this training relations between the system and local teacher training institutions must be greatly strengthened.

9. Pre-primary programs of instruction should be introduced on a city-wide basis, serving children as young as three years.

10. Special schools and programs, particularly those for maladjusted and retarded students, should be studied independently and the findings should be made public. A stronger policy for retaining more such students in their regular schools should be pursued.

11. State and Federal support, fiscal and administrative, should be provided to the city to accomplish these necessary changes. This support should begin after the Board of Education has demonstrated its new initiative and commitment by

taking some of the steps toward desegregation which do not involve additional municipal expenditures.

Our proposals do, we trust, make plain the fact the substantial forces must be reckoned with and redirected if desegregation is to be achieved. If these proposals are adopted and implemented we are confident they will effect some immediate desegregation. More importantly, they would help prevent an increase in the rate of segregation within the schools. To accomplish this, however, they would have to be introduced promptly, progressively, and in an ever more extensive network during the next five years.

May 29, 1964

PUPILS THIS FALL FOR INTEGRATION

8 SCHOOLS PAIRED

*Rezoning and Shift of 6th and 9th Grades
to Affect Others*

By Leonard Buder

A broad integration program that will give hundreds of thousands of pupils their first school contact with children of other races will take effect here next September.

Accompanying the integration efforts will be other school measures intended to improve the quality of education and to meet the special needs of children in underprivileged areas.

Details of the city system's plans were announced yesterday by Dr. Calvin E. Gross, the Superintendent of Schools.

"The time for action is now," he said.

Unofficial estimates placed the number of school children who will be transferred or assigned under the plan at 40,000. This figure includes pupils transferred because of grade changes and school pairings, those attending junior high schools that will be rezoned, and those taking part in voluntary transfer programs.

SUMMARY OF THE PLAN

The plan, which drew immediate criticism from officials of the Parents and Taxpayers movement here, provided for these things:

»The transfer of 5,804 sixth-grade pupils from 44 elementary schools to fill the vacancies created in the 10 junior high schools.

»The pairing of four predominantly Negro and Puerto Rican elementary schools with nearby schools that are now largely white. This would involve bus transportation for nearly 1,000 pupils.

»The establishment of prekindergarten classes for 3- and 4-year-olds at 23 schools and the expansion of kindergarten programs at 18 schools.

»The reduction in the number of pupils receiving short-time instruction in 14 schools and the addition of an hour of class for first-graders at 17 schools.

»The redesign of four high schools, which are scheduled for construction next year, to make them comprehensive schools —offering both academic and vocational programs.

OPPONENT IS SHOCKED

Mrs. Rosemary R. Gunning, executive secretary of the Parents and Taxpayers Coordinating Council, which is opposed to the assignment of children to schools outside their neighborhood, declared:

"We are shocked by this plan. It will not only destroy the rights of many children to go to their traditional neighborhood schools in September, but obviously envisions wholesale involuntary transfers in the future.

"Implementation of this plan will create chaos and turmoil, since parents of all races will refuse to allow their children to be forced out of their own neighborhoods."

Civil rights groups withheld comment pending study.

However, the Rev. Dr. Milton A. Galamison, who directed two citywide school boycotts in recent months to dramatize demands for greater integration, said: "We're happy to see some signs of motion at the Board of Education."

June 4, 1964

SCHOOL INTEGRATION PLAN VOTED, 6–0, BY CITY BOARD

*Donovan Joins Colleagues in Backing Proposal
For 'Quality Education' After Long, Stormy Session*

By Robert H. Terte

The Board of Education early today unanimously adopted its plan for "quality integrated education."

At the end of a stormy session that lasted almost seven hours, James B. Donovan, president of the board, called on community groups to support the objectives of the plan.

The plan calls for the reassignment of sixth-grade children from 44 elementary schools to 10 junior high schools. Room would be made for them by assigning ninth-grade junior high schools to high schools that are racially balanced.

The plan also pairs eight elementary schools and rezones three junior high schools to improve racial balance.

More than 40,000 pupils are affected.

Mr. Donovan, who explained that he did not usually vote on a rollcall except to break a tie, said he wanted to join his colleagues in approving the plan.

Before it voted, the board was caught in a sharp cross-fire of criticism.

Civil rights leaders denounced the plan at the meeting as "a colossal deception" and threatened extended school boycotts in the fall unless more substantial steps were taken to "desegregate the city's public schools."

Parents and Taxpayers groups and the Joint Council for Better Integration, who oppose any plan that would transfer children from their neighborhood schools, sent large delegations to the meeting at 110 Livingston Street, Brooklyn.

They warned that carrying out the proposals would drive many families from the city. Some said it could lead to a school boycott by parents who felt the plan would violate their rights. They also threatened legal action to block its implementation.

The hall of the Board of Education building was filled to

capacity before the meeting started and hundreds of people, most of them from Parents and Taxpayers, milled outside the entrance. They were prevented by the police from entering.

Dr. Calvin E. Gross, Superintendent of Schools, opening discussion on the integration plan, said:

"It is my considered opinion and that of the staff that all recommendations included are educationally sound. No group of people as yet has proposed a package of proposals better than the one the board has before it tonight."

Five of the civil rights organizations, at a joint news conference yesterday morning, described the plan as "diametrically opposed to the spirit and intent of the Allen recommendation for quality integration."

July 10, 1964

COURT BARS TRANSFER OF 3
IN QUEENS SCHOOL PAIRING

*Calls Shifting of Children From a School
Across Street 'Unreasonable'*

By Leonard Buder

A Supreme Court justice in Queens ruled yesterday that the Board of Education could not transfer three children to a school in another neighborhood as part of its school integration plan.

Although the decision was limited to the three children and took into consideration particular circumstances, the lawyer for the parents who brought the suit asserted that "in practice this will apply to all children and, in fact, nullifies the entire pairing plan" of the school board.

There was no immediate comment from board officials. But observers said that the decision—if not reversed on appeal to a higher court—could place in jeopardy the only element of the school integration plan that involves the transfer of white and Negro pupils to improve the racial composition of schools.

The decision, handed down by Justice Henry J. Latham, was the first in a suit contesting the board's plan to pair five predominantly white schools with largely Negro schools to promote racial balance. Arguments in the case were heard on Tuesday.

The three children directly affected by the decision have been attending an elementary school across the street from their homes—Public School 148 at 89th Street and 32d Avenue in East Elmhurst. One child will be in the third grade next fall, another will be in the fourth grade and the oldest will be in the sixth grade.

Under the pairing plan, a "community zone" is scheduled to be established in September for P.S. 148 and P.S. 127 at 88th Street and 25th Avenue. P.S. 148 is now 87 per cent white while P.S. 127 is 94 per cent Negro and Puerto Rican.

All pupils in the community zone were supposed to attend P.S. 148 for the first and second grades and P.S. 127 for the third, fourth, fifth and sixth grades.

In his ruling, Justice Latham said:

"This court deems it unnecessary to make a decision herein of broad application, but confines itself to the specific rights of the petitioners herein named.

"The specific question presented is whether the respondent Board of Education may, under its plan, compel the transfer of the petitioners' children who are of tender years (grades three to six) and who now attend a school across the street from where they live, to a school approximately nine-tenths a mile away, to and from which, if they return home for lunch, they must walk a total of about four miles a day, and each of the four times they make this trip must cross 12 street intersections, including two heavily trafficked streets (Junction and Astoria Boulevards, the latter a busy six-lane thoroughfare).

"The court finds that the planned compulsory transfer of the named petitioners' children is, in their circumstances, arbitrary and unreasonable, and, consequently, the determination as to them is annulled. . . ."

Ironically, had the children lived one-tenth of a mile further away from P.S. 127, they would have received transportation to the new school, which would have changed the circumstances in the case.

July 14, 1964

PAIRING OF SCHOOLS UPHELD
AFTER EARLIER DEFEAT HERE

Validity of Plan Backed—Ruling
Last Week Barred 'Hardship'

By Leonard Buder

The right of the Board of Education to transfer 11 white pupils to a school outside their neighborhood was upheld in Supreme Court in Queens yesterday.

The decision was the second involving school pairing to be announced within four days.

Last Thursday Justice Henry J. Latham, also in Queens, ruled that the board could not transfer three white children from a school across the street from their homes. The ruling yesterday was made by Justice Charles Margett.

Different schools and different legal grounds were involved in the two suits.

Board officials withheld comment on the new decision. But privately they said they regarded yesterday's ruling as the more significant of the two because the suit that it involved had challenged the constitutionality of the scheduled pairings.

The other suit had attacked the transfers of the three children on the ground that "oppression and hardship" would be imposed on the pupils.

Bernard Kessler, the lawyer for the parents of the 11 children affected by yesterday's decision announced that he would appeal to the Appellate Division.

"If necessary, we will take this case to the United States Supreme Court," he said.

Last Friday school officials indicated they would appeal the decision that went against the board.

At issue in the case decided yesterday by Justice Margett was the pairing of Public School 149 in Jackson Heights with P.S. 92 in Corona. The schools are six blocks, or a fifth of a mile, apart.

P.S. 149 is now 87.8 per cent white, while P.S. 92 is 98.8 per cent Negro. Under the pairing scheduled to take effect in the fall, a joint or community zone will be set up for the two schools.

PAIRING PLAN EXPLAINED

All first-grade and second-grade pupils in the new zone will attend P.S. 92, and all pupils in the third through the sixth grades will attend the other school. This, board officials told the court, will give P.S. 92 an enrollment that will be 52.3 per cent white and P.S. 149 one that will be 74.8 per cent white.

The 11 parents in the case told the court in their petition and when argument was heard June 12, that their children were being assigned to P.S. 92 solely because of race. The same, they said, held true for the Negro pupils being transferred to P.S. 149.

Such transfers, they asserted, violated the children's constitutional and statutory rights.

Justice Margett, in an 11 page decision, cited rulings by the Appellate Division in cases involving school rezonings in Brooklyn and Rochester and said that "a plan of action by a Board of Education, which is otherwise reasonable and lawful, is not rendered invalid because it also attempts to correct racial imbalance in the schools."

COURT FORESEES BENEFITS

The board's presentation showed that after the pairing, P.S. 149 would no longer be overcrowded and that the average class size, now 36.6 pupils, would be reduced to 26.6. Both schools would also receive additional teaching and other personnel, extra services and additional funds for textbooks and supplies.

The planned pairing, Justice Margett asserted, "will result in many benefits to the students."

Justice Margett noted that some children in the community

zone would have to walk—at the most—nine-tenths of a mile to get to their new school.

Editorial, July 15, 1964

THE SCHOOL PAIRING TANGLE

In the latest decision on the pairing of elementary schools for purposes of better integration, Justice Charles Margett of the State Supreme Court in Queens declared the Board of Education's action constitutional. He thus took a broader view of the basic issue—the so-called Princeton Plan—than did Justice Henry J. Latham, also of the State Supreme Court in Queens, last week.

The suit before Justice Latham did not deal with the more intricate questions of integration and constitutionality. He therefore merely ruled that to order three youngsters who lived across the street from one school to attend another school almost a mile from their homes was an arbitrary act.

What emerges from the new and by no means final round is the judicial view that pairing of schools for purposes of integration is constitutional but must not be oppressive in violation of a child's rights or detrimental to his education. The question remains whether the courts can disentangle the conflicting issues and offer enough clarity to assure that the pairing experiment will not invite needless administrative confusion.

September 3, 1964

REZONING OF P.S. 6 UPHELD BY COURT

Parents Lose Fight to Block Transfer
of White Pupils Out of Select School

By Robert E. Tomasson

The Board of Education's plan to rezone a predominantly white public school on the East Side to make room for pupils from crowded East Harlem schools was upheld in court yesterday.

State Supreme Court Justice Vincent A. Lupiano dismissed a petition filed by three parents of pupils attending Public School 6 to overturn the board's rezoning, which is part of an effort to achieve racial balance in city schools.

P.S. 6, at 81st Street and Madison Avenue, has been known for 60 years as the best among public elementary schools.

In their suit, the parents said that the board was effecting the rezoning "solely to provide vacancies at the school for Negro and Puerto Rican children."

SEES NO DISCRIMINATION

This, they said, was in violation of the due process and equal protection clauses of the state and Federal Constitutions and contrary to Section 3201 of the Education Law, which prohibits admission or rejection into schools based on a pupil's race.

Neither the board nor Justice Lupiano has denied that the rezoning will specifically exclude white children from the school.

But the court discounted the charge of racial discrimination.

"It must be stressed that the rezoning affects the redistricting of only white children and thus . . . generates no basis per se for consideration of the asserted element of discrimination."

Justice Lupiano cited as the "pivotal point" in the dispute the matter of whether the board's plan was "arbitrary, capricious or unreasonable."

In studying the rezoning plan, Justice Lupiano said that the court could not say that a constitutional or statutory right was violated.

Long known as the "carriage trade school," P.S. 6 probably has one of the highest proportions of educated and wealthy parents in the school system. It has six classes for intellectually gifted children and an enriched program including instruction in French and Spanish.

In 1960, the Board of Education attempted to transfer about

166 children to P.S. 198 at Third Avenue and 96th Street. After a bitter fight, only 66 pupils went to P.S. 198, the rest having transferred to private schools or moved away.

N.Y. Times Magazine, *p. 20, September 20, 1964*

WHY THEY FIGHT FOR THE P.A.T.*

By Peggy Streit

"The way I see it, it's like this," said the taxi driver. "If I had kids of school age I'd join P.A.T. And I'd keep the kids out of school just as long as we white people didn't get our rights. Now don't get me wrong. I ain't got nothing against colored people. If they want good schools they ought to have good schools. But they ought to go to schools in *their* neighborhoods—just like white kids ought to go to school in *their* neighborhood."

The taxi stopped at a red light. The traffic on Van Wyck Boulevard rumbled by the drab, squat commercial buildings— a bar, a hardware store, a beauty parlor, a real-estate office advertising a six-room, two-story, one-family house for $15,000.

"You know Queens?" he asked. "South Richmond Hill? South Ozone Park?" No. "I was born and raised here," he said proudly. "Just like my folks. There's a lot of second-and-third-generation families out here. It's a real neighborly place—not like New York City where nobody cares who lives next door and nobody owns their own home."

Leaving behind the pounding commercial traffic, the taxi turned off abruptly into a more tranquil world of narrow residential streets lined by modest homes—house after identical house, like rows of ditto marks. But they shared the sedate dignity of a clean, orderly neighborhood, their aging, ungracious architecture softened by the sycamore trees.

"Like I was saying," continued the taxi driver, "you buy a house because you want your kid to go to a school nearby and

* © 1964 by The New York Times Company. Reprinted by permission.

the church is just around the corner. And then, here comes the government or school board and what do they say? They say, "Mister, you can't send your kid to school near you. You got to bus him to school in a Negro neighborhood, 20 blocks away, that's been—what do they call it—paired with a white school because of racial imbalance. Now I ask you, is that right? And I say to you, no—that ain't right. We're losing our free-

---

WHY PAIRING?

In its campaign to end segregation in New York City's schools the Board of Education last spring decided to begin a program of school "pairing." Under this plan, a predominantly white school is linked with a predominantly Negro-Puerto Rican school—some grades attending one school and the remaining grades attending the other, thus achieving a racial mixture in both. This integration, proponents of the plan maintain, would end the "ghetto complex" that has held Negro children back. In some cases, a pairing scheme requires the busing of some children from their neighborhoods. A militant organization called Parents and Taxpayers has sprung up to fight the plan, however. This article records the views of members of one chapter, in South Richmond Hills–South Ozone Park, Queens.

---

doms in this country. Next thing you know, they'll be telling you where to go to church."

The taxi slowed to a halt outside the home of P.A.T. official June Reynolds. "I'm sure glad I'm not that schoolboard guy, Gross," he chuckled, with wry satisfaction. "You know how women's voices go up when they get mad? Tell the ladies: "God bless them!"

*   *   *

"Now," said Mrs. Reynolds, "what would you like to know about our group?" Her cluttered desk was the only disorder in a living room like countless others in the neighborhood—wall-to-wall carpets, meticulously vacuumed; modern furniture gleaming with polish; earthenware lamps, their orange shades still protected by plastic wrappers; a large-screen television set;

reproductions of oriental art on the walls . . . a picture of modest but proud possession.

Size? "There are about 2,700 of us," she replied, "with 300 hard-core members doing most of the work—the executive board, the telephone girls who call about P.A.T. meetings and poll members, and the block captains who ring doorbells for new members."

Membership? "Mostly parents with elementary-school kids, of course, but some people without children. This is a moral issue, too, not just an educational one."

Purpose? "To protect our children, preserve our neighborhood-school system, and keep our children from being bused into strange districts."

Activities? "Well, we organize protests against pairing and busing, and we've been urging members to write to their newspapers and councilmen. Things like that."

The racial issue? She paused irresolutely. "The racial issue doesn't have anything to do with what we want," she said. "We believe in open enrollment. If Negroes want to go to white schools where there's room, they should be allowed to. And we believe in the improvement of Negro schools. It's not true what people say—that we don't like Negroes and we don't want them in our schools. If they live in our neighborhood they have a right here. But nobody has a right to send our children *away* from our neighborhood."

The telephone jangled again and she turned her young, earnest face back to business. "Membership meeting this evening," she said to the caller with urgency. "Try to make it. This is a battle we're fighting, and without your support we'll lose it. Yes, everybody will be there."

*   *   *

That night, everybody included a trim, distinguished-looking man graying at the temples, who stated the central position of the group, again claiming that the P.A.T. stand has nothing to do with race.

"I'm sick of hearing us all called bigots," he said with exasperation. "What we want is the best possible deal for our children. My wife and I bought a house where we did because we like the neighborhood and the schools close by. Now we think our kids may be offered second best and we'd be rotten parents if we didn't oppose that. Why do people think that all opposition to pairing has to be equated with bigotry? Please believe me when I tell you that there isn't a person out here who would willingly hurt anyone."

Stanley Smigiel, president of the South Richmond Hill-South Ozone Park P.A.T. and a grease monkey by trade, was also there. A man of hefty body and voice, he was faintly nervous in his new role as civil leader, mopping his steaming brow with a handkerchief.

"When they told me, 'You got to do this and you got to do that,' that's when my dandruff went up," he said. "I lived in South Jamaica in a Negro area for 30 years. I don't have nothing against Negroes, but the only thing I care about is this: I don't want my child traveling no further than he has to to school. What if the bus breaks down? What about snowy days? What if he gets sick and it's an emergency and my wife can't get to him? And furthermore, I don't like him going into classes with a lot of slow readers who will pull down his I.Q. I was a drop-out in school and I learned my lesson. I don't want nothing going wrong with my son's education."

*   *   *

June Reynolds, a young, fresh-faced, bright-eyed, dedicated dynamo, doesn't have anything against Negroes either. "I went to school with Negroes when I was a girl," she said. "If I were a Negro, how would I see to it that my kids got a better education and a chance in the world?" She answered herself without hesitation, "I'd move into an interracial neighborhood. I wouldn't live in Harlem for anything in the world. I'd scrub floors, I'd take in laundry. I'd get any kind of job to get out of Harlem—and I know I'd succeed because I believe that in the United States anybody can do anything if he tries hard enough.

"Look at my father. Negroes can at least speak English, but when my father came here from Italy he had to learn the language, so he went to night school. Then he got a job as a wrapper in a bakery. He worked there 47 years and was a supervisor when he retired. The way I see it," she added with finality, "if a Negro lives in Harlem, it's because he likes it there and because he doesn't want to work hard enough to get out of that environment."

Hannah Edell, a round, small, blond woman with soft pink cheeks and a troubled voice, was a little less dogmatic.

"Yes, I think the Negro has been discriminated against," she said, "and I think they should be helped along. But I don't think their problem is educational. It's social. I know that some Negroes think, 'Why should I bother to get an education if I can't get a job afterwards.'—and that's what I mean by a social problem. It's up to large corporations to give them jobs."

She acknowledged the obvious question with a long hard sigh. "Yes, I know," she said, "Why *shouldn't* large corporations give their jobs to the best-educated—and they are usually white."

She paused then reflected sadly: "It's a vicious circle, isn't it? One hardly knows where to begin. But one thing I *do* know," she went on, gaining assurance. They shouldn't begin with our children. Integration isn't a problem for children to solve—or their parents. It's up to the politicians, big corporations—other people. And the Board of Education. This problem has existed for a long time. Why didn't the board do something to improve Negro education a long time ago, so things wouldn't have got to this state?"

*   *   *

Joe Lamanna, project manager for a contractor, saw the problem differently. A large young man, dark-eyed, handsome, well-turned-out and the possessor of a college degree earned after five and a half years of night school, he is proud of his Italian ancestry, of his home in one of Ozone Park's more affluent districts and of a gigantic new car, which he won in a church raffle.

"This is most of all a moral issue," he said. "What right does anybody—*anybody*—have to tell me what to do? Where does it all end? I worked with Negroes on a construction job for seven years. They don't work hard or help their children in school or care about their families or keep their homes clean. But that's not the issue. I just won't tolerate anybody telling me I've got to send my son into another neighborhood to school."

His small, chic wife agreed. "I don't think I have a moral obligation to anyone—to my family, my husband and child maybe, but no one else. If Negroes have been deprived of some rights it's because they haven't worked for them. They don't deserve them. And the only way they're finally going to get them is through hard work—not by having our children bused into their schools." Her voice rose in distress.

"People just aren't psychologically ready for all this—this mixing," she complained. "We're not bad people out here in Ozone Park. We don't want to hurt anybody. We are decent, hard-working, church-going, law-abiding people—but we're bewildered. Bewildered by this bombshell of radical integration. Why do things have to change overnight? Why can't it be gradual?"

Though differently expressed the views of P.A.T. Members coincide on most questions.

Slavery? Sure Negroes were slaves once and that was terrible. But they haven't been slaves for 100 years. How could they use that anymore as an excuse for not getting ahead?

Color? It wasn't their color that was holding them back. It was the kind of people they were and the things they did and the things they didn't do.

Discriminated against? Not really. In the South, maybe, but there was no segregation in New York City. They could go into any restaurant. Look at the Jews. They lived in ghettos once. They couldn't get certain kinds of jobs once. They had been discriminated against much longer than the Negroes, and look how well they had done.

Substandard schools? But why hadn't they *done* something about their schools before now? White mothers would have. Why had they been so apathetic all these years?

"If I were God, what would I do to improve the lot of the Negro?" echoed a P.A.T. supporter; "If I were God, I'd make everybody white."

*   *   *

Liberty Avenue is a crawling, congested business artery of Richmond Hill flanked by two-story buildings and dotted with the red and purple patterns of tomatoes and eggplants on the fruit stands. It has the vibrant air of a not-too-distant Italy or Germany or Ireland or Israel. The elevated trains roar and rattle overhead, quaking the buildings that border the tracks.

In a two-flight walk up, John and Felicia Petosa live in six cramped but immaculate rooms. There was a miniature organ against one wall of the living room and a television set, to which a small boy was glued, against another. A narrow hall led to small bedrooms miraculously clean despite the gray elevated, an arm's reach beyond the windows.

Felicia Petosa, married to a cook, is a warm, ardent woman. Her breathless commentary on the world and its problems was stalled only occasionally by the need for a fresh breath. She has two children, the eldest of whom spent his first years in a school in East Brooklyn—an area 70 per cent Negro and Puerto Rican.

"Pathetic," began Mrs. Petosa, taking a deep breath. "The school had no hallway. You got to the second classroom by walking through the first two. P.T.A. meetings were held next to the boiler room. I could never get interested. Fights all day. When the kids finished fighting at school they fought at home. Just on our block there were over 75 kids. The Puerto Rican lady who lived next door had 5 and 15 people lived in four rooms. We paid our own exterminator bills, but finally the man said he wouldn't do our place no more because it wouldn't do no good unless the whole block got done. We lived upstairs and the landlord lived down and every day he'd complain about the noise my kids made and I'd say to him, 'Excuse me, I'll go put them in a freezer and take them out for supper.'

"Finally, my husband was getting along better in his business and we moved and the first day my little boy went to school here his conduct improved so much I took his temperature. I don't have anything against Negroes," added Mrs. Petosa, "but I believe in the neighborhood school system. Why do our children have to be inconvenienced, just to satisfy the Negroes' whims?"

She picked up her bag, turned the fire off under the kettle, cautioned her young son to behave himself and said: "I'm going out into the neighborhood to distribute P.A.T. literature. I do it whenever I have a free minute. Come along."

The narrow, elderly streets seemed comfortable and secure in their monotonous uniformity, with cement driveways squeezed between identical houses, small patches of neat green yard, stone stoops. A statue of the Virgin Mary stood in one yard, an empty, dry birdbath in another. A Good Humor man with his tinkle bells trailed children behind him.

"I don't want to buy anything today," called an irritated housewife from her kitchen.

"No, my mommy isn't home. She's at the hospital having another baby."

* * *

"Yes, I know about Parents and Taxpayers." This was the indignant voice of a grandmotherly woman, baby-sitting for two youngsters securely attached to her skirts. "It's terrible, I think, just terrible what people are trying to do to our neighborhood. There was a girl where we used to live—she must have been Polish or something—who married a colored man and had one of those chocolate-colored babies. Terrible. When you start mixing people up, that's when the trouble begins."

A woman paused on the street, a large, brown-paper shopping bag in her arms, and said: "What do they think they're going to accomplish with the pairing? They say they want to bring white and Negro kids together so they can get to know each other. And the Board of Education thinks Negroes will get a better education in schools with white children. But what's really going to happen? Just sitting next to each other isn't going to change things.

"There's a little boy on our street," she went on, "who uses bad language and doesn't do his school work and won't behave. He goes to school with our kids, but he doesn't change just because he sits next to a well-behaved child. He stays the way he is because that's the way his parents are. And as for raising the educational standards, give me one example—just one example—where mixing Negroes and whites hasn't pulled standards down to the Negro level rather than raising them to the white level. I don't know why the Negroes are behind. But they are, and I don't want them hurting my child's chances in school."

*   *   *

Farther down the street, now quiet with the heavy calm of a late-summer afternoon, an elderly lady sat on a camp chair in her front yard, her plump arms stretching the short sleeves of her housedress.

"If the Negroes come into our neighborhood schools, does that mean they will be moving in?" she asked with a worried frown. "Eight years ago we paid $12,000 for this house. We scraped together every penny we had and borrowed more. Now it's worth at least $16,000. My husband and me we worked so hard to get it and it's all we have. And now, if the Negroes start coming into the neighborhood it won't be worth a cent."

A yapping dog subsided into friendliness behind a screen door and his mistress said: "I'm worried, I've got a 10-year-old boy and I don't want him going to school in no Negro neighborhood. Maybe nothing would happen. Then again, maybe it would. What if there's a riot, like there was in Harlem? And what if he goes into a drugstore and some of the older kids give him a jelly apple with dope in it? You never know, do you?"

"People keep saying that we members of Parents and Taxpayers just don't like Negroes," said a neat, brushed young man, seated amidst his bowling trophies. "But that isn't the issue. The fact is, I want my children to go to school where I went to school, and that's just two blocks away. My sister—she lives two doors up the street—she went there. My two cousins who

live just around the corner, they went there. We know the
principal—a fine woman. This is our neighborhood."

A cluster of children on tricycles moved politely out of the
way. In the street, two more youngsters chalked in the outlines
for a game of hop-scotch. On a porch, a woman, her hands in a
pail of water, paused from her window washing.

"Yes, I'm one of P.A.T.'s telephone girls," she said. "Recently I've been polling people on their feelings towards the
boycott. Oh, everybody was for it. People kept saying, 'Well,
it's about time. We've been conducting ourselves like ladies
and gentlemen and where has it got us?' And then you know
what they said—without my even asking? They said, 'I'm going
to vote for Goldwater.' If other communities are like ours,"
she said, with satisfaction, "Goldwater's going to be our next
President."

*   *   *

"I don't know what to think," said an elderly woman plain-
tively. "Please come in and sit down." She settled onto an
ancient divan covered with a green tasseled throw.

"My son comes home a couple of weeks ago and when I say
I think it's shocking, the thought of busing our neighborhood
children into Negro schools and Negro children into our
schools, my son gets furious and he says, 'You're a bigot.' Then
he says to me, 'Don't you know Negroes were slaves once and
they have been discriminated against for 150 years? That people
haven't given them decent jobs and have forced them to live in
Negro ghettos? Can you imagine what that does to people
psychologically?' he says to me. And I say, 'But look how dirty
they are and how bad their morals are and would you want
your children going to school with Negroes?' And he gets mad
again and he says I ought to be ashamed. 'Don't you understand
that if you don't give people a decent education, or home, or
chance, they lose hope and don't bother to work or study or
keep their homes clean? If you treat them inferior, they act
inferior,' he says. And then he says, 'If a Negro and white
person asked you for a job and both were equally qualified,
which would you choose?' I didn't know what to say, but

finally I said I guessed the white person. And then,"—and the old lady shook her hand in distress and disbelief—"then he said, 'You're a bigot!' and he walked out."

The shadows and sounds of the afternoon grew longer and mellower. Someone was having a piano lesson. A car door slammed and a child cried, "Mommy, daddy's home." Home-owners came out on the stoops to take the air, and in the distance, a church bell chimed.

*   *   *

Standing before his church, a rector talked about his parishioners. "I've worked here much of my life," he said, "and I know that by most of the world's standards, these are good people, endowed with many of the great American virtues. They are hard-working and thrifty. They're honest and devoted to their families. But many of them have worked their way out of real poverty and in the process they haven't had much time or inclination to worry about other people's problems or think about the Negro and why he is the way he is; why they made out and the Negro hasn't. And they're not yet secure enough socially or economically to add to their American virtues the great human virtues of understanding, tolerance and compassion.

"Now," he continued, "they're scared. For years, Van Wyck Boulevard has been a psychological Berlin Wall. The Negroes tended to live on one side, the whites on the other, and the whites fear the wall will be breached if busing goes through. Many people here feel that their most precious possessions are in jeopardy, that their children may be endangered educationally and socially and their property devalued. These fears may be unfounded but that doesn't make them any less real. And then, you know, mothers do genuinely find comfort in having their little ones as close to home as possible. And I can't blame them.

"People come to me and ask, 'Why does integration have to begin with our chidren?' " he said sadly, "and I tell them it has to begin somewhere. But they're not very satisfied with these answers. . . ."

October 20, 1964

HIGH COURT LETS CITY
ZONE SCHOOL FOR INTEGRATION

Justices Refuse to Review State Ruling
Permitting Consideration of Race

BROAD DISCRETION SEEN

Case Suggests Decisions on Housing
Patterns May Differ by Localities

By Anthony Lewis

SPECIAL TO THE NEW YORK TIMES

Washington, Oct. 19—The Supreme Court declined today to review a decision allowing the New York City Board of Education to minimize racial imbalance in zoning a new school.

The decision at issue was handed down by the New York Court of Appeals last May 7. It is considered one of the most significant on the general problem of racial imbalance arising from housing patterns.

This is the second major decision in the field that the Supreme Court has declined to review. Last May 4 the court left standing a ruling that the school authorities in Gary, Ind., were not constitutionally obliged to end de facto segregation.

The Supreme Court's refusal to review a case does not ordinarily signify its approval or disapproval. But these two actions fall into a pattern that may indicate the tendency of the court's thinking.

BROAD DISCRETION SEEN

Taken together, the two lower court decisions suggest that local school boards have broad constitutional discretion to deal with racial patterns as they deem wisest.

School boards apparently may consider the race of pupils in laying out school zones and may try to avoid dominance by one race in a school. But the school boards apparently do not have to consider race.

The contention made in the case decided today was that school boards may not, constitutionally, consider race at all and may not attempt to overcome segregated housing patterns. The Court of Appeals had rejected that view by a vote of 6 to 1.

March 30, 1965

NEGRO SCHOOLS INCREASING HERE

Report Also Shows a Rise in Integrated Classes

By Leonard Buder

The number of public schools that are predominantly Negro and Puerto Rican has risen sharply in the last four years, the Central Zoning Unit of the city school system reported yesterday.

But despite the rise in segregated schooling, the zoning group said, the school system has scored gains in its campaign to correct racial imbalance in the schools. More Negro pupils are now attending formerly all-white schools, giving more pupils of both races their first opportunity for an integrated education.

And, the unit declared, the recently proposed school integration plan, if implemented, "should improve ethnic distribution of pupils for 1965–66" and bring further improvements in the years ahead.

"If not for the conscious efforts that have been made to improve integration, this city would be well on its way to having a school system composed largely of two types of schools—all-Negro schools and all-white," asserted Dr. Jacob Landers, assistant superintendent in charge of the school integration program.

The report, an annual compilation of ethnic statistics and observations on trends, noted that the number of Negro and Puerto Rican pupils in the system had increased from 322,059 in 1958–59 to the present 476,866. These pupils now comprise 45.5 per cent of the total school population, as compared with 33.2 per cent six years ago.

"Reflecting the increase in minority group population in

the city and its concentration in certain geographic areas," the report said, the number of predominantly Negro and Puerto Rican schools has increased from 118 in 1960–61 to 187 in 1964–65.

The number of predominantly white schools has decreased from 327 to 237 during the same period. Practically all of the 90 schools that have gone out of the predominantly white category, the unit added, "became midrange schools, affording all pupils in these schools opportunities for quality integrated education."

In 1960–61, the first year for which such statistics are available, 337 of the city's 782 regular elementary, junior and senior high schools were midrange in ethnic composition—that is, they were neither largely all white nor predominantly Negro and Puerto Rican in enrollment. A total of 417,308 pupils, or 42.5 per cent of the total enrollment attended these schools.

This year, 387 of the 811 regular schools, with 47.3 per cent of the system's pupils, are in the midrange schools. Officials said that this represented a significant gain.

"... it is apparent that individuals are responsive to the
standards of those with whom they desire to associate ..."

REVIEW OF EVIDENCE RELATING

TO EFFECTS OF DESEGREGATION

ON THE INTELLECTUAL

PERFORMANCE OF NEGROES*

Irwin Katz

In this article, Katz presents a scholarly summary of
the studies relevant to the process of desegregation, as
well as some implications from theories in social
psychology that are useful to consider in the absence
of any considerable body of research evidence. Although one must fight one's way past a severely technical vocabulary, it is an extraordinarily useful review of significant findings, which everyone must
take into account in coming to a reasonable position
on the issue of school integration.

* From Irwin Katz, "Review of Evidence Relative to the Effects of Desegregation," *American Psychologist* **19,** 1964, 381–399. Copyright 1964 by the American Psychological Association, and reproduced by permission.

Of the three positions on desegregation described in the introduction, the evidence Katz cites seems, at least on the surface, to give most support to the conservative. Is it necessarily damaging to the militant position? How can that position be reconciled with it?

THIS IS a review of evidence regarding the effects of educational desegregation on the scholastic achievement of Negroes. It focuses on the problem of identifying the important situational determinants of Negro performance in the racially mixed classroom. Only a few studies have dealt directly with this problem, so that much of the evidence to be surveyed is only inferential. Included are the following: reports on the academic progress of Negro children attending integrated schools, evidence on aspects of the minority child's experience in desegregation that presumably affect his motivation to learn, relevant research on the behavioral effects of psychological stress, and, finally, a series of experiments on Negro productivity in biracial settings.

Negro Americans. In this paper the term "Negro Americans" refers to a minority segment of the national population that is more or less distinguishable on the basis of skin color, hair texture, etc., and that occupies a subordinate position in American culture. The extent of subordination varies in different regions and localities, but usually includes some degree of restriction on educational and economic opportunities, as well as social exclusion by whites and an attribution by whites of intellectual inferiority. While the term "race" will be used for convenience, no meaning is intended other than that of distinctiveness of appearance and commonality of experience; the issue of whether there are consequential differences in the genetic endowment of Negroes and whites will not be considered. Thus the present discussion should be more or less applicable to any American minority group whose status is similar to that of Negroes.

Desegregation. Educational desegregation is a politico-legal concept referring to the elimination of racial separation within school systems. As such it embraces a great variety of transitional situations having diverse effects upon the scholastic performance of Negro children. The meaning of desegregation has been broadened in recent years to include the reduction of racial clustering due to factors other than legal discrimination —i.e., de facto segregation. A number of recent court decisions in the North have ruled that "racial imbalance" in a school (a predominance of minority-group children) constitutes de facto segregation (United States Commission on Civil Rights, 1962a, 1962b). Also described as de facto segregation by various social scientists are the racially homogeneous classes often found in schools where children are grouped according to ability (Deutsch, 1963; Dodson, 1962; Tumin, 1963).

The present concern is mainly with instances of desegregation that are marked by a substantial increase in the proportion of white peers, or both white peers and adult authorities, in the immediate environment of the Negro student. (In the South integration with white classmates is usually also the occasion of initial contacts with white teachers, while in the North the proportion of white teachers may be high even in schools where Negro students predominate.) Almost invariably in this type of desegregation experience the minority-group child is confronted with higher educational standards than prevail in segregated Negro schools (United States Commission on Civil Rights, 1962a, 1962b). Both aspects of the Negro's experience—change in the racial environment and exposure to relatively high academic standards—are likely to have important influences on his scholastic motivation.

POSTULATED SITUATIONAL DETERMINANTS OF NEGRO PERFORMANCE IN DESEGREGATION

Social threat.   Social threat refers to a class of social stimulus events that tend to elicit anxious expectations that others will inflict harm or pain. One may assume that novel types of contact with white strangers possess a social-threat component for members of a subordinated minority group. The degree of threat should be a direct function of (*a*) the amount of evidence of white hostility (or the extent to which evidence of white friendliness is lacking) and (*b*) the amount of power possessed by whites in the contact situation, as shown by their numerical predominance, control of authority positions, etc. It seems likely that Negro children would be under some degree of social threat in a newly integrated classroom. Mere indifference on the part of white peers may frustrate their needs for companionship and approval, resulting in lowered self-esteem and the arousal of impulses to escape or aggress. In more extreme instances, verbal harassment and even physical hazing may elicit strong fear responses. These external threats are likely to distract the minority child from the task at hand, to the detriment of performance.

In addition, psychological theory suggests that the Negro's own covert reactions to social threat would constitute an important source of intellectual impairment. In discussing the effect of psychological stress on the learning of skills, Deese (1962) mentions distraction by the internal stimuli of autonomic activation, as well as disruption of task responses by neuromuscular and other components of the stress reaction. Mandler and Sarason (1962) and others call attention to the disruptive role of task-irrelevant defensive responses against anxiety. Spence (1958) and Taylor (1963) propose that anxiety, conceptualized as drive, increases intratask response competition. And according to Easterbrook (1959), emotion lowers efficiency on complex tasks by narrowing the range of cue utilization. Also relevant is Bovard's (1959) hypothesis of a specific physiological mechanism to account for the apparent lowering of the stress threshold under conditions of social isolation.

Another way in which social threat may impair performance is by causing Negro children to abandon efforts to excel in order not to arouse further resentment and hostility in white competitors. That is, the latter may possess what French and Raven (1960) refer to as "coercive power." When academic success is expected to instigate white reprisals, then any stimulus which arouses the motive to achieve should also generate anxiety, and defensive avoidance of such stimuli should be learned. This response pattern would not be wholly nonadaptive in a situation where a small number of Negro students stood relatively powerless against a prejudiced white majority—if one assumes that evidence of Negro intellectual competence might have an ego-deflating effect on these white students. The Group for the Advancement of Psychiatry (1957) has put the matter this way:

A feeling of superior worth may be gained merely from the existence of a downgraded group. This leads to an unrealistic and unadaptive kind of self-appraisal based on invidious comparison rather than on solid personal growth and achievement ... [p. 10].

Finally with regard to possible social threat emanating from a white teacher—given the prestige of the adult authority, any expression by a white teacher of dislike or devaluation, whether through harsh, indifferent, or patronizing behavior, should tend to have unfavorable effects on Negro performance similar to those just described, and perhaps of even greater intensity.

Social facilitation. When the minority newcomer in a desegregated school is accepted socially by his white classmates, his scholastic motivation should be influenced favorably. It was noted earlier that achievement standards tend to be higher in previously all-white schools than in Negro schools. From studies based on white subjects, it is apparent that individuals are responsive to the standards of those with whom they desire to associate (reviewed by Bass, 1961; French & Raven, 1960; Thibaut & Kelly, 1959). That Negro children want friendship with white age mates was shown by Horowitz (1936), Radke, Sutherland, and Rosenberg (1950), and Yarrow (1958). Another study, by Criswell (1939), suggests that Negro children in racially mixed classrooms accept white prestige but increasingly withdraw into their own group as a response to white rejection. Thus, if their desire for acceptance is not inhibited or destroyed by sustained unfriendliness from white children, Negro pupils should tend to adopt the scholastic norms of the high-status majority group. Experimental support for this supposition comes from Dittes and Kelley (1956), who found with white college students that private as well as public adherence to the attitudinal standards of a group were highest among persons who had experienced a fairly high degree of acceptance from the group, with a possibility of gaining even fuller acceptance, while those who received a low degree of acceptance showed little genuine adherence to group norms.

Friendliness and approval on the part of white teachers should be beneficial to Negro motivation by increasing the incentive strength of scholastic success. Assuming that white teachers have more prestige for the minority child than do Negro teachers, the prospect of winning their approval should be more attractive. Hence, when such approval can be expected as a reward for good performance, motivation should be favorably influenced.

Probability of success. When the minority child is placed in a school that has substantially higher scholastic standards than he knew previously, he may become discouraged and not try to succeed. This common sense proposition is derivable from Atkinson's (1958a) theory of the motivational determinants of risk taking and performance. For individuals in whom the tendency to approach success is stronger than the tendency to avoid failure, task motivation is assumed to be a joint function of the subjective probability of achieving success and the incentive value of success. From a postulated inverse relationship between the latter two variables (assuming external influences on incentive strength are held constant) he derives a hypothesis that the strength of motivation is at a maximum when the probability of success is .50, and diminishes as this probability approaches zero or unity. The hypothesis is supported by findings on arithmetic performance of white college students (Atkinson, 1958b), and white elementary-school children (Murstein & Collier, 1962), as well as on digit-symbol performance of white high-school students (Rosen, 1961). (In these studies, the effect occurred regardless of whether subjects had scored relatively high or low on a projective personality measure of the motive to approach success.) It follows that if the Negro newcomer perceives the standards of excellence in a desegregated school as being substantially higher than those he encountered previously, so that the likelihood of his attaining them seems low, his scholastic motivation will decline.

Failure threat. Failure threat is a class of stimulus events in an achievement situation which tend to elicit anxious expectations of harm or pain as a consequence of failure. High probability of failure does not by itself constitute failure threat

—it is necessary also that the failure have a social meaning. Thus in Atkinson's formulation, the negative incentive strength of failure varies inversely with the subjective probability of failure, so that fear of failure is most strongly aroused when the probability of failure is at an intermediate level. This leads to the paradoxical prediction that as the probability of failure increases beyond .50, fear of failure declines. The paradox is resolved when one recognizes that Atkinson's model deals only with that component of incentive strength that is determined by the apparent difficulty of the task. Sarason, Davidson, Lighthall, Waite, and Ruebush (1960) call attention to the important influence of anticipated disapproval by parents and teachers on the negative valence of failure. (While their primary interest is in text anxiety as a personality variable, their discussion seems applicable to the present problem of identifying situational determinants of fear of failure.) Presumably, the child's belief that his failure to meet prevailing standards of achievement will bring adult disapproval is relatively unaffected by his own perception of the difficulty of a given task. Hence, fear of disapproval should increase as it becomes more probable— i.e., as the subjective probability of failure increases. Sarason and his associates suggest that a high expectancy of failure arouses strong unconscious hostility against the adults from whom negative evaluation is foreseen. The hostility is turned inward against the self in the form of self-derogatory attitudes, which strengthen the expectation of failure and the desire to escape the situation. Distraction by these and other components of emotional conflict may cause a decrement in the child's performance.

REPORTS ON ACADEMIC ACHIEVEMENT OF NEGROES IN DESEGREGATED SCHOOLS

There is a dearth of unequivocal information about Negro performance in desegregated schools. A number of factors have contributed to this situation.

1. Many desegregated school systems have a policy of racial nonclassification, so that separate data for Negroes and whites are not available.

2. Where total elimination of legal segregation has occurred, it has usually been accompanied by vigorous efforts to raise educational standards in *all* schools; hence the effects of desegregation per se are confounded with the effects of improved teaching and facilities.

3. In several Southern states only small numbers of highly selected Negro pupils have been admitted to previously all-white schools, and since before-after comparisons of achievement are not usually presented, reports of "satisfactory" adjustment by these Negro children shed little light on the question of relative performance.

Taking the published information for what it is worth, most of it presents a favorable picture of Negro academic adjustment in racially mixed settings. Stallings (1959) has reported on the results of achievement testing in the Louisville school system in 1955–56, the year prior to total elimination of legal segregation, and again 2 years later. Gains were found in the median scores of all pupils for the grades tested, with Negroes showing greater improvement than whites. The report gave no indication of whether the gains for Negroes were related to amount of actual change in the racial composition of schools. Indeed, Stallings stated, "The gains were greater where Negro pupils remained by choice with Negro teachers." A later survey on Louisville by Knowles (1962) indicated that Negro teachers had not been assigned to classrooms having white students during the period covered by Stallings' research. This means that the best Negro gains observed by Stallings were made by children who *remained in segregated classrooms,* and can only be attributed to factors *other* than desegregation, such as a general improvement in educational standards.

In both Washington and Baltimore, where legal segregation was totally abolished in 1954, the United States Commission on Civil Rights found "some evidence that the scholastic achievement of Negroes in such schools has improved, and no evidence of a resultant reduction in the achievement of white students [*Southern School News,* 1960]." A detailed account of academic progress in the Washington schools since 1954 has been given by Hansen (1960). The results of a city-wide testing program begun in 1955 indicated year-to-year gains in achievement on every academic subject tested at every grade level where the tests were given. The data were not broken down by race. As in the case of Louisville, it seems reasonable to attribute these gains primarily to an ambitious program of educational improvement rather than to racial mixing. For several years the Washington schools have had a steadily increasing predominance of Negro pupils (over 76% in 1960); this, combined with a four-track system of homogeneous ability grouping which has the effect of concentrating Negroes in the lower tracks, has resulted in a minimal desegregation experience for the majority of Negro children.

Little relevant data have been published on other Southern states where desegregation has been initiated. In 1960, 12 administrators of desegregated school systems testified at a Federal hearing on whether integration had damaged academic standards (United States Commission on Civil Rights, 1960). They unanimously replied in the negative, but only one official (from Louisville) mentioned gains in the achievement of Negro pupils. Reports of widespread academic failure on the part of desegregated Negro children are rare. Among those that have appeared recently is one by Day (1962) on Chapel Hill, North Carolina. Referring to a total of about 45 Negroes in predominantly white schools, he stated that the experience of 2 years of desegregation has shown "a disturbing portion of Negro children attending desegregated schools have failed to keep pace with their white classmates. . . . The question remains as to how to raise the achievement of Negro pupils disadvantaged by their home background and lack of motivation [p. 78]." Wyatt (1962) quoted the Superintendent of Schools in Nashville, Tennessee, as stating there was substantially more difficulty with Negro students entering desegregated situations in the upper grades. The official ascribed most of the difficulties to problems of social adjustment, although the cumulative effect of the generally lower achievement in the Negro schools was credited with some responsibility for the situation.

The academic achievement of Negro graduates of segregated Southern high schools who attended integrated colleges has been reviewed by the National Scholarship Service and Fund for Negro Students (NSSFNS, 1963). In a period of 15 years, NSSFNS helped over 9,000 Negro students to enrol in interracial colleges, situated mostly in the North. The report stated:

> Tabulations of the academic progress of former NSSFNS counselees and scholarship holders show that 5.6% of these students had a scholastic average of A or A−; 50.3% B+, B, or B−; 32.4% C+, C, or C−; and .7% D or below. Not listing grades were 11%. Fewer than 5% withdrew from college for any reason. This record of college success of an educationally and economically underprivileged group is far above the national average, which shows an over 40% incidence of dropouts from all causes [p. 9].

It should be noted that these students were carefully selected by NSSFNS for their academic qualifications. Nonetheless, the NSSFNS experience demonstrates that qualified Southern Negro youth can function effectively in predominantly white colleges of good quality. Later, there will be mention of additional material on these students which suggests that academic success was associated with social acceptance on the campus.

EVIDENCE OF DESEGREGATION CONDITIONS THAT MAY BE DETRIMENTAL TO THE PERFORMANCE OF NEGROES

It was proposed that the achievement motivation of Negro children in desegregation may be strongly influenced by the social behavior of their white classmates and teachers (social threat and facilitation), by their level of expectancy with regard to academic success (probability of success), and by their perception of the social consequences of failure (failure threat). In this section, evidence about conditions of desegregation that are assumed to have unfavorable effects will be considered. The focusing on negative factors is not meant to suggest that conditions favorable to Negro performance are lacking in present-day situations of desegregation, but rather that the former have received more attention from social scientists—apparently because they are more salient.

Social Rejection and Isolation

The rationale for assuming that social rejection is detrimental to the minority child's academic behavior has already been discussed. To what extent are Negroes rejected by white classmates? It is clear that this varies greatly from one community to another. The bulk of early studies on the racial attitudes of white school children in the North indicated that from an early age they expressed strong preference for their own racial group (e.g., Criswell, 1939; Horowitz, 1936; Radke et al., 1950; Radke, Trager, & Davis, 1949). Two examples of desegregation that was highly stressful for Negro children have been described by a psychiatrist, Coles (1963). He writes of the first Negroes to enter white schools in Atlanta and New Orleans:

> When they are in school they may experience rejection, isolation, or insult. They live under what physicians would consider to be highly stressful circumstances ... [p. 4].

> During a school year one can see among these children all of the medical and psychiatric responses to fear and anxiety. One child may lose his appetite, another may become sarcastic and have nightmares. Lethargy may develop, or excessive studying may mark the apprehension common to both. At the same time one sees responses of earnest and effective work. . . . Each child's case history would describe a balance of defenses against emotional pain, and some exhaustion under it, as well as behavior which shows an attempt to challenge and surmount it [p. 5].

Out of 13 original students who were studied during the first 2 years of integration, and 47 who became involved in integration 1 year later and were studied during the second year, "only one child has really succumbed to emotional illness."

Coles does not present a systematic analysis of the various specific sources of fear and anxiety, but he suggests that worries about school work were of less importance than reactions to the prejudice of white children. Nor does he present adequate information about academic success, merely noting that very few learning difficulties "were insurmountable."

Severe stress due to social rejection has been experienced also by Negro students at various newly desegregated colleges and universities in the South. For example, several months after entering the University of Mississippi as its first Negro student, during which time he was often in considerable physical danger, James Meredith emphasized that rejection and social isolation were the most difficult features of his experience. He referred to himself as "the most segregated Negro in the world" despite his enrolment at the University. "Through it all," he said, "the most intolerable thing has been the campaign of ostracising me [*Southern School News,* 1963]."

Two Negro students who initiated integration at the University of Georgia experienced rejection and isolation during their entire 2-year enrolment (Trillin, 1964).

As Hamilton [Holmes] began his final ten-week quarter at Georgia, he had never eaten in a University dining hall, studied in the library, used the gymnasium, or entered the snack bar. He had no white friends outside the classroom. No white student had ever visited him and he had never visited one of them [p. 83].

The other student, Charlayne Hunter, eventually entered into friendly relationships with several white classmates, and was generally in the company of other students when walking to and from classes or eating on campus. However, she remained totally ostracized in the dormitory where she occupied a room by herself. She suffered from stomach trouble off and on during her entire stay at the University. Both Negroes have since graduated, Holmes with a distinguished academic record. Charlayne Hunter is now married to a white Southerner who was a fellow student at the University.

Desegregation under more favorable conditions has been investigated by Yarrow (1958). Comparable groups of Negro and white children of both sexes were observed in segregated and desegregated summer camps during 2-week sessions. The campers were from low-income families in Southern and Border states. The biracial camps had integrated adult staffs that were highly motivated to "make desegregation work." It was found that the behavior of children in segregated and integrated groups was quite similar. An initial tendency for both white and Negro children to prefer white friends lessened during the 2-week period studied. Satisfaction with the camp experience, as indicated by the percentage of children who expressed a desire that the camp session be extended, was somewhat higher in the desegregated camps. However, there were also indications of social conflict and emotional tension associated with the integration process. In older groups (ages 12 and 13) white children initially directed almost twice as much aggression toward Negro cabin mates as toward white age peers. At the beginning of contact 29% of all actions by white campers toward Negroes were hostile. On the other hand, Negro children of all ages aggressed more against one another than against whites. Overt manifestations of white prejudice tended to diminish during the 2-week period. Nonetheless, tension symptoms appeared in almost twice as many children in desegregated as in segregated groups (71% compared with 38%). Frequencies were the same for Negroes and whites. But Negro children in desegregation were more likely to manifest covert or internalized signs of distress (enuresis, fears, nightmares, withdrawal, physical symptoms) than those that were more overt (fighting, generally disruptive behavior, obscene language, complaining). Of the Negro campers showing tension, 85% showed reactions of the covert type. For the white children showing tension, neither covert nor overt responses predominated. That Negroes were particularly fearful of white disapproval is suggested by their oversensitiveness in desegregation to aggressive and dominative behavior in other Negroes, and their denial of such impulses in themselves. Both reactions are further evidence of a tendency to conceal tensions in the presence of whites.

Regarding the relevance of this study to school integration, it should be noted that the total period of interracial contacts was brief, but peer interactions were probably more intimate and intense than the usual classroom contacts. A generally favorable picture of race relations in Southern integrated schools is presented in a recent article by a journalist, Tanner (1964):

> On the social side, younger white and Negro children attending desegregated classes seem to accept each other better than the older ones. Negro and white youngsters can be seen playing together on the slides and swings of almost any desegregated Southern elementary school's playground. At Nashville's Buena Vista Elementary School, Negro boys have won two of the three positions of captain on the school's safety patrol. And in Birmingham, often called the most segregated U.S. city, a Negro boy was chosen vice president of a sixth grade class that was desegregated last fall.

> Even in desegregated high schools, some Negroes win quick social acceptance. When a lone Negro was admitted to the 10th grade of one high school in a small Texas town, he was elected vice president of the class his first day. A Negro also has become president of Oklahoma City's integrated Central High School student council.

One investigation has shown that experiences of social acceptance are associated with academic success. In the earlier-mentioned NSSFNS program of placing qualified Negro graduates of Southern high schools in Northern integrated colleges, it was found that those who participated in extracurricular activities, dated, and had a satisfactory number of friends got better marks than those who did not (NSSFNS, 1960). Though this finding is merely correlational, it is consistent with the proposition that acceptance by white peers is beneficial to the achievement motivation of Negro students.

Fear of Competition with Whites

It was suggested that low expectation of success is an important detrimental factor in the performance of minority children attending integrated schools. The evidence is strong that Negro students have feelings of intellectual inferiority which arise from an awareness of actual differences in racial achievement, or from irrational acceptance of the white group's stereotype of Negroes.

Inadequacy of previous training. The low quality of segregated Negro education is well documented. Plaut (1957) has summarized the overall situation:

> Negroes, furthermore, have long been aware that most of their schools in the South, and often the *de facto* segregated schools in the North, are rundown, poorly staffed, and short-handed. Second- and third-rate schooling for Negroes leaves them without the ability to compete with white students and robs them of the initiative to compete. Even the 1955 Speaker of the Georgia House of Representatives admitted recently that "Negro education in Georgia is a disgrace. What the Negro child gets in the sixth grade, the white child gets in the third" [p. 5].

A few specific instances of educational disparity at the grade-school level will be cited. Findley (1956) found in testing for achievement in the Atlanta schools that from 40% to 60% of white pupils met the standards set by the top 50% of a national sample on the different tests; but only 2% to 10% of Negro pupils met this standard on the various tests. In Tennessee, according to Wyatt (1962) Negro students averaged $1\frac{1}{2}$ to 2 years behind grade level when transferred to biracial schools in the upper grades. In earlier grades, transfers performed satisfactorily. The same report described the status of Negro and white teachers in a Tennessee urban area. Only 49% of 901 academically qualified Negro teachers passed the National Teachers Examination; among white teachers, more than 97% of 783 qualified teachers passed the test. The Tennessee survey showed that the academic retardation of the segregated Negro elementary-school pupil is progressive.

The situation in northern Virginia was summarized by Mearns (1962) in a report written for the United States Commission on Civil Rights:

> The Negroes themselves have recognized that the achievement gap exists, but the only obvious reaction among most Negroes

is reluctance to transfer to white schools. The question is raised as to whether Negroes really obtain a better education in desegregated schools where they must compete with better prepared, highly motivated white students. Frustration and failure engulf the ill-prepared Negro pupils . . . [pp. 209–210].

Other data include that the racial gap in achievement continues to widen through high school and college. Roberts (1963) pointed out that less than 3% of Negro graduates of segregated high schools would meet the standards of nonsegregated colleges. Roberts estimated that not more than 10 to 15% of Negro American college youth were capable of exceeding the threshold-level score on the American Council on Education test that was recommended by the President's Commission (100 on the 1947 edition).

Even in the urban North, where schools are legally integrated, the education afforded Negroes tends to be inadequate. Deutsch (1960), for example, found that in time samples of classroom activity, from 50% to 80% of all classroom time in New York City elementary schools with predominantly Negro, lower-class children was "devoted to disciplining and various essentially non-academic tasks." By comparison, only 30% of classroom time was given over to such activities in elementary schools attended mainly by white children of roughly similar economic status.

The foregoing material indicates that when grade-a-year plans of desegregation are adopted, it is obviously desirable from an educational standpoint to begin integration at the lowest grade and work upward. However, many Southern school systems are on grade-a-year plans of reverse order, with integration starting in the twelfth grade and proceeding down.

Unrealistic inferiority feelings. Apparently, the Negro child's feeling of intellectual inferiority is based not only on reality experience, but reflects an emotional accommodation to the demeaning role in American culture that has been imposed upon his racial group by the dominant white majority. The Group for the Advancement of Psychiatry (1957) has summarized the observations of numerous investigators of Negro personality:

Wherever segregation occurs, one group, in this instance the Negroes, always suffers from inferior social status. The damaging effects of this are reflected in unrealistic inferiority feelings, a sense of humiliation, and constriction of potentialities for self-development. This often results in a pattern of self-hatred and rejection of one's own group, sometimes expressed by anti-social behavior toward one's own group or the dominant group. These attitudes seriously affect the levels of aspiration, the capacity to learn, and the capacity to relate in interpersonal situations [p. 10].

Two experiments with Negro male college students suggest the marked extent to which loss of confidence when competing with whites can override reality. Preston and Bayton (1941) found that when students at a Negro college were told that their own scores on intellectual tasks were the same as the average scores of white students, they tended to set their goal levels lower on the next few trials than they did when told that their scores equalled those of other Negro students. The results can be interpreted on the basis of Atkinson's (1958a) theory of goal-setting behavior. Assuming that the Negro subject's motive to succeed tended to be stronger than his motive to avoid failure, he should have set his goal where the probability of success was .50. When a given level of performance was said to represent the white norm its apparent difficulty became greater than when it was supposed to represent the Negro norm, hence the goal level at which the expectancy of success was .50 tended to be lower immediately following the announcement of these norms. In an investigation of small bi-racial work terms at a Northern university, Katz and Benjamin (1960) observed that Negro students who had actually scored as well as their white teammates on various intellectual tasks afterwards rated their own performance as inferior. Here knowledge of white performance levels apparently influenced the Negro subjects' cognitions of their own *actual* performance, rather than just their estimations of *future* performance.

In an experiment suggested by Whyte's (1943) observations of status influence in a white street-corner gang, Harvey (1953) had members of white high-school cliques take turns on a dart-throwing task. After several practice trials, the boys openly estimated their own and their companions' future performance. Guesses were directly related to social rank in the group. Only boys of lowest rank showed a tendency to *under*estimate own performance. Moreover, they were expected by those of middle and high status to perform more poorly than they actually did. It should be noted that it is unclear from Harvey's results whether rank influenced perception of own ability or merely what one was willing to say in front of higher-ranking clique mates who had coercive power (French & Raven, 1960) to keep those of lesser rank "in their place."

EXPERIMENTS ON
STRESS AND PERFORMANCE

Earlier some situational factors were described that presumably are detrimental to Negro academic achievement: social threat, low expectancy of success, and failure threat. Also, evidence was presented (some of it inferential) of their occurrence in actual situations of racial integration. A good deal of experimentation having to do with the influence of these factors on verbal and motor performance has been stimulated by the concept of psychological stress. Applezweig and Moeller (1957) proposed a definition of stress which focuses on the condition of the individual: Stress occurs when a motive or need is strongly aroused and the organism is unable to respond in such a way as to reduce its motivation. Deese (1962) finds it more useful to define stress as a class of stimulus events that elicit a set of correlated responses, among which are feelings of discomfort. He points out that the effects of stress on performance are specific to particular components of the performance under consideration—i.e., responses to stress may be either compatible or incompatible with the responses required in a given task.

Early studies of stress and performance did not employ the type of analytic comparison of stress responses and dimensions of ability in specific skills that Deese suggests. The general trend of findings on verbal performance (reviewed by Lazarus, Deese, & Osler, 1952) has been that stress impairs efficiency on relatively complex and difficult tasks, while on simple tasks stress has sometimes been shown to improve performance. The types of stress that have been used in experiments include failure feedback or threat of failure, exposure to highly difficult tasks (often under time pressure), annoying or painful stimulation such as electric shock, distraction such as flashing lights or noises, disapproval or disparagement.

Many investigations have employed stress inductions that apparently aroused fear of failure. For example, using 9-year-old boys, Lantz (1945) observed an impairment of Stanford-Binet scores following a failure experience, but no such effect after a successful experience. An examination by Lantz of the differential effects of this failure experience upon the various subtests indicated that tasks requiring visual or rote memory were not affected, while those involving reasoning or thinking suffered a decrement. In other studies that were reviewed by Lazarus, Deese, and Osler failure stress produced decrements in scores on the following verbal-symbolic tasks: learning and recall of nonsense syllables, digit-symbol substitution, arithmetic, recognition of briefly exposed sentences, sentence formation, and digit span. Similar effects were obtained on various types of perceptual-motor performance (e.g., card sorting, reaction time).

Turning to some representative studies of stress not directly involving failure, Barker, Dembo, and Lewin (1941) observed regression in the mental age of nursery-school children, as measured by the constructiveness of their play, when the children were frustrated by being denied access to attractive toys. Stress associated with the blocking of hostile impulses against an instigating agent (a teacher who arbitrarily disregarded the expressed desire of students) was found by Goldman, Horwitz, and Lee (1954) to impair performance on three tasks: retention of learned material, digit span, and problem solving. Laird (1923) reported loss of body steadiness in college students who were "razzed" by future fraternity brothers while working on simple motor tasks. Klein (1957) found that a strong task-irrelevant drive (thirst) caused a reduction in the accuracy of visual size judgments; and Callaway and Thompson (1953) obtained a similar effect when their subjects were required to hold one foot in a bucket of ice water.

During the past decade much research has been done on the role of personality factors in reactions to stress, with particular focus on the role of individual differences in chronic anxiety as measured by Taylor's Manifest Anxiety scale and Mandler and Sarason's Test Anxiety Questionnaire. A lengthy review of this work would fall outside the scope of this paper, inasmuch as the primary concern here is with *situational* factors that affect Negro performance. Yet it is of interest to note the general pattern of experimental results. Greater decrements due to stress are found in the performance of high-anxious individuals than in the performance of subjects lower in the anxiety-score distribution. These studies have been reviewed by Sarason (1960) and Taylor (1963).

Speculating about underlying physiological processes in stress, Bovard (1959) places the organizing center of bodily-emotional responses to stress in the posterior and medial hypothalamus. Of particular interest are his hypotheses that (*a*) activity in the anterior hypothalamus tends to inhibit or dampen posterior activity, and (*b*) excitation in the anterior hypothalamus is produced by certain types of social stimuli. *Thus an organism's vulnerability to stress depends upon the nature of its social environment.* Bovard reviewed studies which suggest that the presence of companions or members of the same species has a supportive effect under stress. At the human level it has been observed that separation from the family and evacuation from London was more stressful for London children than enduring the bombings with their family (Titmuss, 1950). Mandlebaum (1952) and Marshall (1951) dealt with the importance of social contact among soldiers in resisting battle stress. Research at Boston Psychopathic Hospital (1955) has shown that lysergic acid diethylamide (LSD) taken in a group situation results in less anxiety and inappropriate behavior than when taken individually. Schachter (1959) reported that fear, as well as hunger, increased the affiliative tendency in college students; and Wrightsman (1960) found that being with others in a similar plight was anxiety reducing for students who were first-born or only children.

Similar phenomena have been observed at the animal level. Liddell (1950) found that the presence or absence of the mother goat determined whether young goats would develop an experimental neurosis in a conditioning situation. In experiments with rats, animals tested together under stressful conditions gave less fear response (Davitz & Mason, 1955) and had less resultant ulceration (Conger, Sawrey, & Turrell, 1957) than animals tested alone. Similarly, monkeys showed fewer fear responses in a strange situation when another monkey was present (Mason, 1960). Monkeys raised in total isolation from age peers were deficient in normal defensive responses to environmental threat (Harlow & Harlow, 1962).

If Bovard's theory is correct, the extreme social isolation that is often experienced by Negroes in predominantly white environments would weaken their resistance to other stress conditions, such as might arise from the inherent difficulty of academic work, time pressure, financial problems, etc.

Various theories have been invoked to account for the tendency of stress to reduce efficiency on complex tasks, but to facilitate performance, or have no effect, on simple tasks. Sarason and others (Child, 1954; Mandler & Sarason, 1952; Sarason et al., 1960) have dealt primarily with the effects of individual differences in vulnerability to failure stress. They emphasize the interference that occurs when expectation of failure generates anxiety which, in turn, acts as an internal stimulus for defensive, task-irrelevant responses. Similarly, Deese (1962) mentions task interference from responses to the internal stimuli of stress-induced autonomic activity.

Some writers have concerned themselves with the effect of drive on specific characteristics of task-relevant behavior. Thus Easterbrook (1959) postulates an inverse relationship between drive level and the range of cue utilization. Complex tasks require a relatively broad awareness of cues for optimal efficiency, whereas simple tasks by definition require apprehension of only a few cues for successful responding. Hence, when drive is very high (as in stress), relevant cues will be missed on hard tasks, but more closely attended to on easy tasks. Hullian theory, as developed with respect to anxiety drive and learning by Spence, Taylor, and others, deals with the energizing effect of drive on task responses. As strength of drive increases the number of habitual response tendencies that can be elicited in a given task increases also. When activation is strong (as in stress) intra-task response competition is heightened. The theory is supported by the results of experiments in which high and low scorers on Taylor's Manifest Anxiety scale were required to learn competitional and noncompetitional paired-word lists (reviewed by Spence, 1958; Taylor, 1963). Thus Easterbrook and the Hullians have each dealt with a particular component of a great number of tasks, and have tried to predict either favorable or detrimental effects of stress from the presence or absence of this component.

Discussing the effects of stress on perceptual-motor skills, Deese (1963) points out the need for systematic analysis of (*a*) the characteristics of motor arousal under stress, in relation to (*b*) the dimensions of psychomotor abilities that are requisite for various task performances. Both Deese and Spence (1958) mention that a fundamental weakness of present thinking about the effects of stress on *verbal* learning is that not enough dimensions of verbal skills have yet been explored to know what kinds of effects to look for.

Summarizing this section, there is a considerable amount of experimental evidence that types of stress which may be present in desegregation (as varieties of social threat and failure threat) impair certain kinds of verbal and perceptual-motor learning. However, there does not exist at present any comprehensive system of variables for predicting the specific effects of different conditions of stress on the Negro child's performance of various academic tasks.

EXPERIMENTS ON
NEGRO PERFORMANCE
IN BIRACIAL SITUATIONS[1]

In recent years this author and his associates have been engaged in a series of experiments on the intellectual productivity of Negro male college students in situations involving white

1. All of the research by the author and his associates that is reviewed in this section was conducted under Contract Nonr 285 (24) between the Office of Naval Research and New York University.

peers and/or white authority figures. The general aim of the research is the identification of underlying psychological factors that have either favorable or detrimental effects on Negro efficiency. In connection with the interpretation of the results that are now to be presented there evolved the set of postulated situational determinants of performance that were discussed in an earlier section of this paper.

Biracial Teams

In two exploratory studies, conducted at a Northern university (Katz & Benjamin, 1960; Katz, Goldston, & Benjamin, 1958), various cognitive and motor tasks were assigned to groups composed of two Negro students and two white students. Initially the men were total strangers. They worked together in several sessions for a total of 12½ hours. In general, it was found that Negroes displayed marked social inhibition and subordination to white partners. When teams were engaged in cooperative problem solving, Negro subjects made fewer proposals than did whites, and tended to accept the latter's contributions uncritically. On all tasks combined, Negroes made fewer remarks than did whites, and spoke more to whites, proportionately, than to one another. White men, on the other hand, spoke more to one another, proportionately, than to the Negroes. These behaviors occurred even when group members could expect a monetary bonus for good teamwork, and were informed that their abilities were higher than those of subjects in other teams. Moreover, in the second experiment Negro and white partners were matched on intelligence, and were even made to display equal ability on certain group tasks (by means of secret manipulation of tasks). Yet on a terminal questionnaire Negroes ranked whites higher on intellectual performance, preferred one another as future work companions, and expressed less satisfaction with the group experience than did whites.

The findings on Negro behavior may have been a result of (*a*) social threat (ie., Negroes were fearful of instigating white hostility through greater assertiveness), (*b*) low task

motivation in confrontation with white achievement standards (as derived earlier from Atkinson's model, or (c) failure
threat (high expectancy of failure combined with anxious anticipation of disapproval and rejection by white peers and the
white experimenter). The experimental data provide no basis
on which to reject any of these factors as irrelevant.

In the next experiment, Katz and Cohen (1962) attempted
to modify Negro behavior toward white partners in the direction of greater assertiveness and autonomy. It was predicted
that (a) when Negroes were compelled to achieve on a task that
was performed cooperatively with a white peer, they would subsequently display an increased amount of achieving behavior on
another shared task of different content, and (b) Negro subjects
who were not compelled to achieve on the first task would show
an opposite tendency. Negro-white student dyads at a Northern
university engaged in cooperative solving of problems adapted
from the Raven Progressive Matrices. Some of the problems
were made easy, to insure that both participants would perceive
the correct answer. On other problems the subjects unknow-
ingly received different information, so that one person had an
insoluble version. Each subject had the easy version half the
time. On every problem partners had to agree on a single team
answer, after which the experimenter announced the correct
solution. Before and after the problem-solving experience a
disguised measure of social influence between the two men
was obtained on a task which required group estimates of certain quantitative characteristics of briefly exposed photographs
(e.g., the number of paratroopers in the sky).

In a control condition, the rules of the problem-solving
situation did not require that each person openly propose an
answer to every problem. It was found that Negroes tended to
accept passively the suggestions of their white companions *even
when they held the easy version and the teammate had to be in
error.* Regarding intellectual efficiency, the private responses of
Negroes, which they wrote down before each discussion began,
showed *more errors than were made on the same problems at
an earlier, individual testing session.* White subjects, on the
other hand, made *fewer* private errors than they had made

previously. As a consequence of the problem-solving experience in the control condition, Negroes showed increased social compliance on the picture estimations.

In an "assertion-training" condition the men were given their answer sheets from the previous session when they had worked alone. On every problem the two partners were required to read aloud their previous answers before negotiating a team reply. Thus, Negro subjects had the experience of openly announcing correct solutions in about half of all instances of disagreement (both men read off approximately the same number of correct answers). In the subsequent interactions over picture estimation there was an *increase* in the amount of influence Negroes had over the white partner. Further, Negro subjects were now inclined to accept the other person's influence only to the extent that he had displayed superior accuracy on previous pictures.

Thus, unless *forced* to express opinions at variance with those of a white peer, Negro students tended to suppress their own ideas in deference to the other person, and to show increased compliance on another task. But when they were *forced* to act independently on one task, they achieved greater autonomy in the second situation. The responses of white subjects on a postexperimental questionnaire indicate there may have been some hostility aroused against Negro partners who displayed intellectual competence. After working in the assertion-training condition whites tended to downgrade the Negro's performance and to accept him less as a future co-worker. However, since there were no all-white control groups, it is not known whether these reactions of white subjects were specifically interracial.

The results suggest that Negro submissiveness with the white companion was an effect primarily of social threat, and that probability of success was a relatively unimportant factor. As already mentioned, in both the assertion-training and control condition disagreement was experimentally arranged on almost all problems, with random alternation between partners in the assignment of easy and insoluble versions (on a few items *both* men had either easy or hard versions). Also, after each team decision the experimenter announced the correct answer (fictitious when both men had hard items) so that subjects could check the accuracy of their own private response and of the solution the partner had openly proposed. While there was a stable tendency in control teams for whites to make slightly fewer private errors than Negroes (all partners had been matched on pretest scores), it is doubtful that the average race difference of about two private errors on 49 items could have been discriminated by the average Negro subject. Hence the relative accuracy of own and partner's solutions was much the same for Negro subjects in the two experimental conditions, and the only difference between conditions was that in assertion training the Negro subject was forced to *disagree openly* with the partner. The disinhibiting effect of this experience on the Negro subject's behavior on another task seems attributable to a reduction in anxiety about instigating white hostility.

The Effect of Induced Threat in Different Racial Environments

In the next experiment, Katz and Greenbaum (1963) examined more directly the influence of threat on Negro verbal performance by systematically varying the level of threat in different racial environments. Individual Negro students at a predominantly Negro college in the South were given a digit-symbol substitution task in the presence of two strangers who were both either white or Negro—an adult administrator and a confederate who pretended to be another student working on the same task. In order to minimize the amount of uncontrolled threat implicit in the white condition, there was no social interaction between the Negro subject and his white peer, and the task was described as a research instrument of no evaluative significance.

In addition to the variation of racial environment, the students were exposed to a condition of either high or low threat. Since the purpose of the threat variation was to determine whether individual Negroes were more vulnerable to debilitative effects of stress when they were alone with whites than when they were with other Negroes, it seemed desirable to use a threat stimulus that would not lead to intentional suppression of responses, by changing the social meaning of the task situation. The experimenters used an announcement that severe electric shock (high-threat condition) or mild electric shock (low-threat condition) would be administered to the subject and the co-worker at random times during the task. No shocks were actually delivered.

The results indicated that Negro students' scores on the digit-symbol task depended upon the particular combination of stress and racial-environment conditions under which they worked. When only mild shock was threatened they performed better in the presence of whites than of other Negroes. But when told to expect strong shock their efficiency in the Negro condition improved, while in the white condition it went down. Apparently, the prospect of successful competition against a white peer, and of approval from a white authority figure, had greater incentive strength than the corresponding prospect in the all-Negro situation. This is reasonable on the assumption that the whites (particularly the experimenter) had higher prestige for the subject than their Negro counterparts. Since in all experimental conditions the instructions for the task played down its intellectual significance, Negro subjects in the white-environment -low-shock threat condition would not have experienced strong failure threat. Hence, they could respond to the stronger incentive strength of success in the white condition.

There are a number of ways of looking at the effects of shock threat. First, if Negro subjects cared more about performing well in the white condition they would have been more fearful lest the strong shock disrupt their task responses (failure threat). The expected stimulus would thus become more salient and distracting. An upward spiral of debilitation could then be set in motion as distraction and fear made the task seem more difficult, and this in turn aroused further emotion. Subjects in the Negro environment, on the other hand, had a relatively relaxed attitude toward the task in the low-threat condition (*too* relaxed for good performance). Hence they would not have been fearful of possible decrements due to shock, but perhaps just enough concerned to work harder than before. Also relevant to these data is Bovard's earlier-mentioned notion that the ability to withstand stress is strengthened by the presence of familiar social stimuli that have nurturant associations (in this case other Negroes).

The Hullian conception of the energizing effect of drive is also applicable: Efficiency declined in the white condition because the subject's initial stimulation in this racial environment, in combination with the additional stimulation of the strong shock threat, produced a total drive strength that exceeded the optimum for the assigned task. In the Negro condition, initial stimulation was relatively low, so that the increment in arousal due to strong threat brought the total drive level closer to the optimum than it had been under mild threat.

Effects of IQ versus Non-IQ Instructions

In a follow-up on the preceding experiment, Katz, Roberts, and Robinson (in press) investigated the effects of three factors on Negro students' efficiency; the race of the task administrator, the difficulty of the task, and the evaluative significance of the task. All subjects were students at a Southern Negro college. Half of them were tested individually by a Negro adult and the other half were tested by a white adult. In addition, one-third of the total sample worked on a relatively easy digit-symbol code, one-third were given a code of medium difficulty, and one-third had to do a relatively hard code. In order to attach a relatively nonthreatening significance to the situation, the task was described as a research instrument for studying eye-hand coordination, a nonintellectual characteristic. Unlike the Katz and Greenbaum experiment, there was no experimental confederate who posed as a second subject. The findings were consistent with results obtained in the low-threat condition of the earlier study—Negro subjects worked more efficiently when tested by a white adult than when tested by a Negro adult. However, the favorable influence of the white administrator was apparent only on the most difficult of the three tasks. On the two easier codes there were no statistically reliable differences in achievement associated with the skin color of the experimenters. Apparently the easier tasks were too simple to reflect the differences in motivation.

Then two additional groups of Negro students were tested by the same Negro and white administrators on the most difficult task only. But instead of being told that the task measured eye-hand coordination, it was presented to these subjects as a test of intelligence. Now the subjects did not attain higher scores in the presence of a white experimenter; rather, the effect of the IQ instructions was to slightly elevate performance with a Negro tester and to lower scores markedly in the white-tester group, so that the means for both testers were at about the same level. Thus in this experiment, making the most difficult task relevant to intellectual ability had effects not unlike those of strong threat in the previous study by Katz and Greenbaum. On the assumption that intellectual instructions were more highly motivating than the motor-test instructions, one can again apply the Hullian interpretation that motivation in the IQ-test–white-administrator treatment was excessive.

More directly relevant is Atkinson's (1958a) conception of motivation as a joint function of the subjective probability and incentive value of success, which was discussed earlier. Assuming again that a white experimenter has higher prestige for the Negro student than does a Negro experimenter, the prospect of eliciting the white person's approval would be more attractive. It follows that when the likelihood of winning approval by scoring well is equally high whether the tester is Negro or white, the subject will work harder for the white person. Thus in this experiment Negro students performed better with a white adult than with a Negro adult when the task was supposed to assess an ability which Negroes are not stereotyped as lacking (eye-hand coordination). Presenting the task as an intelligence test ought to have raised the incentive value of achievement in both racial conditions, with perhaps an even greater increment occurring when the experimenter was white (since *intellectual* approval by a white adult might be uniquely gratifying to the Negro students' self-esteem).

But suppose that on the intellectual task the Negro subject

saw very little likelihood of meeting the white experimenter's standard of excellence. Unless the incentive strength of success increased enough to counterbalance the drop in subjective probability, Atkinson's model would predict a reduction in task motivation. As an additional source of impairment in this situation, low expectancy of success could have aroused fear of earning the white tester's *dis*approval (failure threat).

Turning now to the situation where the tester is Negro, there is no reason to assume that the subject's expectation of success would be markedly lower when the task was described as intellectual than when it was presented as a motor test. In both instances the racial identity of the tester would tend to suggest to the subject that he was to be compared with other Negroes. Accordingly, performance with the Negro tester ought to go up under IQ instructions. The fact that it rose only slightly in our experiment may be ascribed to the subject's unclarity about the tester's frame of reference for evaluating his score. That is, he was not actually informed whether he would be compared with norms for Negro students only, or with norms for *all* college students. The next study deals directly with this issue.

Effects of Variations in Anticipated Comparison

Katz, Epps, and Axelson (1964) investigated the effects on Negro students' digit-symbol performance of being told that they would be compared intellectually with other Negro students, or with white students. Hard and easy versions of the digit-symbol task were administered to different groups of students at a Southern Negro college under three different instructions: no test, scholastic aptitude test with own college norms, and scholastic aptitude test with national (i.e., predominantly white) college norms. Scores in all three conditions were reliably different from one another, with highest achievement occurring in the Negro-norms condition, intermediate achievement in the white-norms condition, and lowest achievement when no comparison was expected. These differences tended to be larger on the hard task than on the easy one.

Again referring to Atkinson's model, Negro performance was lowest in the no-test condition because of low incentive, while the difference between the two test conditions was due to higher subjective probability of success (closer to .50) when Negro subjects believed they were competing with members of their own race than when they expected to be compared with whites.

White students from a nearby state university were tested under comparable instructions on the hard task only. It was found that scores of the two norms groups—i.e., own college and national—did not differ, and *both* groups were more efficient than subjects in the no-comparison condition.

Future research can determine the usefulness of this application of Atkinson's theory for understanding Negro behavior in integrated schools. For example, the present formulation predicts that if the subjective probability of success were held constant, Negro subjects would perform *better* on certain types of intellectual test when the administrator was white than when he was Negro, or when they were competing with white peers rather than with Negro peers.

A Pilot Experiment on the Effect of Probability Feedback

In a recent pilot study (unpublished), done in preparation for a larger experiment, students at a Southern Negro college were individually given a digit-symbol task by a white administrator under two conditions of probability of success. All subjects performed an initial trial under instructions that the task measured intelligence. Upon completing the first trial, every subject was informed that his final score would be compared with racially integrated norms. Half of all the subjects were told, in addition, that on the basis of their first-trial scores there was a statistical probability of about 60% that their final scores would exceed the mean for their age group. Then a second trial was administered to everyone. It was found that subjects who were given the probability information performed better on the second trial than those who were not. This preliminary investigation gives further weight to the suggestion that the perceived probability of success is an important determinant of Negro reactions to competition with whites.

Emotional Reactions to Test Situations

Another line of investigation has to do with the appraisal of Negro subjects' emotional reactions to various test situations. In connection with the earlier discussion of failure threat, reference was made to the research of Sarason and his associates (Sarason, 1960; Sarason et al., 1960) on emotional factors in the test-taking behavior of white school children. In their view, the child who chronically experiences anxiety when tested is reacting with strong unconscious hostility to the adult tester, who he believes will in some way pass judgment on his adequacy. The hostility is not openly expressed, but instead is turned inward against the self in the form of self-derogatory attitudes, which strengthen the child's expectation of failure and his desire to escape the situation. Thus he is distracted from the task before him by his fear of failure and his impulse to escape.

Sarason has not as yet presented direct evidence that situations of adult evaluation arouse hostility in highly test-anxious children. However, in clinical studies by Lit (1956), Kimball (1952), and Harris (1961), difficulty in expressing aggression openly was found to be associated with scholastic underachievement. Rosenwald (1961) found that students who were relatively unwilling to give aggressive responses on a projective test showed greater impairment in solving anagrams after a hostility induction than did students who showed less inhibition of aggression on the projective test. Mention has been made of a study by Goldman, Horwitz, and Lee (1954), which demonstrated an association between the degree to which strong hostility against an instigator was denied expression and the amount of disruption of intellectual functioning.

These studies are pertinent to the problem of Negro children's learning efficiency in integrated classrooms, because these children often have to suppress strong hostility. It was seen that Yarrow (1958) found a much higher incidence of covert symptoms of emotional disturbance in Negro children than in white children at a desegregated summer camp. White children, it will be recalled, aggressed openly against their Negro cabin mates, but the latter did not respond in kind. Rather, they tended to deny aggressive impulses in themselves and to show heightened alertness to aggressive behavior in other Negro children. Another investigator who has reported stronger trends toward denial of hostile impulses in Negro children than in white children is Karon (1958), who examined individual personality by means of a projective technique, the Picture Arrangement Test.

It was suggested earlier that when the administrator of an intellectual test is white, or when comparison with white peers is anticipated, Negro subjects tend to become fearful of failure. Anticipation of failure would tend to generate feelings of victimization and covert hostility against the white tester. Since hostility against white authorities is dangerous, the hostile impulse would be strongly inhibited. Katz, Robinson, Epps, and Waly (in press) undertook to find out whether suppression of hostile responses occurs when a white adult makes Negro students take an intelligence test. Negro male students at a segregated high school in the South were given a test of aggression disguised as a concept-formation test. It consisted of 58 four-word items, with instructions to "circle the word that does not belong with the others." In half of the items one word had aggressive meaning, one word was nonaggressive, and two words were ambiguous. Hence the subject could choose either a hostile or a neutral concept. Two equivalent forms of the test were administered on successive days. On the first day it was given informally to all subjects by a Negro teacher. The following day the entire sample was divided into four groups, each of which was tested by either a white or a Negro adult stranger, with instructions that described the task as either an intelligence test or a research instrument.

The results show that when neutral instructions were used on the second day, average scores in both the white-tester and Negro-tester groups were the same as on the pretest. But in the intelligence-test condition, hostility scores *increased* over the previous day when the experimenter was a Negro, and they *decreased* when the experimenter was white. The authors' interpretation is that both administrators instigated hostile impulses in the subjects when they announced that the task would be used to evaluate intelligence; when the adult authority was a Negro person, students revealed their annoyance by responding to the aggressive connotations of ambiguous words, but when the adult was a white person, the need to deny hostile feelings resulted in avoidance of aggressive word meanings. (The "denial" interpretation is of course inferential, since the results merely show that hostility scores in the white-adult–IQ-test condition went down; there was no *direct* evidence of increased emotional conflict in this condition.)

Assuming that these findings actually reflect variations in ability to express hostile impulses under different testing conditions, they furnish an interesting clue as to the nature of emotional processes attendant upon the disruption of Negro students' performance in the white-adult–IQ-test condition of an earlier experiment (Katz, Roberts, & Robinson).

SUMMARY

This paper brings together evidence relating to the effect of school desegregation on the academic performance of young Negroes. Negro Americans are defined as a subordinated minority group, and the focus of attention is on their adjustment in schools where white age peers and teachers predominate. In situations of this type there appear to be a variety of favorable and detrimental influences on Negro performance.

Low probability of success. Where there is marked discrepancy in the educational standards of Negro and white schools, or where feelings of inferiority are acquired by Negro children outside the school, minority-group newcomers in integrated classrooms are likely to have a low expectancy of academic success; consequently, their achievement motivation should be low. *Social threat*—given the prestige and power of the white majority group, rejection of Negro students by white classmates or teachers should tend to elicit emotional responses (fear, anger, and humiliation) that are detrimental to intellectual functioning. *Failure threat*—when academic failure entails disapproval by significant others (parents, teachers, and perhaps also classmates), low expectancy of success should elicit emotional responses that are detrimental to performance.

On the other hand, *acceptance* of Negroes by white peers and adults should have a *social facilitation* effect upon their ability to learn, by motivating them to adhere to white standards of academic performance; anticipation that high performance will win white approval should endow scholastic success with *high-incentive value.*

Reports on the academic progress of Negro children in desegregated schools are on the whole inadequate for drawing any conclusions about the effects of biracial environments upon Negro performance. However, other types of evidence indicate that any or all of the situational factors mentioned above may be operative in specific instances. Research on psychological stress generally supports the assumption that social threat and failure threat are detrimental to complex learning.

Experiments on Negro male college students by the author and his associates have shown that in work teams composed of Negro and white students of similar intellectual ability, Negroes are passively compliant, rate their own performance as inferior even when it is not, and express less satisfaction with the team experience than do their white companions. These results are seen as due to social threat and/or failure threat. Later studies have sought to identify specific situational determinants of Negro behavior in biracial settings.

Forcing Negro subjects into attempts to influence nonhostile white partners in problem solving had the effect of increasing their ascendancy on another task with the same white partner, apparently mainly through reduction of their fear of instigating hostility.

Experimentally creating a verbal-task situation that was low in both social threat and failure threat resulted in better performance by Negroes in the presence of whites than in the presence of other Negroes, suggesting that the incentive value of success was greater in the white environment. But when threat of strong electric shock was introduced, the white setting became less favorable to performance than the Negro one. Thus *vulnerability* to stress was greater in the white condition, even though it was not apparent until a strong explicit threat was introduced.

The evaluative significance of a verbal task (e.g., whether it was described as a perceptual-motor test or an intellectual test) interacted with race of the tester in determining Negro performance, in a manner consistent with the notions that (a) the incentive value of success was higher with a white tester than with a Negro tester, and (b) the probability of success was lower with a white tester than with a Negro tester only when the task was defined intellectually.

Anticipated intellectual comparison with Negro peers was found to produce a higher level of verbal performance than anticipated comparison with white peers, in accordance with the assumption that the subjective probability of success was lower when the expected comparison was with whites. Also, performance was facilitated when a white tester raised the subject's expectancy of attaining a white standard of performance by giving him suitable "information" about his score on a previous trial.

Finally, suppression of hostile impulses appeared to occur in Negro students who were tested by a white adult, but not in those who were tested by a Negro adult.

Further research is needed to clarify the effects of the various situational factors mentioned above on the cognitive functioning of Negroes in biracial settings. However, it is possible even now to point out some implications for educational practice of the findings that have been reviewed.

IMPLICATIONS FOR
EDUCATIONAL PRACTICE

The foregoing is relevant to a number of recent suggestions by social scientists on ways to foster movement toward equal education for all children (e.g., Klopf & Laster, 1963):

1. Educational standards of Negro schools should be raised

to the level of white schools, so that minority-group children who transfer to previously all-white schools will have a reasonable chance of succeeding academically. This means, among other things, that the quality of training received by Negro teachers and the criteria used in selecting them for jobs must be raised to white levels, and racial integration of school faculties must be carried out.

2. Programs should be instituted for contacting parents and helping them to understand what they can do to prepare children for schooling, and to foster achievement once children are in school.

3. There should be in-service training of teachers and other personnel in newly integrated schools to develop awareness of the emotional needs of children in biracial situations. The training should include the imparting of techniques for helping children get acquainted with one another.

4. The widely accepted practice of assigning children to homogeneous ability groups (the "track" system) should either be abandoned entirely or modified to afford maximum opportunity for periodic re-evaluation of potentiality. Ability grouping tends inevitably to freeze teachers' expectations as well as children's own self-images, hence it is particularly dangerous to intellectual development in the early grades.

5. Where grade-a-year plans of desegregation are adopted, the process should begin at the lowest grades, where Negro children have the smallest educational handicap and where unfavorable racial attitudes are least strongly learned.

REFERENCES

Applezweig, M. H., and Moeller, G. The role of motivation in psychological stress. *Off. Naval Res. tech. Rep.,* 1957, No. 3.

Atkinson, J. W. Motivational determinants of risk taking behavior. In J. W. Atkinson (ed.), *Motives in fantasy, action, and society.* New York: Van Nostrand, 1958. Pp. 322–340. (a)

Atkinson, J. W. Towards experimental analysis of human motives in terms of motives, expectancies, and incentives. In J. W. Atkinson (ed.), *Motives in fantasy, action, and society.* New York: Van Nostrand, 1958. Pp. 288–305. (b)

Barker, R., Dembo, Tamara, and Lewin, K. Frustration and regression: An experiment with young children. *U. Ia. Stud. Child Welf.*, 1941, 18, No. 1.

Bass, B. M. Conformity, deviation, and a general theory of interpersonal behavior. In I. A. Berg and B. M. Bass (eds.), *Conformity and deviation*. New York: Harper & Row, 1961. Pp. 38–100.

Boston Psychopathic Hospital. Experimental psychoses. *Scient. American*, 1955, 192 (6), 34–39.

Bovard, E. W. The effects of social stimuli on the response to stress. *Psychol. Rev.*, 1959, 66, 267–277.

Callaway, E., and Thompson, S. V. Sympathetic activity and perception. *Psychosom. Med.*, 1953, 15, 443–455.

Child, I. L. Personality. In C. P. Stone and Q. McNemar (eds.), *Annual Review of Psychology*. Stanford, Calif.: Annual Reviews, 1954. Pp. 149–170.

Coles, R. *The desegregation of southern schools: A psychiatric study*. New York: Anti-Defamation League, 1963.

Conger, J. J., Sawrey, W. L., and Turrell, E. S. An experimental investigation of the role of social experience in the production of gastric ulcers in hooded rats. *Amer. Psychologist*, 1957, 12, 410. (Abstract)

Criswell, Joan H. A sociometric study of rat cleavage in the classroom. *Arch. Psychol., N.Y.*, 1939, No. 235.

Davitz, J. R., and Mason, D. J. Socially facilitated reduction of a fear response in rats. *J. comp. physiol. Psychol.*, 1955, 48, 149–151.

Day, R. E. Part 2, North Carolina. In United States Commission on Civil Rights, *Civil Rights U.S.A.—public schools, Southern states*. Washington, D.C.: United States Government Printing Office, 1962. Pp. 57–104.

Deese, J. Skilled performance and conditions of stress. In R. Glaser (ed.), *Training research and education*. Pittsburgh: Univer. Pittsburgh Press, 1962. Pp. 199–222.

Deutsch, M. Minority group and class status as related to social and personality factors in scholastic achievement. *Soc. Appl. Anthropol. Monogr.*, 1960, No. 2.

Deutsch, M. Dimensions of the school's role in the problems of integration. In G. J. Klopf and I. A. Laster (eds.), *Integrating the urban school*. New York: Teachers College, Columbia University, Bureau of Publications, 1963. Pp. 29–44.

Dittes, J. E., and Kelley, H. H. Effects of different conditions of acceptance upon conformity to group norms. *J. abnorm. soc. Psychol.*, 1956, 53, 100–107.

Dodson, D. Statement read at *Conference before the United States Commission on Civil Rights: Fourth annual education conference on problems of segregation and desegregation of public schools*. Washington, D.C.: United States Commission on Civil Rights, 1962. Pp. 137–141.

Easterbrook, J. A. The effect of emotion on cue utilization and the organization of behavior. *Psychol. Rev.,* 1959, 66, 183–201.

Findley, W. G. *Learning and teaching in Atlanta public schools.* Princeton, N.J.: Educational Testing Service, 1956.

French, J. R. P., Jr., and Raven, B. The bases of social power. In D. Cartwright and A. Zander (eds.), *Group dynamics.* (2nd ed.) Evanston, Ill.: Row Peterson, 1960. Pp. 607–623.

Goldman, M., Horwitz, M., and Lee, F. J. Alternative classroom standards concerning management of hostility and effects on student learning. *Off. Naval Res. tech. Rep.,* 1954.

Group for the Advancement of Psychiatry. *Psychiatric aspects of school desegregation.* New York: GAP, 1957.

Hansen, C. F. The scholastic performances of Negro and white pupils in the integrated public schools of the District of Columbia. *Harvard educ. Rev.,* 1960, 30, 216–236.

Harlow, H. F., and Harlow, Margaret K. Social deprivation in monkeys. *Scient. American,* 1962, 207 (5), 136–146.

Harris, I. *Emotional blocks to learning.* New York: The Free Press, 1961.

Harvey, O. J. An experimental approach to the study of status relations in informal groups. *Amer. social. Rev.,* 1953, 18, 357–367.

Horowitz, E. The development of attitudes toward the Negro. *Arch. Psychol., N.Y.,* 1936, No. 194.

Karon, B. P. *The Negro personality: A rigorous investigation of the effects of culture.* New York: Springer, 1958.

Katz, I., and Benjamin, L. Effects of white authoritarianism in biracial work groups. *J. abnorm. soc. Psychol.,* 1960, 61, 448–456.

Katz, I., and Cohen, M. The effects of training Negroes upon cooperative problem solving in biracial teams. *J. abnorm. soc. Psychol.,* 1962, 64, 319–325.

Katz, I., Epps, E. G., and Axelson, L. J. Effect upon Negro digit-symbol performance of anticipated comparison with whites and with other Negroes. *J. abnorm. soc. Psychol.,* 1964, 69, in press.

Katz, I., Goldston, Judith, and Benjamin, L. Behavior and productivity in biracial work groups. *Hum. Relat.,* 1958, 11, 123–141.

Katz, I., and Greenbaum, C. Effects of anxiety, threat, and racial environment on task performance of Negro college students. *J. abnorm. soc. Psychol.,* 1963, 66, 562–567.

Katz, I., Roberts, S. O., and Robinson, J. M. Effects of difficulty, race of administrator, and instructions on Negro digit-symbol performance. *J. abnorm. soc. Psychol.,* in press.

Katz, I., Robinson, J. M., Epps, E. G., and Waly, Patricia. Effects of race of experimenter and test vs. neutral instructions on expression of hostility in Negro boys. *J. soc. Issues,* in press.

Kimball, Barbara. Sentence-completion technique in a study of scholastic underachievement. *J. consult. Psychol.,* 1952, 16, 353–358.

Klein, G. S. Need and regulation. In M. R. Jones (ed.), *Nebraska symposium on motivation: 1957.* Lincoln: Univer. Nebraska Press, 1957. Pp. 224–274.

Klopf, G. J., and Laster, I. A. (eds.) *Integrating the urban school.* New York: Teachers College, Columbia University, Bureau of Publications, 1963.

Knowles, L. W. Part 1, Kentucky. In United States Commission on Civil Rights, *Civil Rights U.S.A.—public schools, Southern states.* Washington, D.C.: United States Government Printing Office, 1962. Pp. 19–56.

Laird, D. A. Changes in motor control and individual variations under the influence of "razzing." *J. exp. Psychol.,* 1923, 6, 236–246.

Lantz, Beatrice. Some dynamic aspects of success and failure. *Psychol. Monogr.,* 1945, 59(1, Whole No. 271).

Lazarus, R. S., Deese, J., and Osler, Sonia F. The effects of psychological stress upon performance. *Psychol. Bull.* 1952, 49, 293–317.

Liddell, H. Some specific factors that modify tolerance for environmental stress. In H. G. Wolf, S. G. Wolff, Jr., and C. C. Hare (eds.), *Life stress and bodily disease.* Baltimore: Williams & Wilkins, 1950. Pp. 155–171.

Lit, J. Formal and content factors of projective tests in relation to academic achievement. *Dissert. Abstr.,* 1956, 16, 1505–1506. (Order No. 16,311)

Mandlebaum, D. G. *Soldier groups and Negro soldiers.* Berkeley: Univer. California Press, 1952.

Mandler, G., and Sarason, S. B. A study of anxiety and learning. *J. abnorm. soc. Psychol.,* 1952, 47, 166–173.

Marshall, S. L. A. *Men against fire.* Washington, D.C.: Combat Forces Press, 1951.

Mason, W. A. Socially mediated reduction in emotional responses of young rhesus monkeys. *J. abnorm. soc. Psychol.,* 1960, 60, 100–104.

Mearns, E. A., Jr. Part 4, Virginia. In United States Commission on Civil Rights, *Civil Rights U.S.A.—public schools, Southern states.* Washington, D.C.: United States Government Printing Office, 1962. Pp. 155–217.

Murstein, B. I., and Collier, H. L. The role of the TAT in the measurement of achievement as a function of expectancy. *J. proj. Tech.,* 1962, 26, 96–101.

National Scholarship Service and Fund for Negro Students. *Annual report 1959–1960.* New York: NSSFNS, 1960.

National Scholarship Service and Fund for Negro Students. *Annual report 1962–1963.* New York: NSSFNS, 1963.

Plaut, R. L. *Blueprint for talent searching.* New York: National Scholarship Service and Fund for Negro Students, 1957.

Preston, M. G., and Bayton, J. A. Differential effect of a social variable upon three levels of aspiration. *J. exp. Psychol.,* 1941, 29, 351–369.

Radke, Marian, Sutherland, Jean, and Rosenberg, Pearl. Racial attitudes of children. *Sociometry,* 1950, 13, 154–171.

Radke, Marian, Trager, Helen G., and Davis, Hadassah. Social perceptions and attitudes of children. *Genet. psychol. Monogr.*, 1949, 40, 327–447.

Roberts, S. O. Test performance in relation to ethnic group and social class. Report, 1963, Fisk University, Nashville. (Mimeo)

Rosen, M. Valence, expectancy, and dissonance reduction in the prediction of goal striving. *Dissert. Abstr.*, 1961, 21, 3846. (Order No. 61-2062)

Rosenwald, G. The assessment of anxiety in psychological experiments. *J. abnorm. soc. Psychol.*, 1961, 63, 666–673.

Sarason, I. G. Empirical findings and theoretical problems in the use of anxiety scales. *Psychol. Bull.*, 1960, 57, 403–415.

Sarason, S. B., Davidson, K. S., Lighthall, F. F., Waite, R. R., and Ruebush, B. K. *Anxiety in elementary school children.* New York: Wiley, 1960.

Schachter, S. *The psychology of affiliation.* Stanford: Stanford Univer. Press, 1959.

Southern School News. Untitled. *Sth. sch. News,* 1960 (Aug.), 7, 6(Cols. 1–2).

Southern School News. Untitled. *Sth. sch. News,* 1963 (Apr.), 9, 11(Col. 2).

Spence, K. W. A theory of emotionally based drive (D) and its relation to performance in simple learning situations. *Amer. Psychologist,* 1958, 13, 131–141.

Stallings, F. H. A study of the immediate effects of integration on scholastic achievement in the Louisville Public Schools. *J. Negro Educ.,* 1959, 28, 439–444.

Tanner, J. C. Integration in action. *Wall Street J.,* January 26, 1964, 64, 1.

Taylor, Janet A. Drive theory and manifest anxiety. In Martha T. Mednick and S. A. Mednick (eds.), *Research in personality.* New York: Holt, Rinehart & Winston, 1963. Pp. 205–222.

Thibaut, J., and Kelley, H. H. *The social psychology of groups.* New York: Wiley, 1959.

Titmuss, R. M. *Problems of social policy.* London, England: His Majesty's Stationery Office and Longmans, Green, 1950.

Trillin, C. *An education in Georgia.* New York: Viking Press, 1964.

Tumin, M. The process of integration. In G. J. Klopf and I. A. Laster (eds.), *Integrating the urban school.* New York: Teachers College, Columbia University, Bureau of Publications, 1963. Pp. 13–28.

United States Commission on Civil Rights. *Second annual conference on education, Gatlinburg, Tenn.* Washington, D.C.: United States Government Printing Office, 1960.

United States Commission on Civil Rights. *Civil Rights U.S.A.—public schools, cities in the North and West.* Washington, D.C.: United States Government Printing Office, 1962. (a)

United States Commission on Civil Rights. *Civil Rights U.S.A.—public schools, Southern states.* Washington, D.C.: United States Government Printing Office, 1962. (b)

Whyte, W. F. *Street corner society; the social structure of an Italian slum.* Chicago: Univer. Chicago Press, 1943.

Wrightsman, L. S., Jr. Effects of waiting with others on changes in level of felt anxiety. *J. abnorm. soc. Psychol.,* 1960, 61, 216–222.

Wyatt, E. Part 3, Tennessee. In United States Commission on Civil Rights, *Civil Rights U.S.A.—public schools, Southern states.* Washington, D.C.: United States Government Printing Office, 1962. Pp. 105–130.

Yarrow, Marian R. (Issue ed.) Interpersonal dynamics in a desegregation process. *J. soc. Issues,* 1958, 14(1, entire issue).

EQUALITY THROUGH EDUCATION
A REPORT ON GREENBURGH
SCHOOL DISTRICT NO. 8*

Naomi and Arnold Buchheimer

One finds successful efforts at school integration
mainly in small cities or suburban areas that do not
have the problems presented by the large ghetto
areas of metropolitan centers. Even where physical
integration has been achieved, however, few systems
have moved beyond it to the reconstruction of the
educational structure necessary to make the integrated situation an effective one for the Negro child.

Greenburgh School District No. 8, in New York's
Westchester County, has devoted itself so intensively
to solving the educational problems that accompany
deliberate integration efforts that the Anti-Defamation League commissioned a study of the District's
program and how it developed. The excerpts below
give some of the history of the integration project
and a most interesting listing of criteria for effective
integration about which the educational personnel
involved seem to agree.

* Naomi and Arnold Buchheimer, *Equality Through Integration*, Anti-
Defamation League of B'nai B'rith, undated. Printed with permission from the
Anti-Defamation League of B'nai B'rith, 315 Lexington Ave., N.Y., N.Y. 10016.

... *THESE TWO* events, one negative, the other positive, were important milestones on the way to transforming a New York school district from one that was segregated and inferior to a model of integrated and quality education. Located about 25 miles north of New York City in prosperous Westchester County, Greenburgh District 8 is tied together only by its educational system; the many separate neighborhoods are not incorporated into a single political unit. There are 12,000 residents including 2,600 pupils in this five-square mile area.

The dates of 1932 and 1947 are both related to the fairly large concentration of Negroes in Greenburgh. The original Negro population was brought in during World War I as laborers. They settled near the center of Greenburgh in a swampy area with poor drainage; an area they still occupy. Some of their grandchildren still have trouble crossing over the mud on their way to school. At present, Greenburgh is approximately 35 per cent Negro. Not all of these are descendants of the first settlers; after World War II a group of middle-class Negroes bought homes in the area. In addition, there is now a low-income housing project where many Negroes live. More than one real estate agent, however, discourages white people from buying homes in District 8 by saying that the schools are 90 per cent Negro.

Today, the population includes a wide range of religions, of nationalities, of races, and of educational and economic levels. Scattered throughout this combined rural and suburban community (though not living next door to each other) are people with Ph.D.'s and those who are barely literate; people who have paid $45,000 for their homes and those who live in slums; people who work as executives in large corporations and those who subsist on welfare allowances; and members of most national and ethnic groups. About ⅓ of the population is Protestant, ⅓ Jewish, and ⅓ Catholic. One element lacking in Greenburgh, an element evident in some of the surrounding towns, is a substantial upper class.

As people move in and out of the school district, and as the school population grows (it recently hit the 2500 mark), the racial balance continues to be about 65 per cent white and 35 per cent Negro. During 1963, 80 new elementary school children entered District 8 and 54 children left. Of those who entered, 42 per cent were Negro and 58 per cent were white. Of those who left, 37 per cent were Negro and 63 per cent were white.

The opening of a brand new school, just before the outbreak of World War II, caused a deterioration of the racial situation.

For years, the Negro and white children of Greenburgh had attended the same elementary and junior-high schools. In 1939, a new two-story brick elementary school was completed, right in the heart of the Negro area. The school was automatically segregated. From that time on, until the war was over, circumstances remained static.[1] No new building was taking place because most building materials were allotted to the armed forces; war-time rationing of gasoline prevented people from moving to a suburb like Greenburgh because of its distance from New York City. . . .

By 1947, the war years were past. Hundreds of new families were crowding into every Westchester community. The dairy farms in Greenburgh were sold to developers; houses sprang up where trees and hills and barns had once stood. As the building boom got under way, white, middle-class commuters bought up the newly-constructed homes. The influx of white people brought the ratio of Negroes to its present 35 per cent. Necessity drove the citizens of Greenburgh to search for a solution to a segregation problem; idealism, money, and common sense provided an answer.

Dr. Bailey was the administrator of three schools. The older of the two elementary schools was predominantly white and very over-crowded. The newer elementary school, the one built in the Negro ghetto in 1939, had many empty classrooms. The third school, a junior high, was also under-utilized

---

1. Until 1946, the district maintained its own high school. At that time, because of a drop in population, students were sent to a neighboring high school on a tuition basis. In 1960, District 8 constructed a new Junior-Senior high school.

and heavily Negro. In March 1951, Dr. Bailey presented four plans to the Board of Education, each designed to alleviate the over-crowding and to provide for desegregation.

Plan Number 1 called for building a new school. By carefully choosing an interstitial or fringe location, a new elementary school would draw children from both Negro and white areas. This idea brought strong opposition from those who were not interested in spending money for new buildings when sufficient desk space already existed.

Plan Number 2 called for the transfer of some white pupils to the all-Negro school. "Whose kid will be transferred?" was the question frequently asked, followed by "How do I know it won't be mine?"

Plan Number 3, essentially, would have eliminated attendance areas and permitted students to go to either school on a first come, first served basis.

It was Plan Number 4, known as the Princeton Plan, that eventually reorganized the entire school system. Under this proposal every child in the district would attend kindergarten, first, second, and third grade in the formerly all-Negro school. Every child would then attend the "white school" from grades four through six. The third school would continue to be a junior high for all of District 8. . . .

By far the greatest single problem involved in integrating the schools was to change the attitudes and feelings of the teachers. How could they possibly teach children likely to vary so much? How would they handle interracial tensions which they were positive would occur? It was a fact that many emotionally-disturbed Negro youngsters had been placed with foster families in Greenburgh by the New York City Welfare Department. Would they present serious discipline problems?

Every conceivable source of aid was brought into play to assist the teachers to overcome their real and imaginary reservations. The New York State Department of Education helped set up elementary school classes that were balanced in terms of race and ability. Universities in the metropolitan area were asked to send in educational consultants to aid teachers in finding techniques to reach every child in their class. A consulting psychologist and a guidance expert were hired to assist teachers in dealing with emotionally-disturbed pupils. The adult education program established earlier by Dr. Bailey had already laid the groundwork for cooperation between many Negro and white parents in the community.

Because of the Princeton Plan, most children live too far to walk all the way to school. The Board of Education provides bus service for any child who lives more than one-half mile from his elementary school or one mile from high school. Actually, the Warburg tract is not at all centrally located, so about 85 per cent of the total student population goes to school by bus. With the exception of only two Board of Education owned buses, the rest are obtained on contract. The cost is not prohibitive—less than $50 a year per child, because the state of New York covers 80 per cent of the total cost. The Princeton Plan is a money saver because no school has to provide equipment like books, tables, and chairs for more than two grades. . . .

It is the consensus of Greenburgh school officials that the Princeton Plan is merely a desegregation device, one which suited their community. They feel, however, that the mechanical side of desegregation is best decided in each locality. Moreover, they also believe that "saturating" or trying to upgrade schools without desegregating them first is, at best, a piecemeal effort. The elementary supervisor reverses this either-or alternative between saturation and integration by saying, "Yes, first integrate, and then saturate every school with new ideas, new materials." He is convinced that Negro and white children must sit in the same classrooms before it is possible to teach either group how to be good citizens in a multi-racial society. The net result of integration, he says, is "better teaching and better schools."

A school social worker expresses this sentiment in other words: "The earlier you start to work with all children, the more they respect each other and accept differences. Saturating without integrating is education in a vacuum."

When the staff in Greenburgh is asked what is transferrable from their district to other school systems, they insist that physical desegregation should come first. They then indicate a number of specific procedures to achieve true integration. There are at least fourteen of these steps:

1. Heterogeneous grouping to create a cross-section of the entire community in each classroom.

2. Early remediation to bridge the cultural gap. The elementary schools recommend early compensatory education for children from economically disadvantaged homes. This "saturation" is specifically geared to developing and enriching the verbal concepts of young children. Improvement of communication skills also widens the horizons of the so-called "culturally-advantaged."

3. Grouping in the high school according to potential rather than by tested achievement. At the secondary level, effective counseling plus remediation and enrichment narrow the achievement-potential gap.

4. Re-evaluation and reconstruction of the entire curriculum, to take into account the diversity of cultures and races. Implementing the new curriculum with materials with bi-racial content.

5. The re-education of teachers, administrators, parents and community leaders. This is accomplished by means of workshops and discussion groups with searching self-examination of attitudes towards all differences.

6. Hiring psychologists, social workers, and other special service personnel in order to develop competent and comprehensive programs and to lend support to the regular teaching staff.

7. Hiring those teachers who already have positive interracial attitudes and for whom teaching is truly a profession, who approach it with a commitment.

8. Establishing a maximum class size of 25 students in order to permit teachers to individualize instruction to a greater extent.

9. Setting up a policy of inclusion rather than exclusion, to create the kind of school where every child is maintained in a constructive and meaningful program as long as possible.

10. Intelligent, sensitive management of situations with

racial overtones, to combat them openly and without defensiveness and to turn them into positive learning experiences.

11. At every grade level, but especially in the secondary school, to involve the students in dealing frankly and constructively with learning and social situations which may arise.

12. Terminating the educational experience by assuming the responsibility for post-high school planning and placement, either on a job or into further schooling.

13. Creating an apolitical Board of Education that is primarily concerned with its role as educational policy-maker without being impeded by political considerations.

14. Enlightened and courageous community commitment. It was a small but active nucleus of Negro and white citizens in Greenburgh who first led the way to the Princeton Plan and later to voting the funds essential to carry out a sound program of integration.

The Greenburgh experiment has demonstrated that when these steps are followed the results are gratifying. The community at large has approved of the Greenburgh plan, because they have seen the self-concept of children of all groups improve. They know that teachers' attitudes have grown better. They realize that their children's achievement levels have risen significantly.

Integration, like education, is a process of continuing change and one not limited to the classroom. Just as each Greenburgh classroom is a microcosm of the community, so the educational system, as a whole, should be a reflection of an open, democratic society.

EQUAL SCHOOLS OR
EQUAL STUDENTS?*

James S. Coleman

In 1966 the U.S. Office of Education completed a vast
survey of the nation's schools, to determine the extent
of educational inequality experienced by five ethnic
minorities. Coleman's analysis of the findings of that
study concentrates on two positive conditions that he
finds are necessary to close the gap in educational
achievement: a decrease in the ethnic and cultural
homogeneity of the individual schools, and a change
in the self-conception of the minority-group child.
The thoughtful reader may find more to perplex
than to enlighten him in these suggestions:

> *The study finds that differences between schools
> are related not to physical factors sometimes con-
> sidered to be part of quality education, but to the
> social environment of other pupils and teachers. Pre-
> sumably this means that Negro children in middle-
> class schools achieve better than those in lower-class
> schools. Can this difference be unqualifiedly attrib-*

* James S. Coleman, "Equal Schools or Equal Students?" *The Public Interest,*
Summer 1966, pp. 70–75. Reprinted by permission of *The Public Interest.*

uted to the social environment of the school? What other explanation is possible?

Coleman links the improvement in Negro self-conception no doubt correctly to participation in the Negro civil rights revolution. Recent directions of the more activist sections of that movement emphasize an improved self-image and a more homogeneous school environment; what are the consequences for education achievement likely to be?

THE CIVIL RIGHTS ACT of 1964 contains a section numbered 402, which went largely unnoticed at the time. This section instructs the Commissioner of Education to carry out a survey "concerning the lack of availability of equal educational opportunities" by reason of race, religion or national origin, and to report to Congress and the President within two years. The Congressional intent in this section is somewhat unclear. But if, as is probable, the survey was initially intended as a means of finding areas of continued intentional discrimination, the intent later became less punitive-oriented and more future-oriented: *i.e.,* to provide a basis for public policy, at the local, state, and national levels, which might overcome inequalities of educational opportunity.

In the two years that have intervened (but mostly in the second), a remarkably vast and comprehensive survey was conducted, focussing principally on the inequalities of educational opportunity experienced by five racial and ethnic minorities: Negroes, Puerto Ricans, Mexican Americans, American Indians, and Oriental Americans. In the central and largest portion of the survey, nearly 600,000 children at grades 1, 3, 6, 9, and 12, in 4000 schools in all 50 states and the District of Columbia, were tested and questioned; 60,000 teachers in these schools were questioned and self-tested; and principals of these schools were also questioned about their schools. The tests and questionnaires (administered in the fall of 1965 by Educational Testing Service) raised a considerable controversy in public school circles and among some. parents, with concern ranging from Federal encroachment on the local education system to the spectre of invasion of privacy. Nevertheless, with a participation rate of about 70% of all the schools sampled, the survey was conducted; and on July 1, 1966, Commissioner Howe presented a summary report of this survey. On July 31, the total report, *Equality of Educational Opportunity,* 737 pages, was made available (Government Printing Office, $4.25).

The summary of the report has appeared to many who have read it to be curiously "flat," lacking in emphases and policy implications. Much of the same flatness can be found in the larger report. The seeming flatness probably derives from three sources: the research analyst's uneasiness in moving from description to implications; the government agency's uneasiness with survey findings that may have political repercussions; and, perhaps more important than either of these, the fact that the survey results do not lend themselves to the provision of simple answers. Nevertheless, the report is not so uncontroversial as it appears. And some of its findings, though cautiously presented, have sharp implications.

Perhaps the greatest virtue of this survey—though it has many faults—is that it did not take a simple or politically expedient view of educational opportunity. To have done so would have meant to measure (a) the objective characteristics of schools—number of books in the library, age of buildings, educational level of teachers, accreditation of the schools, and so on; and (b) the actual extent of racial segregation in the schools. The survey did look into these matters (and found less inequity in school facilities and resources, more in the extent of segregation, than is commonly supposed); but its principal focus of attention was not on what resources go into education, but on what product comes out. It did this in a relatively uncomplicated way, which is probably adequate for the task at hand: by tests which measured those areas of achievement most necessary for further progress in school, in higher education, and in successful competition in the labor market—that is, verbal and reading skills, and analytical and mathematical skills. Such a criterion does not allow statements about absolute levels of inequality or equality of education provided by the schools, because obviously there are more influences than the school's on a child's level of achievement in school, and there are more effects of school than in these areas of achievement. What it does do is to broaden the question beyond the school to all those educational influences that have their results in the level of verbal and mathematical skill a young person is equipped with when he or she enters the adult world. In effect, it takes the perspective of this young adult, and says that what matters to him is, not how "equal" his school is, but rather whether he is equipped at the end of school to compete on an equal basis with others, whatever his social origins. From the perspective of society, it assumes that what is important is not to "equalize the schools" in some formal sense, but to insure that children from all groups come into adult society so equipped as to insure their full participation in this society.

Another way of putting this is to say that the schools are successful only insofar as they reduce the dependence of a child's opportunities upon his social origins. We can think of a set of conditional probabilities: the probability of being prepared for a given occupation or for a given college at the end of high school, conditional upon the child's social origins. The effectiveness of the schools consists, in part, of making the conditional probabilities less conditional—that is, less dependent upon social origins. Thus, equality of educational opportunity implies, not merely "equal" schools, but equally effective schools, whose influences will overcome the differences in starting point of children from different social groups.

THE WIDENING EDUCATIONAL GAP

This approach to educational opportunity, using as it does achievement on standardized tests, treads on sensitive ground. Differences in average achievement between racial groups can lend themselves to racist arguments of genetic differences in intelligence; even apart from this, they can lead to invidious comparisons between groups which show different average levels of achievement. But it is precisely the avoidance of such sensitive areas that can perpetuate the educational deficiencies with which some minorities are equipped at the end of schooling.

What, then, does the survey find with regard to effects of schooling on test achievement? Children were tested at the beginning of grades 1, 3, 6, 9, and 12. Achievement of the average American Indian, Mexican American, Puerto Rican, and Negro (in this descending order) was much lower than the average white or Oriental American, at all grade levels. The amount of difference ranges from about half a standard deviation to one standard deviation at early grade levels. At the 12th grade, it increases to beyond one standard deviation. (One standard deviation difference means that about 85% of the minority group children score below the average of the whites, while if the groups were equal only about 50% would score below this average.) The grade levels of difference range up to 5 years of deficiency (in math achievement) or 4 years (in reading skills) at the 12th grade. In short, the differences are large to begin with, and they are even larger at higher grades.

Two points, then, are clear: (1) *these minority children have a serious educational deficiency at the start of school, which is obviously not a result of school;* and (2) *they have an even more serious deficiency at the end of school, which is obviously in part a result of school.*

Thus, by the criterion stated earlier—that the effectiveness of schools in creating equality of educational opportunity lies in making the conditional probabilities of success less conditional—the schools appear to fail. At the end of school, the conditional probabilities of high achievement are even *more* conditional upon racial or ethnic background than they are at the beginning of school.

There are a number of results from the survey which give further evidence on this matter. First, within each racial group, the strong relation of family economic and educational background to achievement does not diminish over the period of school, and may even increase over the elementary years. Second, most of the variation in student achievement lies within the same school, very little of it is between schools. The implication of these last two results is clear: family background differences account for much more variation in achievement than do school differences.

Even the school-to-school variation in achievement, though relatively small, is itself almost wholly due to the *social* environment provided by the school: the educational backgrounds and aspirations of other students in the school, and the educational backgrounds and attainments of the teachers in the school. *Per pupil expenditure, books in the library, and a host of other facilities and curricular measures show virtually no relation to achievement if the "social" environment of the school—the educational backgrounds of other students and teachers—is held constant.*

The importance of this last result lies, of course, in the fact that schools, as currently organized, are quite culturally homogeneous as well as quite racially segregated: teachers tend to come from the same cultural groups (and especially from the same race) as their students, and the student bodies are themselves relatively homogeneous. Given this homogeneity, the principal agents of effectiveness in the schools—teachers and other students—act to maintain or reinforce the initial differences imposed by social origins.

One element illustrates well the way in which the current organization of schools maintains the differences over generations: a Negro prospective teacher leaves a Negro teacher's college with a much lower level of academic competence (as measured by the National Teacher's Examination) than does his white counterpart leaving his largely white college; then he teaches Negro children (in school with other Negro children, ordinarily from educationally deficient backgrounds), who learn at a lower level, in part because of his lesser competence; some of these students, in turn, go into teacher training institutions to become poorly-trained teachers of the next generation.

Altogether, *the sources of inequality of educational opportunity appear to lie first in the home itself and the cultural influences immediately surrounding the home; then they lie in the schools' ineffectiveness to free achievement from the impact of the home, and in the schools' cultural homogeneity which perpetuates the social influences of the home and its environs.*

A MODEST, YET RADICAL PROPOSAL

Given these results, what do they suggest as to avenues to equality of educational opportunity? Several elements seem clear:

a) For those children whose family and neighborhood are educationally disadvantaged, it is important to replace this family environment as much as possible with an educational environment—by starting school at an earlier age, and by having a school which begins very early in the day and ends very late.

b) It is important to reduce the social and racial homogeneity of the school environment, so that those agents of education that do show some effectiveness—teachers and other students—are not mere replicas of the student himself. In the present organization of schools, it is the neighborhood school that most insures such homogeneity.

c) The educational program of the school should be made more effective than it is at present. The weakness of this program is apparent in its inability to overcome initial differences. It is hard to believe that we are so inept in educating our young that we can do no more than leave young adults in the same relative competitive positions we found them in as children.

Several points are obvious: It is not a solution simply to pour money into improvement of the physical plants, books, teaching aids, of schools attended by educationally disadvantaged children. For other reasons, it will not suffice merely to bus children or otherwise achieve pro forma integration. (One incidental effect of this would be to increase the segregation within schools, through an increase in tracking.)

The only kinds of policies that appear in any way viable are those which do not seek to improve the education of Negroes and other educationally disadvantaged at the expense of those who are educationally advantaged. This implies new kinds of educational institutions, with a vast increase in expenditures for education—not merely for the disadvantaged, but for all children. The solutions might be in the form of educational parks, or in the form of private schools paid by tuition grants (with Federal regulations to insure racial heterogeneity), public (or publicly-subsidized) boarding schools (like the North Carolina Advancement School), or still other innovations. This approach also implies reorganization of the curriculum within schools. One of the major reasons for "tracking" is the narrowness of our teaching methods—they can tolerate only a narrow range of skill in the same classroom. Methods which greatly widen the range are necessary to make possible racial and cultural integration within a school—and thus to make possible the informal learning that other students of higher educational levels can provide. Such curricular innovations are possible—but, again, only through the investment of vastly greater sums in education than currently occurs.

It should be recognized, of course, that the goal described here—of equality of educational opportunity through the schools—is far more ambitious than has ever been posed in our society before. The schools were once seen as a supplement to the family in bringing a child into his place in adult society, and they still function largely as such a supplement, merely perpetuating the inequalities of birth. Yet the conditions imposed by technological change, and by our post-industrial society, quite apart from any ideals of equal opportunity, require a far more primary role for the school, if society's children are to be equipped for adulthood.

SELF-CONFIDENCE AND PERFORMANCE

One final result of the survey gives an indication of still another—and perhaps the most important—element necessary for equality of educational opportunity for Negroes. One attitude of students was measured at grades 9 and 12—an attitude which indicated the degree to which the student felt in control of his own fate. For example, one question was "Agree or disagree: good luck is more important than hard work for success." Another was: "Agree or disagree: every time I try to get ahead someone or something stops me." Negroes much less often than whites had such a sense of control of their fate—a difference which corresponds directly to reality, and which corresponds even more markedly to the Negro's historical position in American society. However, despite the very large achievement differences between whites and Negroes at the 9th and 12th grades, *those Negroes who gave responses indicating a sense of control of their own fate achieved higher on the tests than those whites who gave the opposite responses. This atti-*

tude was more highly related to achievement than any other factor in the student's background or school.

This result suggests that internal changes in the Negro, changes in his conception of himself in relation to his environment, may have more effect on Negro achievement than any other single factor. The determination to overcome relevant obstacles, and the belief that he will overcome them—attitudes that have appeared in an organized way among Negroes only in recent years in some civil rights groups—may be the most crucial elements in achieving equality of opportunity—not because of changes they will create in the white community, but principally because of the changes they create in the Negro himself.

"Citizens everywhere must realize that the effects of over 300 years of oppression cannot be obliterated by doing business as usual."

SHOULD THERE BE "COMPENSATION" FOR NEGROES?*

*Whitney M. Young, Jr.
and Kyle Haselden*

The question of compensation for the Negro applies not only to jobs and housing, but to schooling as well, and most clearly to the issue of school integration, for it is here, one can argue, that the greatest effort, expense, and disruption are demanded. Young's defense of the principle is a clear statement of one of the moral bases for immediate school integration, from one of the members of the civil rights establishment; he is executive director of the National Urban League. Haselden, managing editor of *The Christian Century*, expresses, in his reply, the mood of many white liberals in a period of increasing Negro militancy.

One of Haselden's most interesting arguments, and one often made by sympathetic liberals, is that

* Whitney M. Young, Jr., and Kyle Haselden, "Should There be 'Compensation' for Negroes?" *The New York Times Magazine,* October 6, 1963. © 1963 by The New York Times Company. Reprinted by permission.

preferred status or treatment would have a debilitating effect on the Negro, interfering with the necessary development of self-reliance, etc. Does this justification conflict with his later statement that the Negro's history has left him in a bad competitive position?

'COMPENSATION'—YES

By Whitney M. Young, Jr.

In 1948, by instituting the Marshall Plan to aid the war-torn countries of Europe, the United States took a step unparalleled in history. Recognizing the special need of the nations shattered by World War II, the people of this country committed some $17 billion in money, machines and technical aid to help our neighbors overseas to take their place again in the community of free nations.

This rightful action was in keeping with the long tradition of America's moral, political and economic credo. We have long given special, emergency aid to the oppressed, the sick, the handicapped and deprived. In recent years, we have seen this concept put into action through our aid—in employment, education and welfare—to Hungarian and Cuban refugees. We see it annually carried out in the form of emergency help to "depressed" and "disaster" areas, suffering from joblessness or devastation by hurricanes, drought and other misfortunes. The "G.I. Bill of Rights" after World War II was, in a sense, a recognition of the special need of our discharged veterans for education, housing, employment and other benefits.

Recently, the National Urban League has attracted nationwide attention with its proposal for a temporary "more-than-equal" program of aid for Negro citizens. In the current drive for civil rights, with its demonstrations, marches and sit-ins, this proposal has confused many white Americans. They ask: Is the Negro not to be satisfied by equality alone? Or, is he seeking, not equality, but preference? In the face of these questions, our history should teach us that what the Urban League proposes is not only directly in the American tradition, but has the arguments of racial justice, economic practicality and morality—secular as well as religious—behind it.

On an economic level, the hard but simple fact—borne out by comparative statistics on unemployment, income, mortality rates, substandard housing and education—is that the past of the Negro exists in the present. Citizens everywhere must realize that the effects of over 300 years of oppression cannot be obliterated by doing business as usual. They must know, too, that in today's complex, technological society, a strong back and a will to succeed are no longer sufficient to break the bonds of deprivation, as was the case with minority groups in the past. For, in addition to the ordinary forces affecting one's way of life, the Negro's struggle into America's mainstream has been thwarted by the barriers of discrimination and denial based on the color of his skin.

The facts speak for themselves. Today, the average Negro family earns $3,233, as compared with $5,835 for the white family—a difference of 45 per cent. This gap has widened by two percentage points in the last decade alone. It has widened because the Negro started receiving too little, too late. More than 75 per cent of Negro workers are found in the three lowest occupational categories—service workers, semi-skilled workers, and unskilled and farm labor—the categories most affected by the geometric growth of automation. These same categories include less than 39 per cent of white workers.

By the same token, one out of every six Negro dwellings is substandard, as compared with one in 32 white dwellings. One in every four Negro women with pre-school children is working away from home. Of the school dropouts, 21 per cent are Negro; only 7 per cent of high school graduates are Negroes. Unemployment rates for Negroes are from two and one-half to three times higher than those for white workers.

To overcome these conditions the National Urban League declares that the nation must undertake an immediate, dramatic and tangible "crash program"—a domestic Marshall Plan—to close this intolerable economic, social and educational gap, which separates the vast majority of Negro citizens from other Americans. Unless this is done, the results of the current heroic efforts in the civil-rights movement will be only an illusion, and the struggle will continue, with perhaps tragic consequences.

In its plea for such a domestic Marshall Plan, the Urban League is asking for a special effort, not for special privileges. This effort has been described as "preferential treatment," "indemnification," "special consideration," "compensatory activity." These are "scare" phrases that obscure the meaning of the proposal and go against the grain of our native sense of fair play.

We prefer that our recommendations be seen as necessary and just corrective measures that must be taken if equal opportunity is to have meaning. They are necessary, because only by such means can the majority of Negro citizens be prepared to assume the increased responsibilities that they will face in a more integrated society. They are just, because such an effort alone can repair the devastation wrought by generations of injustice, neglect, discrimination and indifference, based on race.

To put it another way, the scales of equal opportunity are now heavily weighted against the Negro and cannot be corrected in today's technological society simply by applying equal weights. For more than 300 years the white American has received special consideration, or "preferential treatment," if you will, over the Negro. What we ask now is that for a brief period there be a deliberate and massive effort to include the Negro citizen in the mainstream of American life. Furthermore, we are not asking for equal time; a major effort, honestly applied, need last only some 10 years. This crash program must be a cooperative effort by all agencies, institutions and individuals, public and private.

The elements of the crash program, or domestic Marshall Plan, would include:

Education.   For the deprived child—Negro as well as white —provision for first-class schools, with the most modern facilities and the best and most experienced teachers. These are necessary to help him realize his potential and prepare him to take advantage of greater educational opportunity. Necessary also is intensified remedial instruction in the lower grades for culturally deprived and retarded pupils. Schools and colleges must find new ways to seek out Negro youths with undeveloped talents. Similarly adult education programs must be expanded and geared to the needs of citizens lacking the basic literary and technical skills.

Employment.   A planned effort to place *qualified* Negroes in all categories of employment, at all levels of responsibility.

This would mean that employers would consciously seek to hire qualified Negro citizens and would intensify apprenticeship and training programs to prepare new Negro employes and upgrade those already employed. Labor unions, too, must make a conscientious effort to include Negroes in their membership and training programs.

Further, where Negroes have not been employed in the past at all levels, it is essential that there be conscious preferment to help them catch up. This does not mean the establishment of a quota system—an idea shunned by responsible Negro organizations and leaders. But, because we are faced with the hypocrisy of "tokenism," where the presence of two or three Negro employes is passed off as integration, we are forced, during the transitional stages, to discuss numbers and categories. We demand, in all fairness, that the Negro not be expected to bear the brunt of unemployment.

Housing.   Racial ghettos eliminated by providing genuine housing opportunities on the basis of need and financial ability. Programs of redevelopment and relocation, planned to provide both low-income housing and a racial diversity, are needed throughout our communities. This will require the active participation of real estate brokers as well as home-owners.

Health and Welfare.   Public and private agencies seeking to provide the best personnel and facilities in low-income neighborhoods, and increased counseling services to troubled families. Here, particularly, the churches and schools must combine efforts to help Negro families develop a deeper sense of parental and community responsibility.

Finally, qualified Negro citizens should be sought and named to public and private boards and commissions, particularly those which shape employment, housing, education, and health and welfare policies. In achieving this objective, we would develop strong, responsible leadership within the Negro community. Also, we would prompt private foundations, business and government to reassess the extent and aims of their financial contributions to established Negro leadership and organizations.

The program outlined here has a simple, practical aim: to

provide the Negro citizen with the leadership, education, jobs and motivation that will permit him to help himself. It is not a plea to exempt him from the independence and initiative demanded by our free, competitive society. It makes practical economic sense as a measure to reduce unemployment and welfare costs and to increase our productivity and national income by including Negro citizens in the benefits of our rich society. President Kennedy's economic advisers estimate that our gross national product could be raised 2.5 per cent, were the Negro worker's earnings commensurate with the nation's average.

This program makes historical sense as a rehabilitation of the damage inflicted upon the Negro by generations of injustice and neglect. He, too, has given his blood, sweat and tears to the building of our country; yet, where the labor and initiative of other minority groups have been rewarded by assimilation within the society, the black American has been isolated and rejected.

The domestic Marshall Plan has profound moral and religious justification. Our country is in dire jeopardy as long as it has within its body politic a socially and economically deprived group of citizens, whether they be actually enslaved or denied the full benefits of equality and freedom by an insidious economic and psychological slavery. In this sense, the crash programs that we propose are not an effort to impose the guilt and sins of a past generation on our present white community. This is an appeal for all Americans, working together, to rid present-day America of its sickening disease and its moral shame.

The Negro is in revolt today, not to change the fabric of our society or to seek a special place in it, but to enter into partnership in that society. It is a revolt with which every American should sympathize. Already a few educational and business institutions are working with intensified effort, special consideration, if you will, in solving this problem. We have the material and spiritual resources as a country to meet the challenge and accomplish the urgent task ahead. All we need is the will to act and the spirit of decency and sacrifice which abounds in our land.

'COMPENSATION'—NO

By Kyle Haselden

An increasing number of Negro and white Americans agree that securing complete freedom and total equality for the Negro is this nation's No. 1 domestic issue and that justice for the deprived one-tenth of the nation's population is the end toward which the whole society should move speedily. Unanimous in this agreement, they nevertheless disagree as to the permissible and effective means to that end.

Varied in their temperaments, their religious convictions, their sense of what is prudent and practical, these Americans prefer one or another of the various strategies which seek racial justice. The options range from the doctrine of violent rebellion against white domination at one extreme to a patient yet active appeal to the nation's creeds, congresses and courts at the other. Between these extremes fall various nonviolent strategies and schemes, each with its own supporters.

Unfortunately there are, in the ranks of men and women genuinely committed to racial justice, some who insist that unanimity of purpose requires uniformity of plan. They insist that whites and Negroes who share their objective also adopt their methods—however unruly, eccentric and impractical those methods—or accept vilification for Uncle Tomism. This absolutist, autocratic spirit believes that justice for the Negro is the ultimate criterion of all human action and that this end validates any means, whatever practicality or religious principle may dictate to the contrary.

This is a dangerous mood. It divides those who seek justice for Negroes; it alienates influential moderates unnecessarily; and, most serious, this authoritarian spirit lures the Negro into activities which corrupt his purpose and defeat his ultimate hope.

In the struggle for racial justice a technique is not valid simply because it annoys the white man or because it promises some temporary advantage to the Negro. It is valid only if it honors the moral ground on which the Negro makes his claim for justice, respects the right of all men to the same justice, preserves in the human relationship values which are equivalents of justice, and promotes rather than prevents the Negro's progress.

The idea of compensation, which has been suggested as a device to equalize competition between whites and Negroes, fails these crucial tests. By compensation—in the passive rather than the active sense—is meant compensation *for* the Negro rather than *by* the Negro. It has been proposed that the Negro cannot succeed in his search for freedom and equality unless there is an arbitrary—in fact, artificial—removal of the academic, cultural and professional lag forced upon him by over two centuries of slavery and by another of exploitation. It is argued further that the Negroes' years of involuntary, payless servitude established a collectible claim against the descendants of those who enslaved and exploited him.

How can this debt be paid? The proposal is that the Negro be given preference in employment wherever a vacancy occurs, a premium in salary, and a quota system guaranteeing that one-tenth of all people hired by firms, professional enterprises and industries be Negroes. Even though this proposal is obviously unfeasible, what shall we say of it as a theory?

Compensation must be rejected as an equalizer of competition between Negroes and whites for several reasons, all of which rest on the grounds to which the Negro appeals in his demand for freedom and equality.

First. Compensation for Negroes is a subtle but pernicious form of racism. It requires that men be dealt with by society on the basis of race and color rather than on the basis of their humanity. It would therefore as a public policy legalize, deepen and perpetuate the abominable racial cleavage which has ostracized and crippled the American Negro. Racism, whoever may be its temporary beneficiary, should be eliminated from the social order, not confirmed by it.

Second. Preferential economic status for Negroes would penalize the living in a futile attempt to collect a debt owed by the dead. The 20th-century white man is no more to blame for the fact that his ancestors bought and held slaves than are 20th-century Negroes for the fact that some of their ancestors captured and sold slaves. This is the ironic tragedy of exploitation. It leaves with the descendants of the exploiters a guilt they cannot cancel and with the descendants of the exploited a debt they cannot collect.

Third. A scheme which gives Negroes preference in employment and a premium in salary would bestow on Negroes the debilitating social status which has for centuries cursed the initiative and enterprise of the white man in the South. Preferred status for the Negro, however much society may owe him a debt, will inevitably destroy in him the initiative and enterprise required of a minority people in a highly competitive society. Slavery corrupts ambition and self-reliance; so, too, does patronizing social status.

Fourth. Compensation for Negroes would be unfair to other minorities handicapped by their history or by rapid social and industrial change: Puerto Ricans, Mexican-Americans, migrants of all races, Indians, coal miners and others. Negroes are entirely right in demanding that they be hired, paid and promoted on their merit and in boycotting those enterprises which discriminate on a racial basis. But they are not right in demanding an artificial scheme which is unworkable, racist, destructive of initiative and unfair to other struggling Americans.

Our goal should be parity, not preferment, and there are three things we must do, none of them pleasant, none easy, if we are to attain it.

First, there must be a total, across-the-board desegregation of American society. Wherever the white man will not voluntarily surrender the psychic and material advantages of racial discrimination, the Negro must use the law, his power as a consumer, his increasing political leverage, and coercive nonviolent protests to assail and destroy the color structures of our society.

Equality of opportunity is an elemental civil right specifically declared in the sacred documents of the United States. Withholding that right from any people because of their race profanes every tenet in the political and religious creeds of the American people. Denying that right encumbers and humiliates

20,000,000 American citizens. The first business of the nation is the total elimination of racial discrimination and its component, racial segregation.

Such liberation, however, would leave the Negro still handicapped by centuries of poor schooling and by his long exclusion from most trades and professions. A desegregated society would open to the Negro opportunities which are rightfully his and should be granted to him but for which centuries of neglect and abuse leave many of his race inadequately prepared. Even though all racial bars were removed, most Negroes could not, in a free and impartial society, compete on equal terms with most white people for jobs and preferments.

But this, as we have noted, is a handicap which Negroes share with another one-tenth of the population, whose competitive strength has also been sapped by an unfortunate history or by the entrapping eddies of industrial development.

Our second task, therefore, is to undertake a nationwide crash program for the education, training and employment of the underprivileged, underdeveloped one-fifth of the nation, a domestic Point Four which would give to the employable a fair chance and to the unemployable qualifying education and training. Such a program would be based not on race but on need. Negroes would of course be the chief beneficiaries of an educational and economic crash program, because of the predominant number of deprived Negroes. But a domestic Point Four program aimed at the needs of *all* the nation's backward peoples would close rather than widen the nation's racial cleavage.

Finally, irritating as it may be, the fact might as well be faced that no immigrant or minority group has ever made its way into the mainstream of American life without studying and working harder and longer than the general population. This is the third task as it now confronts the Negro.

During their long pilgrimage through slavery and semi-slavery, most Negroes did not have an incentive for the kind of active self-compensation by which other minorities have climbed out of humiliating servitude into respected equality with other ethnic groups. Slavery and peonage do not generally encourage ambition. Even now the Negro must divert himself —his native abilities and his acquired skills, his initiative and enterprise, his devotion and endurance, his ablest leadership— from the pursuits followed by free men to the claiming of those dignities and opportunities which are the birthright of every American citizen. Yet the hard historical fact is that self-compensation is essential if he is to escape that social substratum into which a cruel history and an arrogant, avaricious white man have coerced him.

Along with several million Caucasian Americans, most Negroes need a lift from their Government if they are to overcome the handicaps of a tragic history. More than that, however, Negroes need to throw off the white man's domination if they are to discover at last what they can do for themselves unencumbered in an open society.

INDEX

A

Abolitionism, 190–191
"Academic Instruction and Preschool Children" (Bereiter), 131, 239–249
Acosta, Ralph, 322
Adjustment classes, 53–54
Adolescent Society, The (Coleman), 302
Adulthood, alternative pathway to, 138–140
Adventure of the American People, The (Graff and Krout), 189
Adventures of Huckleberry Finn (Twain), 159–162
Alexander, W. M., 120
Allen, Commissioner James, 282
Allen, Alexander J., 371
Allen, Dr. James E., Jr., 351, 362, 364
Ambition, 30–32

American Association of Colleges for Teacher Education, 132
American Council on Education, 171, 416
American Psychologist, 400
American Red Cross, 202
American Textbook Publishers Institute, 180
Americans for Democratic Action, 321
Anderson, C. Arnold, 230
Anderson, David, 370–372
Anthropomorphism, 174–175
Anti-Defamation League of B'nai B'rith, 443
Applezweig, M. H., 418
Art, 250–265
Asbell, Bernard, 15, 25–47, 48
Ashton-Warner, Sylvia, 7
Atkinson, J. W., 406, 407, 417, 424, 429, 431
Attucks, Crispus, 189, 190

Ausubel, D. P., 16, 130
Automation, 307–308
Auxiliary personnel, 100–117
    attitudes toward teachers, 108–
        109, 110
    benefits of, 104–105, 109–110
    difficulties in the deployment of,
        107–109
    forces increasing the use of, 102
    major findings in study of, 109–
        112
        institutionalization, 111–112
        relationships, 109–110
        role development, 109–110
        training, 110–111
    opportunity for upward mobility,
        116
    purpose of, 103–104
    rationale for, 103–107
    recommendations, 112–117
        development, 112–113
        institutionalization, 115–117
        role definition, 112–113
        training, 113–115
    screening, 106
    training, 107, 109, 110–111, 113–
        115
        higher education, 115
        inservice, 114
        preservice, 113–114
Axelson, L. J., 430

B

Backlash, 201–204
Bailey, Dr., 445–446, 447
Baker, Edward, 352, 353, 363, 364,
    369
Balaban, Isidore, 370
Baldwin, James, 128
Baldwin, Leland D., 188
Ball State University, 132
Baltimore
    ethnic statistics, 28
    teaching experiment in, 42

Bank Street College of Education,
    100, 101, 102
Banneker, Benjamin, 189
Bannerman, Mrs. 50–54
Barker, R., 419
Barrett, Loretta A., 203–204
Bass, B. M., 405
Baxter, Mrs. Zenobia, 34–35
Bayton, J. A., 417
Bell v. School City of Gary, 324,
    326, 329, 363
Benjamin, L., 417, 423
Bereiter, Carl, 131, 239–249
Bernardita, Sister, 360
Bernstein, Basil, 230
Bigart, Homer, 351–353
Bishop, Mrs. Bailey, 39–42
Bookstein, Isadore, 362–364
Borton, Terry, 156–166
Bovard, E. W., 404, 420, 421, 428
Bowman, Garda W., 100–117
Boys Clubs, 146
Branche v. Board of Education, 326
Bridges to Slum-Ghetto Children:
    Case Studies in Learning to
    Become a Teacher (ed. Korn-
    berg), 66–77
Brind, Charles, 362–363
British Journal of Sociology, 230
Brown v. Board of Education, 185,
    332, 339, 340, 344, 364
Browne, Father Henry J., 322
Buchheimer, Naomi and Arnold,
    443–449
Buchwald, Art, 280
Buder, Leonard, 348–349, 365, 377–
    378, 380–384, 398–399
Bunche, Ralph, 105
Bureaucracy, 8, 15, 307–308
Busing, 5–6, 317, 347–348

C

Cahn, Judah, 374
Callaway, E., 419

Callender, Mrs. Lemoine, 355
Canfield, Leon H., 190
Carpenter, Marie E., 185
Carpetbaggers, 194, 195
Carter, Robert L., 364
Carver, George Washington, 197
Casner, Mabel B., 188
Catcher in the Rye (Salinger), 159,
    162–163
Catholic Youth Organization, 146
Catholics, 305, 313, 321
    on transfers, 355–362
Caughey, John W., 189
Center for the Study of Democratic
    Institutions, 309
Changing Education, 192
Channan, Gloria, 21–22
Chicago
    ethnic statistics, 28
    teaching experiment in, 39–42
Child, I. L., 421
Children
    acquiring middle-class values from
        classmates, 287–308
    benefits from auxiliary personnel,
        104, 109–110
    experience of, 33
    games focus of, 61, 64–65
    growth of, 19–20
    importance of routine to, 77
    inability to shift, 63
    inattention of, 33
    potential of, 4
    preschool, 239–249
    respect for, 19
    response to music, 82–84
    reversing handicaps of, 12–13
    -teacher relationships, 17–22
        authority, 17–18
        personal, 17, 18–22
        threatening of, 94–95
*Child's Conception of the World,
    The* (Piaget), 175
Christian Century, The, 460
City University of New York, 66

Civil Rights Act of 1964, 199, 452
Civil rights movement, 198–200
Civil War, 191–192
Clark, K. B., 173
Clark, Kenneth, 4, 16, 374
Clark, Tom C., 346
Classes
    orderliness in, 17–18
    size of, 15, 295–296, 299–300
Cogley, John, 309
Cognition, emotion vs., 58–59
Cohen, M., 424
Coleman, James S., 12–13, 302, 450–
    459
Coles, R., 411
Collier, H. L., 406
"Color Me Brown—I'm Integrated"
    (Dolmatch), 177–181
Columbia University, 277, 348
Communities, in work study pro-
    grams, 147
Conant, Dr. James, 123, 134, 302,
    308
Concept-centered curriculum, *see*
    Curriculum, concept-cen-
    tered
"Conflict and Reform" (Pedersen),
    250–265
Conger, J. J., 421
Congress of Racial Equality, 320,
    370, 372
Criswell, Joan H., 405, 411
Cubans, textbooks reflecting cul-
    tural background of, 127
*Cultural Deprivation—Description
    and Remedy* (Engelmann),
    244
Culturally Deprived Child, The
    (Reissman), 124
Culture of Poverty, The (Reiss-
    man), 55
Curriculum, 119–274
    concept-centered, 266–274
        alternative ways to organize,
        270–272

Curriculum (*Cont.*)
  causation, 274
  creation and manipulation, 273
  expectations, 274
  national workshop, 272–273
  relativism, 273–274
  defined, 120
  ethnocentric biases in, 167–181
  facsimile pages from textbooks, 205–225
  history texts and the Negro, 182–204
    abolitionism, 190–191
    backlash, 201–204
    Civil War, 191–192
    explorers, 187
    extracts from, 186–187
    the freedom movement, 198–200
    indentured servants, 187–188
    Ku Klux Klan, 196–198
    Reconstruction, 192–196
    slave life, 188–190
    slave uprisings, 191
  the humanities in, 148–155
  language learning, 228–238
    drama in, 235
    list of handicaps, 245
    music in, 246
    preschool children, 239–249
  methods of inquiry, 148–155
  moral conflicts in, 4
  national policy, 134–147
    alternative pathway to adulthood, 138–140
    community strategy, 147
    current programs, 140–142
    needed programs, 142–144
    proposals, 140–142
    responsibility of society, 144–145
    work-experience program, 146
  patterns and issues, 119–133
  question of teaching and learning processes, 129–133

reaching the deprived, 156–166
reform, 250–265
textbooks reflecting backgrounds of minorities, 125–129
vocationally oriented, 122–125
  relating subjects to jobs, 124
  work experiences, 123–124
Curriculum Planning for Better Teaching and Learning (Saylor and Alexander), 120
Currivan, Gene, 355–362
Curti, Merle, 187

D

Davidson, Basil, 203–204
Davidson, K. S., 407
Davitz, J. R., 421
Davis, Hadassah, 411
Davitz, J. R., 421
Day, R. E., 409
De facto segregation, 3, 151, 282
  legal decisions affecting, 324–344
Declaration of Independence, 190
Deese, J., 404, 418, 419, 421, 422
Dembo, Tamara, 419
Démocratie en Amérique, De la (Tocqueville), 154
Denmark, 191
Department of Health, Education and Welfare, 306
Desegregation
  effects on Negroes, 400–441
    biracial situations, 422–434
    detrimental conditions, 410–418
    experiments on stress and performance, 418–422
    postulated situational determinants, 403–407
    reports on academic achievement, 407–410
  legal decisions affecting, 324–344
Desmond, Charles S., 367

Deutsch, Dr. Martin, 33–34, 42, 130, 403, 416
Dewey, John, 14
Dialects, 228–238
Disadvantaged Student, The: A Conflict of Cultures in the School (Pedersen), 250
Dittes, J. E., 405
Dodson, Dr. Dan, 337–339, 403
Dodson Report, 337–339
Dolmatch, Theodore B., 177–181
Donovan, James B., 379
Douglass, Frederick, 154, 191
Drama, 153
in language learning, 235
Drew, Charles R., 202
Drexel, Francis Anthony, 361
Drop-outs
current, 290
in 1920, 139
Drummond, Muriel Jean, 188
Duberman, Martin, 154
DuBois, W. E. B., 154, 197, 198
Dunkel, H. B., 133
Dunmore, Lord, 189

E

E.S.E.A., 102
Easterbrook, J. A., 404, 421, 422
Edell, Hannah, 390
Education
cooperative, 140–144
feeling of reward in, 16
most fundamental questions in, 2
progressive, 14–16
widening gap in, 454–456
Education, Economy, and Society (ed. Halsey, Floud, and Anderson), 230
"Education and the Disadvantaged American," 296
Education in the Metropolis (Smiley and Miller), 1, 16, 130

Educational Testing Service, 452
Emotion, cognition vs., 58–59
Engelmann, Siegfried, 244
Enrollment, open, 279, 303, 348
reverse, 279–280
Epps, E. G., 430, 433
"Equal Schools or Equal Students" (Coleman), 450
Equality of Educational Opportunity, 452
Equality Through Integration (Buchheimer and Buchheimer), 443–449
Evans decision, 342–343
Examinations, 60–61
Experience charts, 81–82
Experimenters in the Classroom (Morrison), 154

F

Farmer, James, 370
Farms, migrations from, 290–293
Faulkner, William, 293
Field trips, 90
Filipinos, insensitivity to, 151
Findley, W. G., 415
First semester, 78–99
Fischer, John H., 374
Fish, Brother Francis K., 359
Floud, Jean, 230
Ford Foundation, 23, 27, 28, 29, 42, 296, 305
Fourteenth Amendment, 341
Francis, Mrs. Verdelle, 358
Frank, Virginia, 266–274
Frankfurter, Felix, 342, 343–344
Franklin, John Hope, 189, 202, 203
Freedmen's Bureau, 194
Freidel, Frank, 190
French, J. R. P., Jr., 404, 405, 418
Fund for the Advancement of Education, The, 120

G

Gabriel, Ralph H., 188
Galamison, Reverend Milton, 281,
    352–353, 371, 372, 378
Gans, Herbert, 132
Garber, Lee O., 324–332
Garrison, William Lloyd, 190, 191
Gavian, Ruth W., 190
George III, King, 190
George-Barden Act, 142
G.I. Bill of Rights, 462
Goals, 36–38
    minimal, 64–65
Goddard-Riverside Settlement
    House, 322
Gold, Mrs. Gloria, 353
Goldman, M., 419, 432
Goldston, Judith, 423
Goldwater, Barry, 395
Gomez, Aramis, 322
Goodlad, J. I., 120
Graff, Henry F., 189
Grant, Gerald, 201–204
Great Cities School Improvement
    Studies, 28
Greenbaum, C., 426, 429
Greenburgh School District No. 8,
    443–449
Gross, Dr. Calvin D., 347, 351, 377,
    380
Group for the Advancement of
    Psychiatry, 404–405, 416
Growth of America, The (Liebman
    and Young), 185
"Guide to African History, A"
    (Davidson), 203–204
Gunning, Mrs. Rosemary R., 378

H

Haggard, Ernest A., 38
Halsey, A. H., 230
Hamlet (Shakespeare), 153

Hamm, William A., 190
Hampton, Mason, 363
Handbook of Social Psychology
    (ed. Lindzey), 173
Handicaps, reversing, 12–13
Hansen, C. F., 409
Harding, John, 173
Harlow, H. F., 421
Harlow, Margaret K., 421
Harris, I., 432
Harvey, O. J., 417, 418
Haselden, Kyle, 460, 467–471
Haverty, Msgr. John Paul, 356–357
Havighurst, Robert J., 134–147, 149
Head Start program, 101, 120, 129–
    130
Henry, Mrs. Enid Brann, 358
Henry, Patrick, 189
Higher Horizons, 42–43
Hilgard, 19
Hill, Norman, 372
History of Our Republic (Baldwin
    and Warring), 188
Holley, Mr., 50–54
Holmes, Hamilton, 412
Horowitz, E., 405, 411
Horwitz, M., 419, 432
Howard, Lawrence C., 148–155, 156
Howe, Harold, Jr., 275–277, 281,
    452
Hull, Clark L., 57
Humanities, 148–155
Humphrey, Hubert, 145
Hunt, DeWitt, 141
Hunter, Charlayne, 412
Hunter College, 78

I

Imbalance of Schools, 275–471
    case study of integration, 345–
    399
    equality of students, 450–459

Imbalance of Schools (*Cont.*)
Greenburgh School District No.
8, 443–449
legal decision affecting desegregation, 324–344
de facto segregation, 326–332
New Rochelle decision, 333–
344
Negroes, 309–323
compensation for, 460–471
intellectual performance under
desegregation, 400–441
slums and, 287–308
cost of, 297–302
democratic aspect, 305–307
politics of social integration,
302–305
school vs. the home, 294–297
tragedy of, 307
upper-middle- vs. lower-mid-
dle-class, 292–294
transfers, 349–351
In White America (Duberman), 154
Indentured servants, 187–188
Indians (American), 28, 39, 103,
469
achievement of average, 454–455
as depicted in textbooks, 125–
129, 169–170
insensitivity to, 151
sense of time, 34
Inquiry, methods of, 148–155
Institute for Developmental Studies,
33, 42, 130
Institutionalization of auxiliary personnel, 111–112, 115–117
Instructional style, 13–17
differences in, 48–54
the motivator, 14–17
the taskmaster, 13–17
technical approach, 55–65
animals and men, 59–61
awareness and utilization, 62–
63
cognition vs. emotion, 58–59

illustrative model, 57–58
minimal goals, 64–65
strategies of modification, 61–
62
strength over weakness, 63–64
Integration, 151–152, 275–286
case study of, 345–399
educational parks, 280–281
new school spotting, 280
open enrollment, 279, 303, 348
reverse, 279–280
pairing, 280
politics of, 302–305
redistricting, 279
slum schools, 287–308
specific procedures to achieve,
448–449
Intelligence quotient (IQ), 5–6, 27,
29, 37–38
of alienated youth, 137
ignoring, 40
raising, 38, 43
"Intergroup Relations in Teaching
Materials" (Wilson), 171
Interracial Parents Committee, 354–
355

J

Jefferson, Thomas, 189
Jencks, Christopher, 282, 287–308
Job Corps, 125
Jobs, 123–124
for juveniles, 139–140
as a social policy, 145
moral equivalent of, 140
for Negroes, 45–47
relating subjects to, 124
See also Work experience
Johnson, Edward A., 184
Johnson, Fred, 322
Johnson, Lyndon B., 309
Jones, Ernest, 45–47
Jones, Frederick, 371

Jones, Leander, 357
Journal of Negro History, 192
Juvenile delinquents, 137, 139
    work experience programs and,
        146

K

Karon, B. P., 433
Katherine, Reverend Mother, 361
Katz, I., 282, 400–441
Kaufmann, Bel, 20
Kaufman, Judge Irving R., 333,
        334, 344
Kelley, H. H., 405
Kennedy, John F., 199–200, 466
Kessler, Bernard, 353, 371–372, 382
Kihss, Peter, 353–354
Kimball, Barbara, 432
Klein, G. S., 419
Klineberg, Otto, 6, 167–176, 177–
        178
Klopf, Gordon J., 100–117, 348, 436
Knowles, L. W., 408
Kornberg, Leonard, 66–77
Kransdorf, Esta, 322
Krout, John A., 189
Krug, Mark, 192
Ku Klux Klan, 196–198

L

Laird, D. A., 419
Lamanna, Joe, 390–391
Land of the Free (Caughey, Frank-
        lin, and May), 189
Landers, Dr. Jacob, 350, 398
Language
    oral, as instrumental to learning,
        244
    painting as non-verbal, 254
*Language of Elementary School
        Children: A Study of the*
*Use and Control of Lan-
        guage Effectiveness in Com-
        munication, and the Re-
        lations among Speaking,
        Reading, Writing, and Lis-
        tening* (Loban), 232
Language learning, 228–238
    drama in, 235
    preschool children, 239–249
    list of handicaps, 245
    music in, 246
*Language Programs for the Dis-
        advantaged: Report of the
        NCTE Task Force on Teach-
        ing English to the Disad-
        vantaged,* 131, 228, 239
"Language and Social Class"
        (Bernstein), 230
Lantz, Beatrice, 419
Lass, Abraham H., 365
Laster, I. A., 436
Latham, Henry J., 381, 382, 384
Lazarus, R. S., 418, 419
Learning
    aural, 61, 64–65
    cognitive categories of, 58
    oral language as instrumental to,
        244
    question of process of, 129–133
    reading as instrumental to, 243–
        244
    the style of, 55–65
    teacher-education courses in, 59
    visual-physical, 57
    warm-up period, 63–64
    See also Language learning
Lee, F. J., 419, 432
Levine, Professor, 185
Lewin, K., 419
Lewis, Anthony, 346–347, 366–367,
        397–398
Lewis, Oscar, 132
Liddell, H., 420–421
Liebman, Rebekah R., 185

"Life is Fun in a Smiling, Fair-Skinned World" (Klineberg), 167–176
Lighthall, F. F., 407
Lindzey, G., 173
Link, Arthur S., 193
Lit, J., 432
Loban, Walter, 228–238, 239–240, 248
Lord of the Flies (Golding), 159, 163–164
Loyola, Mother, 361
Lupiano, Vincent A., 385
Lurie, Mrs. Ellen, 355
Lyford, Joseph P., 309–323
Lysergic acid diethylamide (LSD), 420

M

M.D.T.A., 102
McKeon, Richard P., 152
McLaughlin, Frederick C., 372
MacLeish, Archibald, 150
McNeese v. Board of Education, 326, 328
Making of Modern America (Canfield and Wilder), 190
Mama's Bank Account, 164–165
Mandlebaum, D. G., 420
Mandler, G., 404, 421
March on Washington, 199
Margett, Charles, 382, 383–384
Marshall, S. L. A., 420
Marshall Plan, 462
Mary Francilda, Sister, 314
Mason, D. J., 421
Mason, W. A., 421
May, Ernest R., 189
Mays, Willie, 30–32
Mead, Margaret, 132, 169
Mearns, E. A., Jr., 415
Meredith, James, 412
Metraux, Rhoda, 169

Metropolitan Museum of Art, 257
Mexican-Americans, 28, 103, 138, 469
achievements of average, 454–455
insensitivity to, 151
textbooks reflecting cultural background of, 125–129
Michigan Department of Public Instruction, 179
Miller, Harry L., 130
Miller, Arthur, 153
Milwaukee, teaching experiment in, 42
"Mitch Miller Sing Along Folk Songs" (record), 82–83
Moeller, G., 418
Montessori, Maria, 130–131
Morrison, Philip, 154
Motivator, the, 14–17
Murphy, Vincent D., 202–203
Murrow, Edward, 19
Murstein, B. I., 406
Museum of the City of New York, 90
Music
children's response to, 82–84
in language learning, 246
poetry set to, 153
Muzzey, David S., 193
Myrdal, Gunnar, 150

N

National Association for the Advancement of Colored People, 196, 303–304, 319–320, 321, 348, 364–365, 370–371
lack of rapport with low-income families, 319
official pronouncements of, 318
National Council of Teachers of English, 228, 232, 239
National curriculum workshop, 272–273

National Education Association, 18–19

Educational Policies Commission, 296

National Institute for Advanced Study in Teaching Disadvantaged Youth, 266, 268

National NDEA Institute for Advanced Study in Teaching Disadvantaged Youth, 132

National policy for alienated youth, 134–147
  alternative pathway to adulthood, 138–140
  community strategy, 147
  current programs, 140–142
  needed programs, 142–144
  proposals, 140–142
  responsibility of society, 144–145
  work-experience program, 146

"National Policy for Alienated Youth" (Havighurst and Stiles), 134–147

National Scholarship Service and Fund for Negro Students (NSSFNS), 410, 414

National Teachers Examination, 415, 456

Neglected History: Essays in Negro History (Wesley), 184, 187

"Negro as an American, The" (Johnson, Weaver, Lyford, and Cogley), 309–323

"Negro in American History Textbooks, The," 184, 185, 200

Negro in Modern American History Textbooks, The (Sloan), 185

Negro Self Concept (ed. Patterson), 187

Negroes, 16, 30–32, 103, 138, 150, 275–276, 309–323, 470
  achievement of average, 454–455
  average earnings, 463
  child potential, 4

  compensation for, 2–3, 460–471
    affirmative approach, 460–466
    negative approach, 467–471
  as depicted in textbooks, 171, 173, 179, 180
  effects of desegregation, 400–441
    biracial situations, 422–434
    detrimental conditions, 410–418
    experiments on stress and performance, 418–422
    postulated situational determinants, 403–407
    reports on academic achievement, 407–410
  employment, 464–465, 469
  fear of competition with whites, 414–418
  health and welfare, 465
  housing, 463, 465
  intellectual performance under desegregation, 400–441
  job picture for, 45–47
  preoccupation with freedom, 154
  providing substitute influences for, 44
  self-confidence and performance, 458–459
  statistics on school enrollments, 28
  textbooks reflecting cultural background of, 125–129, 182–204
    abolitionism, 190–191
    backlash, 201–204
    Civil War, 191–192
    explorers, 187
    extracts from, 186–187
    the freedom movement, 198–200
    indentured servants, 187–188
    Ku Klux Klan, 196–198
    Reconstruction, 192–196
    slave life, 188–190
    slave uprisings, 191

Neighborhood-school concept, 3–4

New Careers for the Poor (Pearlman and Reissman), 100–101
"New Improved American, The" (Asbell), 25–47
New Republic, The, 287
New Rochelle decision, 333–344
New World Foundation, The, 167
New York City
  ethnic statistics, 28
  teaching experiment in, 42–43
New York City Welfare Department, 446
New York Historical Society, 90
New York State Department of Education, 446–447
New York Times, The, 275–276, 345–399, 460–471
New York University, 422
North Carolina Advancement School, 457

O

Office of Economic Opportunity, 100, 101, 102
Office of Juvenile Delinquency and Youth Development, 78
Office of Naval Research, 422
Olympic Games, 197
On Becoming a Person (Rogers), 154
"On Rewriting of the Story of Reconstruction in the United States History Textbooks," 192
O'Neill, Eugene, 153
Open enrollment, 279, 303, 348
  reverse, 279–280
Oral language as instrumental to learning, 244
Oriental Americans, achievement of average, 454–455
Osler, Sonia F., 418, 419
Our American Republic (Link and Muzzey), 193

Our Nation from Its Creation (Platt and Drummond), 188

P

Painting, 250–265
  as a non-verbal language, 254
Pairing, 280, 380–384, 387
Paperback books, 50–51
Parents and Taxpayers of Jackson Heights (PAT), 354, 386–396
Parker, Mrs. Rubie, 357–358
Parks, educational, 280–281
Passamanich, Miss, 53–54
Patterson, Franklin, 187
Pearlman, Arthur, 100–101
Pedersen, Douglas, 250–265, 266
Petosa, John and Felicia, 392–393
Pettigrew, Thomas, 151
Phi Delta Kappan, 134
Philadelphia, ethnic statistics, 28
Piaget, J., 175
Pierce, Marylynn G., 335
Pierce School, 26
Platt, Nathaniel, 188
Plaut, R. L., 415
Poetry, 163–164
  set to music, 153
Politics, 7–8
  overcompensation for the Negro and, 2–3
  of social integration, 302–305
Ponder, Edward, 35–36
"Prejudice and Ethnic Relations" (Harding), 173
"Prejudice and Your Child" (Clark), 173
Preschool children, 239–249
Preston, M. G., 417
Pribram, 18
Princeton Plan, 280, 367, 446, 447
Project BRIDGE, 66–77
Project TRUE, 78–99
Prosser, 191
PTA Magazine, The, 48

Public Interest, The, 450
Puerto Ricans, 28, 103, 138, 275, 309–323, 469
 achievement of average, 454–455
 compensation for, 460–471
 intellectual performance under desegregation, 400–441
 racial pride, 72–76
 statistics on school enrollments, 28
 textbooks reflecting cultural background of, 125–129, 173
Punishment, 39, 90
 for errors on tests, 60

R

"Racial Imbalance in Public Education in New Rochelle, New York," 337–339
Racial prejudice, 71–76
 in textbooks, 167–181
 as underdeveloped morality, 150
 See also Desegregation; Segregation
Racial pride, 71–76
Radke, Marian, 405, 411
Raven, B., 404, 405, 418
"Reaching the Culturally Deprived" (Borton), 156–166
Reading, 37–38, 43
 as instrumental to learning, 243–244
 levels in, 5
 selecting material, 153
 separate courses, 121–122
 teaching, 64
 textbooks for, 167–176
  anthropomorphism in, 174–175
  racial prejudice in, 167–181
  socioeconomic-centrism in, 173–174
  upgrading selections, 159–165
Reconstruction, 192–196, 204
Redistricting, 279

Reissman, Frank, 16–17, 55–65, 100–101, 124, 132
Religion, 73–74, 91, 126, 313, 321
 private schools of, 305
 in textbooks, 171–172
 on transfers, 355–362
Ressentiment, 20–22
"Review of Evidence Relative to the Effects of Desegregation" (Katz), 400–441
Revolutionary War, 189–190
Reynolds, June, 387–388, 389–390
Rezoning, 351–353, 362–365, 367–370, 384–386, 397–398
Ribicoff, Abraham, 306
Rincon de Gautier, Felisa, 105
Rise of the American Nation, The (Todd and Curti), 187, 188
Roberts, S. O., 406, 428, 434
Robinson, J. M., 428, 433, 434
Robinson, Jackie, 197
Rogers, Carl, 154
Rosen, M., 406
Rosenberg, Pearl, 405
Rosenthal, Dr. Robert, 38
Rosenwald, G., 432
Ross, Betsy, 203
Rubin, Max J., 347–348
Ruebush, B. K., 407
Ryan, William, 321

S

Sadowsky, Edward L., 354
St. Louis, 43–47
Santayana, George, 179
Sarason, S. B., 404, 407, 420, 421, 432
Saturday Review, 128, 148, 156, 167, 177
Sawrey, W. L., 421
Saylor, J. G., 120
Schachter, S., 420
Scholarships, federal, 304, 305

School Curriculum Reform in the United States (Goodlad), 120
School History of the Negro Race in America, A (Johnson), 184
School Review, 133
Schools
  bureaucracy in, 8, 307–308
  the taskmaster and, 15
  democratic aspect of, 305–307
  Dewey's conception of, 14
  ethnic statistics, 28
  first semester, 78–99
  lifting attendance, 43
  the nature of, 5
  pairing, 280, 380–384, 387
  physical conditions, 26
  private, 304–305, 306
  as resistant to change, 8
  reversing handicaps, 12–13
  rezoning, 351–353, 362–365, 367–370, 384–386, 397–398
  sites for new, 280
  slums and, 287–308
    cost of, 297–302
    democratic aspect, 305–307
    politics of social integration, 302–305
    school vs. the home, 294–297
    tragedy of, 307
    upper-middle- vs. lower-middle-class, 292–294
  supplies, 98–99
  transfers, 346–347, 349–351, 353–354, 380–382
    Catholics, 355–362
  See also Desegregation; Imbalance of schools; Integration; Segregation
Segregation, 126
  busing and, 5–6, 317, 347–348
  de facto, 3, 151, 282
  legal decisions affecting, 324–344
  as morally indefensible, 3
Settlement Houses, 146

Sexton, Patricia, 124
Shagaloff, June, 364–365, 370–371
Shepard, Samuel, Jr., 43–47
Shepard v. Board of Education, 326, 327
"Should There be Compensation for Negroes?" (Young and Haselden), 460–471
Sibley, John, 362–365
Skinner, B. F., 57
Slavery
  life under, 188–190
  uprisings, 191
Sloan, Irving, 182–200
"Slums and Schools" (Jencks), 287–308
Slums and Suburbs (Conant), 123
Smigiel, Stanley, 389
Smiley, Marjorie B., 15, 48–54, 130
Smith-Hughes Act, 141, 142
"Social Class and Linguistic Development: A Theory of Social Learning," 230
Society, responsibility of, 144–145
Socioeconomic-centrism, 173–174
"Some Sociological Determinants of Perception," 230
Southern Education Foundation, 266
Southern School News, 409, 412
Spence, K. W., 404, 421, 422
Stallings, F. H., 408
Stangel, Mrs. Marguerite, 29–32, 38
Stevens, Thaddeus, 194
Stiles, Lindley J., 134–147, 149
Story of the American Nation (Casner and Gabriel), 188
Story of Our Country, The (Ver Steeg), 187
"Strategy of Style, The" (Reissman), 55–65
Streit, Peggy, 386–396
Strycker's Bay Neighborhood Council, 319, 321, 322
Student culture, 299–301

"Study of Culture at a Distance,
    The" (Mead and Metraux),
    169
Style of learning, 55–65
Sumner, Charles, 194
"Sustained Program of Language
    Learning, A" (Loban), 228–
    238
Sutherland, Jean, 405
Sutton, Percy, 319–320, 321
Syracuse University, 23

T

"Talk to Teachers, A" (Baldwin),
    128
Tanner, J. C., 414
Taskmaster, the, 13–17
    bureaucracy and, 15
Taylor, Reverend Gardner, 320
Taylor, Janet A., 404, 420, 421, 422
Taylor et al. v. New Rochelle
    Board of Education, 327,
    332, 333–344
"Teach them the Arts of Freedom"
    (Howard), 148–155
Teacher (Ashton-Warner), 7
Teachers, 11–117
    absolute authority of, 254
    attitudes toward auxiliary per-
        sonnel, 107–109, 110
    benefits from auxiliary personnel,
        104
    as civil servants, 293
    creating goals, 36–38
    deterrents to the development of,
        66–77
    diagnosis by, 55–65
    expectations of, 11–12
    hostility of, 39
    innovations and, 8
    insensitivities of, 25–47
    instructional style, 13–17
        differences in, 48–54
        the motivator, 14–17

the taskmaster, 13–17
technical approach, 55–65
kindness of, 18
parents' charges against, 12–13,
    16
providing substitute influences,
    44
-pupil relationships, 17–22
    authority, 17–18
    personal, 17, 18–22
re-examining role of, 113
selection of, 22–24
setting up own library, 50–51
summer institutes for, 23
training of, 6–7, 14–15, 22–24,
    66–77, 295
    education courses, 59
Teachers College Record, 55
Teaching
the art of freedom, 148–155
experimentation in, 11
oversimplifying materials, 92
question of process of, 129–133
technical approach to, 55–65
    animals and men, 59–61
    awareness and utilization, 62–
        63
    cognition vs. emotion, 58–59
    illustrative model, 57–58
    minimal goals, 64–65
    strategies of modification, 61–
        62
    strength over weakness, 63–64
"Teaching Strategy for Culturally
    Deprived Pupils, A: Cogni-
    tive and Motivational Con-
    siderations" (Ausubel), 130
Technology, 290–291
Terte, Robert H., 349–350, 379–380
Tests, 60–61
Textbooks, 205–225
    anthropomorphism in, 174–175
    history, 182–204
    racial prejudice in, 167–181
    reflecting cultural backgrounds

Textbooks (*Cont.*)
  of minorities, 125–129
  religion in, 171–172
  socioeconomic-centrism in, 173–174
  standardized, 7
Thibaut, J., 405
Thompson, S. V., 419
Threatening, 94–95
Time, sense of, 34
Titmuss, R. M., 420
Tocqueville, Alexis de, 154
Todd, Lewis Paul, 187
Tomasson, Robert E., 384–386
Trager, Helen G., 411
Training
  auxiliary personnel, 107, 109, 110–111, 113–115
  higher education, 115
  inservice, 114
  preservice, 113–114
  of teachers, 6–7, 14–15, 22–24, 66–77, 295
  education courses, 59
Treatment of the Negro in American History School Textbooks, The (Carpenter), 185
Trillin, C., 412
Tubman, Harriet, 191
Tumin, M., 403
Turner, Henry McNeal, 154
Turner, Nat, 191
Turrell, E. S., 421

U

Underground Railroad, 190
Unemployment, 139–140
Union League, 194
United States Commission on Civil Rights, 403, 408, 409, 415–416
United States Department of Health, Education and Welfare, 78

United States History (Gavian, Hamm, and Freidel), 190
United States Office of Education, 23, 132, 141, 450
United States Supreme Court, 126, 324–344, 346, 364, 366–367, 397–398
University of California, 203
University of California at Berkeley, 184, 185
University of Chicago, 202
University of Georgia, 412
University of Illinois, 247
University of Illinois Institute for Research on Exceptional Children, 244
University of Mississippi, 412
University of North Dakota, 38
Up the Down Staircase (Kaufmann), 20
Upward Bound programs, 125, 129, 131–132, 250–265
Urban League, 197, 277, 320, 321, 348, 371, 460, 462, 463
  lack of rapport with low-income families, 319
  official pronouncements of, 318

V

"Value Decisions and the Public Schools" (Dunkel), 133
Van Voorhis, John, 368, 370
Ver Steeg, Clarence L., 187
Vocational education, 122–125
  relating subjects to jobs, 124
  work experiences, 123–124

W

Wagner, Robert F., 320, 347
Waite, R. R., 407
Waly, Patricia, 433
Warren, Earl, 340

Warring, Mary, 188
Washington, Booker T., 197, 198
Washington, George, 189
Washington, D.C., ethnic statistics, 28
"We Shall Overcome!" (song), 154
Weaver, Robert C., 309
Weiss, Theodore, 321
Welfare, 28, 73, 78, 103, 298, 446, 465
Welfare Administration, 78
Wesley, Charles H., 184, 187
Wheatley, Phillis, 189
White, Bertha O., 335
"Who Would Teach Here . . ." (Smiley), 48–54
Whyte, W. F., 417
Wilder, Howard B., 190
Wilson, H. E., 171
Work experience
  communities in, 147
  federal program, 145–146
  juvenile delinquency and, 146
  limitations of, 146
  moral equivalent of, 140
  programs and proposals, 140–142, 143
  responsibility of society, 144–145

secondary schools, 141–142
senior high schools, 142–144
three stages of, 143–144
vocational schools, 123–124
  See also Jobs
Work Experience Education Programs in American Secondary Schools (Hunt), 141
World Journal Tribune, 201
Wrightsman, L. S., Jr., 420
Wyatt, E., 409, 415

Y

Yarrow, Marian R., 405, 412, 432
Yearbook of School Law 1962, 327, 332
Yearbook of School Law 1963, 327
Yearbook of School Law 1964, 324
Young, Gertrude A., 185
Young, Whitney, 281, 318, 319
Young, Whitney M., Jr., 460–466
Young Men's Christian Association, 146
Youth Conservation Corps, 145
Youth Development Program, 145